Sanborn's Travelog Series:

MEXICO'S PACIFIC COAST
& COPPER CANYON
A Driver's Guide

by "Mexico" Mike Nelson

Wanderlust Publications, McAllen, Texas

Inquiries should be addressed to: Wanderlust Publications, 2009 South 10th Steet, McAllen, TX 78503-5405 Ph: (956) 682-7433 Fax: (956) 686-0732.

Our web page address: http://www.hiline.net/sanborns
E-mail: wanderlust@sanborns.hiline.net

First Edition: May, 1996
Second Edition: May, 1997

Printed in the United States of America
01   00   99   98   97   7   6   5   4   3   2

Library of Congress Cataloging-in-publication Data

Nelson, Mike 1950-
     Mexico's Pacific Coast & Copper Canyon: A Driver's Guide
     by "Mexico" Mike Nelson
     p. cm. — (Sanborn's Travelog Series)
     Preassigned LCCNumber: 96-60879
     ISBN: 1-878166-10-7

     1. Sinaloa (Mexico: State) — Guidebooks. 2. Sonora (Mexico:
     State) — Guidebooks. 3. Automobile travel — Mexico — Guidebooks.
     I. Title.
     F1341.N45 1997   917.21704'835
                    QBI96-40139

Table of Contents

GENERAL INFORMATION v
    AA AND OTHER 12 STEP PROGRAMS ix
    AMERICAN LEGION POSTS IN MEXICO xi
    AMERICAN CONSULATES xii
    CONVERSION TABLES xv
    TOLL ROAD RATES xvii
    FERRY INFORMATION xix
    SANBORN'S AGENTS xx

Maps and Special Reports

MAP OF NOGALES 1
PADRE KINO SPECIAL REPORT 8
MAP OF MAGDALENA 8
MAP OF HERMOSILLO 11
MAP OF GUAYMAS 14
MAP OF CD OBREGON 17
MAP OF LOS MOCHIS 21
MAP OF CULIACAN 24
MAP OF MAZATLAN 27
MAP OF MAZATLAN NORTH BEACH 28
MAP OF TEPIC 33
MAP OF PUERTO VALLARTA 36
SPECIAL REPORT ON THE TOWN OF TEQUILA 41
MAP OF TEQUILA 42
MAP OF GUADALAJARA 44
MAP OF KINO BAY 47
MAP OF CREEL 56
MAP OF SAN CARLOS 62
MAP OF ALAMOS 63
MAP OF EL FUERTE 65

Southbound Logs

LOG 1   START: Nogales, Az   END: Imuris, Son 2
LOG 2   START: Douglas, Az   END: Imuris, Son 3
LOG 3   START: Imuris, Son   END: Santa Ana, Son 7
LOG 4   START: Santa Ana, Son   END: Hermosillo, Son 9
LOG 5   START: Hermosillo, Son   END: Guaymas, Son 12
LOG 6   START: Guaymas, Son   END: Navojoa, Son 15
LOG 7   START: Navojoa, Son   END: Los Mochis, Sin 19
LOG 8   START: Los Mochis, Sin   END: Culiacán, Sin 22
LOG 9   START: Culiacán, Sin   END: Mazatlán, Sin 23
LOG 10   START: Mazatlán, Sin   END: Tepic, Nay 30
LOG 11   START: Tepic, Nay   END: Pto. Vallarta, Jal 34
LOG 12   START: Tepic, Nay   END: Guadalajara, Jal 37

Specials

SPECIAL A   START: Hermosillo, Son   END: Kino Bay, Son 45
SPECIAL B   START: Kino Bay, Son   END: Hermosillo, Son 46
SPECIAL C   START: Kino Bay, Son   END: Jct Hwy #15 49
SPECIAL D   START: Jct Hwy #15   END: Kino Bay, Son 50

SPECIAL E   START: Hermosillo, Son   END: La Junta, Chih 50
SPECIAL F   START: Cuauhtémoc, Chih   END: Creel, Chih 53
SPECIAL G   START: Creel, Chih   END: Divisadero, Chih 55
SPECIAL H   START: Creel, Chih   END: Tejabán, Chih 55
SPECIAL I   START: Creel, Chih   END: Batopilas, Chih 57
SPECIAL J   START: Batopilas, Chih   END: Creel, Chih 58
SPECIAL K   START: Creel, Chih   END: Cuauhtémoc, Chih 59
SPECIAL L   START: Guaymas, Son   END: San Carlos, Son 61
SPECIAL M   START: Navojoa, Son   END: Alamos, Son 61
SPECIAL N   START: Los Mochis, Sin   END: El Fuerte, Sin 65
SPECIAL O   START: Cd. Obregón, Son   END: Sn NicolOás, Son 66
SPECIAL P   START: Hermosillo, Son   END: Douglas, Az 66
SPECIAL Q   START: Imuris, Son   END: Douglas, Az 69
SPECIAL R   START: Jct. Hwy #l5   END: San Blas, Nay 70
SPECIAL S   START: Tepic, Nay   END: San Blas, Nay 71
SPECIAL T   START: Las Varas, Nay   END: Santa Cruz, Nay 72
SPECIAL U   START: Santa Cruz, Nay   END: Las Varas, Nay 73
SPECIAL V   START: Compostela, Nay   End: Chapalilla, Nay 74
SPECIAL W   START: Chapalilla, Nay   END: Compostela, Nay 74
SPECIAL X   START: Douglas, Az   END: Hermosillo, Son 75

Eat & Strays and General Info

Hermosillo 78
Kino Bay 79
San Carlos 82
Guaymas 84
Ciudad Obregón 86
Navojoa 87
Alamos 88
Los Mochis 90
El Fuerte 92
Culiacán 93
Mazatlán 94
Creel & the Copper Canyon 102
Tepic 105
San Blas 106
Rincón de Guayabitos 108
Puerto Vallarta 110
Guadalajara 118

Northbound Logs

LOG 13   START: Guadalajara, Jal   END: Tepic, Nay 125
LOG 14   START: Pto Vallarta, Jal   END: Tepic, Nay 129
LOG 15   START: Tepic, Nay   END: Mazatlán, Sin 132
LOG 16   START: Mazatlán, Sin   END: Culiacán, Sin 135
LOG 17   START: Culiacán, Sin   END: Los Mochis, Sin 138
LOG 18   START: Los Mochis, Sin   END: Navojoa, Son 140
LOG 19   START: Navojoa, Son   END: Guaymas, Son 141
LOG 20   START: Guaymas, Son   END: Hermosillo, Son 145
LOG 21   START: Hermosillo, Son   END: Santa Ana, Son 147
LOG 22   START: Santa Ana, Son   END: Imuris, Son 149
LOG 23   START: Imuris, Son   END: Nogales, Az 150
Index 153

WELCOME TO MEXICO!

WHY DRIVE?

If you had a friend from a foreign country visit you, how would you show him the United States of America? Would you fly him to New York, Chicago, Atlanta, Los Angeles and Seattle? Would he be able to go home and tell his friends that America is a wonderful place, full of big cities and grand airports?

Wouldn't it be better to set out with him in your car and show him the glories of a sunrise over a Kansas wheat field, contrast the two very different majesties of the Appalachians and the Rockies, take him for a hike and overnight in the Grand Canyon and the Olympic rain forest? Admittedly he could bus to the same destinations, but if he drove, he could stop wherever his fancy took him and he could be a lot more comfortable.

For one person it will cost more to drive. For two it will be just a little more expensive. For three, it will be cheaper. For anyone it is a lot more convenient. I've taken buses and trains, but I'd much rather drive.

I've met people who will say that they have "seen" Mexico because they've flown to Cancún, Acapulco, Ixtapa, or Los Cabos. Those are great places and worth seeing, but they are only a fraction of what Mexico has to offer. Some people think that Mexico is just two beaches with a desert in-between. They are missing the point.

The Mexico we will show you has centuries-old castles and monasteries that are now serving as hotels. It has mountains and forests that will make you think you are in the Rockies or in Switzerland. It has spas that can soothe you and rejuvenate you for about half the cost of their U.S. or European counterparts. It is a land of startling contrasts, rugged beauty and elegant softness. Millions of Monarch butterflies migrate to Angangueo, Michoacán every year. Hundreds of American and Canadian expatriates live idyllic lives in San Miguel de Allende, Guanajuato, Guadalajara and Chapala, Jalisco.

Small towns often have one or two attractions that are quite worthwhile. Stop and ask. You'll find that the people of Mexico are her real treasures. They will go out of their way to make you feel at home, even if you don't speak the language. Are we that accommodating in the US? Buy a soft drink at a tienda in a small town and go sit in the square. Before long you will be the focus of attention. Little children may come up to you and ask you what you are doing, particularly if you have a camera. A local person, who speaks a little English and may have lived in the States once, may approach you and ask if he can help you. I've been lost and people have not only gotten me on the right road, but invited me to their home for dinner before I set out. These are the experiences that can happen to you if you drive. Take these back to your friends who have "seen" the beaches and watch them turn green with envy.

HOW TO READ THIS BOOK

First of all, take some time to get familiar with our format. The information is presented in varying detail, depending on where you are in your journey. In cities, we tend to give you several landmarks, in case one has disappeared since our last visit.

For goodness sakes, read ahead in the log! You should look at it the night before to plan your trip and mark appropriate highlights. Look at the "Mexico" Mike Specials. They are eclectic like me. You may find them fascinating, or you may find them awful. Some of them are easy drives with the family sedan and some require a truck or four wheel drive. I'll tell you in advance. After you've taken a few, you'll know if they are your cup of tea, or if, by your standards, I'm as crazy as a loon. On the road, the navigator should read ahead about four or five entries, but don't give them all to the driver. I may just be dim-witted, but I can't handle more than two items at a time. Work this out with your pilot.

With this *Travelog*, we have attempted to include every route that you could take while exploring this section of Mexico. Since there is sometimes more than one way you could go, we've included alternate routes. Every time you come to a major intersection or a major new highway, there should be a new log.

Topes or speed bumps are described in another section. All you really need to know about them is that you do not want to hit them going over five miles an hour. Both pilot and navigator should keep an eye out for them as you approach any small town. They will be at the entrance and somewhere in the middle. We used to list every one, but they moved around so much that we gave up. Don't be lulled into a false sense of security by the fact that some of them have signs marking their location. If traffic is slowing down for no apparent reason, more will be revealed when you get closer.

The mileage numbers represent miles and kilometers respectively. We've listed both so our Canadian friends can use this book. The numbers start at 0.0 at a major intersection. You should reset your car's odometer whenever we change our numbering. The "KM XXX" stands for the kilometer markings you'll see on Mexico's highways. They aren't always visible, but when they are, they give you a great reference point.

We gave up listing exact prices years ago. That's the one thing that people are most likely to complain about in any guidebook. Prices change, but often stay within the same range. A moderately priced restaurant or hotel will stay in the same category relative to others in the same city. With the dramatic devaluation of Dec. 1994, and the subsequent free fall of the peso, prices are lower in dollar terms than they had been in years. First of all we'd like to say that we feel compassion for our friends in Mexico. It is a very tough time and they didn't deserve what happened. Many lives were affected, careers ruined and dreams dashed. Perhaps the lesson is that one man's (ex-president Carlos Salinas de Gortari) ambition shouldn't be allowed to devastate a whole country. Some people on both sides of the border have blamed NAFTA, but thinking citizens of both countries believe that Mexico will make it through this unpleasantness and some good will come out of it. Be kind and generous in all your dealings. One of the saddest things I've ever seen is an American "bargaining" with a Mexican artisan in a loud and rude voice. True, they will get the item from a poor woman for a few pesos less, but at how high a cost to their soul? Bargaining is no longer the fun it used to be for Mexicans, even among themselves. If an item is a good deal, take it. If it's overpriced and you feel like you're being ripped off, then say so. Just don't try to squeeze that last *centavo* from someone who is barely able to put food on her family table.

Now that my preaching is over, the good news for American and Canadian tourists is that your dollar buys more. Many locally owned hotels (unlike the multinational resorts) didn't raise their rates, or if they did, not by much. Restaurants did raise their rates a little, but they are still a bargain for us. There is no animosity towards Americans for the disaster, so don't feel guilty. I have to admit I am getting my windshield cleaned more often, though. Pay with your credit card whenever possible, to take advantage of the best exchange rate.

Not every gas station is listed. There are just too many of them these days. The ones we list all have unleaded gasoline. Diesel is found at all the larger ones. Neither is every little town listed, a departure from our original way of doing things.

The scenic ratings of roads are subjective, with me and my roadlogger being the subjects and final authority. A "5" is very close to heaven. A "0" is either hell or a toll road. These have nothing to do with driving ease. Some toll roads are actually pretty, but most are not. Take the scenic route if you want to dawdle. Take the direct route if you just want to get from point A to point B.

EAT AND STRAY LEGEND

AE = American Express, MC = MasterCard, VI = Visa, SATV = satellite TV, SAC = Sanborn's Amigo Club

PRICES – please don't take these as gospel – prices increase at least once a year, but we give you a fighting chance to hold on to your bucks. Always look at the room first and ask for the best price. If a hotel has a disco and you want to sleep, ask for a room far, far, away – in another galaxy, perhaps. If the room's too noisy, think nothing of asking to change. Be sure to ask for the *sub-gerente* since the *gerente* will be home asleep. Prices are in US dollars.

ECON – under $25   MOD – $25-$60   UPPER $60 & above

Restaurants are rated for quality and service. Prices are approximate, for two folks to eat dinner there. Drinks, tips & appetizers are not included. If breakfast is the specialty, cut prices in half.

ECON – under $10   MOD – $10-$25   UPPER – $25 & above

For RV parks, we list approximate rates when known.

ECON – under $8   MOD – $8-10   UPPER – $10 & above

GAS AND GAS STATIONS

GAS — (the kind you put in your car) & DIESEL — There is so much unleaded gas in Mexico that you would have to work at it to run out. I know you've read articles that disagree (I even saw one in a recent photography magazine), but they simply do not know what they are talking about. I play a game sometimes (okay, I don't have good sense, but I'm a writer and it's not a job requirement) where I try to run the tank down between 1/8 and "E" and see if I get stuck. So far I haven't. You'd be smarter to fill at a somewhere between half a tank and 1/4, unless you are really out in the boonies (or deficient in brain power like the author). Unleaded gas is called Magna Sin and comes from a green pump. There is only one brand (at this writing, though this will change, thanks to NAFTA), PEMEX, which stands for PEtroleos MEXicanos. Prices are the same throughout the interior. Both leaded and unleaded cost about the same. The government is trying to encourage people to use unleaded to reduce pollution. Diesel is found at most stations. The diesel pumps are in a different part of the station and are red. The dirtier the diesel area, the better the diesel is. We fill up where the big trucks do. The best diesel is *centrifugado*, or centrifuged. The new Diesel Sin has lower sulfur content.

Forget what you've read in other books about only asking for a specific amount of gas (XX liters). That's a holdover from the days when the real bandits were operating the Pemex pumps. Nowadays the stations have pretty honest personnel (for the most part), pumps with accurate gauges and plenty of unleaded gasoline. Say, "*lleno, por favor*." That means "fill 'er up." It's still a good idea to make sure that the pump has reset to zero before the attendant starts pumping, and to hang around until the operation is finished. Don't just rush off to the bathroom. Except in some areas on the West Coast, they do not take credit cards — only pesos or U.S. dollars. The bathrooms used to be filthy, but lately they have embarked on a cleanup effort. I usually travel with a lady friend, often one who has never been to Mexico before. They are generally pleasantly surprised by the bathrooms. Just like in the U.S., there are some I wouldn't use in a pinch, but mostly, they are much better than they used to be. Often there will be an attendant. Tipping him/her is a nice thing to do. A personal supply of toilet paper is smart, though not always necessary.

Speaking of restrooms, in Mexico *his* will be called *Caballeros* and *hers* will be *Damas* (sometimes W.C. for water closet). In the bathrooms of many Mexican hotels you'll notice the initials C on one faucet and F on the other. Since we don't want you to be scalded under what you thought was going to be a refreshing cold shower, bear in mind that C means *caliente* (hot) and F means *fría* (cold).

The attendants are a lot more honest than in the past. A fellow stopped in my office one day and asked when I was going to Matehuala again. It seems he had accidentally cheated a Pemex attendant and wanted to make amends. The Gringo swore that his tank didn't hold as much as the attendant had pumped and paid only part of the bill. About halfway to Saltillo, he realized that he had miscalculated the number of liters in a gallon and had shortchanged the poor kid.

A longtime reader recently told me that the old-style stations still operated by Pemex were up to their old tricks of padding the bill by thirty pesos. They would distract you, saying. "Gee, that tire needs air," or "Was that your wife I saw you with last night?" While you were confused (was it your wife?), they would add some pesos to the bill. These guys are definitely the minority, but it still pays to be alert. With the current economic hardships going on in Mexico, there is likely to be a return to the old days when you had to watch the pump jockey. Please remember to tip the honest ones the peso equivalent of a quarter. We feel this will help the tourist behind you. When the attendants realize that treating tourists honestly is a source of income, they will be more prone to be honest. A new wrinkle returning travelers have told me about is that the guy will pump, say 102 pesos worth and then say it was 120. When you point to the pump, his buddy will have erased the evidence. What to do? As soon as the pump stops dinging, point to it and say the amount. If you don't speak Spanish, point to the amount and make eye contact. That should clear up any misunderstanding.

AUTO PARTS AND REPAIRS

You'll find lots of spare parts in Mexico, though not always the right ones. Fords, Chevys, Dodges, Nissans are all made there. Many of the parts are interchangeable. The best thing to do is to have a good honest mechanic check out your car before you go and to pay particular attention to the brakes, tires, front end, U-joints, belts (carry spares) and any "computer" parts. Please do not even think about messing with your catalytic converter. Get a tune-up including new spark plug wires etc. Your car is going to be your servant for the next few thousand miles. Don't let it be the other way around.

If you do have car problems, don't worry. I've driven a lot of wrecks that should never have left the garage, much less braved a four thousand mile trip. I've always made it back with the car, usually in better shape than when I left. Goodyear is in every town and can do a good job with brakes, front ends, etc. I've found shade tree mechanics, identified by a *"taller mecánico"* sign beside the road. Taller has nothing to do with his height. It means shop. I've had fuel pumps fixed with silicone or silly putty, I'm not sure. All I know is that it worked. I've had water pumps rebuilt. I've seen parts made that U.S. machinists swore couldn't be done. If they don't have the brake pads you need, they will make 'em. They will work fine until you return, but be sure to have 'em replaced with regulation equipment when you get back. I've had dealers fix "computer" problems. I've had automatic transmissions rebuilt. The list could go on, but I hope you get the picture.

Carry: belts (all), fuel filters (4), air filters (2), a good set of tools, windshield washer fluid (lots), auto transmission fluid (1 qt.), fuel injector cleaner (5 bottles). Diesels should have (5) filters and any additive that might combat water and the buildup of sulfuric acid in your crankcase.

I've tried octane booster and found it a waste of money. Others swear by it. A spare gas can should only be necessary if you are going four wheeling. Carrying gas is too dangerous and smelly. Ninety-nine per cent of folks won't need it. Also make sure your tires (including spare) are in good shape. Mexican tires are excellent, but the sizes are slightly different.

RENTING A CAR

Over 3,000,000 people fly to Mexico, then rent cars for all or part of their trip. 1,500,000 drive from the U.S. or Canada. These "more than average" tourists have realized that driving is the most practical way to get around, offering unlimited freedom. Renting a car in Mexico is similar to renting one anywhere in the world, with a few caveats. You must have a major credit card. All the major rental car agencies are located at major airports. Their rates vary, so shop around. I've found that you will get one price if you reserve a car from the States and another if you just show up at the counter. There is no rhyme or reason to this, because it could be cheaper either way. I suggest that you make a reservation, then, when you arrive, "forget" that you have one and ask what the rate will be. If it is higher, "remember" that you have a reservation, otherwise keep your short-term memory loss. There are also some independent rental car agencies at many airports. Sometimes they offer a better deal and sometimes not. Again, shop around.

You absolutely must have an auto insurance policy issued by a Mexican insurance company. I have asked at rental car agencies, arguing that my gold card covered me. They said, "Fine, You don't have to buy our insurance." Only after I pressed them did they explain that what they would do in case of an accident is charge the value of their car to my credit card. "What would happen if I didn't have that high a limit?" I asked. "Oh, Señor Mike, you would have to find a way to pay us before you could leave the country." Even if you may have a higher credit limit than I, you must have liability insurance issued by a Mexican insurance company. So my advice is to just buy the insurance from your rental car company.

Please check the vehicle carefully! Any little ding not noted will be charged to you as if you damaged their car on purpose. Make sure all lights, signals, and especially the horn work. I got a Volkswagen one time that had a busted speedometer, which lowered my per kilometer charge for sure. Unlimited mileage is the exception rather than the rule, so be sure to ask if it is available. In Mexico City, all vehicles are prohibited from circulating one day a week, based on the last number of their license tag. This applies to rental cars, too. A good rental car company will swap cars so you don't lose a day's driving. We have heard that some rental companies will try to switch license tags and tell you it's okay. It's not. Make sure they agree to give you another legal car for that day. There should be a decal in the back window with the license tag number on it. Be sure they match or refuse the car. Renting in one city and then dropping off in another is expensive. The car rental company will charge you a per kilometer fee that may double you bill.

INSURANCE

If you drive your own car or a rental car from the border, you must buy insurance issued by a Mexican company. If you are renting a car within Mexico, the rental agency will provide it (for a fee). Besides auto insurance, medical, air evacuation and legal service policies are smart. Foreign liability insurance is not recognized in Mexico. We recommend Sanborn's Insurance, but not just because of our relationship. Many other guidebooks recommend them, because they are the best in many ways. They are not the cheapest, though they are competitive. What is important about Sanborn's is that they will pay promptly and fairly. Sanborn's has been insuring tourists driving to Mexico since 1948 and has a good reputation. They have offices at most border crossings in Arizona, and Texas with offices in Houston, San Antonio, Phoenix, Tucson and El Centro, CA. The main office is: Sanborn's Mexico Insurance, P.O. Box 310, McAllen, TX 78505-0310 For a quote call: 956-686-0711. Ask about "Sanborn's Amigo Club" which provides discounts at many hotels, RV parks and a few restaurants. They have an inexpensive annual policy and a six month policy that are considerably cheaper than a daily rate policy. They also offer medical, air evacuation and legal assistance coverage. Visit our web site: http://www.hiline.net/sanborns.

CAR PERMITS AND IMMIGRATION DOCUMENTS

If you are driving your car or a rented car from the border, you'll need a vehicle permit to drive to the interior of Mexico with the exception of Baja California (If you fly to the interior and rent a car you won't need a permit). Getting one is a piece of cake. Don't be like the lady who said, "I just waved at the border guards and they waved back. My, I thought, they sure are friendly here." When she reached the 21 Kilometer checkpoint, they were just as friendly, but told her to go back and get a permit. Someday, maybe they will also ask, "Didn't you read 'Mexico' Mike's books?"

To get your permit, you'll need the vehicle title or registration, which must be in the same name as your credit card (Visa©, MasterCard©, American Express©, or Diner's Club©). If your chariot is financed, you'll need a notarized letter of permission from the lien holder to take it into Mexico. You can't loan you car to a friend. If you have a boat and a trailer, they must also be in the same name as the vehicle. You need the credit card to pay a $12 fee to Banjército for your permit. If you don't have a credit card, you can still get a permit by posting a bond, but it's a lot more trouble. Get a credit card if you possibly can. The permit is good for multiple entries during 180 days.

You must turn in your permit and tourist card before you leave the country for the last time. Forgetting to do so could result in your being refused entry again or subject you to a high fine. You must turn in your permit at the Banjército office, either at the 21 Kilometer checkpoint or at the border station. The Banjército offices are generally close to the bridge. Sometimes you have to park a block or two away and scout it out first. Don't expect to just get in line at the bridge going to the U.S. and expect the toll taker to help you out. That's not his job or department. You do not need to return to the U.S. at the same border crossing where you started.

Everyone must have proof of citizenship, or a picture ID with a birth certificate, voter's registration card or a notarized proof of citizenship. Even little children must have birth certificates. If a child is traveling with only one parent, it is necessary to have notarized permission of the absent parent (even if divorced). Pets need current vaccination records and health certificates.

MONEY MATTERS

Credit cards like Visa©, MasterCard© are accepted almost everywhere. Discover© is not accepted anywhere. American Express©, Diner's Club© and Carte Blanche© are accepted only at the finer establishments. ATM's can give you money on your debit card, but they are sometimes quirky, so have some cash available. You can get cash advances on the Visa© and MasterCard© at some ATM's. I've never gotten one to work, but other people have. Pesos bills come in denominations of 10, 20, 50, 100, 500, 1000, 10,000 and probably bigger, but I've never had that much money. Coins are 10¢, 20¢, 50¢ (*centavos*) and 1, 2, 5, 10, 20 pesos.

At press time the peso was trading at about 7.8 to the dollar. In late Dec. 1994 and early 1995, it underwent a serious devaluation and it's still floating. We did a spot-check of hotels in a dozen towns and most were not raising their rates as much as the peso went down against the dollar. This means that Mexico is a true bargain, with prices at about the 1970 levels. I've been to several towns since the devaluation, and have been pleasantly surprised. You can now find bargains like $20 hotels and $8 cabrito. We cannot predict how long this will last (I've lost more money on Wall Street than I've made and bought pesos just before the Christmas devaluation, so I'm not a very good prognosticator), but we think the situation will last long enough for tourists to enjoy some benefits. Always try to pay with your credit card, so as to get the best rate. Gas stations and toll booths take only cash.

Getting money from home can be a rip-off. The very best bet is for you to have an ATM card that works. The rates are good and the charges minimal. However, if you are like me, and use yours so seldom that it becomes deactivated, you will have to find alternative means of getting money in a pinch. While the Western Union/Electra alliance seemed like a good idea, there are drawbacks. Electra, as you know, is the nationwide chain of furniture/department stores. The advantage is that they are everywhere. The disadvantage is that the transaction will cost an arm and an leg. For $700 sent to me, the sender paid a $75 fee. Although I got the money within hours (not the minutes as promised as the store ran out of money, the computer was down etc.), I had to pay a premium for it. You have to know the name of the sender, by the way, to retrieve your money, so make sure you find out exactly who is sending it to you. Anyway, when the exchange rate was 7.8 pesos to the dollar from a *casa de cambio*, Electra gave me 6.8. Combine the two and you find out that you lose 20-23% for the service. Now that's *mordida* (a little bite)!

TRAVEL TIPS

If you wish to catch up on the news in the States, there are 2 daily English language newspapers published in Mexico City called *The News* and *The Mexico City Times*. They carries all the latest U.S. and world news as well as sports, columns and your favorite comics.

Many of the hotels in Mexico have self-operated (do-it-yourself) elevators. When you push the button to go down remember that the main floor is PB, not 1.

Along the road in Mexico you'll see an occasional cross on the side of the road. It means that someone was killed there. Sometimes the crosses are decorated with flowers – usually on the Day of the Dead (November 1st), the equivalent of our own Memorial Day when we decorate our graves. Sometimes, in the case of wealthier persons, the marker will be fairly elaborate, like a monument or even a small shrine. You may also come across a sign with the name of a village with nothing more than a house or two nearby, and wonder why your roadlogger left that village out of the log. Well, the sign doesn't indicate a village but a bus stop. You see, many of the bus lines won't stop to pick up passengers (or drop one off) except at signs. So, if you see a sign that says Santa Rita, Escondido, Rancho Pancho or something else, but there's nothing else around, it means that the spot is a bus stop; not necessarily a little village worthy of being mentioned in the *Travelog*.

Most railroad crossings in Mexico have STOP signs. It doesn't follow that you have to stop, but some joker behind you might plow right into your rear end. The sign means that if you should get hit by a train, it would obviously be you own fault. If you had observed the stop sign, you would not have been hit... a very logical conclusion.

Commonly nicknamed "Moctezuma's Revenge", diarrhea is sometimes developed by tourists while visiting Mexico. One must realize that traveler's diarrhea can be caused by several factors and can occur anywhere in the world. Over-eating, over-drinking and over-exertion at high altitudes are typical causes. But drinking impure water is the main cause for contracting the *turista*. Avoid tap water (even for brushing your teeth). Use purified water or *agua purificada* available in gas stations and small stores, just like in the States. In supermarkets, it can be purchased in one-gallon plastic containers. Mineral water, while perfectly safe, has the effect of a mild laxative on some individuals due to its mineral content. So be sure and ask for purified water at hotels, motels and restaurants. Do not eat from street carts and sidewalk vendors.

NEED TO CALL HOME?

While calling back home from Mexico has gotten easier, it has also given rise to scam artists who will take advantage of you. We recommend that you use AT&T to call home from your hotel or a pay phone. Call: **95-800-462-4240** for an English-speaking operator. Avoid like the plague the places with signs: "Call the USA with your Visa©, MasterCard© ...."etc. These places are the true *banditos* in Mexico. They charge about $8 a minute for a call to the U.S. Hotels that advertise the same services charge the same amount. They blame it on higher Mexican taxes, but in fact it is just plain greed. A short phone call cost me $69.00 recently

SAFETY

I know that many of you are hesitant to drive in Mexico because you've read dire warnings in other books, or heard so many "horror stories" about *banditos* and bad roads. Folks, I've been driving Mexico since 1969 and have never seen a bandit. Sanborn's insures about 250,000 people who drive Mexico's highways every year. In the last several years, we've heard of only a very small handful of problems. I know many people who have been driving to Mexico for years who tell me that they are far more fearful in the United States where we have drive-by shootings, car- jackings, assaults in rest areas and angry motorists who carry guns. Our motels and hotels are not immune from robberies and assaults. A lady who traveled with me once said, "You know I was so surprised. I felt so much safer in Mexico. It's good to be out of the United States where I feel I have to carry a gun for protection." Believe me, not only will you not have to carry a gun but under no circumstances should you bring a gun into Mexico.

POLICE

You've probably heard nothing but bad stories about Mexican cops. Again, I disagree with that. In all my dealings with cops, most of them have been helpful, polite and honest. While it's true that many years ago, mordida (a little bite, meaning a bribe) was a way of life, things have changed. Now, to be truthful, you cannot change a country overnight. There are still pockets of corruption. My advice is to approach each policeman with the attitude that he is honest and just doing his job. If, however, you encounter one of the old school who is looking for a bribe, ask for his badge number. I always carry a note pad and a pen.

Most cops are honest. Some travelers have told me about policemen who went out of their way to help them or guide them out of town when they were lost. Should you encounter one who's not so liberated, don't panic. Get his badge number and insist you want to see his *jefe*. One couple told me that they spoke no Spanish, but pointed to a place in the Sanborn's *Travelog* where I've put that phrase in Spanish. The cop backed off. The phrase is *"Vamos a la comandancia."* Another is, *"Hablemos con su jefe."* Usually that will start a negotiating process. Stick to your guns, so to speak, as long as you are sure you didn't do anything wrong. If you insist on going to the police station, bogus infractions will vanish. One wrinkle, though, is that if you have broken a law, the cop has every right to take your license plates. You must go to the station to pay your fine. If it's a weekend, you'll probably have to wait until Monday. Although we do not recommend it. Old-timers prefer to pay the fine "on the spot" to save the aggravation. If a cop asks you for a bribe, report him. The government is very concerned about cops on the take and take all reports seriously. You should report the cop's badge number and when and where the incident occurred. Send any complaints about cops, other officials, hotels, restaurants, etc., (or praise for those who went out of their way to help you) to: Departamento de Quejas, Dirección General de Turismo, Presidente Masaryk #172, Mexico, DF. You can also call toll free in Mexico: 91-800-00148. In Mexico City, call: 604-1240. The Policia Federal de Caminos are quite professional and honest. They can be your best friend in an emergency.

AA AND OTHER 12 STEP PROGRAMS

You'll find AA throughout Mexico, even in small towns. NA has a sizable presence in the larger towns. Alanon is almost everywhere. OA, SALA and other programs are less likely to be encountered outside major cities. AA is very visible. I have noted where there are meetings in many cases, but like here, they move or change. Look for the AA symbol inside a triangle and a circle, usually on a blue background jutting out from buildings. Meetings are usually at 8:00 or 8:30 PM in Spanish. Even if you don't speak the language, you will be welcome and often asked to speak. Go ahead. It will do you good. Meetings last an hour and a half and there are often refreshments and birthdays are celebrated like here, except you might get tamales instead of cake or both. Have a ball.

Just in case you forgot your International Directory, we've included a list of all the English-speaking meetings we know about, arranged alphabetically. Just like in the U.S., they change, though, so, if a meeting is no longer where I said it was, you have two courses of action (aside from giving up and giving in). Believe me, looking for a meeting is often a better choice than going back to your hotel where the "Chug tequila till you barf" contest is going on. The first is to check the local English-language newspaper if there is one. The second is to find a Spanish meeting and ask. For Alanon and NA etc. these places will be able to direct you as well, though NA is not as "popular." You'll be welcome at any AA meeting. There are two different types of AA in Mexico. One is *"Grupos de 24 Horas"* (24 hour groups). These are more like institutional settings and the message here is hard core, "put the plug in the jug" type. The other is more like what you are used to. Be prepared for emotional meetings, with long orations and lots of slang. You will be asked to say something. Do your best and take care of yourself. If the above fails and you can't find a meeting, try putting up signs in your hotel and other tourist spots about a meeting in your room. Then stay there.

While we are on the subject of drinking, forget the myth that some folks will tell you that it is a shooting offense to refuse a drink offered by a Mexican. You can refuse to do anything you want if you do it politely. Many times Mexicans are only offering to share something with you because they are being polite. They would never expect you to do something that would cause you harm. If you simply say, *"No gracias, no bebo cerveza* (tequila, ron etc. or simply alcohol), *pero quisiera un refresco,"* you'll probably get a soft drink instead and no one will be offended. If the guy insists that you have a drink with him, be as polite as possible, and just as insistent. Plead illness, medication or whatever you are comfortable with. Saying *"tengo alérgia al alcohol"* sometimes does the trick, but saying you are an alcoholic usually elicits a blank stare. If all fails, get up and walk away. Offending a drunk does not rank as a punishable offense in any country and you have to remember what's really important.

Be especially careful ordering tonic water or *agua quina* in bars or restaurants. You'll often end up with gin and tonic, because the waiter thought you didn't speak Spanish well enough. Stick with Agua Mineral or Coke or 7-Up, or a local soft drink. There are some great ones and we mention them in the text. Toni-Col on the west coast, especially near Mazatlán is one of the best.

When asking if a dish has alcohol in it, be sure to ask if it has wine, too. For some reason, wine is not considered alcohol by waiters. Often they will say, "Oh, no, there is no alcohol, only a little wine." I subscribe to the school that it does not cook out. Even if you don't believe that to be true, believe it in Mexico. Trust me.

Coffees with fancy names like "Spanish, German or Lithuanian (just kidding)" are suspect. If the price is more than plain coffee (*Americano*), then it's a booze drink. It's rare, but I have had Amaretto poured over *flan*, the great dessert. Always use the sniff test before eating anything with a sauce on it. If you accidentally imbibe something with booze spit it out and don't worry about it. It happens to the best. Just don't take a second swig or taste and forget about it.

If you have an AA medallion or ring and wear it, you'll be surprised at the people you'll meet. If we ever meet in person, I'll tell you a story that was related to me about that.

That's all the sobriety wisdom that my sources have given me, but the main thing to remember is that you are not alone even in Mexico and that you can still have a great trip and not lose your program.

We've included this because so many customers wanted to be able to plan their trip based on a routine they're used to back home. Your help in getting new Info is appreciated. You'll see a circle with a triangle and "AA" at Spanish-speaking meetings everywhere. You are always welcome, even if you don't speak Spanish. Spanish for "meeting" is *reunión* or *"sesión"*. The phone numbers below were either provided by the contact person or came from newspapers.

BAJA

CABO SAN LUCAS – Hotel Hacienda, around back, 2nd floor – Sun-Wed-Fri 6 PM. Ph: Barbara (684) 3-2726.

ENSENADA AREA– PUNTA BANDA – Men's AA Catholic Church, La Jolla Beach Mon, 10 AM. – Women's 12 Step, Train Room, Casa De Riker, La Jolla Beach. Mon. 10 AM. – Catholic Church, La Jolla, Tue. 8 AM. – Catholic Church, La Jolla, Thu. 8 AM. – "Going to Any Length" AA, Train Room, Casa De Riker, La Jolla. Sat. 8 AM.

LA PAZ – "Group Esperanza" AA Daily 9-10 AM. Calle Madero between Navarro & Encinas. Contact" 2-93-13 or Casa Blanca Trailer Park.

MULEGE – 1 block east of Canada store – Fri. 3 PM.

MANEADERO, BC – Cultural Social Salón (on Hwy #1), 10.6 MI south of Ensenada at junction with paved roads to Bufadora. Sun, 10 AM. Ask for Albert.

ROSARITO BEACH, BC – Calle Escondido #110 Baja Trade winds. Thurs, 7 PM. – Group 12 Traditions (English) at 72 Calle de La Palma, near police station in middle of town. (If you can't find it, inquire at Red Cross Hospital or Space 100 in KOA Campground). Saturdays, 3 PM; Sundays, 10 AM; Wednesdays, 6 PM; Mondays, 2 PM. Men's meeting Thursdays in KOA Space 100, 5 PM. – AA Breakfast Meeting (English) at Don Guiseppes restaurant back room, Mondays, 9 AM. – Mixed Bar Ladies (English-speaking women's group of multiple 12 step issues) 72 Calle de La Palma, Friday 10 AM.

SAN FELIPE, BCN - There is a meeting hall in the highway thru town, on the left by a car wash, about halfway thru town. Some meetings are women only, so check the schedule on the front door before barging in.

TODOS LOS SANTOS, BC – There are a couple of loners here. Ask around.

WEST COAST

ACAPULCO – English speaking group meets at Horacio Nelson #250. Nelson runs from the Wal-Mart store to the church behind Baby'O's disco. Turn (away from water) off Costera at intersection with Oceanic 2000 on beachside and with 100% Natural and Banca Confía across street on corners. Go one block to Calle Horacio Nelson, and turn right. AA Club is about mid-block at #250 on beachside of street across from Splash Car Wash. Wed, Fri, 5 PM. Call Richard. Ph: (74) 84-1022 or 84-6854 Fax: 84-6854. In the winter there are four or five meetings a week. There are Spanish-speaking meetings at the same locations every day from 6:30 PM till 8:00 PM. Cristo Del Rey Catholic Church at Calle del Caracol #73, has ALANON – Mon, Wed 6 PM. Call Linda: (748) 84-7196. ACOA/CODA – Mon, 7 PM. Call Gail: (748) 84-2087. French-speaking AA – Tues, Fri 6:30 PM. Acapulco Children's Home, on Gran Vía Tropical, Mon 6 PM (tea time). At University, Mon 6 PM and Wed Fri 7 PM.

KINO BAY, SON – Club Deportivo – Wed & Sat, 7 PM. El Saguaro Trailer Park, rec room. Chuck or Gloria (624) 2-0141.

MANZANILLO, COL – On the beach in front of Willy's Restaurant. Wednesday, 10 AM

MAZATLÁN, SIN – 333 Sabalo, Suite 6, across from Guadalajara Grill in shopping center next to Las Palmas T.P. Mon, Wed, & Fri from 6:30 till 7:30 PM; (Nov-Mar) Sun, 10-11 AM. Contact Barbara R. 16-1568 or Ed. L. 14-0174. Also Spanish meeting daily, 8:00 to 9:30 PM and 8:30-10:00 AM, Wed-Sat.

PTO VALLARTA, JAL – meets at Edificio Cine Bahía (in older section of town, across the Río Cuale at 181 Insurgentes (near Madero), second floor at end of hall, RM #208. Daily, 6:30 PM. Mon, Sat, 9 AM; Sun, 11:30 AM. Most meetings are nonsmoking. There's an 8:00 smoking meeting some nights. NA, Tues, Thurs, Sat, 5:00 PM. OA, Tues, 8:00 PM. ALANON, Mon, 5:00 PM. CODA 8:00 PM, Fri. Ph: Helen (322) 5-5919; Paul (322) 2-6060 ext. 204; Angelo (322) 2-3906.

SAN BLAS, NAY – Check at McDonald's restaurant for times. 6 PM, M W F. 9:30 Sun. Calle Sinaloa #19 (sort of). Little shopping center across from police station. All the way in back. Go thru gate to back patio.

SAN CARLOS, SON – At Catholic Church by marina. Mon - Fri 7:30 PM. Sat, 9:30 AM. Thanks to B. C.

YELAPA, JAL. – Wed, Sat, 5:30 PM. Ask at Mike's house on the beach.

ZIHUATANEJO/IXTAPA, GRO – Go on the canal road towards Playa Madero. Pass La Boquita bakery. Turn right towards Hotel Solimar. On one side of the plaza is the Spanish meeting club. Across the plaza is the English speaking group. Meet at 6 PM on Thurs. Call Alanon # Ph: (743) 4-3767.

COLONIAL MEXICO

CHAPALA, JAL – AJIJIC AREA – Sun, Jocotepec, call Bill (376) 5-2575. Mon – Little Chapel, 4 PM. Tues – Río Zula #1, Wed – ACOA, Hidalgo #63, Ajijic, ALANON, Río Zula #1, 4 PM. Thurs – Río Zula #1, 4 PM. Sat – ALANON, Río Zula #1, 9:30 AM.

CUERNAVACA, MOR – Ph: (73) 13-9013 (Francis) or (73) 13-7831 (Minerva). Chilpancingo #8, Colonia del Empleado. It's near the school for the blind (Escuela para los Ciegos) and the Starry Gym at Guerrero #8 near Starry Gym. Meetings Tues. and Thurs. at 5:30 PM.

GUADALAJARA, JAL. – Clubhouse, Filadelfia #2015 (off López Mateos & Las Américas, near Brazz Restaurant) – Mon, Wed, 7:30 PM. Call Bill (36) 63-1417 or Vick (36) 625-2613 for info.

MEXICO CITY, DF – Río Danubio #39 (upstairs), M W F 2 PM. Tues Thurs, 8 PM. Sat, 4 PM. Sun, 6 PM. Union Church, Reforma 1870 – M W F, 8 PM. Ladies Meeting, Nuestra Señora de Guadalupe, Corner Prado Sur y Virreyes (Basement) – Wed, 4 PM. Ph: (5) 568-5104, 525-9090.

OAXACA, OAX – Sun 12 Noon. Ph: (951) 5-1989 (Enrique).

SAN MIGUEL DE ALLENDE, GTO – Alano Club, Terraplen #17; AA M–F, Sat, Sun, 12 noon. ALANON, Mon, 4:30 PM. ACOA, Wed, 7 PM. Sat, 4:30 PM. OA, M W F, 4 PM (Spanish). Tues, 7:30 PM. CODA, Fri, 6 PM (women). Sat, 7 PM. ARTA, Sun, 6 PM. Ph: (415) 2-0667 or (415) 2-2218.

YUCATÁN

CANCÚN, QR – AA English-speaking meetings at the Cancún International Group, 6:15 PM every day downtown at the Plaza Centro shopping center, Av. Nader, third floor. Call Jim (98) 84-2608 (has answering machine) or Vicki (98) 84-2445.

COZUMEL, QR – Tabla de Salvación, 632 20th Av. South, between 7th & 9th streets. Su M W F, 6 PM.

PUERTO MORELOS, QR – AA (English), 1 Km. beyond Villas Shanti on left just before dead end (it's a sand road). It's a 2-story house and may have "AA" sign. There's a large dog in yard.

AMERICAN LEGION POSTS IN MEXICO

Please note: All phone numbers and addresses are for CONTACT ONLY and not necessarily home or post numbers. If calling long distance in Mexico all phone numbers are preceded by 91.

ACAPULCO, GRO — POST #4, Emilio Carranza — Apdo. Postal #1477, 39300 Acapulco, GRO. Ph: (74) 83-9357 Comm: 84-0022. Meets at the Acapulco Yact Club. Commander: Ken Honett; Adjutant: Dean Geddes (74) 66-0462.

CHAPALA, JAL — POST #7, Lake Chapala — Apdo. Postal #31, 45900 Chapala, JAL. Ph: (3) 765-2259. Commander: Mike Valentine; Adjutant: Bob Martin.

CUERNAVACA, MOR — POST #10 — Apdo. Postal #4-464, 62460 Volcanos Cuernavaca, MOR. Ph: (73) 15-6276 Comm: (73) 17-2509. Commander: Fred Bach; Adjutant: Ken Smythe. Apdo. Postal #1-1623, 62000 Cuernavaca, MOR.

GUADALAJARA, JAL — POST #3, Alvarez Castillo — San Antonio #143, Apdo. Postal 31-401 Col. Las Fuentes 45050 Guadalajara, Jal. Ph: (3) 631-1208. Commander: Bill Gillohm; Adjutant: Royce Wheeler.

MAZATLÁN, SIN — POST #11 — Apdo. Postal #154-B, Central Camionera 82000 Mazatlán, SIN. Ph: (69) 84-1003 or 83-8787. Commander: Frank Montoya; Adjutant: Ray Robbins.

MEXICO, DF — POST #2, Alan Seeger — Celaya #25, Col. Hipódromo Condesa. 06100 Mexico, DF. Ph: (5) 564-3386 Res/Bar: 574-4053 Fax: 564-3386. Has Happy Hours. Commander: Ray F. Buggs; Adjutant: Robert F. Fox.

MEXICO, DF — Post #18, Billy Payne — Chilpancingo #46, Col. Roma Sur 06760 Mexico, DF. Ph: (5) 553-4383. Commander: Marv. Gottlieb; Adjutant: Wm. P. McIntosh.

MONTERREY, NL — POST #5, Steve Fordham — Apdo. Postal #280 Col B. del Valle, 66250 Garza García, NL. Ph: (83) 56-8293 Fax: (83) 42-5517. Commander: Ernersto De Karatry; Adjutant: Raymond Orrell.

SAN MIGUEL DE ALLENDE, GTO — POST #6, Thomas V. Price — Apdo. Postal #331, 37700 San Miguel de Allende, Gto. Ph: (415) 52-0764. Commander: John V. Fleming; Adjutant: Simón B. González.

SAN MIGUEL DE ALLENDE, GTO — POST #8, Raymond Howard — Apdo. Postal #218, 37700 San Miguel de Allende, GTO. Ph: (415) 2-3115. Commander Tom Proulx; Adjutant: Jack Hines.

TAMPICO, TAM — POST #1 — Apdo. Postal #664, 89000 Tampico, TAM, Ph: (12) 13-3721 or 13-3722. Commander: George Pelford; Adjutant: Burton Grossman; Secretary: Alicia Cruz Gómez.

U.S. CONSULATES

CD. JUÁREZ, CHIH — López Mateos #924-N CP. 32000 Ph: (16) 13-4048 or 13-5050 Fax: (16) 16-9056 Duty Officer: (915) 526-6066 (in El Paso, TX) Office Hours: 08:00 to 15:45 Mailing Address: American Consulate Apdo. Postal #1681 32000 Cd. Juárez, Chih.

GUADALAJARA, JAL — Progreso #175 CP. Ph: (3) 625-2998 Fax: (3) 626-6549 Duty Officer & after hours calls: (3) 626-5553 Office Hours: 8:00 to 16:30 Mailing Address: Apdo. Postal #39-10 44171 Guadalajara, Jal.

HERMOSILLO, SON — Monterrey #141 CP. 83260 Ph: (62) 17-2575 Fax: (62) 17-2578 Office Hours: 08:00 to 16:45 Mailing Address: American Consulate Apdo. Postal #972, 83260 Hermosillo, Sonora.

MATAMOROS, TAM — Calle Primera #2002 Ph: (891) 2-4402 Fax: (891) 2-2171 Duty Officer: (210) 638-7027 (Celular Phone in Brownsville, TX) Office Hours: 08:00 to 12:00 and 13:00 to 17:00 Mailing Address: American Consulate Apdo. Postal #451, 87350 Matamoros, Tamps.

MÉRIDA, YUC — Paseo Montejo #453 Ph: (99) 25-5011 Fax: (99) 25-6219 Office Hours: 07:30 to 16:00 Mailing Address: American Consulate Apdo. Postal #130, 97000 Merida, Yucatán.

MONTERREY, NL — Avenida Constitución #411 Pte. CP. 64000 Monterrey, N.L. Ph: (83) 45-2120 Fax: (83) 45-7748 Mailing Address: P.O. Box #3098 Laredo, TX 78044-3098

NVO. LAREDO, COAH — Calle Allende #3330 Colonia Jardín CP. 88260 Nuevo Laredo, Tamps. Ph: (871) 4-0696 or 4-0512 Fax: (871) 4-0696 Ext. #128 Duty Officer: (210) 763-1351 (cellular phone in Laredo, TX), Office hours: 08:00 to 12:30 and 13:30 to 17:00 Mailing Address: American Consulate Apdo. Postal #38 88260 Nuevo Laredo, Tamps.

TIJUANA, BCN — Tapachula #96 Ph: (66) 81-7400 Fax: (66) 81-8016 Duty Officer: (619) 585-2000 (Paging Service in San Diego, CA) Office Hours: 08:00 to 16:30 Mailing Address: Apdo. Postal #68 22420 Tijuana, B.C.N.

U.S. CONSULAR AGENTS

ACAPULCO, GRO — Lambert J. Urbanek, Hotel Club del Sol Costera Alemán Esq. Reyes Católicos 19300, Acapulco, Gro. Ph: (748) 5-7207, 5-6600 Fax: 5-7207.

CABO SAN LUCAS, BCS — Robin Hann, Blvd. Marian y Pedregal, local 3 Zona Centro Ph & Fax: (114) 3-3566

CANCÚN, Q ROO — Lorraine H. Lara, Av. Nadar 40-super Manzana 2A Edificio Marruecos, 3rd floor #31 77500 Cancún Q.R. Ph: (98) 84-2411, 84-6399 Fax: 84-8222.

MAZATLÁN, SIN — Gerianne Nelson, Hotel playa, Rodolfo Loyaza #207 Zona Dorada 82100, Mazatlán Ph & Fax: (69) 16-5889 (ask for consular agent).

MULEGE, BCS — Donald J. Johnson, Hotel Serenidad, 23900, Mulege, B.C.S. Ph: (685) 3-0111 Fax: 3-0311.

OAXACA, OAX — Mark Arnold Leyes, Alcala # 201 Desp. 206, 68000 Oaxaca, Oax. Ph & Fax: (951) 4-3054

PTO. VALLARTA, JAL — Jeannette McGill, Parian del Puente, Local 12-A 48300 Puerto Vallarta, Jal. Ph: (322) 2-0069 Fax: 3-0074. Mailing Address: Apdo. Postal #462 Puerto Vallarta, Jal.

SAN LUIS POTOSÍ, SLP — Kathleen Reza, Francisco de P. Moriel #103-10, Col. Centro 96000 San Luis Potosí, SLP Ph & Fax: (481) 2-1528.

SAN MIGUEL DE ALLENDE, GTO — Col. Philip J. Maher, Hernández Macías #72 CP. 37700 San Miguel de Allende, Gto. Ph: (465) 2-2357, 2-0068 Fax: 2-1588. Mailing Address: Apdo. Postal #328 San Miguel de Allende, Gto.

TAMPICO, TAM — Elizabeth Alzaga, Ejército Mexicano # 503-203, Col. Guadalupe 89120 Tampico, Tam. Ph & Fax: (12) 13-2217.

VERACRUZ, VER — Edwin Culp, Víctimas del 25 de Junio #388, 91700 Veracruz, Ver. Ph: (29) 31-5821 Fax: 31-6941.

VEGETARIANS

If you are a true vegan, you will have a limited diet if you eat only in restaurants. There are plenty of fresh fruits and vegetables if you can cook for yourself. If you are a lactovegetarian, then your horizons will open quite a bit: cheese *enchiladas, quesadillas,* pizzas etc. An ovo-lactovegetarian can include *flan, huevos mexicanos* etc. When asking if a dish has meat in it, be very skeptical. Beans *a la charra,* for instance are usually cooked with pork fat, but when a vegan friend of mine asked, she was assured they were *sin carne.* Later, after she had ingested a few bits of pork fat, she said, "Gee, if I was going to eat meat after two years of being a vegan, it could at least have been filet mignon!" Refried beans are usually cooked with lard. *Sopa de verduras* is sometimes prepared with chicken stock, though not always. The main thing to do is to cover all bases. Ask if a dish has: *carne, pollo,* or *puerco.*

NOISE

Motels along the highway (and even in towns) may be noisier than you are used to. I pack a couple of pairs of ear plugs and don't worry about it. An even better solution is to buy a "white noise machine" like the ones sold in travel stores.

Asking for a quiet room is a hit or miss proposition. The desk clerks have probably never seen the inside of their hotel's rooms, so don't depend on their advice. Instead, ask to see it. The bellman who takes you there will know where the quiet rooms are. Tip him well. Always check out the neighborhood before you check in. I asked for a quiet room with a view of the bay in Veracruz and got just what I asked for. I called for a 6:30 AM wake up call and the operator laughed. At 6:01 AM the Navy band from the Naval academy next door began reveille and their daily march to the end of the street. Oh, well, I now have some great pictures of them and a good memory. Remember, "go with the flow!"

GENERAL SOCIAL RULES

If someone invites you to dine with them or come to their house, they are sincere. To refuse without giving good reason is bad manners. In general whenever a specific place and time are mentioned, the invitation is sincere. Their sense of time (except in business situations) is different than ours, so allow thirty minutes to an hour for acceptable tardiness.

Never make fun of someone's station in life or what they have or don't have. People are proud of themselves and their possessions, no matter how meager they may appear to your eyes.

Please, please, don't ask, "How much is it in real money?" Often people will quote you in dollars to be polite. Also, don't worry too much about being short changed. People are a lot more honest than you might suspect.

WAITING IN LINE — chances are that someone will cut in. If you politely say, *"Desculpe, la fila sigue atrás,"* will tell them that the end of the line is somewhere behind you. Unfortunately, Mexicans are no different than people anywhere in the world.Some rude people will just ignore you, but most people are polite and will go farther back in the line and try again.

DRINKING — while it is proper to accept a drink offered in friendship, and to return the favor, but be careful as this can result in a never ending cycle that will drain your new friends' paycheck. Make a polite excuse that you have time for one more, but must meet someone for something pressing. Then keep your word and leave. If you want to see the friend more later at a non-drinking situation, suggest it before you leave.

PHOTOGRAPHS — Almost everyone likes having his picture taken, but ask first. I still remember the old men in the park in Tepic who refused, saying, "We aren't Huichols" (meaning, we aren't someone to be gawked at). Unfortunately, most people get this really serious, stiff appearance for portraits that ruins what you want to do. Sometimes you can fake 'em out with a premature flash. They will lighten up and you can take a second picture if your flash recycles quick enough. There is plenty of print film everywhere. The larger cities will have slide film, but it is usually Ekatchrome©. If you like Velvia© or Fujichrome©, better bring your own, though Fuji is making a stronger presence than in years past. By the way, film is not more expensive than here. In some cases it is cheaper.

RESTAURANTS — If a restaurant owner offers you a free drink or sample of a specialty dish, be aware that you have arrived at a new level of familiarity. Acknowledge this by complimenting him and his offering.If a waiter or chef makes a recommendation, take him up on it. It is probably a local specialty and often quite palatable to a gringo's taste buds.

Chain restaurants like McDonalds, Kentucky Fried Chicken, Church's©, Burger King©, etc. are spread throughout the country. If you are hesitant about going because of a fear of different foods, don't. Other higher-end restaurants like: Applebee's© Denny's©, etc. and others are becoming more prevalent.

KIDS — instead of giving them candy, take a big bag of big balloons and blow one up and offer them around. You will be amazed at how many new friends you will have before you are halfway through the bag.

PARKING ATTENDANTS — in small towns there are still some guys who are wearing khaki clothing and official looking hats that are as old as they are and will direct you to a parking space. They are not cops but will watch your car. Pay them the peso equivalent of fifty cents or so unless they are very helpful. At parking lots you will get a ticket. Don't worry about leaving your keys with them. I've never had anything bad happen. Tip them if they bring car to you, otherwise, no.

PARKING LOTS — Many hotels have underground lots that are narrow and have low ceilings. You will not be able to use them if you have a tall camper. If you have an extended cab pickup with long bed, it will take some maneuvering to get in and out, but it can be done, if you have the patience. Find another open-air lot if possible. Make sure you know the price before leaving and don't loose the ticket.

CAR WASH — These are often available at parking lots and from kids on street. Once in Durango, I conducted an experiment to see how honest the average guy on the street was. I found a guy washing a car late at night. I told him where my truck was. I paid him and went home. The next morning, I had a clean truck.

TIPPING — I usually tip the gas pump jockey, unless he was surly, the peso equivalent of a quarter. Remember that your U.S. coins are useless to anyone in Mexico, so don't use them for tips. The kids who wash my windshield get a quarter, a little more if there is a gang of them. Be sure to pick one as the jefe and pay him and point to the rest, or they will all ask for a donation. Porters get fifty cents a bag. Maids should get a dollar a day. Waiters get 10-15% average and exceptional service, of course, gets up to 20%. Please use common sense and don't overtip like an ugly American or undertip like a cheapskate.

WOMEN TRAVELING ALONE

While many folks enjoy their trips more with a companion, traveling alone in Mexico should be no more daunting than doing so anywhere in the U.S. Use common sense, dress conservatively, don't sleep in you car and you will find the Mexican people to be very hospitable. If you break down on a lonely stretch of road, you're better off than in the U.S. You will probably be helped by a Green Angel (more on them later), a family or a gallant truck driver. There are fewer weirdoes on the highways of Mexico than the U.S., in my humble opinion. I've also been told this by my women friends who have traveled alone. As in any country, how you are treated often depends on the signals you give out. Don't dress provocatively. Wear loose clothing. Don't be overly friendly to any single men. Be aware of your surroundings, but remember that women are more respected in Mexico than here, so don't be too uptight. Many guidebook writers and travel writers are women and they travel alone all the time. I personally know some eighty year old ladies who have been traveling alone all their lives. Places to be careful are ruins and other tourist attractions close to closing time, bars, lonely beaches (please don't camp on one) and anywhere you would not go back home. Use common sense and you'll have a good time. You may very well meet someone else traveling alone who will share the rest of your trip with you if you feel uncomfortable. It's true that in some cities, you will receive catcalls from young guys, but that happened to me and a friend recently, so what good was I?

Don't worry. If you don't want to travel alone, we have a Tripshare service that links people wanting a traveling companion. Send info about where and when you want to travel and who you will and won't travel with. We'll mail you a list of all other participants and you take it from there. Write to: Sanborn's Tripshare, P.O. Box 310, McAllen, TX 78505-0310. It's free.

DON'T DRIVE AT NIGHT!

Please don't drive at night — You are quite safe in terms of personal safety on Mexico's highways. In fact, most people say that they feel safer in Mexico than they do in the U.S. Still, a number of factors make night driving hazardous.

On older, two lane roads, you could hit a chuckhole with no warning that could seriously damage your suspension — if you don't bounce off the pavement or roll over. Shoulders are narrow or sometimes nonexistent. Drivers of broken down vehicles often place rocks on the road to "warn" you that they are taking up a lane ahead. Even if you see the rocks in time, it may be too late. Long after they are gone, the rocks remain, despite signs telling you not to. These rocks can tear up your car or send you careening off a mountain.

Mexico has a lot of open range. Cows, burros, goats and horses think they have the right of way. Even a collision with a little goat can tear up your front end. A horse or cow can kill you. You can't see a black cow at night. Outside of cities, some drivers still drive without headlights, thinking they can see better or that they will conserve their lights by not using them. Others (besides trucks, which have enough lights to wake the dead) may have only one (or no) taillights.

There is often a great drop from the pavement to the shoulder that could send you end over end. The famous Green Angels don't drive at night. Cows, burros etc. don't wear taillights. I nearly hit a black cow the last time I drove at night.

There are exceptions. The toll roads are generally OK to drive at night, but be cautious. Just as U.S. highways turn into deer sanctuaries at night, Mexico's cows and deer can decide to take the toll roads at night. Keep awake. If you find that you MUST drive at night on a two lane road, try to follow (but not too closely), a long-distance bus or a semi-truck. They will clear the way for you. Those cattle catchers on the front of trucks aren't called *mataburros* (burro killers) for nothing.

GREEN ANGELS

These are not related to the Jolly Green Giant or the Hulk. Green Angels are trained mechanics who roam all the major highways to assist disabled travelers. This is a free service provided by Mexico's Department of Tourism. You'll see their bright green panel trucks driving slowly down every major highway. They cover each route twice a day. If you break down, they will find you, or you can call them on your CB, channel 9. There are over 800 "Angels" covering 230 routes. If one of them helps you, his service is free, but he will have to charge you for any parts you need or gasoline. He can also provide emergency medical aid. Whenever I've used their services, I've always given them a tip. It's never been turned down. If you need help and a phone is nearby, call the Green Angel Hot Line: 91-800-90392 or the central radio room 91-5-250-8221.

DRIVING ETHICS

CUTTING IN — This is very common. If you are in a line of traffic and it doesn't seem to be moving and cars are passing you on the dirt on the right, chances are they are cutting in front of the line. You can try it yourself, if you are aggressive. Just remember that the side of the road may be uneven or have big potholes, so go slow. If you can see a railroad crossing ahead, don't try it. In city traffic when someone wants to turn right or left (from any lane), one of the passengers (or driver) will stick arm out and waggle finger in direction of intended turn. It's customary to let them. When you are in a traffic jam and someone acts like they are going to cut in, but point their finger straight in front of them, indicating that they are crossing the line of traffic, not trying to cut in. They are usually telling the truth. Let them in.

BUSES — Passing a long distance bus (not the little local *colectivos* and *lecheros* or second class stop and go varieties) is usually an invitation to a duel. Do so at your own risk, or better yet, don't. They will always go faster than you. Bus drivers really seem to be bothered if you use high beams of even fog lights or drive during the day with your headlights on. They will flash you if they are feeling pleasant, but if not, they will blind you with their forty-seven running lights and two million candlepower sets of quad-headlights. It's an awesome sight on a lonely road.

FLAGMEN — You're bound to encounter a few sets of these. Sometimes the flagman may be only a inattentive young man with a faded red rag who is supposed to warn you about upcoming dangers. Sometimes, like Herman Melville's Ishmael, he may be composing stories instead of paying attention. Whenever you see a guy on the side of the road with a red rag, assume you'd better slow down. Sometimes the road will have been freshly oiled or tarred and if you go too fast, you will have a black vehicle. (When that happens there will usually be an enterprising young man with a bucket of gasoline who will not detail, but de-tar your car. This may not be good for your paint job, though.) There could also be a myriad of dangers ahead, so slow down.

TRAFFIC SIGNALS — When a light changes from green to yellow to red, sometimes the green will start flashing, turn yellow, then red. Mexicans tend to inch forward before the red changes to green. When there are four lights on a signal (and a left turn lane) then one is probably a protected left turn signal. Be careful, if there is no left turn lane because the fourth signal may indicate a right turn or just be an extra green.

RIGHT TURN ON RED — This is not universally allowed, unless there is a sign, usually a right arrow with the words *Continua con precaución.*

LEFT TURNS — You didn't think you'd get off that easily did you? There are at least five kinds. Some sadistic engineer in Mexico City is probably inventing the sixth one right now.

The first is easy — when you are in a city, there will be a left turn lane (usually, not always) and a traffic signal with four lights. The far left one is a protected turn signal. That's simple enough, right? Ah, newcomer to Mexico, listen up. You must wait for the left turn arrow. You cannot turn left when the coast is clear on only a green light. That's why traffic doesn't flow all that well in U.S. border cities because the Mexicans are diligently waiting for the protected arrow and the gringos aren't even waiting for the Indians.

Left turn type two — There is no arrow. If the light has only three lights, it is every man for himself.

Left turn type three — There is a sign with an arrow indicating you should exit, then it turns left in front of traffic. What on earth does that mean? You should exit right onto a lateral or access road on a divided street. Stay in the left lane. Go to a stoplight. Turn left across the street you were just on. It's easier to do than it sounds.

Left turn type four — You are on a two-lane open road. If there is traffic coming, do not put on your left turn blinker and stop in the middle of an intersection to turn left. Just before you get there, you'll see a paved shoulder to the right. You should exit right, pull around until you are heading in the direction you want to turn. When traffic is clear, scoot across the highway.

Left turn type five — This is easy and familiar. You are on a divided highway. There is a break in the median and a sign that says *retorno*. You guessed it — a turn around.

Well, now folks, you have had a really good introduction to what it's really like to drive in Mexico from someone who knows what he's talking about. The bottom line is go and have a good time. All of this stuff comes naturally after awhile. The Mexican people are friendly and don't get all uptight if you make a few mistakes. Just don't go mistaking the road crew up ahead for a group of banditos. I firmly believe that's how all those stories got started. — "Mexico" Mike.

TEMPERATURE CONVERSION TABLE

FAHRENHEIT	100	95	85	80	75	70	65	60	55	50	45	40	35	32
CELCIUS	37.3	35	29.4	26.6	23.8	21.1	18.3	15.5	12.7	10	7.2	4.2	1.6	0

CONVERTING KILOGRAMS TO POUNDS: Simply double the kilogram figure, then add 10%. For example: if a man's weight is 80 kilos, double this (160) and add 10% (16). His weight would be 176 pounds.

CONVERSION OF METRIC WEIGHTS & MEASURES

1 gram = 0.035 ounces	1 millimeter = 0.039 inch
1 kilogram = 2.205 pounds	1 centimeter = 0.393 inch
1 metric ton = 1.102 tons	1 decimeter = 3.937 inches
1 milliliter = 0.033 fluid ounces	1 meter = 3.289 feet
1 deciliter = 3.381 fluid ounces	1 kilometer = 0.621 miles
1 liter = 1.056 quarts	

TIRE PRESSURE:

KILOS	2.1	2	1.9	1.8	1.7	1.6
POUNDS	32	30	28	26	24	22

CONVERTING KILOMETERS TO MILES

KILOMETERS	1	5	10	20	30	40	60	70	80	90	100
MILES	0.62	3.1	6.2	12.4	19	25	31	37	50	56	62

CONVERTING LITERS TO GALLONS

LITERS	1	4	10	15	20	30	40	50	60	70	80	90
GALLONS	0.26	1.06	2.64	3.97	5.28	7.92	10.56	13.2	15.8	18.5	21.1	23.8

SANBORN'S COMPANY BIOGRAPHY

Sanborn's Mexico Insurance traces its roots to 1948 when Dan Sanborn, a newspaperman from Kankakee, Ill., began writing a unique highway guide to Mexico for his friends. He's retired now.

In the early 1950's, he opened a roadside stand to sell citrus juice, curios, Mexico insurance and "horned toads" (lizards that shoot blood from their eyes). With the insurance, each customer got a *Travelog*, Dan's mile-by-smile highway guide of Mexico, custom-made for the customer's itinerary.

Today, Sanborn's has 27 agencies located at major US-Mexico border crossings, and in Mexico. Customers can purchase insurance by using our Faxinsure or Phoneinsure service, in addition to our walk-in and mail order service. We also sell Central American insurance. It's a "family-style" business with old-fashioned values and courtesy. Each customer is "one of the family."

Tourists need Mexican insurance because neither U.S. nor Canadian insurance is recognized in Mexico. We sell Seguros Del Centro insurance. It's sold on a daily or inexpensive yearly group basis. Claims are settled in the U.S. We have adjusters throughout Mexico (Our U.S. claims service will pay to fix vehicle in the U.S.A.).

Today, the *Travelog* is a guidebook to all Mexico and Central America. It is 1,000 pages of incredibly detailed directions, history, customs and folksy humor which gets people where they're going safely and helps them enjoy the historic routes they drive. Detailed maps of most tourist towns are included, as are hotels, restaurants and RV parks. All price ranges are covered. It lists the names of the small towns, including many former *ejidos*. It also explains why the *ejido* system was one of the cornerstones of the Revolution, what *topes* are and why a stop sign is sometimes a "slow down" sign. We also publish a series of guidebooks to various regions of Mexico.

The "*Travelog*" is written by "Mexico" Mike Nelson, who drives 20,000 miles a year to try to keep it up to date. He also helps individuals with route planning and info from the home office in McAllen, TX. He promotes driving in Mexico through his many magazine and newspaper articles, and contributes to other guidebooks. He has been profiled in the *Wall Street Journal, New York Times, Texas Monthly,* and many others, and has promoted driving tourism on radio & TV shows throughout the country.

Our newsletter is distributed to about 800 newspapers in the US, Canada, & Europe. It contains "filler" sized info of interesting facts. The annual subscription is $8.00. Our SANBORN'S AMIGO CLUB offers discounts on hotels & books. Medical air evacuation is a Club benefit included with membership, as is a subscription to the newsletter.

Mexico Travel Document Processing Service – Sanborn's now can fill out your travel documents including tourist cards and vehicle temporary import permits. We offer this service for those who don't feel comfortable getting their own documents.

Let Us Explain Our Services

AUTO INSURANCE —Recommended limits are: $50,000 property damage / $40/80,000 bodily injury liability and $2,000/10,000 medical. These coverages, added to your Fire, Total Theft and Collision coverage give you the total cost of your policy. By special arrangement with our insurance company, a Sanborn's Amigo Club member can purchase a six month or annual policy for less than the regular policy.

BOAT AND AIRCRAFT INSURANCE — Fishin' or flyin' Mexico is accessible, when you travel with our Insurance for your boat or plane.

UNIVERSAL — Assists you through a 24-hour phone service in locating the right kind of medical care nearest you. Directs you to a doctor who speaks your language. Monitors your progress, coordinates communication with your family and doctor in your home country, and arranges for medical air evacuation if necessary. Free with our Mexico auto policies and our Amigo Club.

PHONEINSURE & FAXINSURE SERVICE — For your convenience at selected Sanborn's agencies, you can purchase your insurance, join our club, or order our Travel Books and Famous *Travelog* over the phone or via fax.

PROLIBER — Bail complement that guarantees your liberty and property, and legal defense anywhere in Mexico — Our Mexico auto policy now includes ProLiber to protect Sanborn's insurance customers.

SANBORN'S AMIGO CLUB — Benefits include a membership card, quarterly newsletter, discount guide book with over 500 hotels, motels, and restaurants offering our members substantial discounts, "Universal" medical assistance hot line and air evacuation coverage, Fishing & Hunting guide, RV & camping guide, our famous mile-by-smile *Travelog*, a road map, a "Drive Mexico with Experts" guide, and an official member's window decal. PLUS, members get a DEEP discount on our six month and annual Mexico auto insurance policies. You can choose either our standard plan or our family plan.

THE FAMOUS *TRAVELOG* — OUR PRIDE AND JOY! The *Travelog* is the most detailed Driving Guide to all the major highways in Mexico and Central America that take you mile-by-smile to your destination and back. Tailor made for your itinerary, it's like your own personal guided tour south of the border.

TRIP PLANNING AND ROUTING — Where's the best place to go in December? In March? What's the weather like in Chapala? What's the best route to Veracruz? The Yucatán? These questions and more can be answered to help you plan your trip to Mexico, coupled with our *Travelog* and maps will get you down and back.

TRIPSHARE SERVICE — Don't want to travel alone? Want to share experience with others that have similar interests, but didn't know where to find these people? Maybe our TripShare Service can help. Call for details.

About the Author

"Mexico" Mike Nelson admits to traveling, photographing and living in Mexico for over twenty years, though we suspect it has been longer than that. The name "Mexico" Mike was bestowed on him for his extensive writings and knowledge about the county. Some say he deserves the name because he has spent more time wandering around south of the border than being gainfully employed.

Newspapers and magazines like the *Wall Street Journal, New York Times, LA Times, Associated Press, Orange County Register, U.S. News and World Report, Denver Post, Houston Chronicle and Post, Dallas Morning News, Washington Post, Texas Monthly, American Way Mexico Business, Mexico Travel Monthly Report* and more have published feature stories describing his travels, or quoted him as an expert on the country. Mexico's Tourism Department has recognized his vast knowledge by naming him the official spokesman for their surface tourism program. In his promotion of Mexico, he has appeared on television and radio shows across the county. He is one writer who truly knows Mexico inside out.

His first book, *Mexico From the Driver's Seat*, is a humorous, insightful and knowledgeable armchair reading experience that gives the reader a good taste of travel in Mexico. Besides travel books, he has written articles on the culture of the country.

He also publishes other books, like *Live Better South of the Border* and *More than a Dozen of Mexico's Hidden Jewels*, which should be available at Sanborn's offices. If not, call 1-800-321-5605 for a catalog or to order.

MAJOR TOLL ROAD RATES

These toll rates are subject to change. RV's although technically may be considered 2-Axle, they are actually charged by the number of rear tires (3-Axle rate and possibly at the 5-Axle rate if towing a car). If you verify any changes, please let us know, so we can keep this chart updated. Prices are in Pesos (8 to 1 as of 3/97).

HIGHWAY – TOLL HOUSE	CARS	2-AXLE	3-AXLE
HWY 15 – WEST COAST – NOGALES TO MAZATLAN			
MAGDALENA – HERMOSILLO	$32.00	$64.00	$96.00
HERMOSILLO – GUAYMAS	$32.00	$64.00	$96.00
GUAYMAS – OBREGON	$32.00	$64.00	$96.00
OBREGON – NAVAJOA	$32.00	$64.00	$96.00
NAVAJOA – LOS MOCHIS 1	$32.00	$64.00	$96.00
NAVAJOA – LOS MOCHIS 2	$32.00	$64.00	$96.00
LOS MOCHIS – CULIACAN #1	$10.00	$15.00	$17.00
LOS MOCHIS – CULIACAN #2	$15.00	$23.00	$31.00
CULIACAN - MAZATLAN #1	$63.00	$84.00	$112.00
CULIACAN – MAZATLAN #2	$61.00	$82.00	$110.00
TOTALS	$341.00	$588.00	$846.00
HWY 40 REYNOSA – MONTERREY – SALTILLO – TORREON			
REYNOSA – MONTERREY #1	$105.00	$210.00	$315.00
REYNOSA – MONTERREY #2	$15.00	$30.00	$45.00
REYNOSA — MONTERREY #3	$15.00	$30.00	$45.00
MONTERRREY – ALLENDE#1 (PERIFERICO)	$31.00	$62.00	$93.00
MONTERREY – ALLENDE #2 (PERIFERICO)	$17.00	$34.00	$51.00
MONTERREY – SALTILLO	$11.00	$22.00	$33.00
SALTILLO – MATEHUALA	$18.00	$36.00	$54.00
SALTILLO – TORREON #1	$45.00	$90.00	$135.00
SALTILLO – TORREON #2	$45.00	$90.00	$135.00
HWY 85 LAREDO – MONTERREY			
LAREDO – MONTERREY	$88.00	$176.00	$264.00
HWY 45 ELPASO – CHIHUAHUA – TORREON – ZACATECAS			
EL PASO – CHIHUAHUA (MOCTEZUMA)	$33.00	$66.00	$99.00
EL PASO – CHIHUAHUA (SACARAMENTO)	$16.00	$32.00	$48.00
CHIHUAHUA – JIMENEZ (CONCHOS)	$10.00	$20.00	$30.00
CHIHUAHUA – JIMENEZ (CAMARGO)	$10.00	$20.00	$30.00
JIMENEZ – TORREON #1	$16.00	$32.00	$48.00
JIMENEZ – TORREON (SAVALSA)	$12.00	$24.00	$36.00
JIMENEZ – TORREON (CEBALLOS)	$38.00	$76.00	$114.00
TORREON – ZACATECAS (LEON GUZMAN)	$44.00	$88.00	$132.00
TORREON – ZACATECAS (CUENCAME)	$13.00	$26.00	$39.00
TORREON – ZACATECAS (FRESNILLO)	$9.00	$18.00	$27.00
TOTALS	$201.00	$402.00	$603.00
TORREON – DURANGO			
TORREON – DURANGO #1	$37.00	$74.00	$93.00
TORREON – DURANGO #2	$26.00	$52.00	$65.00
TORREON – DURANGO #3	$27.00	$54.00	$67.00
TORREON – DURANGO #4	$22.00	$44.00	$55.00
TOTALS	$112.00	$224.00	$280.00
HWY 95D MEXICO – ACAPULCO			
MEXICO – ACAPULCO #1 (TLALPAN)	$40.00	$80.00	$120.00
MEXICO – ACAPULCO #2 (ALPULYECA)	$38.00	$76.00	$114.00
MEXICO – ACAPULCO #3 (PASO MORELOS)	$99.00	$198.00	$297.00
MEXICO – ACAPULCO #4 (PALO BLANCO)	$61.00	$122.00	$183.00
MEXICO – ACAPULCO #5 (LA VENTA)	$55.00	$110.00	$165.00
MEXICO – ACAPULCO #6 (METLAPIL)	$25.00	$50.00	$75.00
TOTALS	$318.00	$636.00	$954.00

HIGHWAY – TOLL HOUSE		CARS	2-AXLE	3-AXLE
ZACATECAS – GUADALAJARA				
ZACATECAS – OJOCALIENTE		$11.00	$22.00	$33.00
OJOCALIENTE – AGUASCALIENTES		$18.00	$36.00	$54.00
AGUASCALIENTES – LAGOS DE MORENO		$31.00	$62.00	$77.00
LAGOS DE MORENO – ARANDAS		$38.00	$76.00	$114.00
ARANDAS – ZAPOTLANEJO		$39.00	$78.00	$117.00
ZAPOTLANEJO – GUADALAJARA		$14.00	$28.00	$42.00
	TOTALS	$151.00	$302.00	$437.00
HWY150D MEXICO – VERACRUZ				
MEXICO – VERACRUZ #1		$15.00	$30.00	$45.00
MEXICO – VERACRUZ #2		$13.00	$26.00	$39.00
MEXICO – VERACRUZ #3		$13.00	$26.00	$39.00
MEXICO – VERACRUZ #4		$13.00	$26.00	$29.00
	TOTALS	$54.00	$108.00	$152.00
HWY 45-90D QUERETARO – GUADALAJARA				
QUERETARO – CELAYA		$13.00	$26.00	$39.00
SALAMANCA – IRAPUATO		$14.00	$28.00	$42.00
PUENTE LA PIEDAD		$2.00	$4.00	$6.00
ZAPOTLANEJO – GUADALAJARA		$14.00	$28.00	$42.00
TOTALS		$43.00	$86.00	$129.00
HWY #57 QUERETARO – MEXICO CITY				
QUERETARO BYPASS		$20.00	$40.00	$60.00
QUERETARO – MEXICO #1 (PALMILLAS)		$15.00	$30.00	$45.00
QUERETARO – MEXICO #2 (TEPOZOTLAN)		$15.00	$30.00	$45.00
	TOTALS	$50.00	$100.00	$150.00
HWY #1 TIJUANA – ENSENADA				
TIJUANA – ENSENADA #1		$7.00	$14.00	$21.00
TIJUANA – ENSENADA #2		$7.00	$14.00	$21.00
TIJUANA – ENSENADA #3		$7.00	$14.00	$21.00
TIJUANA – ENSENADA #4		$4.00	$8.00	$12.00
	TOTALS	$25.00	$50.00	$75.00
VERACRUZ - MINATITLAN (3 toll booths)		$132.00	$264.00	$396.00
SAN LUIS POTOSI BYPASS		$20.00	$40.00	$60.00
TAMPICO BRIDGE		$12.00	$24.00	$36.00
TUXPAN BRIDGE		$9.00	$17.00	$25.00
TECOLUTLA BRIDGE		$6.00	$13.00	$16.00
NAUTLA BRIDGE		$8.00	$10.00	$15.00
VERACRUZ BRIDGE		$8.00	$10.00	$15.00
ORIZABA - OAXACA		$80.00	$160.00	$240.00
TOLUCA – IXTAPAN DE LA SAL		$8.00	$16.00	$24.00
GUADALAJARA – COLIMA (4 toll booths)		$91.00	$133.00	$176.00
GUADALAJARA – TEPIC (3 toll booths)		$119.00	$238.00	$357.00
SILAO – GUANAJUATO		$7.00	$14.00	$21.00
LEON – SAN FRANCISCO DEL RINCON		$37.00	$74.00	$111.00
CHAMPOTON – CAMPECHE		$14.00	$28.00	$42.00
PUENTE REYNOSA		$11.00	$22.00	$33.00
GUADALAJARA – MEXICO CITY VIA MORELIA				
GUADALAJARA – MORELIA #1		$12.00	$18.00	$24.00
GUADALAJARA – MORELIA #2		$41.00	$82.00	$123.00
GUADALAJARA – MORELIA #3		$37.00	$74.00	$111.00
GUADALAJARA – MORELIA #4		$56.00	$112.00	$168.00
MORELIA – TOLUCA #1		$14.00	$28.00	$42.00
MORELIA – TOLUCA #2		$6.00	$12.00	$18.00
TOLUCA – MEXICO CITY		$21.00	$42.00	$63.00
	TOTALS	$187.00	$368.00	$549.00

How 'bout them Ferries!

Take seasick preparations if you're inclined to that malady. It can get rough. Don't plan on sleeping in the "*salón*" unless you really like people and kids. Go for the "*turista*" or "*cabina*," Sleeping arrangements are bunks in a comfy room for two with a bathroom. Your rig stays below. You won't be able to return to it, so take get anything you need before you leave the bowels of the ship. Food is served on board. **NO PETS** are allowed to ride in the passenger compartments. Fare is per person, one way, sharing the accommodation. Children under 12 years old pay half price. Children under 2 years old must be registered at no cost. Pregnant women are not allowed aboard.

You need to reserve a few days to a week in advance. The easiest thing to do is have a travel agent do it for you. You can do it by phone, but must pick up your ticket in person. In La Paz, you must pick up ticket at downtown office at G. Prieto #1495, not at the dock. **Hours change**, but try 8-noon. Plan on a long line. Then, you must show up at the dock the day you are to leave and register, about 8 AM (this will vary, so ask and then arrive an hour early). Then you hang around until they begin boarding. There's always a chance of a cancellation, so you can **try** showing up, waiting and asking for a ticket. You **might** get one. At other locations, you can get tickets at the ferry landing. There is a toll-free # for all of Mexico that may take reservations – 91-800-6-9696. The Peso exchange rate is about 8 Pesos / 1 Dollar (as of 3/'97).

FERRY PRICES RATES ARE IN PESOS and are based on length:

PRICE LIST

Vehicle	Mazatlán	Topolobampo	Guaymas
Under 5 meters	$826.40	$503.75	$580.05
5.01 to 6.5 meters	$1075.10	$654.30	$754.50
Motorhome under 9 meters	$1489.40	$907.15	$1044.55
Autos/w/trailer 9.01 to 17 meters	$2813.20	$1712.35	$1971.45
Buses	$1404.40	$860.40	$990.10
Motorcycles	$106.85	$63.20	$85.00
Motorcycle with side car	$180.95	$109.10	$144.05
Passenger Compartments			
Salón	$109.10	$72.85	$72.85
Turista	$218.30	$145.45	$145.45
Cabina	$327.10	$218.30	$218.30
Especial	$436.30	$290.90	$290.90

It doesn't matter how long your vehicle is, as long as your pockets are deep enough. Sometimes the ferry runs, but only for freight, so don't plan too strictly.

FERRY SCHEDULE

Route:	La Paz to Mazatlán	Mazatlán to La Paz	La Paz to Topolabampo	Topolobampo to La Paz	Sta Rosalla to Guaymas	Guaymas to Sta. Rosalla
Frequency and Class:	Thursday to Tuesday, Salón, Turista, Cabina & Especial	Friday to Wednesday, Salon, Turista, Cabina & Especial	Wednesday & Thursday, Salón, Turista, Cabina & Especial	Wednesday & Thursday, Salón, Turista, Cabina & Especial	Sunday & Wednesday, Salón & Turista	Tuesday & Friday, Salón & Turista
Frequency and Class:	Wednesday, Cargo Ferry, Salón	Thursday, Cargo Ferry, Salón	Monday, Tuesday, Friday & Saturday, Salón	Monday, Tuesday, Friday & Saturday, Salón		
Departure:	3:00 PM	3:00 PM	11:00 AM	10:00 PM	8:00 AM	8:00 AM
Arrival:	9:00 AM	9:00 AM	7:00 PM	7:00 AM	3:00 PM	3:00 PM

INFORMATION AND RESERVATIONS

LA PAZ, B.C.S: Guillermo Prieto & 5 de Mayo Ph: (112) 5-3833 & 5-4666 Pichilingue Terminal Ph: (112) 2-9485 Fax: (112) 5-6588

MAZATLAN, SIN: Ferry Terminal Ph: (69) 81-7020 & 81-7021 Fax: (69) 81-7023

TOPOLOBAMPO, SIN: Muelle Fiscal Ph: (686) 20141, Fax: (686) 2-0013

STA. ROSALIA, B.C.S.: Muelle Fiscal Ph: (115) 2-0013 & 2-0013

GUAYMAS, SON.: Muelle Fiscal Ph: (662) 2-3390 Fax: (662) 2-3393

MEXICO CITY: FESTIVAL TOURS, Texas #36, Col. Nápoles, Delegación Benito Juárez, Mexico DF 03810, Ph: (5) 682-7043, 682-6213 Fax: (5) 682-7378

Sanborn's U. S. Agents

Unless noted, agents closed Sundays & holidays, but after hours and 24 hour policy pickup available.

AJO, AZ — PH: (520) 387-6376. AZ 800-293-2560 FAX: 387-6910.

AMARILLO, TX — PH: (806) 374-2818, 1-800-779-0454 FAX: (806) 374-9959.

BASTROP, TX — PH: (512) 321-1131 or 800-531-5440 FAX: 321-6672.

BROWNSVILLE, TX — PH: (956) 542-5457 or 546-6644 FAX: 504-2919.

DEL RIO, TX — PH: (956) 775-3252. FAX: 774-4306.

DOUGLAS, AZ — PH: (520) 364-8496. FAX: 364-5443.

EAGLE PASS, TX — PH: (956) 773-2341. FAX: 773-7791.

EL CENTRO, CA — PH: (619) 352-4643. FAX: 352-6321.

EL PASO, TX — PH: (915) 779-3538, FAX: 772-1795.

HIDALGO, TX — PH: (956) 843-8747 FAX: 843-7414.

HOUSTON, TX — PH: (713) 690-1800, or 1-800-861-5723, FAX: 690-1866.

LA FERIA, TX — PH: (956) 797-2281, FAX: 797-51333.

LAREDO, TX — PH: (956) 723-3657. FAX: 723-0000.

McALLEN, TX — PH: (956) 686-0711. FAX: 686-0732.

NOGALES, AZ — PH: (520) 281-1873 FAX: 761-1215.

PAMPA, TX — PH: (806) 665-6581, 1-800-894-0423 FAX: 665-6582.

PHOENIX (GLENDALE), AZ — PH: (602) 938-1128. FAX: 547-0104.

SAN ANTONIO, TX (Broadway) — PH: (210) 828-3587, FAX: 824-7741.

SAN ANTONIO, TX (Shannon) — PH: (210) 922-6166. FAX: 922-4509.

SCOTTSDALE, AZ — PH: (602) 483-0571 FAX: 905-8135.

SIERRA VISTA, AZ — PH: (520) 458-4950 FAX: 458-0654.

TUCSON, AZ — PH: (520) 327-1255, 888-327-1255 FAX: 327-1303.

WESLACO, TX — PH: (956) 968-9188 FAX: 969-0110.

YUMA, AZ — PH: (520) 726-0300, 1-888-726-0300.

In Mexico & Central America

GUADALAJARA, JAL. — Martin Parker, Callejón Del Arroyo #200, Villa Nova, Ajijic, JAL Apdo. Postal #575, Ajijic 45920 JAL. Ph: (376) 6-0269, 5-4666.

MANZANILLO, COL. — Sr. Ricardo Morín, Independencia #22 Apdo. Postal #84 Manzanillo (Santiago), Colima C.P. 28860 Ph: (333) 3-0720 Fax: (333) 3-0420

PUERTO VALLARTA, JAL. — Sr. Clemente Celis, Near Sheraton at Calle Sierra Rocallosa #379. Corner Ecuador & Rocallosa. Turn east at Sheraton. Go 5 blocks on Américas, left at Ecuador (Lion's Club school). Go 1 block, then left one-half block. Ph: (322) 2-2364.

SAN MIGUEL DE ALLENDE, GTO. — Sr. Abraham Cadena, Calle Ancha San Antonio #21 — almost across from the Instituto. Ph: (415) 2-1638 Fax: 2-2313. Also Apdo. Postal #554 C.P. 37700

GUATEMALA CITY, GUATEMALA — Bill Tanner, 48 Av. 2-4927 Lotificación El Rosario, Guatemala, Guatemala Sect. 0943. P.O. Box 025289 Miami, FL 33102-5289 Ph: 2-91-0416.

Retirement Places, Books, Newspapers?

The communities you're looking for with other Americans are Guadalajara, Lake Chapala, Ajijic, Pto. Vallarta all in Jalisco.

San Miguel de Allende, Gto; Cuernavaca, Mex; and Oaxaca, Oax, are others. John D. Bryant, who wrote Guadalajara, A Great Place to Visit or Retire, told me he's updating his fine little book. It should be good reading. Cost: $15.00. For really up-to-date info on retirement, get the *M.R.T.A. Newsletter*, for $25.00 a year (USA), or a sample for $8.00. You can get either by writing: Mexico Retirement & Travel Assistance, P.O. Box 2190, Henderson NV 89015. We also like *Get to Know Mexico*. Cost: $9.95 retail.

Travelmex, Apdo. Postal 31-750, 45050 Guadalajara, JAL. $15 a year (8 issues). This is a great source of current info.

Aim, a newsletter on retirement and travel in Mexico is published six times a year. This handy newsletter is packed with nitty-gritty information (how much eggs, rent and electrify cost in Oaxaca or San Luis Potosí, or wherever), tips on retiring etc. Order from Apdo. Postal 31-70, 45050 Guadalajara, Jalisco, MEXICO. $16 US, $19 Canadian. Back issues $2.

Amigo Club Membership Application

_________ I wish to apply for or renew my Sanborn's Amigo Club membership which includes UNIVERSAL Coverage. I am enclosing $40.00 for membership fee.

_________ I wish to enroll in the family plan which includes UNIVERSAL Coverage (only spouse and children). I am enclosing $65.00.

Last Name:____ First Name:_____________________________

Address: ____

City: ____State: __________Zip Code:_____________________

Date Of Birth: _______/________/____ Age: ______ Phone: (______) _____________________________

Emergency Contact: ________________________________ Phone: (______) _______________________

List family members to be covered in the family plan:

Last Name: ____ First Name: ___________________________

Last Name: ____ First Name: ___________________________

Last Name: ____ First Name: ___________________________

Last Name: ____ First Name: ___________________________

Insurance Application

Name:____D.O.B.:_______/________/_________

Street____Ph:(______)_________________

City:____ State:____________Zip:_______________

Type(s) of Vehicle: Car   Motorhome   Pickup   Camper

Car: Make: ________ Year: ______ Body:________Vehicle ID # (VIN)_______________________________

Trailer: Make:_______ Year:_______ Length:________ID Number (VIN)____________________________

Boat: Make:________ Year:______ Length:_________ID Number (VIN)_____________________________

Motor: Make:________ Year:______ HP:__________ID Number (VIN)_____________________________

Type of Coverage: ☐ Full   ☐ Liability Only   Insurance Info:_______________________________

____

Amount of Coverage
Property Damage: $50,000
Bodily Injury Liability: $40,000 per person, $80,000 per accident
Medical Payments: $2,000 per person, $10,000 per accident

	VEHICLE	**TRAILER**	**BOAT**	**MOTOR**		**YES NO**
Retail Value:	$________	$________	$________	$________	Legal:	____ ____

Term: _______ Days @ $___________ Per Day

From ____/____/____ at _________ AM / PM To: ____/____/____ at ________ AM / PM

Here's how to complete your Insurance cost.

$_______________ Enter Daily Rate

X______________ Multiply by Number of Days

= $___________ Premuim

- $___________ Discount Percentage

= $___________ Net Premium

+ $ 10.00   Policy Fee

+ $ 5.00   Handling

+ $ 15.50 (Only if Federal Express).

= $___________Total

See the example on our rate sheet for help.

Make checks payable to Sanborn's Insurance. Please allow two weeks for mail order

Credit Card: ☐ DI   ☐ VI   ☐ MC

Card Number:__________________________________

Expiration Date: _______/______/______

Signature:____________________________________

Cut out this form and mail it to Sanborn's or fax it to (956) 686-0732.

FROM:

NO POSTAGE
NECESARY
IF MAILED
IN THE
UNITED STATES

BUSINESS REPLY MAIL
FIRST CLASS PERMIT NO. 57 McALLEN, TEXAS

POSTAGE WILL BE PAID BY ADDRESSEE

SANBORN'S
MEXICO INSURANCE SERVICE
P.O. BOX 310
McALLEN, TX 78505-0310

Wanderlust Publications

P.O. Box 310, McAllen, Texas 78505-0310 Ph: (956) 682-7433 Fax: (956) 686-0732

Mexico's Colonial Heart

This travelog covers all overland routes linking Central Mexico's Colonial region. Highlights inclulde San Miguel de Allende, Guadalajara, Chapala, Guanajuato, Querétaro and Mexico City. Also tips on area spas, hidden side trips and armchair reading are included. ISBN: 1-878166-17-4 — 340 pages — soft cover $19.95 plus $3.00 S & H.

Mexico's Pacific Coast & Copper Canyon

All overland routes from Nogales, Arizona to Mazatlán and back. It includes details on the Copper Canyon, Puerto Peñasco (Rocky Point), Kino Bay, San Carlos, Alamos and El fuerte. ISBN: 1-878166-10-7 — 140 pages — soft cover $15.95 (Can $19.15) plus $3.00 S & H.

Mexico's Gulf Coast & Costa Esmeralda

All overland routes from the the US border at McAllen / Brownsville to Acayucan, Veracruz and back. It includes the beautiful Costa Esmeralda, El Tajin archeological ruins and Jalapa, the capital of Veracruz. ISBN: 1-878166-15-8 — 140 pages — soft cover $15.95 (Can $19.15) plus $3.00 S & H.

Central America by Car

The only highway travel guide that covers all overland routes in Central America. Includes detailed directions for the six countries of Guatemala, El Salvador, Honduras, Nicaragua, Costa Rica and Panama. ISBN: 1-878166-23-9 —140 pages — soft cover $15.95 (Can $19.15) plus $3.00 S & H.

Mexico's Ruta Maya

All overland routes from Acayucan, Veracurz torough the Yucatan Peninsula circle, including Merida Cancun, Villahermosa, Palenque, offbeat beaches and ferries. ISBN: 1-878166-08-5 — 150 pages — soft cover $15.95 (Can $19.15) plus $3.00 S & H.

Mexico's Baja

All overland routes from the border to Cabo San Lucas and back; includes Tijuana, Ensenada, San Felipe, La Paz, and Cabos. ISBN: 1-878166-078-7 — 100 pages — soft cover $15.95 (Can $19.15) plus $3.00 S & H.

Monterrey Saltillo from Laredo, Texas

Enjoy a short trip from the Texas border at Laredo, Eagle Pass or Del Rio to Mexico's third largest city and the beautiful mountains that surround it. ISBN: 1-878166-16-6 — 100 pages — soft cover $15.95 (Can $19.15) plus $3.00 S & H.

Monterrey / Saltillo from McAllen, Texas

Enjoy a short trip from the Texas border at McAllen or Roma to Mexico's third largest city and the beautiful mountains that surround it. ISBN: 1-878166-16-6 — 100 pages — soft cover $15.95 (Can $19.15) plus $3.00 S & H.

Sanborn's RV & Camping Guide to Mexico

The most complete and up-to-date directory of RV facilities in Mexico. Updated annually, this no-nonsense directory will prove invaluable to those people RV'ing or camping in Mexico. ISBN: 1-878166-06-9 — 46 pages — soft cover $5.95 plus $2.00 S & H.

Mexico From the Driver's Seat

"Mexico" Mike Nelson's musings about driving in Mexico. Taken from over 20 years experience in traveling the highways and byways South-of-the-border. Excellent armchair reading. "Mexico" Mike Nelson ISBN: 1-878166-04-2 — 54 pages — soft cover $8.95 plus #3.00 S & H.

Name:____ Phone:__________________

Street:______________________________ City:_______________ State:________ Zip:________

Quantity	Description	Unit Price	Extended Price
_______	__________________________	__________	__________
_______	__________________________	__________	__________
_______	__________________________	__________	__________
_______	__________________________	__________	__________
_______	__________________________	__________	__________
_______	__________________________	__________	__________
	Texas Residents add tax	@8.25%	__________
	(1-2 books = $3.00, 3-4 books = $5.00, 5 or more = $6.00)	S & H	__________
		TOTAL	__________

METHOD OF PAYMENT

_______Please find enclosed a check/money order or _______Bill my VISA_______ MasterCard_______

Name of Cardholder:____

Card No.: ____ Exp. Date: _____/_____/_____

Signature: ____

FROM:

NO POSTAGE
NECESARY
IF MAILED
IN THE
UNITED STATES

BUSINESS REPLY MAIL

FIRST CLASS PERMIT NO. 57 McALLEN, TEXAS

POSTAGE WILL BE PAID BY ADDRESSEE

SANBORN'S

MEXICO   INSURANCE   SERVICE

DEPT. BOOKS
P.O. BOX 310
McALLEN, TX 78505-0310

Other books by "Mexico" Mike

Available at Sanborn's offices or from 1-800-222-0158. Add $3.50 shipping and handling for mail orders. Texas residents add 8.25% tax.

______   *Live Better South of the Border* — ISBN 1-889-48902-6 — 214 pages, 8 1/2 by 5 1/2 — No other book covers living and working in Mexico like this one. It is for people of all ages who want to know what it is really like to live in there. Mike tells the good, the bad and the ugly facts about living there. More than 30 towns are compared. He addresses the concerns of young people, victims of downsizing, gays, lesbians, singles, retirees. $16.95.

______   *More Than a Dozen of Mexico's Hidden Jewels* — ISBN 1-878-166-24-7 — 37 pages, 8 1/2 by 11 — This is a collection of stories about some of the most unusual places throughout the country — places unmentioned by regular guidebooks. Visit: the Zone of Silence where UFO's reportedly land, Xilitla where an eccentric contemporary of Dali built a surrealistic sculpture garden, the bottom of the Copper Canyon, an unspoiled beach a few hours from Mazatlán and many more. $9.95.

______   *Spas & Hot Springs of Mexico* — 137 pages, 5 1/2 by 8 1/2, perfect bound with index and table of contents — Yes, it's finally out. Mike has been promising this book for years and he finally got busy and did it. This has more than forty healthful get-aways. There are several world-class spas that are as good as or better than their counterparts in Europe and the U.S. for 1/2 the price. He has a chapter on spiritual retreats, with yoga, meditation and a generally nurturing environment. For the adventurous, he also tells you about simple hot springs and *balnearios*. These range from mud holes to hot spring resorts where you can spend the night. Water temperatures and chemical composition is noted in most cases. If you are someone who wants to de-stress and rejuvenate or a hot spring junkie, you need this book. $16.95.

Name:____Phone:__________________

Street:____________________________City:______________State:________Zip:________

Quantity	Description	Unit Price	Extended Price
______	________________________	________	________
______	________________________	________	________
______	________________________	________	________
______	________________________	________	________
______	________________________	________	________
______	________________________	________	________
	Texas Residents add tax	@8.25%	________
(1-2 books = $3.00, 3-4 books = $5.00, 5 or more = $6.00)		S & H	________
		TOTAL	________

METHOD OF PAYMENT

______Please find enclosed a check/money order or ______Bill my VISA______ MasterCard______

Name of Cardholder:____

Card No.: ____ Exp. Date: _____/_____/_____

Signature: ____

FROM:

NO POSTAGE
NECESARY
IF MAILED
IN THE
UNITED STATES

BUSINESS REPLY MAIL

FIRST CLASS PERMIT NO. 57 McALLEN, TEXAS

POSTAGE WILL BE PAID BY ADDRESSEE

SANBORN'S

MEXICO   INSURANCE   SERVICE

DEPT. BOOKS
P.O. BOX 310
McALLEN, TX 78505-0310

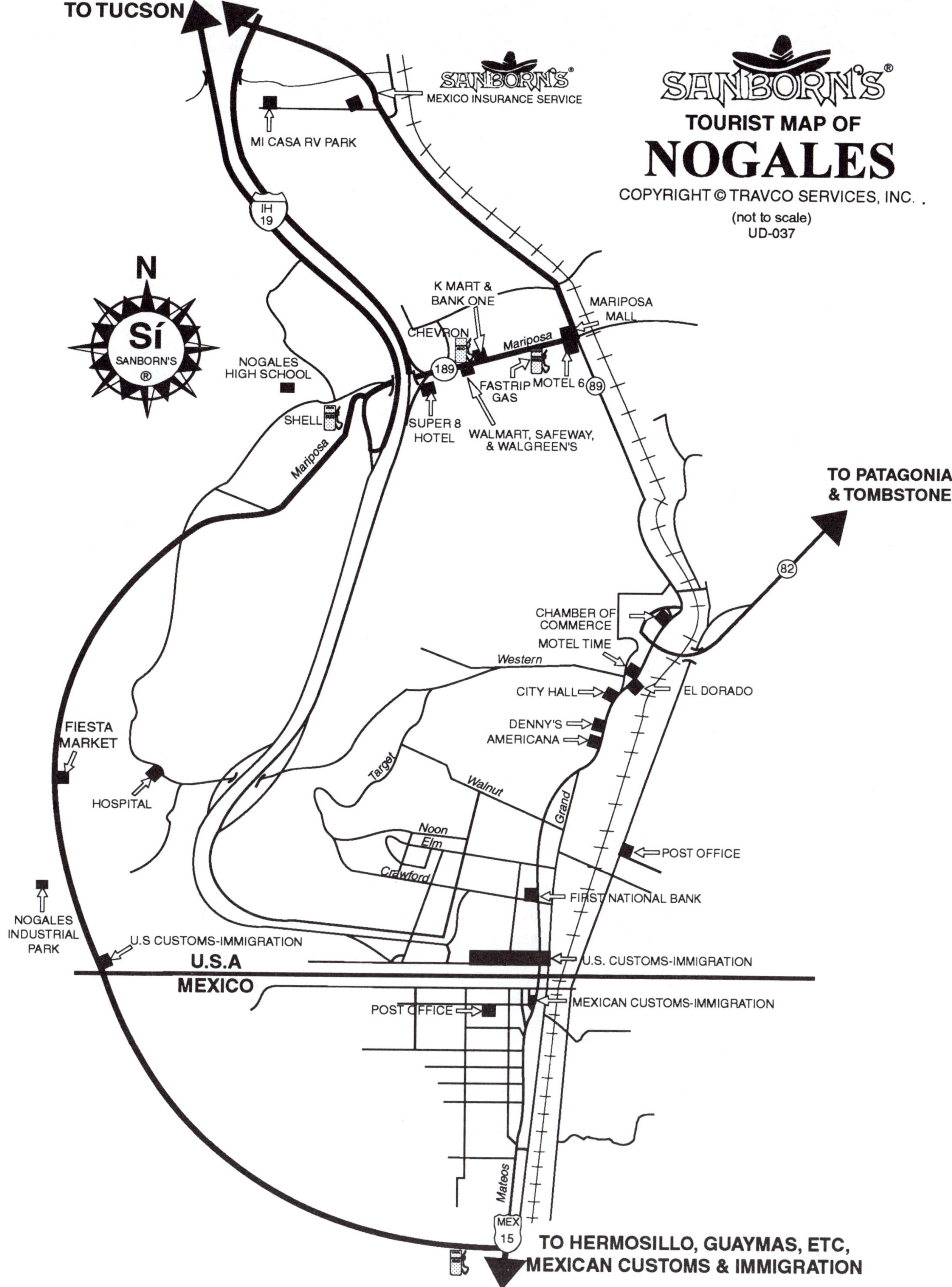
1
TO TUCSON
SANBORN'S
MEXICO INSURANCE SERVICE
SANBORN'S
TOURIST MAP OF
NOGALES
COPYRIGHT © TRAVCO SERVICES, INC. .
(not to scale)
UD-037
MI CASA RV PARK
IH 19
N
Sí
SANBORN'S
®
K MART &
BANK ONE
MARIPOSA MALL
CHEVRON
Mariposa
NOGALES HIGH SCHOOL
189
FASTRIP GAS
MOTEL 6
89
SHELL
Mariposa
SUPER 8 HOTEL
WALMART, SAFEWAY, & WALGREEN'S
TO PATAGONIA & TOMBSTONE
82
CHAMBER OF COMMERCE
MOTEL TIME
Western
CITY HALL
EL DORADO
DENNY'S
AMERICANA
FIESTA MARKET
HOSPITAL
Target
Walnut
Grand
Noon
Elm
Crawford
POST OFFICE
NOGALES INDUSTRIAL PARK
FIRST NATIONAL BANK
U.S CUSTOMS-IMMIGRATION
U.S.A
MEXICO
U.S. CUSTOMS-IMMIGRATION
MEXICAN CUSTOMS-IMMIGRATION
POST OFFICE
Mateos
MEX 15
TO HERMOSILLO, GUAYMAS, ETC,
MEXICAN CUSTOMS & IMMIGRATION

LOG 1 *START:* Nogales, Az *END:* Imuris, Son

UD-017

If entering Mexico from Nogales, use this log. If entering from Douglas skip to Log 2 (page 3) or to Special X (page 75).

48.0 MI or 76.8 KM
DRIVE TIME 50 MIN — 1 1/4 HOURS
SCENIC RATING - 2
Easy, winding stretch of divided highway.

NOTE: The newer border crossing via the "loop" is open from 6 AM till 10 PM only; otherwise, you have to cross at the "old" gateway via Hwy 89 downtown. Since you're not driving at night, it doesn't matter — right? Please read driving tips at front of log.

MI	KM	
0.0	0.0	Leave Sanborn's Mi Casa RV Travel Park and head South down US #89. Pass Nogales Service Center Truck Stop on right.
1.6	2.6	TURN RIGHT onto US-180 (Mariposa Road and 4th light after leaving Sanborn's). Fastrip **GAS** and Motel 6 on left.

IF TO: Old gateway thru downtown Nogales and on to Imuris thru congested downtown Nogales, Sonora, continue straight ahead of US-89. However, this route is not recommended, especially for trailers and RV's.

1.9	3.0	Having elected not to go thru downtown, continue ahead on Mariposa past Mariposa Mall and K-Mart.
2.0	3.2	Pass Wal-Mart, Safeway, and Revco drug stores for last-minute items. Then Bank One and Chevron **GAS** on right.
2.2	3.5	Pass Super 8 Hotel on left and under IH-19 overpass and continue West along truck route.
2.6	4.2	Shell **GAS** and Nogales High School on right.
5.0	8.0	Nogales Industrial Park on right.
5.2	8.3	Straight to border gateway — you're entering Mexico. This is Nogales, Sonora. You'll get your tourist and vehicle permits farther down the pike at mile 19.0. *"Bienvenidos a Mexico!"* (Welcome to Mexico!)

TOPES — Thought we'd better tell you about "TOPES" — before you find out the hard way! They're pronounced TOE' PAYZ. Think of them as speed bumps gone berserk. They're metal or concrete domes attached to the road surface a few inches high. They're meant to slow traffic down. If you don't slow to a CRAWL, they'll TEAR YOUR SUSPENSION APART. We've given up on telling you where every tope in Mexico is located. Just be aware that every small town will have at least two sets, one as you enter town and another as you leave. When we mention them, keep your eyes open for three or four others.

Sonora tourist information office phone number is 1-800-4-SONORA.

5.7	9.1	School at left. Under pedestrian walkway. **KM 6**. Straight ahead thru cut. Pass turnoff, left to downtown Nogales. Pass *La Voz Del Norte* newspaper, right. Then thru housing development.
6.1	9,8	Pass town of Nogales, Sonora, mostly to left.
6.2	9.9	Cross Mariposa Canyon.
6.4	10.2	Curve left. Uphill. Then past customs. You do not get your papers here but farther ahead.
7.3	11.7	**GAS**, right. Municipal auditorium to right.
9.3	14.9	Federal prison, right. **GAS**, and diesel station.
9.8	15.7	Come to stop at intersection with Hwy #15. General Tire at right. TURN RIGHT. Sign, "Nogales centro, straight, Santa Ana left." Hotel Posada Real ahead. You're now on your way down 4 lane divided Hwy #15.
9.9	15.8	Plaza Kino to left. CAREFUL for TOPES, Pedestrian crossing & school at right.
10.0	16.0	Thru traffic lite. Pass Foster Grant Americana. This is a big industrial zone — some big-name American plants are located here. **KM 266**.

They manufacture the first part of their products in Mexico and then ship 'em to their stateside counterparts for finishing touches — less expensive this way. They are called *maquiladoras*. They operated long before NAFTA and Ross Perot's demagoguery about "...that giant sucking sound ..."

MI	KM	
10.5	16.8	Goodyear plant right. **KM 265.**
11.0	17.6	Highway patrol station at right. By the way, Mexican smokeys have ears. That's radar, son, radar, so watch your speed. Frequent *retornos* (turnarounds).
12.0	19.2	Over railroad and follow alongside railroad at right.
13.1	21.0	Beautiful grove to right.
14.0	22.4	Nogales' airport over at right. Sign, "Santa Ana 94 KM. Hermosillo 260 KM." The "KM" numbers we put to the side are the Mexican highway markers which denote the distance to the next major town or highway junction. So now you'll see "KM 260" and realize it's 260 kilometers to Hermosillo or the next intersection with a major road or next major town. Got it? **KM 260.**
18.9	30.2	**GAS**, left.
19.0	30.4	Slow now! Pull off to right and STOP for *MIGRACIÓN & ADUANA* . This is where you get your tourist card and vehicle permit.

REMEMBER — It is good for 6 months, multiple entry. YOU MUST TURN IT IN BEFORE YOU LEAVE THE COUNTRY. You don't do it at the bridge (or crossing) on the way back, but you must find *Hacienda* or *Banjército* office at a checkpoint like this or at frontier city BEFORE you cross into U.S. Failure to turn papers in may result in high fines. There is a "Sonora only" lane here, but this permit takes longer to get and does not allow you to visit Alamos nor the rest of Mexico. If you are only going to Sonora and don't have a credit card, it will do.

27.0	43.2	Bear right thru Cibuta and slow thru school zone. Pedestrians. **KM 240.**
34.2	54.7	Curve left. Now up. Topped 3,500 ft. **KM 229.**
34.9	55.8	We have descended to 3,400 ft.
45.0	72.0	Up past Las Viguitas on right. Speed limit is 90 KMPH.
46.8	74.9	Imuris railroad depot at right. Then into fringe of hilltop town of Imuris (e-moo-rees).
48.0	76.8	Come now to junction left with Hwy #2 from Douglas, Arizona and Agua Prieta, Mexico. **GAS**, right. There is a VERY neat statue at left. Take a few minutes to stop and walk all the way around it. **KM 207.**

IF TO: Magdalena and Santa Ana, straight. Start Imuris — Santa Ana Log (page 7).

IF TO: Cananea, Agua Prieta, and Douglas, left. Start Imuris — Douglas Log (page 69).

End of Log 1. Onward!

LOG 2   *START:* Douglas, Az   *END:* Imuris, Son

UD-125

104 MI OR 166.4 KM
DRIVE TIME 2 — 3 HOURS.
SCENIC RATING — 4

If you want to take the alternate route that goes to Hermosillo via Nacozari, use Special X (page 75).

The most interesting place to stay in Douglas is the historic old Hotel Gadsden with best restaurant in town. Motels are the Desert Inn, El Coronado and the Travelodge. If you wish to overnight in Agua Prieta and get an early start, there's the Hotel Hacienda. There are 2 RV parks. An hour away is Bisbee, AZ, an old mining town. The bed & breakfast Inn At Castle Rock is a "center for expanding consciousness", with *mucho* appeal for those on a journey of discovery. A new age, 60's kind of place.

None of our customers ever forget anything, but they might misplace some things, so please check now for: proof of your citizenship (or notarized affidavit) and proof of ownership of your vehicle (title or registration & driver's license plus an international credit card, AE, DI, MC, VI in the same name). You'll leave a photocopy of your credentials with Mexican officials. If you're not absolutely sure about your credentials, better check back with our Sanborn's office before you head for the border. Make sure before you leave. REMEMBER — The person whose name is on the car permit <u>MUST</u> be in car whenever it is driven. Your permit is good for multiple entries, but you <u>MUST</u> turn it in at any border crossing BEFORE it expires. Also, all kiddies need either both parents with them, or notarized permission from the absent parent.

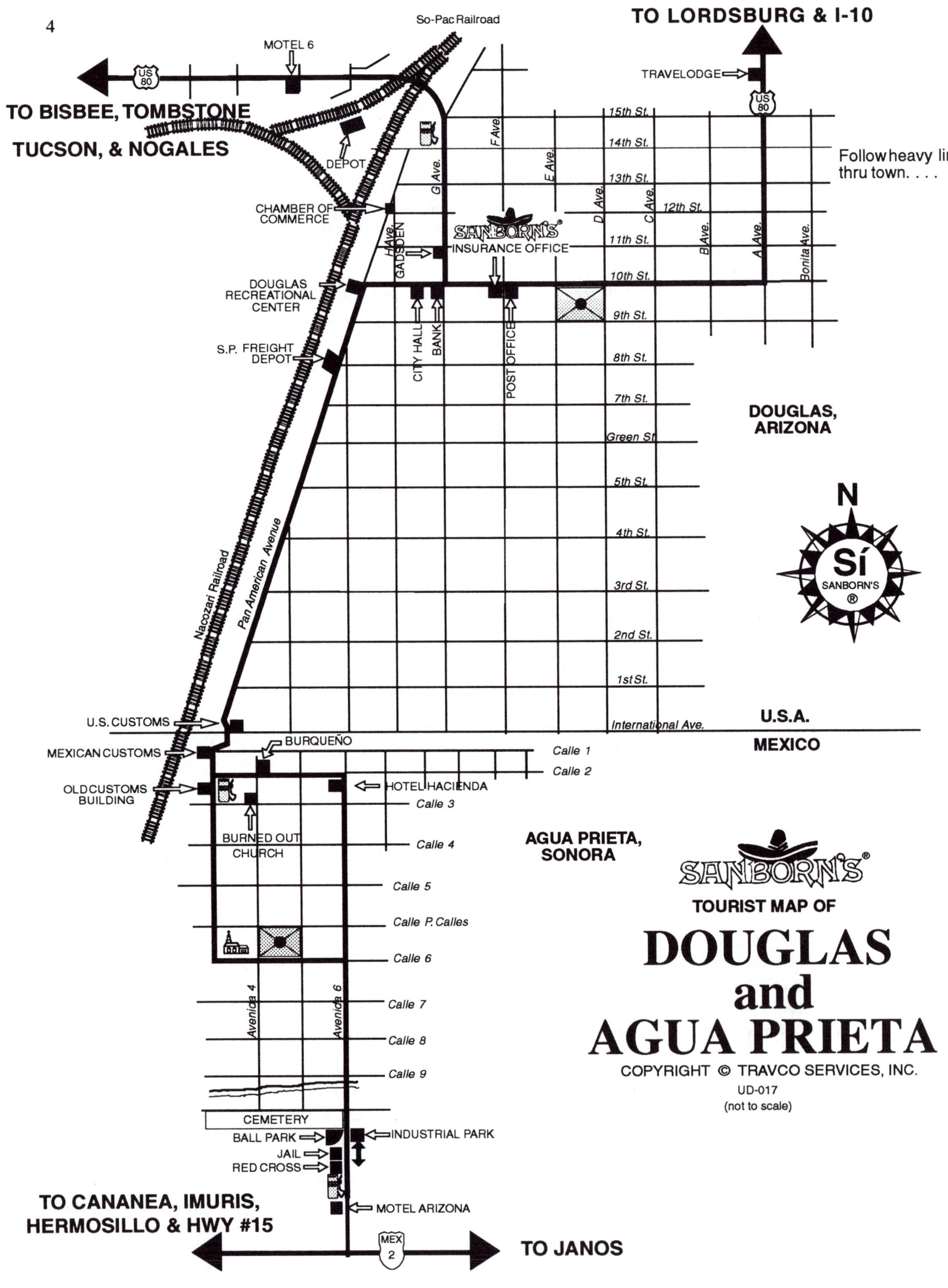

COPYRIGHT © TRAVCO SERVICES, INC.

MI	KM	
0.0	0.0	Leave Jones Associates Insurance Agency (Sanborn's rep) on 10th St. between "G" & "F" Ave. in Douglas, Arizona, heading West on (10th St.) Hwy #80.
0.1	0.2	Straight at light. Pass city hall at left.
0.3	0.5	After two long blocks, come to dead end. Cochise vocational college ahead. TURN LEFT onto wide Pan American Ave. Ahead for about three-quarters of a mile.
1.0	1.6	Wave good-bye to U.S. Customs on your left (don't stop). Cross border (there's no river to cross here) on one-way bridge — you're now in Mexico.

Take far right slot and pull up to Mexican official and tell him you're going to Guadalajara or Guaymas or Kino or wherever you're going. He'll tell you to park diagonally just ahead at right. Then go into Mexican government building at right and head for the counter at MIGRACIÓN (immigration) on right side of building where your tourist cards will be written (or those that you have will be validated). Then cut across the big room to ADUANA (Customs) where you'll get your car permit. They'll put a sticker on your windshield and you're on your way.

Now back out of the diagonal parking spot and careful for incoming traffic. Then head straight down their main street. **GAS**, left on corner. You're now in Agua Prieta, Spanish for "dark water" or "dirty water."

1.1	1.8	Turn left at first corner. Then **GAS** at right. Pinheras Vildosa on left. Go 3 blocks. The 3 story building on right is Hacienda Hotel. Turn right onto Avenida 6.
1.3	2.1	Pass seafood restaurant "Gómez Hnos. (Brothers abbreviated)" and La Fogata at right, then El Mesquite. Continue ahead till you get to Hwy #2. Watch — several stoplights. Cross Calle Porfirio Calles. There are sneaky traffic cops here so be careful.

There are at least 3 kinds of left turns, the most common being that there is a left turn lane with an arrow, just like in the U.S. The difference is that you absolutely must wait for the arrow before turning. Another is on the open road: If there is oncoming traffic on a two-lane road, pull over to the right (careful for drop from pavement) and wait till all is clear, then turn left. Remember, the left turn signal on the open road signals the guy behind permission to pass! On freeways and city driving it's OK to use it to signal a left turn. In city streets, there are often "laterals", or parallel side streets that are for local traffic. If there is no left turn lane, but a left turn arrow, exit from the main street down onto the lateral a block before a traffic light. Wait for the left turn arrow. Cross the street you were just on. This is tricky and scary, so pay attention and watch to see if others are doing the same thing. After the first few times, you'll figure it out. Remember, though, it ain't always so (read the rules of the road in the filler section at the front of book). — MM.

1.6	2.6	Calle 7 Grupo AA at right on corner. Then Goodyear at left. Then stoplight.
1.8	2.9	Past Motel Ruiz at right
2.0	3.2	Cemetery at right. Industrial park at left. Then ball park at right. **GAS** and then **Motel Arizona.**
2.8	4.5	Come now to junction Hwy 2.

IF TO: CANANEA, Imuris, Nacozari, and Hermosillo, TURN RIGHT here.

IF TO: Janos and on to Chihuahua., TURN LEFT and start Agua Prieta - Janos Log (not included in this book).

CAREFUL! There are sometimes policemen here making sure you stop at ALTO sign. As we mention in our cover, you should always be careful at railroad tracks & watch the guy behind you, as not all people stop at them. Here, you should plan to stop.

3.5	5.6	Over **TWO** railroad tracks — line runs to Nacozari, another copper town.
4.3	6.9	Come now to junction with Sonora Hwy #12 and road (left) to Hermosillo.

IF TO: Cananea and on to Imuris, STRAIGHT AHEAD and on to Imuris, 46 miles South of Nogales on Hwy 15.

IF TO: Hermosillo (thru Nacozari, and Moctezuma), turn left and join Douglas - Hermosillo Special at mile 4.3 (page 75). Sign says "118 kilometers to Nacozari" or 73 miles.

13.5	21.6	Curve left and up a little and then wide right around foothills at right.
16.3	26.1	Curve left and over and down big hill on straight stretch. That big mountain ahead at one o'clock is MT. GRANIZO, which means "hail" or "hailstorm."

6

MI	KM	
19.0	30.4	Abandoned customs check at right.
22.0	35.2	Now left and nice straight stretch with good view of Mt. Granizo over at right.
27.8	44.5	Curve right at Kilometer 40 and start straight stretch.
29.5	47.2	Pass side road (right) up to **Naco**, Bisbee's border town. Stop there on way home.
30.8	49.3	**Ejido Cuauhtémoc** over to right.

Cuauhtémoc (1502-1525) was the 11th & last Aztec Emperor. The son of Emperor Ahuizotl & princess Tilalcaptl, he was educated in the Calmecac school for nobles. Cortés made him a prisoner on Aug. 13, 1521 & had him killed by hanging him by his feet like a common criminal, on Feb. 28, 1525. He was 23. He was betrayed by Malinche, who acted as interpreter. To this day, a "Malinche" is a woman who cannot be trusted — that's the polite version.

MI	KM	
31.0	49.6	Slow now and stop for immigration check station. Have your papers ready.
35.3	56.5	Now right curve and up and then thru long rock cut and wind thru hills.
38.0	60.8	Curve right and up thru cut onto mesa (plateau) — note Cananea in distance ahead.
38.8	62.1	Now a long downward stretch and over bridge over Arroyo Claro and up.
41.0	65.6	**Ejido Ignacio Zaragoza** over to right. Nice ranching country thru here. Slow now! Pull over to right and stop for customs check — have car permit ready.
43.8	70.1	Now curve right and down on another straight stretch practically to **Cananea.**
46.3	74.1	**Ejido Emiliano Zapata** to left. (Zapata was the hero of the land revolt.)
52.5	84.0	Pass Motel **Valle de Cobre** —MOD— 38 rooms, CATV, pool, PH: (633) 2-2086 Fax: 2-3808. Also Motel and Restaurant **Mesón**, looks good, near Chrysler/Dodge dealership on right. Then pass side road (left) to **Arizpe** and airport at right.
53.0	84.8	On divided boulevard. Careful now!

IF TO: Bypass Cananea, take right fork (at IMURIS sign) and curve right.

MI	KM	
54.0	85.4	Volkswagen agency at right. Monument at left honoring the strikers killed in 1906 during a labor dispute. **GAS**, right. Then over railroad (LOOK-&-LISTEN). Then curve left and wind down over arroyo and up.

If you have the time and wish to drive into Cananea, this is a pleasant little town with really nice folks. You can visit the old jail, view a museum and just soak up the atmosphere. Motel Zafari (into town 1 mile on left) — MOD— 36 A/C rooms, SATV. PH: (633) 2-1308, 2-1528, 2-1108 Fax: 2-3739. Gives discount on weekends. Take left fork above.

MI	KM	
56.0	89.6	Nice view over to left of famous Cananea copper mine. You can drive to front gate, but no tours or visits.
58.5	93.6	Wind on thru Río San Miguel canyon.
60.5	96.8	Up on winding road. Then left horseshoe curve and on up.
61.5	98.4	Summit - 1840 meters (or 6,036 feet) elevation. Then start winding down.

REMEMBER: On downhill stretches, brake with your motor — not your brakes. A burning smell means you've used your brakes too much. If you can, pull over and let 'em cool for ten minutes or so.

MI	KM	
67.5	108.0	Pretty trees at left. Then slow for sharp right curve.
69.5	111.2	Come now to scattered village of Cuitaca. Detour over Arroyo Cuitaca and start up.
71.0	113.6	Now over and down. Elevation now 4400 feet above sea level.
73.5	117.6	Curve left and down big hill on straight stretch and into green valley.
76.3	122.1	Pass side road (right) to Santa Cruz up near Arizona line. Over another arroyo.
80.1	128.2	Note little church up at right next to ruins of older, bigger church.
85.3	136.5	Nice Rancho El Aribabi in pretty setting at left. . Then curve right and wind up.
89.5	143.2	Slow for sharp left horseshoe curve and down thru cuts.
91.3	146.1	Now sharp left horseshoe curve and start up on other side — and up and up.
94.0	150.4	Note pink color of rocks.
94.3	150.9	Start gradual winding decline from 4300-foot elevation (9 miles to go).
96.5	154.4	Majestic panorama to left.
97.3	155.7	Old road over at right. On down and careful on this deceptive grade.
98.8	158.1	Bottom. Now along past dry gulch at right.
104.0	166.4	Ahead into Imuris (pronounced "e-moo-rees"). Slow for dangerous right curve and take RIGHT FORK and THEN LEFT (follow SANTA ANA signs) and careful as you move slowly onto Highway #15. **GAS**, right.

IF TO: U.S.A. (Nogales) turn right and start Imuris - Nogales Log (page 150).

IF TO: Magdalena, Santa Ana, Hermosillo, Caborca, etc., turn left and start Imuris Santa Ana Log.

There are pretty good motels in Magdalena, Motel Ayabay, Saguaro and Kino Hotel and Trailer Park PH: (632) 2-0983.

End of Log 2

LOG 3   *START:* **Imuris, Son**   *END:* **Santa Ana, Son**

UD-017

26.5 MI or 42.4 KM
DRIVE TIME 30 — 45 MINUTES
SCENIC RATING — 2

MI	KM	
0.0	0.0	Proceed ahead at junction with Hwy #2 from Douglas, Arizona at statue of Father Kino. **GAS**, right. Then down and over bridge over Río de los Alisos. Careful for next 7 winding miles.
4.4	7.0	Careful for curves.
6.5	10.4	Careful for sharp right and left curves.
9.6	15.6	Pass side road (right) to San Ignacio, baseball field on right.
10.4	16.6	Over bridge over Río Tasicuri & under power line. **KM 171**.
12.1	19.4	Pass school at right. Then bypass Magdalena (pop. 41,000), famous as the place where the skeletal remains of the great PADRE KINO were discovered in 1966 (see our special report). A magnificent job has been done beautifying the plaza where his bones are displayed — if you have an extra 20 minutes, don't miss this!

IF TO: Magdalena & Padre Kino's mausoleum, exit here. Left at first fork after Hermosillo sign. Pass VW dealer, right & school, left. **GAS**, left, then **GAS**, right. Fancy restaurant. After viewing remains, straight ahead to rejoin Hwy. Up & merge right.

IF TO: Santa Ana, straight ahead.

MI	KM	
12.3	19.7	Sign says: Hermosillo, 186 KM. Thru series of cuts.
13.1	21.0	TOPES. CAREFUL!.
13.4	21.4	Come to toll house and pay toll (cars $32, extra axle $16) then ahead.
14.0	22.4	**GAS** at left. Then Conasupo grocery store at right.
14.3	22.9	**GAS**, right. Pass Red Cross office then school at left. Cross bridge over Río Magdalena. Motel Ayabay (best in town) & nice restaurant, left. Railroad at right. Turnoff to Kino Motel & Trailer Park to right. **KM 181**.
14.5	23.2	Slight curve to right. **KM 183**.
17.1	27.2	CAREFUL. Curve left! This is where Magdalena road rejoins highway.
18.2	29.1	Propane at right.
24.5	39.2	Now down and over bridge across Arroyo de las Calabazas and enter Santa Ana (Pop. 25,000). **GAS**, right just ahead (More ahead).
26.2	41.	Still divided. Ahead on right is Hotel Elba —MOD— RESTAURANT (OPEN 6 AM TILL 11 PM) with good food (serve 1/2 orders for those who have a small appetite, MC, VI, Ph: (632) 4-0361, 4-0777, or 4-0178. At left is Motel San Francisco, Ph: (632) 4-0322
26.5	42.4	Come now to junction Hwy #2 and end of log. Punta Vista RV Park is ahead on Hwy #15, 0.7 Mile South of junction. It's one of Mickey's favorites with nice view at top of hill.

IF TO: Hermosillo, start Santa Ana — Hermosillo Log (page 9) and curve left and up. **GAS** at right.

IF TO: Caborca, Sonoyta, Mexicali, etc., turn right here at Hwy 2 junction and start Santa Ana — Sonoyta Log (not included in this book).

End of Log 3.

PADRE KINO SPECIAL REPORT

One of the greatest men ever to come to Mexico was the Italian-born, German-educated Father Eusebio Francisco Kino, the Conquistador of the Desert, who came with the Spanish Jesuit order. And one of the greatest archaeological discoveries of our modern times was right here in Magdalena in 1966 when Padre Kino's grave was uncovered.

You can drive to the magnificent new plaza where Kino's remains can be viewed — it's very interesting. You'll be stirred by emotion when you realize you are looking upon the skeletal remains of the man who brought Christianity and civilization to this whole area thru here some 250 years ago.

How did they know the skeleton was Padre Kino's? Well, they knew that the mission church that he and the Indians built was in this immediate area, and they also knew that he died here when he came to dedicate his new mission church (which has long since disintegrated), so it seemed reasonable to assume he was buried nearby.

Historic documents indicated that the good father was badly crippled with arthritis — and the hands of the skeleton they found were badly crippled. There was other proof in addition, thus it has been established beyond doubt that these bones are definitely those of Padre Kino, who established at least 25 missions in Northern Mexico, Arizona, and 'way up into California.

Padre Kino, for your information, labored thru this area for some 25 years from around 1687 until he died on March 15, 1711. Matter of fact, he didn't even get to Mexico until he was 50 years old.

He Christianized seven Indian tribes - the Apaches, Yumas, Seris, Maricopas, Papagos, Pimas, and Cocopas. He built all his missions, which have long since disappeared, but the Franciscans who came 75 years later built new churches either nearby or actually atop the Kino missions. The church just next to the Kino remains is one of the Franciscan missions built around 1775.

Incidentally, Padre Kino brought new farming techniques to the Indians in addition to introducing Christianity. Also, he proved that Baja California was not an island. The good padre was quite a mathematician, astronomer, architect, and cartographer, in addition to being a rancher and economist. He wanted to become a Jesuit missionary in China because he knew the Chinese were interested in mathematics and astrology but instead ended up in Mexico and Bishop of Mexico sent him 'way out here to the wilds. Really quite a guy, this great Padre Kino!

The plaza is easy to find and the streets are mostly paved. If it's late, you won't find a motel in these parts any better than the Motel Kino which is between padre Kino Plaza and the South end of town.

LOG 4   *START:* **Santa Ana, Son**   *END:* **Hermosillo, Son**

UD-017

107.1 MI or 171.4 KM
DRIVE TIME 1 1/2 — 2 HOURS
SCENIC RATING — 2

MI	KM	
0.0	0.0	Here in Santa Ana at junction Hwys #15 & #2, up past **GAS**, right, and proceed ahead.
0.1	0.2	Retorno Nogales/Magdalena — 6 lane divided for .5 miles, then 4 lane.
0.6	1.0	Uphill. Curve to right then school to right. At right is hotel Elba, —MOD— restaurant (open 6 AM till 11 PM) with good food (serve 1/2 orders for those who have a small appetite), MC, VI, Ph: (632) 4-0316, 4-0777, 4-0178 and at left, San Francisco, Ph: (632) 4-0322. Over little bridge. Centro bus station. Turn left.
0.7	1.1	Punta Vista RV park, right. Run by nice folks, Ana & Edgar Osuña. It's one of Mikey's favorites. Restaurant El Zarape and Corona sign. Nice view at top of hill.
2.0	3.2	Plaza Kennedy truck stop (RV parking, sometimes) and Highway patrol, right. Short stretch of winding road.
7.0	11.2	**GAS**, to right. **KM 159.**
8.0	12.8	Restaurant to right. **KM 157.**
13.0	20.8	Pass railroad town of Estación Llano at right. Cemetery with pearly gates at left. "Swing low, sweet chariot....
15.0	24.0	**GAS** and restaurant on left under construction. Cross Río El Alamo (cottonwood).
15.3	24.5	**GAS**, at left, clean bathrooms. Expensive refreshments.
26.3	42.1	**GAS**, left. Then pass side road (right) that leads to railroad junction of Benjamín Hill. The town has an unusual name for a Mexican place especially since there's no "hill." It's named after a general in the Mexican Constitutionalist forces during the Mexican Revolution of 1910-1917. General "Hill" was the defender of the Mexican border town of Naco (South of Bisbee, Arizona) in 1914 and was of British descent.
27.1	43.4	The hand carved art works by the Seri Indians are done with *palo fierro* or iron wood. A non-Indian taught them the skill within the last 20 years. By the way, Libby Langdells of Yuba City, Ca, tells us bargaining is no longer done with them. They've formed cooperatives and sell for fixed prices now. **KM 125.**
28.8	46.1	Now up and over railroad overpass. **KM 123.**
29.5	47.2	Restaurants at left and right.
34.5	55.2	Pass side road left to Querobabi on railroad. Hwy #82. **KM 113.**
41.9	67.0	The Pápago Indians are desert dwellers. Their pottery & wood carvings are sold in "trading posts" in Phoenix & Tucson, AZ. **KM 100.**
51.3	82.1	Over bridge over dry Río Apache. A Texas Aggie had to make an emergency landing with his plane around here. He banged it up pretty badly. When he was pulled from the wreckage, he asked, "Now why would somebody make a runway that's 100 Mi. long and only 20 ft. wide?"
52.0	83.2	Water for radiator sign with place to left. I wouldn't count on finding water though. **KM 84.**
54.3	86.9	Chapel at right and truck stop of "Los Chinos" (the Chinamen), then microwave tower at right.
55.5	88.8	*Parador turístico* to left.
61.3	98.1	Up into El Oasis. **GAS**, right. Emergency motel Oasis, also at right with bus station restaurant. Pass side road left to town of Carbo on railroad.
61.8	98.9	The Yaqui Indians are also natives here. Their "deer dance" is pretty neat. 'Course young folks of all tribes do "dear" dances. Like most Indians, they have a dance to celebrate the important passages in life and the seasons. It's also an excuse to socialize and relax. KM 68.
73.5	117.6	Mount Cuervos over to right.
84.0	134.4	Pass side road (left) to Pesqueíra, named after Ignacio Pesqueíra, a former governor of Sonora. Red Cross. Cafes on both sides.
99.4	159.0	**GAS**, at right. Altitude 1,000 ft. **KM 10.**
99.6	159.4	Statue Capitán de Anza to right. ITESM Technical school to left.
100.0	160.0	Hermosillo straight, then side road, left, to old town of Ures (capital of state of Sonora from 1838-79) and on to Agua Prieta and border town of Douglas, AZ. This is where free road joins Hwy #15. **KM 9.**

IF TO: Douglas, Agua Prieta, turn left and start Hermosillo — Douglas Log (page 66).

101.8	162.9	Note Rodríguez Lake off ahead, together with fertile valley. This is a rich farming area with a lot of allied industry. Pass ice house at left.

MI	KM	
102.2	163.5	Pass town of La Victoria on road over to left.
103.0	164.8	Enter Hermosillo (Population: 449,472), capital of the state of Sonora. It's named for Colonel J. María González Hermosillo in 1828, a leader in the war for independence. For info on accommodations see Hermosillo Eat & Stray (page 78). **GAS**, left. **KM 4**.
103.6	165.8	Ice plant to left. 60 KMPH. Motel Costa del Sol, left.
104.0	166.4	Café Combate plant at right. 5 horses in middle of road.
104.4	167.0	Mercedes Benz dealer at right.
104.5	167.2	Hotel Autoparador at left, nice. *Gruas* (tow trucks), right.
104.6	167.4	Under pedestrian crossing. Railroad station to left.
104.8	167.7	Come to traffic light and junction with bypass around town. Huge **GAS**, right (across intersection). Periférico South, left. "Periférico" means "bypass" or "loop."

IF TO: Bypass town and on to Guaymas or to Copper Canyon, turn LEFT and start bypass stublog below.

Stub Log: Bypass Hermosillo to Guaymas & Kino Bay.

0.0	0.0	Having turned left at junction with Hwy #15, thru town. **GAS**, on right. Following signs to Guaymas. Chevy dealer to right after Periférico Ote. sign. Protected left turn with arrow and pass ice house.
0.1	0.2	Chevy dealer with Fiesta Americana Hotel behind it and Mobile at right.
0.3	0.5	Firestone at left.
0.4	0.6	Pemex gasoline storage facilities at left and right. 50 KMPH.
0.5	0.8	Curve left at Y.
0.8	1.3	Over railroad crossing. Topes. Curve right under pedestrian crossing. Now on one-way heading SE. You are on Calle Sanalona. Careful for children.
1.4	2.2	At "T" turn left. Go one block. At another "T" turn right. **GAS** at left. School on right.
1.8	2.9	TURN RIGHT to airport and Kino Bay. Veer left then right. Then uphill.
2.2	3.5	Over canal and railroad bridge above you on left.
2.4	3.8	Lake Domínguez at left.
3.0	4.8	Railroad crossing.
4.5	7.2	Roll up your windows, Cattle feed lot at left.
4.8	7.7	Junction, left, to Sahuaripa or Tecoripa. Right to Guaymas and Kino Bay. Veer right.

IF TO: Chihuahua or the Copper Canyon, turn left and start Hermosillo — La Junta Log (page 50).

5.0	8.0	**GAS**, left.
5.8	9.3	Goodyear at right. Come to junction with Hwy #15. Stoplight.

IF TO: Kino Bay, straight ahead and continue this stub log.

IF TO: Guaymas, turn left and start Hermosillo — Guaymas Log (page 12) at mile 3.3.

IF TO: DOWNTOWN, TURN RIGHT.

5.9	9.4	Pass Plaza Sur shopping center (you can get slide film from photo stores only).
6.8	10.9	Pass automatic transmission repair shop, right.
7.0	11.2	Pass **GAS** station, left. Stoplight. Cemento Campana, left just before light.
7.8	12.5	Amazing rock formation at left behind Las Palmas shopping center
9.2	14.7	Another shopping center, left.
9.5	15.2	Stoplight. Plaza Satélite, left just past light.
10.1	16.2	Pass big dry cleaner (*tintorería*) at left.

IF TO: Kino Bay, Turn left and begin Hermosillo — Kino Bay Special at mile 2.0 (page 45).

End of Stub Log

104.9	167.8	High-rise Fiesta Americana Hotel and big Ariaza Hotel at left.
105.2	168.3	Well-known motel Gandara at left, 1000 Blvd. Kino. Pretty Bancomer at right.
105.3	168.5	Excellent restaurant Henry's, right. Motel Encanto at left. Ahead down wide divided.
105.5	168.8	Hotel Petic Valle Grande, left. Motel Bugambilia Valle Grande, right.
105.6	169.0	Señorial hotel at left. Motel Siesta, left. Ford dealer at right. Mannix Cafeteria at right (fast service). Laundromat at left. **GAS**, right.

TOURIST MAP OF
HERMOSILLO
COPYRIGHT © TRAVCO SERVICES, INC.
(not to scale)
UD-017
CONVENTION CENTER
(Bypass) Periférico Norte
G. Arriola
Blvd Morelos
TO NOGALES &
SANTA ANA (with
RV Parks, 105 MI)
STADIUM
STADIUM
BUGAMBILIA
VALLE GRANDE
HENRY'S
MANNIX
EL ENCANTO
GANDARA
MEX 15
R.R. STATION
Quintana Roo
Tlaxcala
Aguascalientes
Veracruz
Tamaulipas
Zacatecas
BLOCKY'O CLUB
Blvd. Quinta
LA SIESTA
PITIC VALLE
VALLE GRANDE
FIESTA AMERICANA
Blvd. Transversal
MIYAKO
VALLE GRANDE HERMOSILLO
ARIAZA
MERENDERO LA HUERTA
VILLA FIESTA
TO AIRPORT & KINO BAY
UNIVERSITY STADIUM
Yucatán
HOSPITAL
MUSEUM & LIBRARY
UNIVERSITY OF SONORA
RODEO
JUAREZ GARDEN
EL PALOMINO
REGIONAL HISTORY MUSEUM
CALINDA HERMOSILLO
QUALITY INN
ART GALLERY
SAN ALBERTO
US CONSULATE
KINO
MARKET
CHILDREN'S PARK
PLAZA ZARAGOZA
POST OFFICE/ TELEGRAPH OFFICE
BUS STATION
(Bypass)
CITY HALL
GOVERNMENT PALACE
JO-WAH
PRESA (DAM)
A .L. RODRIGUEZ
Blvd. Fco. Sema
MUSEO COSTUMBRISTA
CERRO DE LA CAMPANA
POPULATION: 500,000
ALTITUDE: 720 Feet
CASA DE LA CULTURA
XOCHIMILCO
Blvd. Agustín de Vildosola
N
Sí
SANBORN'S
®
MEX 15
FORD PLANT
Periférico Sur (Bypass)
INDUSTRIAL PARK
TO GUAYMAS

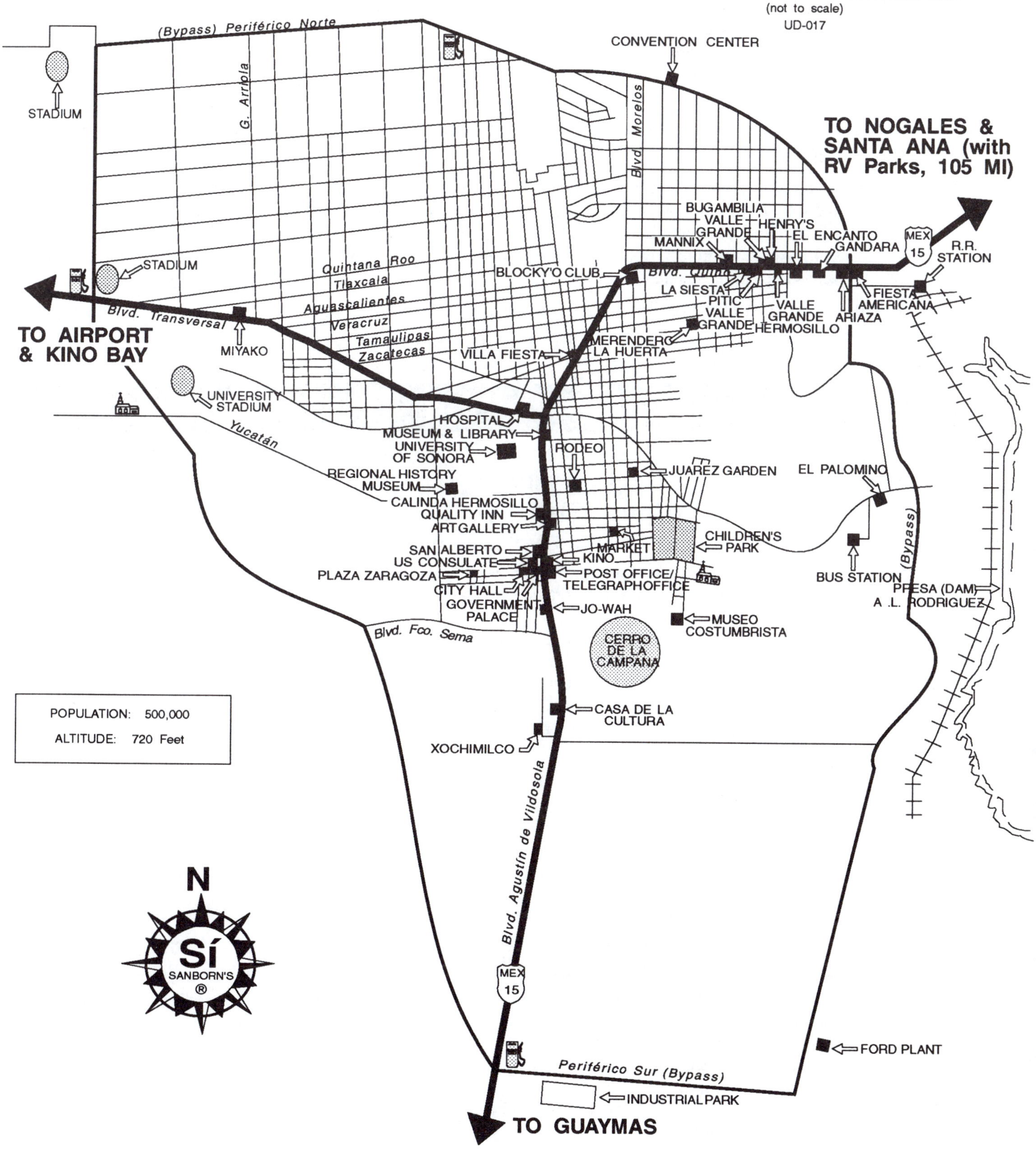

MI	KM	
105.8	169.3	La Fiesta restaurant at right. Chrysler dealer at left.
105.9	169.4	To the right is a grocery store, "Valle Petic." You should veer slightly right here. Do not get into "lateral" lane at far right. Then **GAS**, left.
106.2	169.9	Pass shopping center right. Left to downtown at the light. Chevy dealer and Ford clock tower to right. Sports Palace at left. STAY OUT OF EXTREME LEFT LANE AS YOU MIGHT BE FORCED TO TURN LEFT.
106.5	170.4	Come to monument, at left, to one-armed man — General Alvaro Obregón. He was presidente of Mexico from 1920-24, a native of Sonora state. Pancho Villa shot off his arm during a revolutionary battle at Celaya. Hertz Rent-a-Car, right. You are on Av. A.L. Rodríguez.
106.8	170.9	KFC, left. Then pass Av. Madrid.
107.0	171.2	STOPLIGHT. Japanese Restaurant Mirikon, left.

IF TO: Kino Bay, take right fork just past next monument, but before stoplight. Start Hermosillo — Kino Bay Special (page 45).

107.1	171.4	Come to busy Yánez St. Take LEFT FORK past monument of mounted Capitán de Anza (a native of Sonora and founder of San Francisco, California). Come to STOPLIGHT. Rodríguez Museum and Library at left. Ahead and at your right is plaza of University of Sonora. Rodríguez Museum and Library, Rodríguez Dam and Lake, & Rodríguez Boulevard you were just on, are all named for Abelardo Rodríguez, a Sonora boy who served as presidente from 1932-34.

IF TO: Guaymas, start Hermosillo — Guaymas Log.

End of Log 4.

LOG 5   *START:* Hermosillo, Son   *END:* Guaymas, Son

UD-017

82.5 MI or 132.0 KM
DRIVE TIME 1 1/4 — 2 HOURS
SCENIC RATING — 3

0.0	0.0	Here at university plaza, ahead down wide two-way Avenida Rosales.
0.5	0.8	Hotel Calinda, right. Hotel San Alberto, right. Civic center, right. Then Jo Wah Restaurant.
0.7	1.1	Hotel Kino, left
0.9	1.4	Under pedestrian walkway. Another turnoff to Kino Bay, right.
1.1	1.8	Go over old bypass around city. Up and over dry bed of Río de Sonora. Big Rodríguez Dam which feeds Lake Rodríguez behind it, is upstream to left.
1.5	2.4	Hotel Grenada at right. Note monument at right to *Los Tres Pueblos* in memory of three little villages on Río de Sonora that were washed away years ago by a big flood. **GAS**, left.
3.0	4.8	Large shopping plaza, right.
3.3	5.3	Come to **GAS**, left (watch 'em). Whenever you see "watch 'em" that means several of our customers have had bad experiences here. We change the info when enough folks write us that they got good service at the same place. Then junction with periférico or loop around town. Welcome to those folks joining us from periférico.

IF TO: Santa Ana & El Novillo Dam (and lake), 95 miles (good bass fishing), turn LEFT.

IF TO: Kino Bay, turn right and start Kino Bay stublog below. Otherwise continue straight.

Stub Log: Kino Bay Via Bypass

0.0	0.0	Having turned onto periférico heading West, pass Plaza Sur shopping center (you can get slide film from photo stores only).
0.4	0.6	Pass Palo Verde business park, left.
0.9	1.4	Pass automatic transmission repair shop, right.
1.1	1.8	Pass **GAS** station, left. Stoplight. Cemento Campana, left just before light.
1.9	3.0	Amazing rock formation at left behind Las Palmas shopping center
2.1	3.4	Road goes over usually dry river and freeway to nowhere.

MI	KM	
2.8	4.5	Fuel injection service, right.
3.3	5.3	Another shopping center, left.
3.6	5.8	Stoplight. Plaza Satélite, left just past light.
4.2	6.7	Pass big dry cleaner (tintorería) at left.

IF TO: Kino Bay, Turn left and begin Hermosillo — Kino Bay Special (page 45) at mile 2.

End of Stub Log

3.4	5.4	Shopping plaza at right with store selling slide film.
3.9	6.2	Motel Cid at right. AA sign.
4.0	6.4	Conasupo at right. Tecate agency at left. Left to Hermosillo Ecological Park — a very worthwhile place. **KM 248.**
4.9	7.8	Police Institute, left. Mexico is working hard to modernize it's police forces and hires some consultants from the US and other places.
13.2	21.1	Notice camel-hump hill over to left.
15.0	24.0	SHARP left and over bridge over little dry Río La Poza. KM 233.
22.4	35.8	Shirley Temple mountains to right.
28.0	44.8	Those rugged mountains ahead to left are called *El Pilar* (The Pillar).
35.5	56.8	Whistle stop of La Pintada at left where there are supposed to be caves whose walls are carved with prehistoric hieroglyphics (though nobody seems to know about them, so look for them only if you are adventurous and speak Spanish). CAREFUL, there will be some fairly sharp curves ahead. Also, the smokeys have ears here, dear. Go the speed limit. Nice as we are, we won't pay your traffic tickets.
40.9	65.4	SHARP "S" CURVE. There's about a mile more of them.
44.3	70.9	Slow! Brown-&-white cow in middle of road. This is the original brown cow from Dan's day.
54.3	86.9	**GAS**, right. WELCOME TO THOSE JOINING US FROM KINO SHORTCUT. Pass side road right back to Kino Bay.
61.1	97.8	WATCH OUT for posts on left side of road. Dangerous.
71.6	114.6	Series of well-marked curves for a mile or two.
73.5	117.6	Wide spot of El Caballo (The Horse), left. Truck inspection station, left. **KM 141.**
74.5	119.2	**GAS** & Diesel, right Then careful as you come to junction with toll bypass around Guaymas. Get in left lane for toll bypass.

IF TO: San Carlos, straight ahead and skip stublog.

IF TO: Bypass of town, VEER LEFT following CD. OBREGÓN sign and follow stublog below. Otherwise skip down to mile 78.3. The free bypass is OK, unless you're in a hurry.

Stub Log: Toll Bypass around Guaymas

0.0	0.0	Having veered left at OBREGÓN sign, continue ahead on 4-lane bypass around Guaymas. **KM 21.**
1.1	1.8	Come to toll house and pay toll ($28). Then under overpass. Sign says "Cd. Obregón 129 KM."
3.0	4.8	Truck-stop restaurant Los Faroles, left.
11.8	18.9	Restaurant in middle of road.
12.0	19.2	Pass big Fertimex plant at left. Then **GAS** at right and up and over railroad. Topes. Then come to junction with HWY #15.

IF TO: Downtown Guaymas, turn left.

IF TO: Navojoa, Mazatlán, continue straight and join Guaymas — Navojoa Log at Mile 10.5 (page 15).

End of Stub Log

78.3	125.3	Come to side road (right) to San Carlos.

IF TO: SAN CARLOS, exit RIGHT here and start Guaymas — San Carlos Special (page 61) — it's quite a nice place, sort of a gringo oasis. It's about 5 miles straight ahead on a fine road — you won't get lost. Be CAREFUL, watch your speed. They really have traffic cops now.

78.5	125.6	Come to overpass. **KM 132.**

IF TO: GUAYMAS, under overpass and ahead.

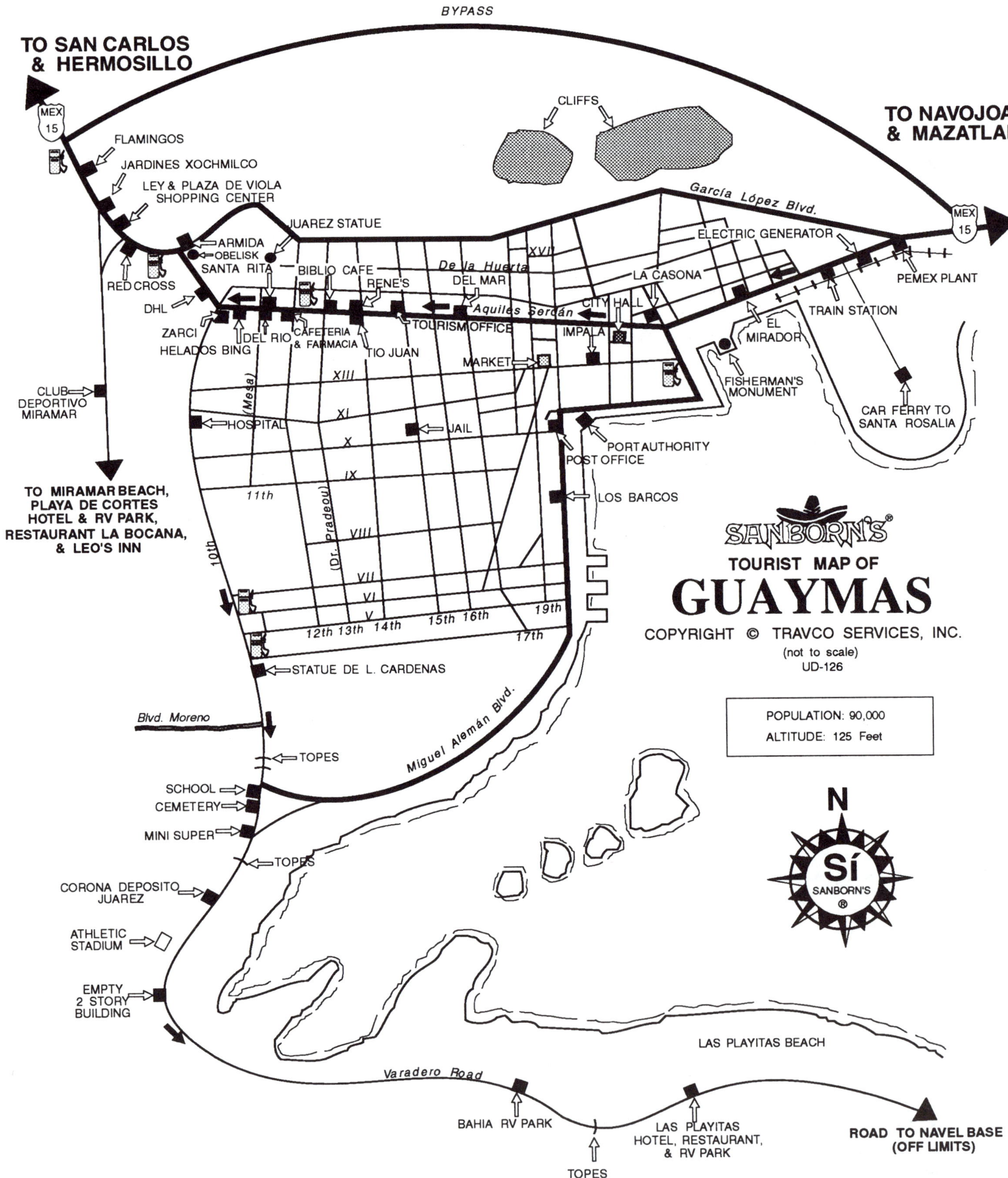
BYPASS
TO SAN CARLOS
& HERMOSILLO
TO NAVOJOA
& MAZATLAN
CLIFFS
MEX 15
FLAMINGOS
JARDINES XOCHMILCO
LEY & PLAZA DE VIOLA
SHOPPING CENTER
JUAREZ STATUE
García López Blvd.
ELECTRIC GENERATOR
ARMIDA
OBELISK
SANTA RITA
BIBLIO CAFE
De la Huerta
XVI
LA CASONA
MEX 15
PEMEX PLANT
RED CROSS
RENE'S
DEL MAR
DHL
Aquiles Serdán
CITY HALL
TRAIN STATION
ZARCI
HELADOS BING
DEL RIO
CAFETERIA
& FARMACIA
TIO JUAN
TOURISM OFFICE
IMPALA
EL MIRADOR
CLUB
DEPORTIVO
MIRAMAR
(Mesa)
XIII
MARKET
FISHERMAN'S
MONUMENT
XI
HOSPITAL
X
JAIL
PORT AUTHORITY
POST OFFICE
CAR FERRY TO
SANTA ROSALIA
TO MIRAMAR BEACH,
PLAYA DE CORTES
HOTEL & RV PARK,
RESTAURANT LA BOCANA,
& LEO'S INN
IX
11th
(Dr. Pradeou)
VIII
LOS BARCOS
SANBORN'S
TOURIST MAP OF
GUAYMAS
COPYRIGHT © TRAVCO SERVICES, INC.
(not to scale)
UD-126
VII
10th
VI
V
12th 13th 14th
15th 16th
19th
17th
STATUE DE L. CARDENAS
POPULATION: 90,000
ALTITUDE: 125 Feet
Blvd. Moreno
Miguel Alemán Blvd.
N
TOPES
SCHOOL
CEMETERY
SÍ
SANBORN'S
MINI SUPER
TOPES
CORONA DEPOSITO
JUAREZ
ATHLETIC
STADIUM
EMPTY
2 STORY
BUILDING
LAS PLAYITAS BEACH
Varadero Road
BAHIA RV PARK
LAS PLAYITAS
HOTEL, RESTAURANT,
& RV PARK
ROAD TO NAVEL BASE
(OFF LIMITS)
TOPES

MI	KM	
80.0	128.0	There's Guaymas airport over to left.
81.5	130.4	**GAS** at right (do not accept credit cards).
82.0	131.2	Motel Flamingos at left. Tecate agency at right and enter city of Guaymas. For info on accommodations see Guaymas Eat & Stray (page 84)
82.5	132.0	Miramar exit, right to Bacochibampo Bay, Playa de Cortés Hotel & RV park. This Hotel is a wonderful old place with plenty of charm. Also down the road is economical Leo's Inn. Careful for big topes.

IF TO: Navojoa, Alamos, Los Mochis, Mazatlán, etc., STRAIGHT. Start Guaymas — Navojoa Log (page 15).

IF TO: Ferry Baja California, proceed ahead and then bear right onto main street a short mile ahead (see Guaymas map). You just keep going straight through town until you see ferry compound on your right. See "How 'Bout Them Ferries!" in front section of your *Travelog*.

IF TO: Guaymas RV Parks, start Guaymas RV Stub Log below:

Stub Log: To Guaymas RV Parks

Note: They were building a new bypass when we were there. If you see a sign to "Playitas" on the highway, it will get you there and avoid the first two miles of this log. Otherwise, this log works well. Watch your speed.

0.0	0.0	Having veered right just past light, continue on past spire obelisk monument, left,
0.1	0.2	Modelo beer distributor, right.
0.2	0.3	Stoplight. VH shopping center on right just beyond light. TURN RIGHT onto Calle Diez (even though it looks like a one-way the other way).
0.5	0.8	IMSS hospital, left. Then stoplight and **GAS** at left.
0.6	1.0	Statue of Lázaro Cárdenas, left.
1.0	1.6	Veer right at second light, then take left fork at intersection with divided Blvd. Go uphill with trees and small plaza at right.
1.2	1.9	Stoplight. You're now on Benito Juárez.
2.6	4.2	Veer left. Follow Las Playitas sign. Beer distributor on right.
2.7	4.3	Athletic stadium, right. Large stucco commercial building, right. Then cemetery on right. After cemetery turn right following Las Playitas sign
2.8	4.5	Bay at left. Watch speed thru here (20 kph). Then veer left. Right goes to subdivision.
3.5	5.6	Bahía RV Park, left.
3.8	6.1	Industrial Park, right.
3.9	6.2	Naval club, left.
4.1	6.6	Las Playitas Motel and RV Park, left.

End of Log 5.

LOG 6   *START:* Guaymas, Son   *END:* Navojoa, Son

UD-017

121.7 MI or 194.7 KM
DRIVE TIME 2 — 2 1/2 HOURS
SCENIC RATING — 2

0.0	0.0	Having passed exit right for Bocachibampo Bay (Bay of the Sea Serpents), & neat Hotel Cortés, with large RV park, continue ahead under overpass on divided 4-lane.
0.4	0.6	"Ley" shopping plaza, left.
0.5	0.8	Las Villas Subdivision at right. Then Nissan and Ford dealers, right. Also VW and Chrysler/Dodge Then **GAS**, right.
1.0	1.6	Hotel Armida, left. Under pedestrian crossing. Then traffic light. Stay left and veer left at obelisk.

IF TO: Cd. Obregón, Navojoa, VEER LEFT here.

IF TO: Guaymas, RV parks on bay, TURN RIGHT.

MI	KM	
1.1	1.8	HAVING DECIDED NOT TO GO TO DOWNTOWN GUAYMAS, STRAIGHT AHEAD. Monument at right to Héroes of Guaymas. Chevy dealer.
1.3	2.1	"Topes, topes, topes" General Tire, right. Coca Cola bottling co., left.
1.5	2.4	Monument to Benito Juárez on hilltop to right. SLOW thru SCHOOL ZONE.
2.0	3.2	**GAS** left. You're skirting edge of town. Another SCHOOL ZONE.
2.3	3.7	Careful for merging traffic. Then slow for school zone.
3.6	5.8	Veer left past junction with road to ferries. Mexico calls the Gulf of California *Mar de Cortés* (Sea of Cortés).
3.8	6.1	Power plant, right. LP gas, left and right. **KM 120.**
5.3	8.5	Onto causeway alongside railroad track, right. CAREFUL.
6.5	10.4	End of causeway — LOOK-&-LISTEN for DOUBLE railroad crossing. AHEAD on Hwy 15. Left fork is to railroad town of Empalme (population, 70,000) And there, left stands old engine 70 of the *Ferrocarril de Sonora* ("Sonora Railroad"), a monument to Empalme and its railroad industry. Then slow for another railroad crossing — LOOK-&-LISTEN.
6.7	10.7	Mount Dolly Parton to right? Restaurant to left.
7.3	11.7	TOPES! Then big Anderson-Clayton complex, also, right. And one more railroad switch line LOOK-&-LISTEN. Then white palm trees lining highway.
8.0	12.8	*Ferrocarril del Pacífico* station (Pacific Railroad station), left. Railroad crossing.
8.1	13.0	**GAS** (watch 'em), right. Highway patrol, left. **KM 11**
10.5	16.8	Pass side road (right) to beachfront community of El Cochori, 2 miles (no accommodations) and careful for merging traffic from TOLL bypass, left.
13.0	20.8	Pass side road (left) to Ortiz. Down this road a short mile is where famous NASA space capsule tracking station was located (the place that a couple of the early astronauts referred to when they remarked as they passed over, "Hello, Guaymas! Send us up some enchiladas!"). This station is no longer used by NASA.
15.0	24.0	Pass side road (right) to Playa del Sol, a beachfront development.
15.5	24.8	Pass Cruz de Piedra (Cross of Stone) over to left on railroad. Note disabled and outdated railroad cars now used as homes. Here is where a big Yaqui Indian reservation starts and runs for 50-odd miles to the Yaqui River just North of Cd. Obregón. The Yaquis had a big uprising back in the late 1920's and Mexico gave them this territory for a reservation.
21.0	33.6	Thru rock cut of Boca Abierta (Open Mouth).
22.8	36.5	Livestock-shipping community of Las Guásimas.
27.3	43.7	Slow for sharp right curve.
36.7	58.7	Pass side road (left) to Pitahaya.
42.5	68.0	Pass side road (right) to Potam. Note irrigated countryside thru here — very fertile soil. Main crops — cotton, wheat soya, sunflower oil, sorghum. There's a drug check point at this junction.
48.0	76.8	Slow thru little town of Vicam. Red Cross, right. **GAS**, left.
52.5	84.0	Community of Cárdenas and site of the famous YAQUI INDIAN VOCATIONAL AND AGRICULTURAL SCHOOL, where "knowhow" is taught to Yaqui Indian kids. Emergency hotel "Yaqui Aggies"?, right, with long distance phone and laundry. "Ehwee" in Yaqui means "Yes."
54.1	86.6	Pass side road right to Torim.
57.0	91.2	Sign advising there will be a choice of either toll road or free (*libre*) road in 10 KM. This log takes the toll road.
59.0	94.4	Truck weigh station. Yaqui masks are made of desiccated deer heads, wood & dried goat skin.
61.8	98.9	Come to junction (right) with free road.

IF TO: Cd Obregón via toll road continue straight, but if via free road veer right, you're on your own.

61.9		Having taken toll road continue ahead on 4-lane divided. **KM 26.**
62.9	100.6	Pass another road, left to Bacum.
68.0	108.8	Thru scattered settlement of Loma de Guamúchil.

Guamúchil is a tree, very common in this part of Mexico, with thorny leafstalks, hairy white globe-shaped flower clusters, and black shiny seeds in spirally twisted pods from 5-6 inches long.

69.8	111.7	CAREFUL! Settlement of Tajimaroa to right. Side road left to Est. Corral, 3 km. Bend right and slow for *Salida de Camiones* (yield to trucks) merging with highway traffic).

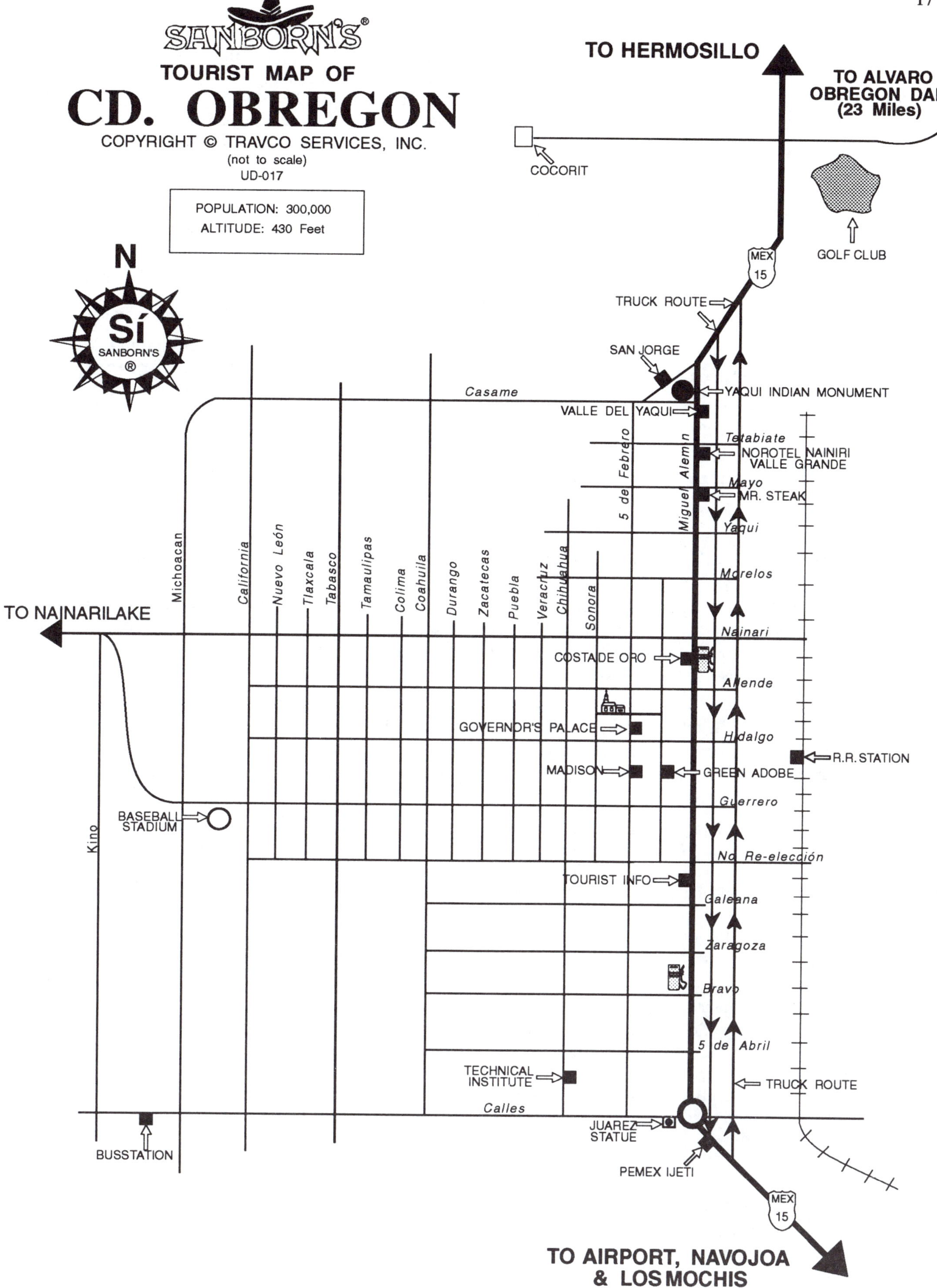
SANBORN'S ®
TOURIST MAP OF
CD. OBREGON
COPYRIGHT © TRAVCO SERVICES, INC.
(not to scale)
UD-017
POPULATION: 300,000
ALTITUDE: 430 Feet
N
Sí
SANBORN'S
®
TO HERMOSILLO
TO ALVARO OBREGON DAM
(23 Miles)
COCORIT
GOLF CLUB
MEX 15
TRUCK ROUTE
SAN JORGE
Casame
YAQUI INDIAN MONUMENT
VALLE DEL YAQUI
Tetabiate
NOROTEL NAINIRI VALLE GRANDE
5 de Febrero
Miguel Alemn
Mayo
MR. STEAK
Yaqui
Morelos
Michoacan
California
Nuevo León
Tlaxcala
Tabasco
Tamaulipas
Colima
Coahuila
Durango
Zacatecas
Puebla
Veracruz
Chihuahua
Sonora
Nainari
TO NAINARILAKE
COSTA DE ORO
Allende
GOVERNOR'S PALACE
Hidalgo
R.R. STATION
MADISON
GREEN ADOBE
Guerrero
Kino
BASEBALL STADIUM
No Re-elección
TOURIST INFO
Galeana
Zaragoza
Bravo
5 de Abril
TECHNICAL INSTITUTE
TRUCK ROUTE
Calles
BUSSTATION
JUAREZ STATUE
PEMEX IJETI
MEX 15
TO AIRPORT, NAVOJOA & LOS MOCHIS

MI	KM	
70.8	113.3	Cross over famous Río Yaqui whose course from the state of Chihuahua to the Sea of Cortés is 419 miles long. This is also where the Yaqui Indian Reservation ends.
72.8	116.5	Stop and pay toll ($28). **GAS**, left (has Diesel Sin). Careful for stoplights.
73.8	118.1	Skirt edge of Esperanza (Hope). Pass side road (right) to Cocorít, while side road (left) goes to Tezopaco de Rosario and to Presa (dam) Alvaro Obregón which has a reputation for the best bass fishing in North America. **GAS**, right, but there's a better one ahead in Cd. Obregón, 5 miles.
74.4	119.0	Military base, left.
75.8	121.3	Pemex tank farm, left.
77.5	124.0	Enter prosperous town of Cd. (abbreviation for *ciudad* "city") Obregón, the agricultural heart of the Yaqui Valley (known as the Bread Basket of Mexico) with a population of 450,000. This was formerly called Cájeme after the famous chief of the Yaqui Indians, but the name was later changed in honor of Presidente Obregón. His family was originally of Irish lineage.
77.7	124.3	TURN LEFT onto bypass around Cd. Obregón just beyond statue of soldier and ahead on divided.

IF TO: Cd. Obregón continue straight. There is a **GAS** station 1/2 mile towards town that takes credit cards (when manager is in), several new hotels, a Holiday Inn Ph: (64) 14-0936 Fax: (64) 13-4194, 91-800-62333 and a good restaurant, Mr. Steak, where they roll a cart of beef out and cut your steak to your request. See Cd. Obregón Eat & Stray (page 86) for more info on accommodations.

78.3	125.3	Pass Mobile, right. Then Corona left.
78.8	126.1	VW agency on left.
79.3	126.9	Very nice Travelodge on right (70 rooms, pool, Ph & Fax: 14-5044).
79.5	127.2	**GAS**, right.
79.8	127.7	Over railroad crossing (Look-&-Listen).
80.6	129.0	Here is where the bypass rejoins highway. TURN LEFT at traffic lights. **GAS** on right after turn.
81.3	130.1	Ley shopping center, left.
81.5	130.4	Coca-Cola bottling plant, right. Then big Gamesa (Galletas Mexicanas, S.A.), left, one of Mexico's largest cookie producers - sort of like Nabisco in the States. SLOW-LOOK-&-LISTEN at bumpy railroad crossing. Many cotton grain-related industries here. Industrial park, right. **KM 222**.
82.0	131.2	Pass turnoff (right) to Villa Juárez.

If you have a generous and compassionate heart and would like to visit an orphanage, you will find Hogar de Refugio Infantil Villa Juárez by turning right onto side road to Villa Juárez, go 26 miles on paved road, turn right for another mile, then turn left following signs to the orphanage. Bob Mason, the director, welcomes visitors. They are able to accommodate motor homes, trailers etc. and have a crude dumping station as well as electrical hookups.

84.0	134.4	**GAS**, right (accept credit cards), but watch 'em. **KM 210**.
88.8	142.1	Pass side road (right) to airport.
90.0	144.0	Enormous shrine to the Virgin of Guadalupe over at left. **KM 203**.
95.5	152.8	**GAS**, right. Exit right to take free road bypass around Navojoa and follow stublog below, otherwise jump down to continuation of log (MI 97.9). At press time car toll was $28.00. Free road is OK. It takes 15 minutes longer.

Stub Log: Free Road To Navojoa

96.5	154.4	Having turned right at "V. Juárez/Navojoa" sign, continue ahead on 2-lane road.
105.5	168.8	Thru village of Jecopaco, store with phone. "Topes" and more "topes" Texaco sign, left.
111.4	178.2	Come to "T." For Navojoa, TURN LEFT. Villa Juárez, is to the right. Suddenly you are at KM 28.
113.0	180.8	Village of Bacobampo and calle 26 to right. Then over canals at **KM 26**.
113.5	181.6	Thru Agua Blanca and "topes." Farm equipment yard, left, then more "topes." **KM 24**.
116.6	186.6	Pass side road (right) to Buaysiacobe. **KM 20**.
122.4	195.8	Pass village of Bacame Nuevo to left.
128.9	206.2	Come to "T" and REJOIN HWY #15 AT MILE 119.1 BELOW. TURN RIGHT and ahead to Navojoa.

End of Stub Log

97.9	156.6	Toll booth. Stop and pay toll ($28). KM 195.
110.8	177.3	Cotton community of Sibolibampo.

MI	KM	
112.5	180.0	Pass side road (right) to Villa Juárez, 30 km. (18 miles).
118.0	188.8	**GAS**, right. If taking the free road to Los Mochis, turn right here.
119.1	190.6	Motel Rancho (there are better choices) down, right. Just past it is good bed & breakfast Hotel Cazadores — 16 rooms. Pollo & Elsa Acosta, owners. Ph: (642) 2-9360. Then thru little community of Guaymitas. KM 1.
119.6	191.4	Over bridge.

IF TO: Alameda RV Park, exit right immediately after bridge.

119.9	91.8	Turn right into RV Alameda just after bridge. Motel Del Río at right. Restaurant Los Arcos at right. Tecate store at left. Corona distributor at right.
120.0	192.0	The bypass is not worth taking, go thru town. Enter Navojoa (Population: 122,390), a clean agricultural boom town and birthplace of LA Dodgers' pitcher, Fernando Valenzuela. Straight on thru on nice wide main street. Very good **GAS**, left. This has SELF-SERVICE lanes! What's Mexico coming to? Neat little coffee shop Alamos, next door with packaged ice, etc. Then Asadero Restaurant (tasty "*carne asada*"), left. Friends of Bill W. in town (Spanish only) Tel: 2-5953. AA at Pesqueíra #105 Nte.

Navojoa means "place among the tunas" in Mayo Indian, tuna being a prickly pear.

120.6	193.0	**GAS**, left. Restaurant/bar Los Coporales at left. 2 smiling elephants at right. Goodyear left. Nissan right. Chevy left. General tire at right. Restaurant Jo Wah to right. ISSTE clinic at right.
120.9	193.4	Uniroyal at left and Firestone at right.
121.2	193.9	Pass side road (right) to San Ignacio and Tetanchopo.
121.4	194.2	Several photo supply stores at right.
121.5	194.4	Pass Nissan dealer right. Funeral parlor and General tire at left. Stoplight.
121.7	194.7	V H shopping center at left. Come to junction with road to Alamos. Semi-Llantas on right just past light. Ahead on right is a highly recommended Dodge dealer (he helped me out). For info or accommodations, see Navojoa Eat & Stray (page 87).

IF TO: Los Mochis, start Navojoa — Los Mochis Log.

IF TO: Alamos, one of the neatest old mining towns in Mexico, start Navojoa — Alamos Special (page 61).

End of Log 6.

LOG 7 *START:* Navojoa, Son   *END:* Los Mochis, Sin

UD-017

98.0 MI or 156.8 KM
DRIVE TIME — 2 HOURS
SCENIC RATING — 2

0.0	0.0	In Navojoa at STOPLIGHT and junction (left) with side road to Alamos, head South/Southeast on Hwy 15. Tips' Restaurant, left. On right, Goodrich, VW dealer and Chrysler/Dodge (I highly recommend this Dodge dealer — he helped me out). Pass **GAS**, left..
0.3	0.5	Over railroad tracks. Social security hospital (ISSTE) at right. Curve right. Big flour mill (Conasupo) also at right. Motel Colonial at right. Then over Canal Las Pilas, **KM 155**, and take leave of Navojoa as you pass industrial park on left. Then pass Navojoa Medical Center
1.0	1.6	**GAS**, right. Exit for free road, right. Free road is 15 KM longer than toll road. If you want to avoid tolls, follow "Libre" signs. We prefer the toll road if you can afford it. Ask locals regarding the condition of the free road. **KM 153.**
5.2	8.3	Pass airfield at left.
6.0	9.6	Railroad tracks follow road at left.
10.0	16.0	Rest area El Abajeno at right, restaurant — popular with truck drivers. Then small shrine at right. **KM 139.**

By the way, these shrines are places where someone died in an accident. The families often visit them and put flowers on them on saints' days and birthdays. During the week of the "Day of the Dead" (*Día de los Muertos*) around our Halloween, most every one in Mexico has flowers on it.

16.5	26.4	Slow for toll booth. Stop and pay toll ($32).

MI	KM	
17.0	27.2	Pass side road (right) to Huatabampo "Willow Tree in the Water", a nice little city located in a large, prosperous irrigated district. Four miles South of town is Huatabampito, a little resort on the Gulf of California with miles and miles of inviting sandy beach. Then at left is Ejido Luis Echeverría, named after one of Mexico's ex-presidentes (1970-1976).
26.3	42.1	Pass another side road (left) to Masiaca, 6 miles and (right) to Las Bocas, 7.5 miles, a beach resort on the Sea of Cortés. KM 118
30.3	48.5	Truck stop restaurant Carmelita, right.
35.0	56.0	Mexico's always attracted dreamers & visionaries, for instance Albert Kinsey Owens, who founded a Utopian community in Los Mochis. He wanted to grow sugar cane & build a railroad to the U.S. in 1872. **KM 100.**
39.0	62.4	Railroad station community of Estación Luis at left. Then pass side road (left) to Ejido Tierra y Libertad (Land and Liberty).

"Tierra y Libertad" was Emiliano Zapata's cry as he seized and burned the haciendas in his home state of Morelos and divided the land among his white—clad Indian followers, paving the way for Article 27 of the Mexican Constitution, upon which all subsequent land reform laws have been based.

MI	KM	
44.9	71.8	Big Ejido Francisco Sarabia at right. Bumpy railroad crossing! Watch for animals and bicycles along highway. Then huge Conasupo farmers' co-op at right. **GAS**, right, clean restrooms, **KM 93.**
47.4	75.8	Note pig farm at right (the smell is hard to miss).
52.0	83.2	Thru village of Estación Don. ("Don" is pronounced "Doan", sort of like Doan's back pills, except it's pronounced crisper.) **KM 72.**
54.0	86.4	**GAS**, left and agricultural inspection station. **KM 70.**
54.5	87.2	Come now to state line. Leave state of Sonora and enter state of Sinaloa.

You've been traveling in the state of Sonora, which must be the longest state in Mexico. It's 433 miles from Nogales down to this point; and if you came by way of San Luis Río Colorado, you've been in Sonora for the last 665 miles. Sinaloa is also pretty lengthy — 397 miles. Please be aware that, seat belts are required by law in Sinaloa.

MI	KM	
54.6	87.4	Veer right and slow down for agricultural station to left.
56.0	89.6	SLOW and pull over to right. Be ready to stop for truck agricultural inspection station. There is also a drug inspection checkpoint here.
59.0	94.4	Big Ejido Talamantes at right. Pass side road (left) to San Francisco microwave tower.
63.7	101.9	Ejido El Carrizo at right, headquarters town for irrigation district of huge El Fuerte irrigation project. Red Cross. **GAS**, left. CAREFUL — THERE'S A SHARP DROP FROM THE HWY TO THE SHOULDER. **KM 55.**

By the way, an *ejido* is a government-sponsored community agriculture project — you'll pass many of these on your Mexico motor trip. They usually have fancy names, like famous revolutionary heroes, ex-presidentes or historical dates. There are about 30,000 *ejidos* throughout Mexico. The concept of some land for every Mexican was one of the tenets of the Revolutionary struggle in Mexico. The ejido system has been eliminated in modern times, but the names and signs live on.

MI	KM	
65.6	105.0	Pass Restaurant La Posta, left. **KM 52.**
65.8	105.3	Pass side road (left) to El Fuerte and Chiox, but there's another shorter route at Los Mochis.
79.5	127.2	Curve left and start winding thru Cerro Prieto Pass carefully. Devil's Canyon over at right.
85.4	136.6	Prepare to pay toll ($12) at "caseta puente San Miguel." **KM 20.**
87.3	139.7	Burned-out cotton gin at left with "no smoking" (*prohibido fumar*) still visible on side of building. Then side road, right, to nice, pleasant Río Fuerte RV Park and Hacienda de Zamora. Bumpy bridge over Río Fuerte, the principal river in these parts.
88.1	141.0	Now thru edge of little town of San Miguel Zapotitlán. **KM 16. GAS**, left sometimes they try to charge more for it, so watch 'em. Over main irrigation canal. Vibradores. KM 15.
91.0	145.6	Cavalry's 18th regiment barracks at right. If you go through on leave day, don't be alarmed. There will be hundreds of soldiers hitchhiking.
98.0	156.8	Come now to Los Mochis interchange. **GAS**, left but watch 'em.

IF TO: Los Mochis, take right turnoff and head into town. See map. For accommodations see Los Mochis Eat & Stray (page 90).

IF TO: Culiacán or Mazatlán, start Los Mochis — Culiacán Log. Go under 2 overpasses.

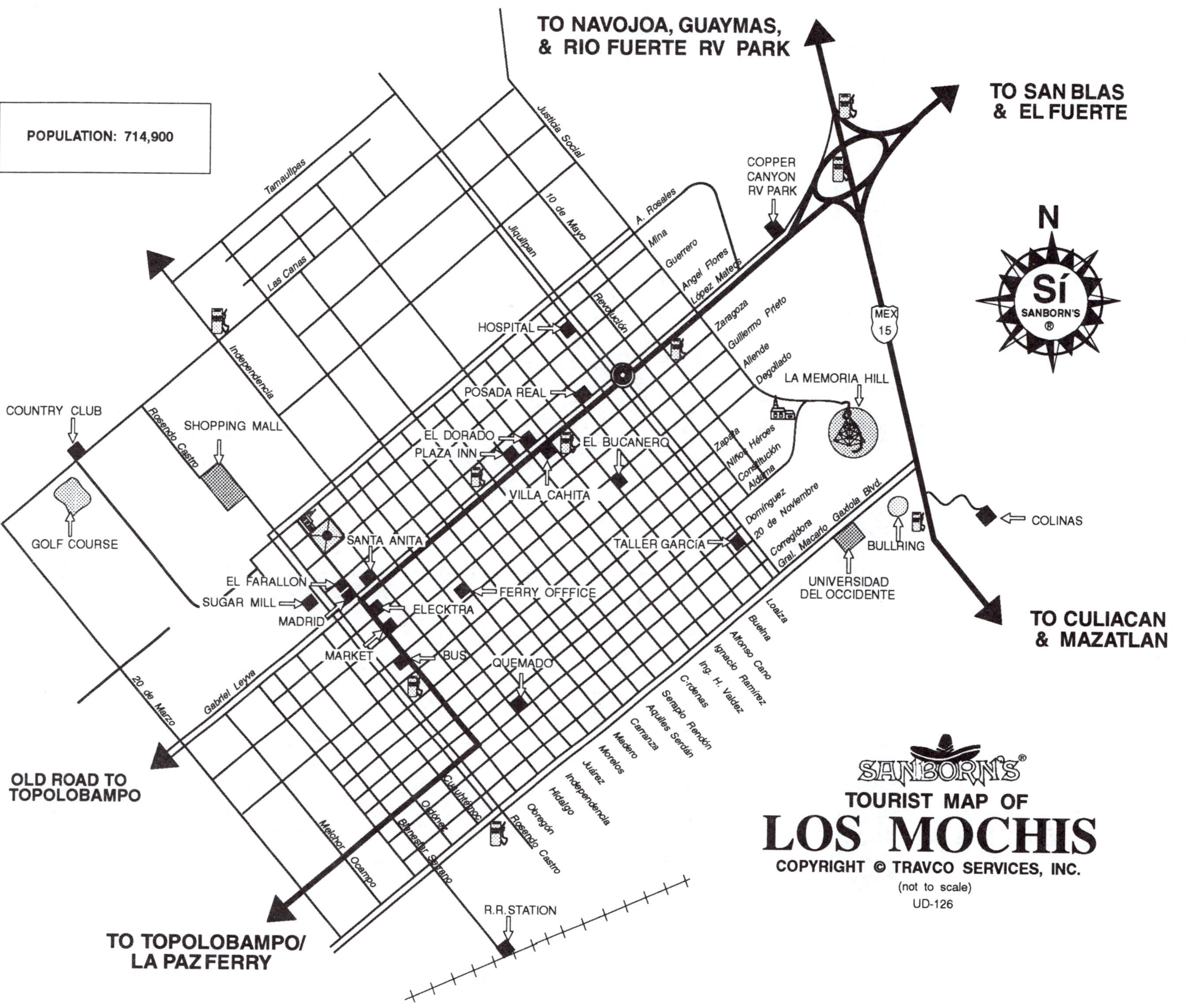

TO SAN BLAS & EL FUERTE
TO NAVOJOA, GUAYMAS, & RIO FUERTE RV PARK
TO CULIACAN & MAZATLAN
TO TOPOLOBAMPO/ LA PAZ FERRY
OLD ROAD TO TOPOLOBAMPO
N
SANBORN'S
SÍ
SANBORN'S
TOURIST MAP OF
LOS MOCHIS
COPYRIGHT © TRAVCO SERVICES, INC.
(not to scale)
UD-126
POPULATION: 714,900
COLINAS
BULLRING
UNIVERSIDAD DEL OCCIDENTE
Gral. Mercado
Carregidora
20 de Noviembre
Domínguez
Gaxiola Blvd.
Loaiza
Buelna
Alfonso Cano
Ignacio Ramírez
Ing. H. Valdez
Cárdenas
Serapio Rendón
Aquiles Serdán
Carranza
Madero
Morelos
Juárez
Independencia
Hidalgo
Obregón
Rosendo Castro
R.R. STATION
Cuauhtémoc
Ordóñez
Bienestar Serano
Melchor Ocampo
MEX 15
LA MEMORIA HILL
COPPER CANYON RV PARK
Guillermo Prieto
Allende
Degollado
Zaragoza
Constitución
Niño Héroes
Aldama
Zapata
López Mateos
Angel Flores
Guerrero
A. Rosales
Mina
TALLER GARCÍA
EL BUCANERQ
Revolución
Justicia Social
10 de Mayo
Jiquilpan
HOSPITAL
POSADA REAL
EL DORADO
PLAZA INN
VILLA CAHITA
FERRY OFFICE
ELECKTRA
QUEMADO
BUS
MARKET
SANTA ANITA
EL FARALLON
MADRID
SUGAR MILL
Independencia
SHOPPING MALL
Rosendo Castro
Las Cruces
Tamaulipas
COUNTRY CLUB
GOLF COURSE
20 de Marzo
Gabriel Leyva
TO TOPOLOBAMPO/ LA PAZ FERRY
OLD ROAD TO TOPOLOBAMPO

IF TO: El Fuerte and nearby lakes of Hidalgo and Domínguez (plentiful black bass and catfish & hunting) take right turnoff, and start Los Mochis — El Fuerte Special (page 65). The twin lakes are about 40 miles NE of Los Mochis, via a paved road, a few miles from the town of El Fuerte. The two lakes are about 5 miles apart. They have some of the best fishing South of the border.

Lupi Nieblas & Tom Jenkins, Box 11, El Fuerte, SIN or Hidalgo Lodge PO Box 3036, Burbank, CA PH: (213) 388-4157. Nice Hidalgo Lodge there for hunting/fishing. PH: (706) 813-0657 in El Fuerte, Box 11. In U.S. P.O. Box 3036, Burbank, CA 91504, PH: (213) 388-4157. 24 units. A/C. Hunting/fishing packages. Also a smaller hotel for non-hunters — La Posada El Fuerte. Thanks to Ingrid Bautista for her help.

Incidentally, the Chihuahua-Pacific (Copper Canyon) Railroad passes near El Fuerte — you might wish to combine a little fishing with this very scenic train ride through the Sierra Madre Occidental.

End of Log 7

LOG 8   *START:* Los Mochis, Sin   *END:* Culiacán, Sin

UD-017

135.5 MI or 216.8 KM
DRIVE TIME 2 — 2 1/2 HOURS
SCENIC RATING — 1

MI	KM	
0.0	0.0	Starting here in Los Mochis at junction with Hwy to El Fuerte, proceed ahead on Hwy 15, a nice divided four-lane highway. If you want to take the old *libre* routes, and aren't in a hurry, just follow the *Libre* signs. Some folks prefer 'em. On this route, though, you're better off paying your way.
1.0	1.6	**GAS**, on right. Mountain at right is called *Cerro de la Memoria*. Turnoff, left, is to nice Hotel Colinas & RV Park, left, on hilltop (67 spaces EWS, 30 AMP, PH: (681) 2-0101, 2-0134)). It was formerly a Holiday Inn. *Lienzo del Charro* arena at right where the Mexican "charro" (cowboy) performs in the rodeo, usually on Sunday. Turnoff to Topolobampo, right.
2.0	3.2	Curve right around hill, then up and over Chihuahua-Pacífico Railroad overpass which is the same line that goes up into the Sierra Madres thru scenic Copper Canyon. Sanborn's logs the road. You can drive from Cd. Obregón or Hermosillo to Creel and on to Chihuahua on the other side.
5.5	8.8	Northrup-King seed plant at right. Then rice factory at right. Then pass entrance to industrial park at right.
9.5	15.2	Cross Río Estero and curve, right, past *Ejido Las Vacas* (The Cows) at right. Heading due East.
11.0	17.6	Big town of Juan José Ríos, the largest *ejido* in Mexico at right. **GAS**, right. Then agricultural experiment school (Ciapan), left. **KM 186.**
14.1	22.6	Careful at crossroads, right, to Bachoco. Occasional farm equipment and bicycles on road.
17.1	27.4	**GAS**, to left. Unfriendly (watch 'em)
18.0	28.8	Little town of Ruiz Cortines, at right, named for a past presidente of Mexico (1952-58).
25.0	40.0	Pass side road (right) to Huitusi over on Bahía de San Ignacio. Pass LP **GAS** to left.
28.3	45.3	Pass side road (right) to Las Barritas.
30.3	40.0	Road left to Est. Naranjo. **GAS** on road to Est. Naranjo.
32.5	52.0	Pass Trébol Park Motel, left.
35.0	56.0	Curve left and pass ball park at right (Guasave belongs to the powerful Mexican Pacific League).
36.1	57.7	Now thru edge of boom town of Guasave, founded in 1595 (population: 257,821). Shopping center to left. Then ahead over Río Petatlán. **KM 145.**

GUASAVE has three hotels and a great mechanic, Taller Bojórquez (see map inset). The best hotel is El Sembrador at Guerrero & Zapata. It has 85 nice quiet rooms, 10 suites, restaurant, bar, parking and is very reasonably priced. SATV (English & weather channel, HBO, CNN, etc). Ph: (682) 2-4062, 2-3141, Fax: 2-3131.

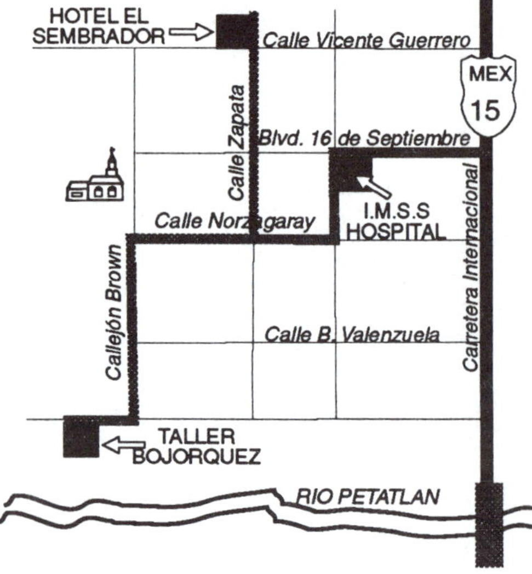

If you have a notion to go fishing at Lake Baccarito (Presa Díaz Ordaz) we recommend that you change your mind. There is no reason to visit that out-of-the-way lake. It has been gill-netted out and there have been assaults on the road.

MI	KM	
44.0	70.4	**GAS**, right.
45.0	72.0	Come to toll house and pay toll ($9, $4 extra axle).
51.0	81.6	Veer left (follow CUOTA sign). Exit, right, is old two-lane "libre" highway which goes thru Guamúchil. Veer left for Culiacán.
56.7	90.7	Under overpass. **KM 119.**
62.0	99.2	Come to toll house and pay toll ($15, $8 extra axle). Pass side road (right) to Angostura and left Guamúchil. **GAS**, right. **KM 110.**
70.0	112.0	Thru rich farmland with mountains on horizon. Excellent road thru here.
84.6	135.4	**GAS** at right. **KM 75.**
91.1	145.8	Pass side road (right) to La Reforma and Zapatillo. Then under overpass. **KM 63.**
91.7	146.7	Pass Restaurant El Bacatete, left.
103.5	165.6	Curve left and cross bridge over Río Pericos. Nice cattle farm over to left on Hwy #259.
110.5	176.8	Exit right to La Palma and Vitaruto a couple of miles over to left.
111.5	178.4	Toll booth if you exit.
115.5	184.8	Under overpass. Then **GAS** at left.
122.5	196.0	Over bridge and exit right to San Pedro and La Curva. **KM 13.**
127.5	204.0	Come to toll house ($15, $8 extra axle) and pay it again, Sam. **GAS** at left and restaurant with good food, nice rest area with swings for kids. Then proceed ahead.
129.5	207.2	Come to junction with Hwy 15 "Libre" from downtown Culiacán, Sin (population: 602,000).

IF TO: Culiacán, turn left and follow map to hotels. For accommodations see Culiacán Eat & Stray (page 93)

IF TO: Mazatlán, toll road, turn right just after **GAS** station.

IF TO: Mazatlán, free road, start Culiacán — Mazatlán Log, continuing straight just past **GAS** station.

End of Log 8.

LOG 9   *START:* Culiacán, Sin   *END:* Mazatlán, Sin

UD-017

136.8 MI or 218.9 KM
DRIVE TIME 3 — 3 1/2 HOURS
SCENIC RATING — 2

Note: This log covers the free road and the toll. The toll road is rather expensive. There are 2 toll booths, one at KM 22 and the other at exit to Mazatlán. Some say it's worth it (if you're in a hurry) saving at least an hour of driving time and is safer. Others feel like it's "highway robbery" since they can fill up twice for the cost of the toll and enjoy the more scenic free road.

0.0	0.0	Here at the junction of Hwy #15 and the toll road, with Pemex **GAS** on left (Beware! Scam at this Pemex station — guy will install weather stripping for 18 pesos a meter; it'll end up costing about one hundred dollars. MM was taken in by this. A woman wouldn't have fallen for it).

IF TO: Toll road, exit right, after bridge (also to Culiacán) and follow stub log below:

Culiacán — Mazatlán Toll Road

0.0	0.0	Having veered right just past toll house and **GAS** station, proceed ahead.
0.7	1.1	Go under overpass.
2.8	4.5	Los Comales restaurant, right If you want to go there get in lateral lane well before.
4.5	7.2	Pass chicken processing plant at right. **GAS**, right. Then pass exit (right) to Villa Juárez.
6.5	10.4	**GAS**, left.

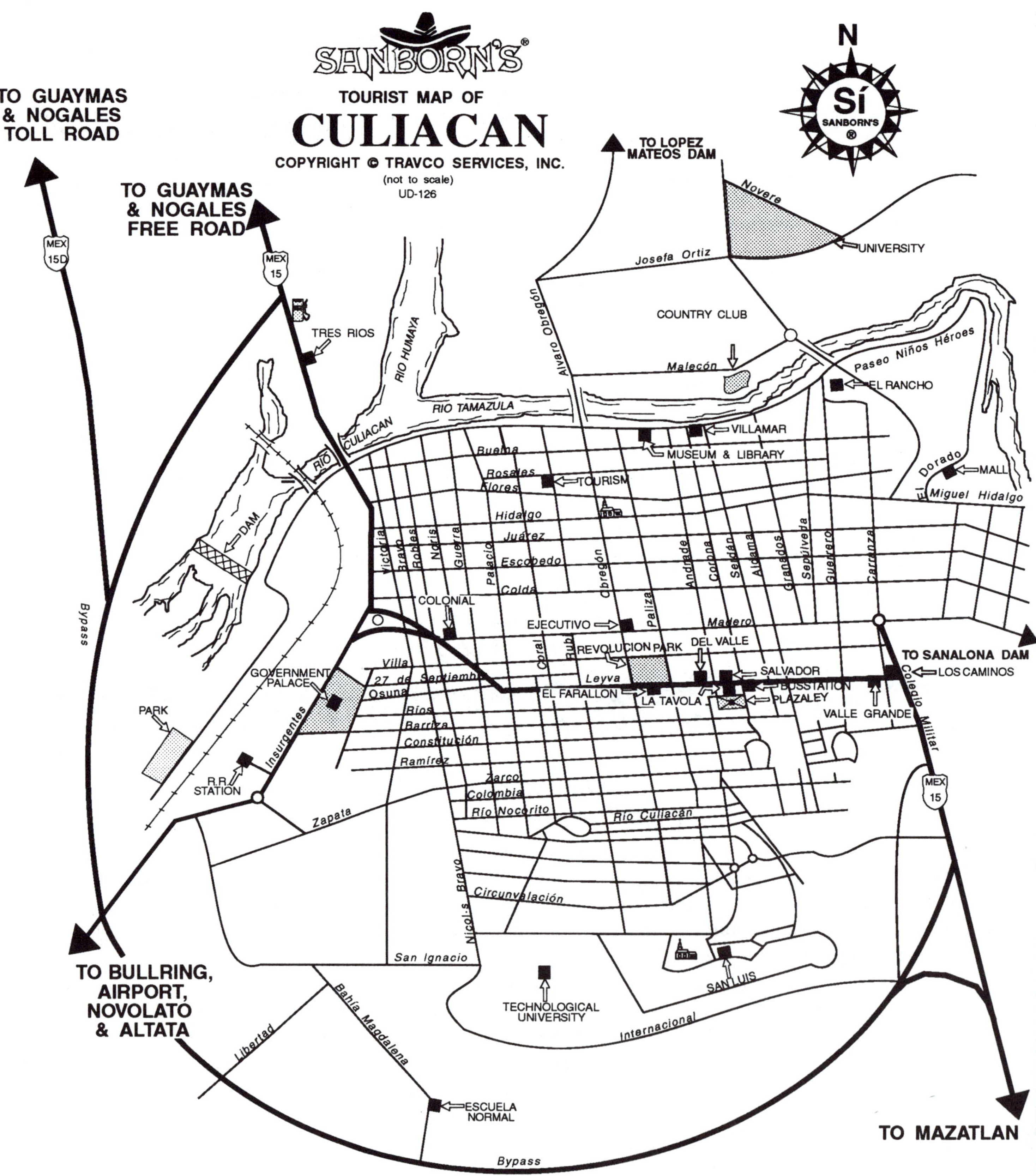

SANBORN'S
TOURIST MAP OF
CULIACAN
COPYRIGHT © TRAVCO SERVICES, INC.
(not to scale)
UD-126
N
Sí
SANBORN'S
TO GUAYMAS & NOGALES TOLL ROAD
TO GUAYMAS & NOGALES FREE ROAD
TO LOPEZ MATEOS DAM
TO SANALONA DAM
TO BULLRING, AIRPORT, NOVOLATO & ALTATA
TO MAZATLAN
MEX 15D
MEX 15
MEX 15
Bypass
Bypass
TRES RIOS
RIO HUMAYA
RIO TAMAZULA
CULIACAN
RIO
DAM
PARK
R.R. STATION
GOVERNMENT PALACE
Insurgentes
Zapata
Libertad
Bahía Magdalena
San Ignacio
ESCUELA NORMAL
TECHNOLOGICAL UNIVERSITY
Circunvalación
Internacional
SAN LUIS
Nicolás Bravo
Zarco
Colombia
Río Nocorito
Río Culiacán
Ramírez
Constitución
Barriza
Ríos
Osuna
Villa 27 de Septiembre
COLONIAL
Victoria
Bravo
Robles
Noris
Guerra
Palacio
Buelna
Rosales
Flores
Hidalgo
Juárez
Escobedo
Colda
EJECUTIVO
Obregón
Cobral
Bub
REVOLUCION PARK
EL FARALLON
Leyva
LA TAVOLA
Peliza
Madero
DEL VALLE
SALVADOR
PLAZALEY
BUSSTATION
Andrade
Corona
Seldán
Aldama
Granados
Sepúlveda
Guerrero
Carranza
VALLE GRANDE
LOS CAMINOS
Colegio Militar
Josefa Ortiz
Alvaro Obregón
Novere
UNIVERSITY
COUNTRY CLUB
Malecón
Paseo Niños Héroes
EL RANCHO
VILLAMAR
MUSEUM & LIBRARY
TOURISM
Dorado
MALL
Miguel Hidalgo

MI	KM	
7.1	11.4	Agriculture Experimental school, left.. You are now passing thru rolling hills and farm country.
9.6	15.4	Veer right, following Mazatlán El Dorado sign. Straight ahead for Costa Rica. At top of overpass stay in left lane. Then down, following Mazatlán - La Cruz sign.
10.5	16.8	**GAS**, right. KM 180.
11.3	18.1	Come to toll house and pay toll (Car - $56, extra axle - $28). They accept AE, MC, VI. KM 179.
25.1	40.2	Pass exit (right) to Quila and El Dorado.

There is a nice pastoral spot 4.1 miles West of here on highway #19. It's Los Cascabeles, on the lake of the same name. 20 fenced acres with 10 cabins, boats, pool, hunting and fishing. RV section (MOD) with 44 spaces, electricity and water. Dump station. Medical services. Palapa. BBQ pits. Security. Store. Laundry. Restaurant. FAX: (67) 13-6418 or in Culiacán (671) 3-6418, 3-6822.

71.1	113.8	Pass exit (right) to La Cruz and Cueta. This is also the exit to take if you want to go to Cosalá.

Cosalá, founded in 1516, is a small Spanish colonial town with cobblestone roads and churches over 250 years old. There are two OK (two Mexican star) hotels and some restaurants. The Sabinal river feeds the *Vado Hondo* spa (not reviewed) with clear water. 20 KM North is Lake Comedero chock-full of largemouth bass. We stayed at the hotel Conde (hot water). Also a Museum of the History of Mining. The Balneario and waterfall are 8 KM off the highway on a dirt road. Do not attempt this road when it's been raining. It is 6.5 miles before town, on the left.

PRESA LÓPEZ PORTILLO (LAKE COMEDERO) — One of Mexico's two hottest lakes, Comedero was opened to fisherman only since in 1987. Comedero has fast become a legend in the number of fish caught per man per day. With catches from 100 to 200 bass per day common it is easy to see why this remote lake has become a prime destination for the traveling angler. Turn East on the Cosalá turnoff to the town of Cosalá (50 miles). The lake is 30 miles from town on a dirt road that winds up in the steep mountains to the village of Higueras de Urea.

The San Lorenzo river is the source of Lake Comedero and the lake is one of the prettiest in the northern hemisphere. Towering mountains surround the lake with lush subtropical jungle right up to the waters edge. Comedero's banks are lined with some brush and cover, however the lake is large and very open and it's also very, very deep. With depths approaching 300 feet in places, Comedero's fish tend to school up and suspend. Sometimes in water as deep as 60 feet. At present there's only one full time camp on the lake. Full packages are available as well as room and board. Contact: Ron Speeds S & W Tours, 1013 Country Lane, Malakoff, TX, 875148 (903) 489-1656.

104.0	166.4	Come to toll house and pay toll ($58, extra axle $28). There are restrooms and tourist information. **KM 27**.
106,7	170.7	Over Río Quilete.
116.7	186.7	Pass exit (right) to North beach (Playas). This is the exit for North end RV parks and Zona Dorada hotels.
121.0	193.6	Exit right for Mazatlán. This is junction with free road. After exit, Quaker State to left. Tecate Agency to right. Ahead on two-lane road.
122.0	195.2	**GAS**, right. Monterrey Tech. to left. Veer right for Mazatlán, left for airport, Durango and Tepic. There is a stoplight just beyond where you veer right. Motel Relax on right.

IF TO: Downtown Mazatlán, see stub log at end of free road log (page 29).

End Culiacán — Mazatlán Toll Road

2.0	3.2	Motel Cabañas del Rey.
5.3	8.5	Pass little town of El Ranchito.
6.3	10.1	Come to "T." Mazatlán to right, Culiacán to left.
6.8	10.8	Pass a truck and bus wrecking yard, right. **KM 208.**
7.5	12.0	Huge field of wrecked car, left ("used auto parts"). **KM 206.**
8.5	13.5	Pass restaurant Los Caminantes, left.
12.3	19.7	Laguna Colorada at left.
16.1	25.8	Seafood restaurant. Pass side road (right) to Costa Rica. Careful for slow-moving farm traffic.

There is a nice pastoral spot 4.1 miles West of here on highway #19. It's Los Cascabeles, on the lake of the same name. 20 fenced acres with 10 cabins, boats, pool, hunting and fishing. RV section (MOD) with 44 spaces, electricity and water. Dump station. Medical services. Palapa. BBQ pits. Security. Store. Laundry. Restaurant. FAX: (67) 13-6418 or in Culiacán (671) 3-6418, 3-6822.

MI	KM	
16.4	26.2	Restaurant Centro Recreativo Los Cascabeles. **GAS**, both sides of the road.
17.3	27.7	Thru San Miguel. Cattle ranches thru here (also, careful for people on bicycles on road).
27.0	43.2	El Dorado to the right. To right is also another entrance to toll road if you want to take it.
27.5	44.0	Topes! Topes! Topes! Up thru town of El Salado and over couple of bridges over Río Salado.
33.8	54.1	Now curve right and over Río San Lorenzo and thru Tabala. Note ruins of ancient church at left with burial tombs. Cactus growing out of spiral on church. **KM 165**.
38.9	62.2	Pass side road (right) to Oso (bear).
40.6	65.0	Thru village of Las Flores. Then curve right and over North fork of Río Obispo.
43.3	69.3	Pass side road (right) to Obispo (bishop).
46.5	74.4	Curve right and cross South fork of Río Obispo and pass village of Higueras de Abuya.
55.4	88.6	Thru settlement of El Avión. **KM 130**.
61.7	98.7	Pass Las Tinas at left. **KM 121**.
63.1	101.0	Thru El Espinal. More "topes." **KM 118**.
66.8	106.9	Thru El Aguaje and curve right. Pass Glass House Resort hotel — MOD — 36 rooms, Restaurant, Pool, English spoken; looks brand new and very nice. **KM 112**.
69.7	111.5	Pass side road (left) to picturesque ex-mining town of Cosalá, 33 miles, on Hwy #D-1.

Cosalá, founded in 1516, is a small Spanish colonial town with cobblestone roads and churches over 250 years old. There are two OK (two Mexican star) hotels and some restaurants. The Sabinal river feeds the *Vado Hondo* spa (not reviewed) with clear water. 20 KM North is Lake Comedero chock-full of largemouth bass. We stayed at the hotel Conde (hot water). Also a Museum of the History of Mining. The Balneario and waterfall are 8 KM off the highway on a dirt road. Do not attempt this road when it's been raining. It is 6.5 miles before town, on the left.

PRESA LÓPEZ PORTILLO (LAKE COMEDERO) — One of Mexico's two hottest lakes, Comedero was opened to fisherman only since in 1987. Comedero has fast become a legend in the number of fish caught per man per day. With catches from 100 to 200 bass per day common it is easy to see why this remote lake has become a prime destination for the traveling angler. Turn East on the Cosalá turnoff to the town of Cosalá (50 miles). The lake is 30 miles from town on a dirt road that winds up in the steep mountains to the village of Higueras de Urea.

The San Lorenzo river is the source of Lake Comedero and the lake is one of the prettiest in the northern hemisphere. Towering mountains surround the lake with lush subtropical jungle right up to the waters edge. Comedero's banks are lined with some brush and cover, however the lake is large and very open and it's also very, very deep. With depths approaching 300 feet in places, Comedero's fish tend to school up and suspend. Sometimes in water as deep as 60 feet. At present there's only one full time camp on the lake. Full packages are available as well as room and board. Contact: Ron Speeds S & W Tours, 1013 Country Lane, Malakoff, TX, 875148 (903) 489-1656.

71.2	113.9	Pass side road (right) to La Cruz. Red Cross. **KM 105.**
79.7	127.5	Pass side road (left) to nearby town of Elota. Cross Río Elota.
80.0	128.0	Slow for sharp right curve and pass so-so-restaurant-bus stop. Then right and wind up.
84.4	135.0	La Minita (The Little Mine) up at left. The mill here grinds ore in from Mexico's interior, separating zinc, copper, and lead.
86.8	138.9	Village of Piaxtla off to left.
88.3	141.3	Cross Río Piaxtla and right and up.
90.6	145.0	Settlement of Crucero de Piaxtla. Then side road right to Hacienda Piaxtla.
95.2	152.3	Pass side road (left) to San Ignacio, 32 KM.

San Ignacio is a very picturesque town. Founded in 1582 as San Ignacio de Loyola. Painted palm trees line the road into town with a grand mauve entrance that, when you pass through it, opens to a bridge that crosses a rather large river.

95.6	153.0	**GAS** left. Diesel, but be ready for lots of kids here.
97.7	156.3	Pull off to right. Over bridge, then start winding with sharp curves.
99.1	158.6	Pass side road (left) to El Limón.
99.4	159.0	Pull off for view watches to right.
111.5	178.4	El Moral off to left and then a straight stretch for a change.

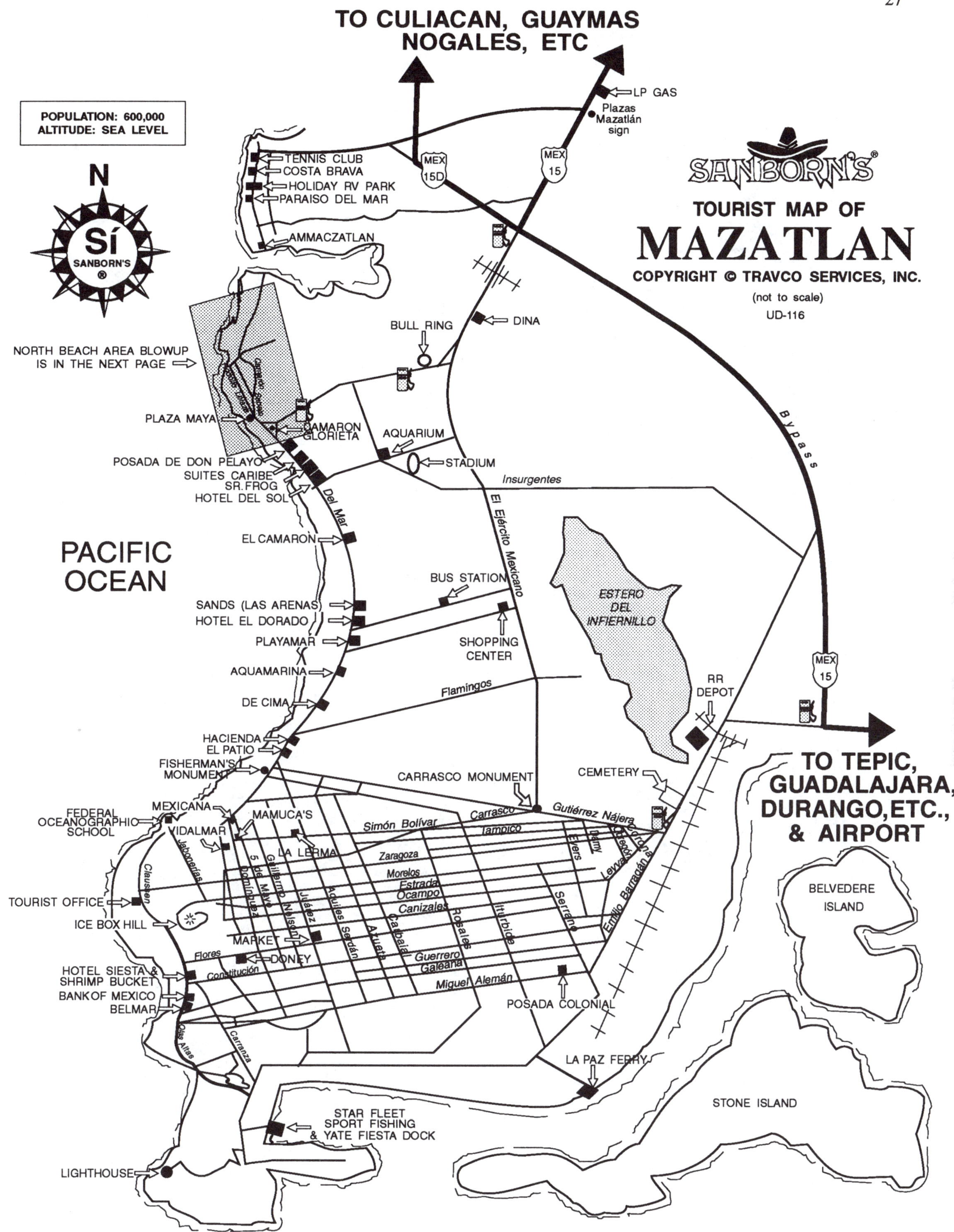

TO CULIACAN, GUAYMAS NOGALES, ETC
POPULATION: 600,000
ALTITUDE: SEA LEVEL
N
SÍ
SANBORN'S
NORTH BEACH AREA BLOWUP IS IN THE NEXT PAGE
LP GAS
Plazas Mazatlán sign
SANBORN'S
TOURIST MAP OF
MAZATLAN
COPYRIGHT © TRAVCO SERVICES, INC.
(not to scale)
UD-116
TENNIS CLUB
COSTA BRAVA
HOLIDAY RV PARK
PARAISO DEL MAR
AMMACZATLAN
MEX 15D
MEX 15
DINA
BULL RING
PLAZA MAYA
CAMARON GLORIETA
AQUARIUM
POSADA DE DON PELAYO
SUITES CARIBE
SR. FROG
HOTEL DEL SOL
STADIUM
Insurgentes
Del Mar
El Ejército Mexicano
Bypass
PACIFIC OCEAN
EL CAMARON
BUS STATION
ESTERO DEL INFIERNILLO
SANDS (LAS ARENAS)
HOTEL EL DORADO
PLAYAMAR
SHOPPING CENTER
AQUAMARINA
DE CIMA
Flamingos
RR DEPOT
MEX 15
HACIENDA EL PATIO
FISHERMAN'S MONUMENT
CARRASCO MONUMENT
CEMETERY
TO TEPIC, GUADALAJARA, DURANGO, ETC., & AIRPORT
FEDERAL OCEANOGRAPHIC SCHOOL
MEXICANA
VIDALMAR
MAMUCA'S
Simón Bolívar
Carrasco
Gutiérrez Nájera
Tampico
Jabonerías
LA LERMA
5 de Mayo
Guillermo Nelson
Zaragoza
Morelos
Estrada
Ocampo
Canizales
Evers
Damy
Serrano
Leyva
Emilio Barragán
BELVEDERE ISLAND
Clausen
Juárez
Aquiles Serdán
Azueta
Calbajal
Rosales
Iturbide
TOURIST OFFICE
ICE BOX HILL
Domínguez
MARKET
DONEY
Flores
Guerrero
Galeana
HOTEL SIESTA & SHRIMP BUCKET
BANK OF MEXICO
BELMAR
Constitución
Miguel Alemán
POSADA COLONIAL
Olas Altas
Carranza
LA PAZ FERRY
STONE ISLAND
STAR FLEET SPORT FISHING & YATE FIESTA DOCK
LIGHTHOUSE

SANBORN'S®
TOURIST MAP OF
MAZATLAN
NORTH BEACH AREA
COPYRIGHT © TRAVCO SERVICES, INC.
(not to scale)
UD-116

N
SÍ
SANBORN'S
®

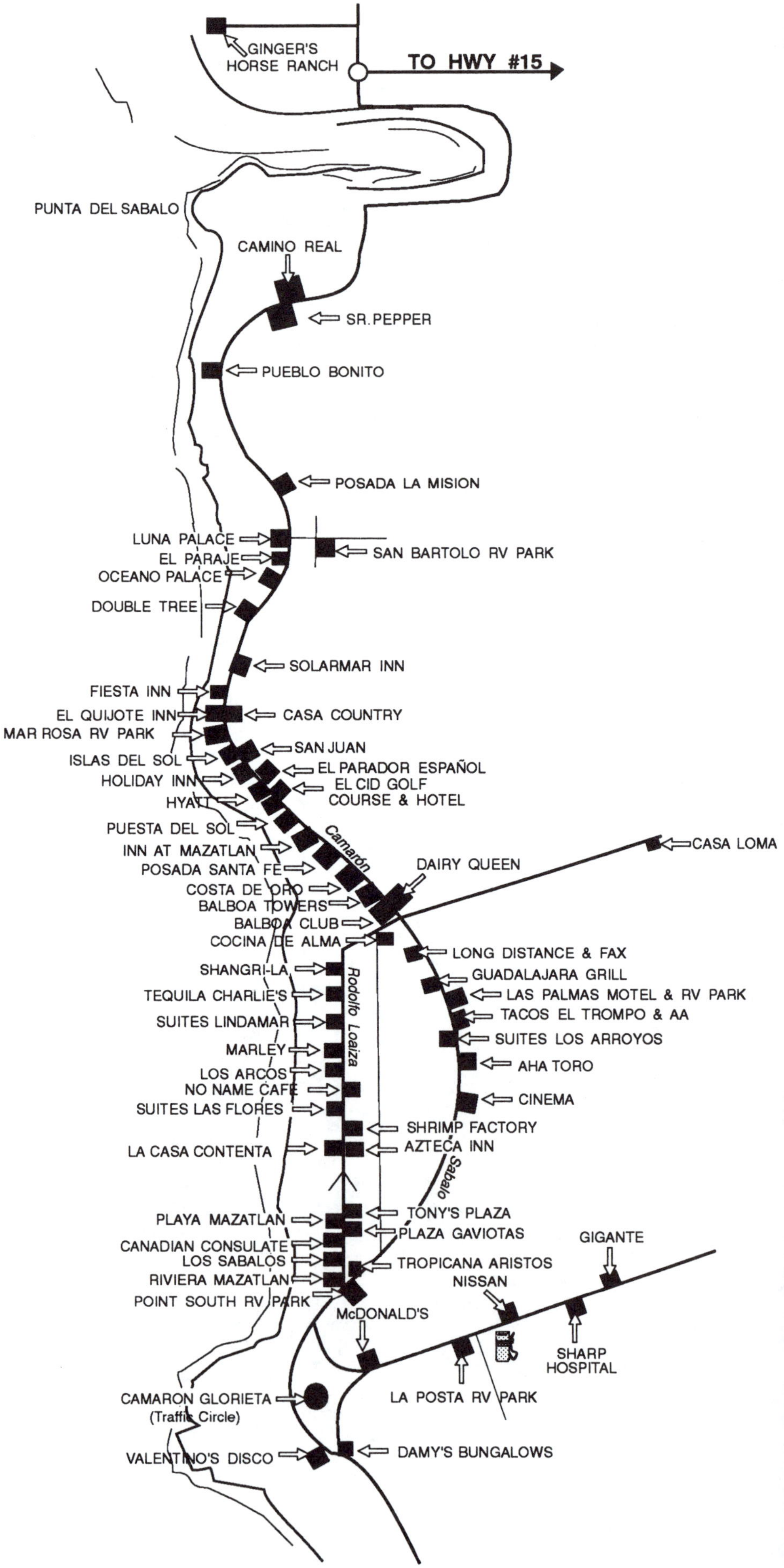

GINGER'S HORSE RANCH
TO HWY #15
PUNTA DEL SABALO
CAMINO REAL
SR. PEPPER
PUEBLO BONITO
POSADA LA MISION
LUNA PALACE
EL PARAJE
SAN BARTOLO RV PARK
OCEANO PALACE
DOUBLE TREE
SOLARMAR INN
FIESTA INN
EL QUIJOTE INN
CASA COUNTRY
MAR ROSA RV PARK
SAN JUAN
ISLAS DEL SOL
EL PARADOR ESPAÑOL
HOLIDAY INN
EL CID GOLF
COURSE & HOTEL
HYATT
PUESTA DEL SOL
Camarón
INN AT MAZATLAN
CASA LOMA
POSADA SANTA FE
DAIRY QUEEN
COSTA DE ORO
BALBOA TOWERS
BALBOA CLUB
COCINA DE ALMA
LONG DISTANCE & FAX
SHANGRI-LA
GUADALAJARA GRILL
Rodolfo Loaiza
TEQUILA CHARLIE'S
LAS PALMAS MOTEL & RV PARK
SUITES LINDAMAR
TACOS EL TROMPO & AA
MARLEY
SUITES LOS ARROYOS
LOS ARCOS
AHA TORO
NO NAME CAFE
SUITES LAS FLORES
CINEMA
SHRIMP FACTORY
LA CASA CONTENTA
AZTECA INN
Sabalo
PLAYA MAZATLAN
TONY'S PLAZA
PLAZA GAVIOTAS
CANADIAN CONSULATE
GIGANTE
LOS SABALOS
RIVIERA MAZATLAN
TROPICANA ARISTOS
POINT SOUTH RV PARK
NISSAN
McDONALD'S
SHARP HOSPITAL
CAMARON GLORIETA
(Traffic Circle)
LA POSTA RV PARK
VALENTINO'S DISCO
DAMY'S BUNGALOWS

MI	KM	
116.6	186.6	Come to crossroads. Mazatlán, straight. Left is to Quelite.
117.0	187.2	Curve right past side road (right) to Mármol (marble) and then over Río Quelite. I've always wanted to go there. Wonder if there's any marble?
122.6	196.2	Los Zapotes off to left and El Recreo off to right.
123.5	197.6	Come now to TROPIC OF CANCER — note marker at right. As you may know, many folks let their libido loose from here on
127.0	203.2	Pass side road (right) to El Potrero. Note bust of General Juan Carrasco at right.
127.1	203.4	Pass side road (left) to La Palma.
130.0	208.0	Come to junction.

IF TO: Beach. Side road (right) to Playa Cerritos and shortcut beach road to Mazatlán. (If heading to North beach hotels, RV parks, etc., go ahead & turn here. When you come to ocean, turn left and head toward town.)

IF TO: Downtown Mazatlán, Tepic, Durango, straight.

132.6	212.2	Hilltop restaurant at left. **KM 7.**
134.6	215.4	Big mango grove at right. Then highway police station at right.
134.8	215.7	Begin 4-lane Divided (Toll road to Culiacán, exit right here), then under bridge. Toll road from Culiacán rejoins Hwy #15 here.
135.0	216.0	Be ready to turn left soon, if bypassing Mazatlán, going South.
136.1	217.8	**GAS**, right. Then at left is Ciudad de los Niños ("boys' town" or "orphanage", not to be confused with the "red-light district"). Centro de Bodegas at left. Gamesa Plant at left.
136.8	218.9	Careful now as you approach bypass left around Mazatlán. Get into left lane for left turn for bypass if continuing on Hwy #15. **GAS**, right. Restaurant La Palmita, left.

IF TO: Durango, veer left just before stoplight and start Mazatlán — Durango Log (not included in this book).

IF TO: Tepic, Guadalajara, Airport, etc., veer left just before stoplight and start Mazatlán — Tepic Log (not included in this book).

IF TO: Beachfront, downtown Mazatlán, follow stub log below:

STUB LOG TO DOWNTOWN MAZATLÁN

0.0	0.0	Continue straight with Motel Relax at right and Pacific beer at left.
0.4	0.7	Up and over railroad.
0.6	1.0	Come to intersection and turn right just past bus station at right.
1.1	1.8	Bullring at right. Then Gigante at right.
1.2	1.9	Sharp hospital at left. Then **GAS** that takes credit cards at left.
1.4	2.2	La Posta Trailer Park, left.
1.5	2.4	Hotel San Diego on left, McDonald's on right and come to ocean boulevard (see map). Don't bypass Mazatlán if you have the time — it's well worth a look-see. Friends of Bill W. in town. For info on accommodations, see Mazatlán Eat & Stray (page 94).

End of Log 9

LOG 10   START: Mazatlán, Sin   END: Tepic, Nay

UD-106

173.5 MI or 277.6 KM
DRIVE TIME 4 1/2 — 5 HOURS
SCENIC RATING — 2

Some divided, mostly two lane. Heavy truck traffic. Stretches of poor surface. Tobacco country. Scrub jungle near ocean. Birder's paradise.

MI	KM	
0.0	0.0	Having turned left off Hwy #15, (following Tepic, *Aeropuerto* signs) ahead on nice divided bypass around Mazatlán. Gamesa plant and Corona distributor, right. Basketball field, left. Divided, six lanes. Palm tree lined. There will be a stoplight here in the future.
0.3	0.5	Pass up motel Real, a motel *del paso* (rents by the hour).
0.5	0.8	Cemetery at right. Pass multicolored Colonia (subdivision) Lic. Mario A. Arroyo.
1.3	2.1	Community of Colonia Echeverría at right. Over bridge. Then thru Colonia S. Allende. Parque Industrial. Stoplight. Church ahead on left.
1.8	2.9	General Tire, left.
2.5	4.0	ISESM Campas Mazatán, subdivision, left. Farmer's market (Central de Abastos), left. Pass Café Marino plant left. Up & over overpass. Then right & down. Road narrows to four lanes divided. Thru suburb of Rincón de Urias. Then curve right and past school at left.
3.0	4.8	End of bypass. Come to intersection. Stop sign. LEFT, following "Tepic, Aeropuerto" signs. In front of you is Corona distributor. Ahead and right is Pepsi agency, "Bebidas Purificadas." AFTER turning, John Deere, left and Goodyear, right. Then Aga plant, left. Sign says: "Aeropuerto 14 KM, Tepic 286 KM."
3.2	5,1	Under overpass. **GAS**, right. LP gas, left.
3.2	5.1	Overhead sign says "Durango & Tepic straight ahead."
3.3	5.3	Tractores de Occidente, left. Golf course, left. Divided 4 lane.
3.5	5.6	LP gas.
4.0	6.4	Under *Buen Viaje* arch. Follow "Tepic, Aeropuerto" signs, straight.
5.5	8.8	Colonia La Sirena, right. Salt flats, right.
6.3	10.1	Begin long curve, right. Big power plant, right. Then side road, right, to El Castillo. Speed limit 70 KM.
8.5	13.6	Large penitentiary, left. Speed limit 80 KM. Pass "el Zipi-Zape" veggie packers, then over bridge. **KM 272.**
10.9	17.4	Experimental Farm station at right.
11.3	18.1	Pass side road, right, to Mazatlán's airport. **KM 275.**
13.4	20.8	Divided ends. Then El Pozole, right. **KM 271.**
14.0	22.4	Cross Río Presidio. Slow thru town of Villa Unión. Hotel El Kino, right. I ate there. OK. Slow thru town. TOPES. SPEED 30 KM.
15.3	24.5	End of town. Curve left and out.
15.5	24.8	Motel El Piño, left, OK. **GAS**, right.

IF TO: Hwy #40 to Durango, Torreón, Saltillo, Monterrey etc., left here. Start Mazatlán — Durango Log (not included in this book).

IF TO: Tepic, ahead on Hwy #15 for you.

26.5	42.4	Village of El Huajote, at right, with its baseball field.
29.0	46.4	Ejido El Tablón, mostly at right.
29.5	47.2	Thru Tablón #1.
31.0	49.6	Village of Potrerillos down at right. Then experimental fruit station.
32.5	52.0	Pass side road (left) to Presa (dam) Las Higueras and then cross *río* and pass village of Las Higueras off to left.
36.5	58.4	Over bridge and then settlement of Los Otates (The Bamboos), left.
38.6	61.8	Mango Orchard to left.
41.5	66.4	That's Mount Yauco dead ahead.
42.5	68.8	Pass LP gas, left, and skirt town Rosario (50,000 population). Hotel Los Morales at left. **GAS**, left. Nice snack stands soft drinks etc. Ice house, right and down, then cross Río Baluarte on half-mile-long bridge. Up past village of Chilillos and onto particularly bad stretch of road. Goodyear on left.

MI	KM	
48.5	77.6	Pass side road (right) to Chametla. Very long, bumpy bridge.
50.6	81.0	Cross South fork of Río Baluarte.
53.3	85.3	Rest area. San José restaurant on right.
54.0	86.4	Mango orchard to right. Restaurant to left. If you want a smack, you can eat at a bus stop restaurant without fear. KM 202.
54.5	87.2	Good enough Motel Virginia on left.
55.6	89.0	Over bridge and enter town of Escuinapa (population 60,000). Then careful and at the stoplight, turn right (follow TEPIC signs) onto one-way street. At end of two blocks, turn left and ahead thru Escuinapa on one-way street. **GAS**. Come to junction with road (right) to Teacapan.

IF TO: Teacapan, turn right,

TEACAPAN, Sinaloa is a little off the beaten track, 26 miles away, a sleepy tropical village with nice white beaches. This is a birder's paradise area. Efforts are underway to have the government declare it a sanctuary and park. And just for your info, Country/Western singer Loretta Lynn has a vacation home here. A great place to go if you have a spirit of adventure and you are tired of the party atmosphere of Mazatlán. Naturalists will enjoy the place and the (so far) unspoiled beaches. You can fish, go birding and loaf. Wildlife includes white & pink heron and pichihuila and deer. This is a small town with friendly folks and beautiful scenery. There are two good hotels: In town on plaza is Hotel Denisse, which is small (5 rooms) & inexpensive; farther out is the Rancho Los Angeles (after 15.8 miles, turn right at mini-Super Los Angeles sign; use gate entrance to right of arch; enter and veer right, follow dirt road 1.5 miles to hotel) with the best restaurant (excellent Bar-B-Q fish) in town, perhaps in Mexico. It is for a more affluent crowd with private bungalows and a swimming pool. The only RV park is The Oregon, on the beach, near Señor Wayne's restaurant. Hotel Palmeras (under construction) will be a nice place once it's finished. Jejenes (no-see-ems, or sand fleas) do exist here but are not as bad as in San Blas. They only come out for about an hour in the morning and an hour at dusk. Also there are few mosquitos (the city sprays).

		Back on one-way Hwy #15.
56.5	90.4	Parador Turístico just on the other side of the village to the left. Clean restrooms and shower.
57.0	91.2	Turn right as one-way street comes to end and merges with Hwy #15. **GAS**, left. Empacadora (packing company) de Escuinapa, right.
58.5	93.6	Loma Linda restaurant at left and chapel across street. And thru 1.3-mile long mango grove. At end, LP gas, left.
61.0	97.6	Santa Anita fumigation station at right.
63.0	100.8	Village of Tecualilla , off to right, behind trees.
70.0	112.0	Big Ejido La Campaña, left. Pick up railroad on right.
75.0	120.0	Thru village of Palmillas.
78.1	125.0	Up alongside mountain with salt marshes on right. Then slow for sharp left curve.
79.1	126.6	Community of Las Mulas (The Mules). Careful for couple of sharp curves ahead.
83.4	133.4	Pass railroad village of Copales.
88.0	140.8	Inspección de Sanidad Fitopecuaria Y Forestal. No pigs allowed!
87.5	140.0	Thru village of La Concha. Then curve right and slow past truck inspection, right. Over Río Cañas and cross state line — leave Sinaloa and enter Nayarit. **KM 143**.
92.3	147.7	Up and over bridge over railroad.
92.8	148.5	Pass side road, left, to Acaponeta, founded in 1584 by the Franciscans (about 1.3 miles away where there's OK motel Cadenales at entrance to town). **GAS**, right. Then paved side road, right to Tecuala and on to Novillero (22 miles), a rather solitary village on the Pacific coast with miles and miles of open beaches known as "Playas de Novillero."

You'll find the accommodations somewhat inadequate and primitive — Margarita 2-story, 33-room hotel within walking distance of beach; ceiling fans, restaurant, covered parking and Bungalows Paraíso 12 kitchenette units on beach, space for few RV's with no hookups, tenting permitted. We heard that some gringos have moved in and are offering accommodations.

95.0	152.0	Pass side road (right) to Sayulita. Then slow for sharp left curve and over steel bridge. Limit of 50 tons, strictly enforced.
96.4	154.2	Over Río Acaponeta and thru San Francisco.
103.4	165.4	Village of San Miguel, mostly to left. KM 113.
107.7	172.3	Up thru village of Tierra Generosa (Generous Land). TOPES. TOPES. **KM 110.**

MI   KM

120.0 192.0   **GAS**, right. Truck stop of El Mil (1000) at right. Then couple of bridges and railroad at left. Tobacco field, on right, just past **GAS**. New 4 lane road ahead 57 KM.

121.2 193.9   Cross Río Rosamorada. Railroad bridge, left and railroad town of Rosamorada (Purple Rose), left.

132.5 212.0   Pass side road (right) to Chilapa. Then cross bridge over Río El Bejuco. Road improves.

132.0 211.2   Come now to side road, right, to little island town of Mexcaltitán, Mexico's mini-Venice. Helo's 24 hour on right. You can get purified water there for RV's.

If you insist on visiting Mexcaltitán, go approximately 29 miles over a rough gravel road to a place called "*El Embarcadero*", where you'll park, then hire a dugout canoe for the 15-minute trip to the island town of about 3,500 inhabitants, many of whom have never left the island. This side-sortie is suggested only for the adventuresome as Mexcaltitán isn't ready yet for the normal course of tourist traffic but the shrimp is fresh, jumbo-size, and delicious.

133.0 212.8   Cross Río San Pedro and thru roadside market community of Peñitas. Careful for side road (right) to Tuxpan. **GAS**, left.

138.0 220.8   Community of Heróico Batallón de San Blas up road, left.

141.1 225.8   Pass side road (right) to Santiago Ixcuintla and on to Los Corchos (The Corks) on beach. **GAS**, in town. **KM 55**.

If you're interested in the Huichol Indians' weaving and beadwork, this is the place where the Huichol Center for Cultural Survival and Traditional Arts is located. Susana Valadez, who helps organize things will be glad to arrange classes for interested groups. She runs a hospital and cultural center there, so please be considerate. She's not ready for troops of tourists to drop by and visit, but if you have a sincere interest, or a fledgling importer who wants to buy some really unique art, please call and make an appointment to see her. She's usually gone in late June-July. She'll put on demonstrations for tour groups also. The hotel Bugamvillas is the best, just on the outskirts of town. There is an OK hotel, Casino, in town, basic, but clean. You can call her at (323) 5-1171 Fax: 5-1006, or write: 20 de Noviembre #452, Santiago Ixcuintla, Nay.

When you get back, if you want to buy some of their art work, they have a US outlet: 801 2nd Ave., Suite 1400, Seattle, WA 98104. Ph: (206) 622-4067 Fax: (206) 622-0646. The Huichols are shy, artistic people who are becoming extinct due to TB & other diseases. They have a 50% infant mortality rate. IF you want to help with medical supplies or donations, they are tax-exempt: IRS # 95-3012063.

143.0 228.8   Thru village of Capomal. Cemetery on left. **KM 52**.

143.5 229.6   Pass side road (left) to Estación Yago on railroad.

144.0 230.4   Cross Río Grande de Santiago on big steel bridge. This is a bad-acting river. Large tobacco fields on right. **KM 50**.

145.5 232.8   Wind past tobacco town of Valle de Lerma at left. Note tobacco fields thru here.

152.0 243.2   Pass side road (right) to another tobacco town of Villa Hidalgo.

151.3 242.1   El Paraíso at right. Note big stand selling freshly squeezed fruit juices.

154.6 247.4   Careful now! **GAS**, right and come to junction, right, with side road down to famed old-time seaside town of San Blas. If you have a couple of hours to spare, run down for a quick look-see at this tropical historic place. Friends of Bill W. sometimes in town.

IF TO: San Blas, See SAN BLAS SPECIAL Log (page 70)

154.7 247.5   On highway after San Blas turnoff, pass restaurant Amalia at left at TOME FANTA sign — cold cokes, package snacks, plus a zoo of sorts including jaguars, parrots, etc. Veer right onto divided, then straight ahead and start climbing. Your are now at 1,000 ft. At 1,100 ft. go back to 2 lanes.

156.6 250.6   Constructing a 4 lane to the right.

157.2 251.5   Tepic (Quota) Toll road to right. Tepic Libre (free road) to left. Altitude 1,600 ft. Now divided 4 lane. Road gets much better at this point.

62.3 259.7   Community of Trapichillo to left. Then Summit at 2,600 ft.

166.1 265.8   Toll gate 2,300 ft. PAY TOLL (car — $12; 2 (rear) axles — $24; extra axle — $6). Free highway still to the left.

169.1 270.5   Divided ends.

169.3 270.8   Under overpass. Come now to nice Periférico (loop) around Tepic.

IF TO: Downtown Tepic, on old Hwy #15, exit at right (follow TEPIC signs). If you need gas, there's a big station down old highway.

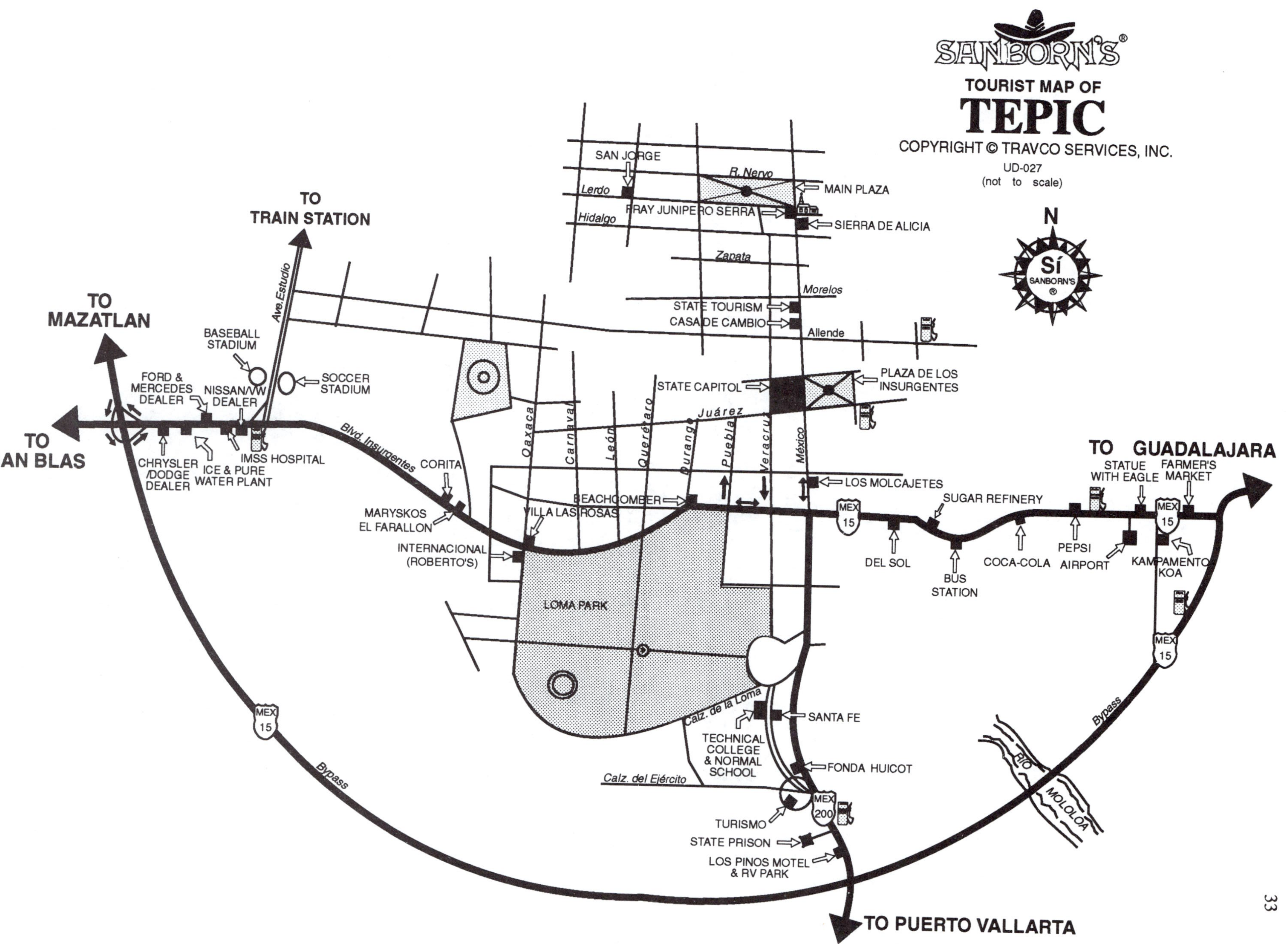
SANBORN'S
TOURIST MAP OF
TEPIC
COPYRIGHT © TRAVCO SERVICES, INC.
UD-027
(not to scale)
N
Sí SANBORN'S
TO MAZATLAN
TO SAN BLAS
TO TRAIN STATION
TO GUADALAJARA
TO PUERTO VALLARTA
SAN JORGE
Lerdo
Hidalgo
R. Nervo
MAIN PLAZA
FRAY JUNIPERO SERRA
SIERRA DE ALICIA
Zapata
Morelos
STATE TOURISM
CASA DE CAMBIO
Allende
PLAZA DE LOS INSURGENTES
STATE CAPITOL
Juárez
Oaxaca
Carnaval
León
Querétaro
Durango
Puebla
Veracruz
México
LOS MOLCAJETES
Statue WITH EAGLE
FARMER'S MARKET
SUGAR REFINERY
MEX 15
DEL SOL
BUS STATION
COCA-COLA
PEPSI AIRPORT
KAMPAMENTO KOA
MEX 15
MEX 15
BEACHCOMBER
VILLA LAS ROSAS
MARYSKOS EL FARALLON
INTERNACIONAL (ROBERTO'S)
CORITA
Blvd. Insurgentes
BASEBALL STADIUM
SOCCER STADIUM
Ave. Estudio
FORD & MERCEDES DEALER
NISSAN/VW DEALER
CHRYSLER /DODGE DEALER
ICE & PURE WATER PLANT
IMSS HOSPITAL
LOMA PARK
Calz. de la Loma
SANTA FE
TECHNICAL COLLEGE & NORMAL SCHOOL
Calz. del Ejército
FONDA HUICOT
TURISMO
MEX 200
STATE PRISON
LOS PINOS MOTEL & RV PARK
MEX 15
Bypass
Bypass
RIO MOLOLOA

MI   KM

169.8 271.7   Housing project to right. Suburb and school to left. **KM 12.**

IF TO: Downtown Tepic (Centro, Miramar sign), exit right.

IF TO: Vallarta, go straight.

170.0 272.0   Note Tepic at left.
172.0 275.2   Curve right. Col. del Bosque to left. **KM 8.**
172.1 275.4   Cement block factory to left.
172.4 275.8   Cuauhtémoc Suburb to right.
173.1 277.0   Thru rock cut. **KM 6.**
173.5 277.6   Come now to junction with Hwy #200. Distributor de Radiadores Sanher at right. **KM 5.**

IF TO: Guadalajara, straight ahead and start Tepic - Guadalarara Log (page 37).

IF TO: Puerto Vallarta, turn right and start Tepic - Puerto Vallarta Log.

IF TO: Downtown Tepic (and to Los Pinos and Linda Vista RV Parks), turn left here.

Don't hesitate to stop if you've a little time to spare and visit Tepic, capital of the state of Nayarit, a very nice town of 150,000 at the foot of inactive Sanganguey Volcano. Of interest are its cathedral (built in 1750) and its regional museum of anthropology.

End of Log 10

LOG 11   *START:* Tepic, Nay   *END:* Pto. Vallarta, Jal

UD-106

103.5 MI or 165.6 KM
DRIVE TIME 3 1/2 – 4 1/2 HOURS
SCENIC RATING – 3

0.0   0.0   Having taken PUERTO VALLARTA exit at right, proceed ahead and up. Slow as you merge with traffic coming from Tepic.

1.5   2.4   Thru little town of Xalisco. **GAS** at right. Then pretty plaza at right.

4.5   7.2   Thru settlement of El Testerazo, mostly at left. Thru sugar cane country.

15.1   24.2   Pass side road (left) to coffee-growing El Refilión. Then over bridge over Río Refilión.

19.8   31.7   Take RIGHT FORK here and curve right thru cut for bypass around town of Compostela (10,000 population), biggest place between Tepic and "PV" with a couple of emergency hotels on plaza. Of interest here is the old church built with red "tezontle" (volcanic rock) in 1539.

21.8   34.9   Pass Autonomous University of Nayarit branch at right. Then come to junction left with Hwy #68-D Toll Road that cuts across East to Chapalilla on Hwy #15, a nice shortcut for motorists traveling between Puerto Vallarta and Guadalajara (page 74).

32.3   51.7   Thru village of Mesillas and then thru redlands. It's becoming more tropical now.

38.8   62.1   Thru village of Las Piedras (The Stones). Then over Río Las Piedras.

40.5   64.8   Thru little settlement of La Cuata (The Female Twin) and over Río Viejo and careful for topes.

41.8   66.9   Now thru booming little tobacco town of Las Varas. Note red brick tobacco factory and Tabaco Mexicano office ahead on right. Side road (right) to Zacualpan. Then **GAS,** at right.

43.5   69.6   Pass side road (right) to Chacala and over Río Las Varas. This used to be magnificent jungle – but look at the price of progress.

49.0   78.4   Pass side road (right) to Lima de Abajo and Puesta de la Lima. Then over Río de la Lima. Note tobacco-drying racks.

54.3   86.9   **GAS,** at right. Then side trail right to La Peñita RV Park, a nice cliff-side layout overlooking the Pacific.

54.5   87.2   Slow for topes and into seaside brick-making village of La Peñita de Jaltemba (simply known as "La Peñita"). Pass divided boulevard to right to downtown La Peñita.

 IF TO: Russell Motel & RV Park, go to end of boulevard and then a block North (or right).

55.0   88.0   Over Río La Peñita. Ice house a few blocks off to left. Then over Río de Jaquey.

MI	KM	
56.3	90.1	There! You can catch a glimpse of the Pacific off to right.
56.5	90.4	Come to side road (right) to Rincón de Guayabitos (see Eat & Stray, page 108), a popular resort development.
59.8	95.7	Pass edge of village of El Monteón at right.
62.0	99.2	Thru settlement of Chula Vista.
64.5	103.2	Pass side road (right) to Lo de Marcos and to nice El Caracol RV Park.
70.8	113.3	Settlement of San Francisco at right with its own hospital and vocational fishing school. Also Hotel Costa Azul sport resort. Adriana's Bed & Breakfast is one block from plaza. Then thru banana plantations.
72.5	116.0	Thru deep rock cut – and there's the pacific!
73.5	117.6	Pass side road (right) to Playa Sayulita and Sayula RV Park on beach, 1.5 miles (not recommended for large RV's because of rough entrance road).
83.3	133.3	Pass side road (right) to La Cruz de Huanacaxtle and to its nautical institute. There is also a Japanese resort Pinta Mitaketmar.
84.3	134.9	Bungalows Vista del Bahía at right on beach. 8 nice kitchenettes. Pool. Pets OK. Portable fans only. 5 RV spaces, all hookups, shower, toilet. Bungalows Los Picos, also at right on beach. Complex of 6 buildings, each with two 3-bedroom, 2-bath apartments. Portable fans only. Pets
84.5	135.2	Thru seaside village of Bucerias and over Río de Bucerias. Slow for topes.
85.5	136.8	Costa Dorada at right, a very nice a/c 5-story, 15-apartment condominium (oceanview rooms; piped-in music; pool; restaurant-bar; laundromat).
86.0	137.6	Pass side road (right) to Hotel Playa de Bucerias and to Bucerias RV Park. 25 spaces with hookups, 30 more with electricity and water, showers, toilets, laundromat, rec room.
88.0	140.8	Nice Club de Golf Los Flamingos at right, open to public. Restaurant-bar. Pool. Pro shop. Sauna. Massage. Green fee. Electric cart fee. Caddy fee.
90.5	144.8	Pass side road (right) to Nuevo Vallarta, a resort city in the making.
91.5	146.4	Now past side road (right) to Jarretaderas. Then up and over big, long toll bridge over Río Ameca. This is also state line – leave Nayarit and enter Jalisco. Likewise, this also marks a time zone - leave Central Time and enter Mountain Time. You gain an hour – set your watches and dashboard clock BACK an hour (you become an hour younger). Come to toll house and pay toll. Then pass Policia Federal de Caminos.
93.8	150.1	Pass side road (left) to Las Juntas, 2 kilometers.
95.5	152.8	Pass Puerto Vallarta's international airport at right. LP and gas at left.
97.5	156.0	Bumpy side road (left) to Tacho's RV Park. Car-passenger ferry terminal at right. **GAS** down at right. Then Hacienda del Lobo Hotel and Tennis Club at right. Side street right to big Posada Vallarta Hotel and Village, Hotel Playa de Oro, and Miller Travel Service, located across street from Posada Vallarta.
98.5	157.6	Highrise Ramada Inn, Fiesta Americana (outstanding), and Los Tules Resort, all at right. La Onda Disco at right and side road (right) to Econ-hotel Los Pelícanos and Hotel Las Palmas. Side road left to Puerto Vallarta RV Park. Careful for stoplight. *"Libramiento"* under construction at left, a bypass around Vallarta.
98.8	158.1	Sports field at left. Then excellent Sheraton Hotel at right.
100.3	164.5	Over bridge over Arroyo Camarones (shrimp) and start one-way cobblestone street. Enter Puerto Vallarta and pass big gas station at left. For accommodations see Puerto Vallarta Eat & Stray (page 110).
100.5	160.8	Bend right slightly past little plaza at left. Hotel Rosita at right and ahead on waterfront boulevard, known locally as the "malecón."
101.0	161.6	Hotel Océano at left overlooking Pacific, a Puerto Vallarta old-timer with mucho ambience – some scenes of the movie "Night of the Iguana" were filmed here. Then jog left and right and past little lighthouse at left. Post office at left – and jillions of shops.
101.1	161.8	Waterfront boulevard ends. Puerto Vallarta's main plaza and city hall at left and straight ahead for you. Turismo (tourist office) at left. Then Hotel Río, another of Puerto Vallarta's old-timers.
101.5	162.4	Up over bridge over Río Cuale. Then note houses back at left built up alongside river. That's famous "Gringo Gulch", a colony of expatriate Americans and plush homes. Actress Liz Taylor and Richard Burton used to have a house up there, as they were here when the film "Night of the Iguana" was made down at Mismaloya, 8 miles South of town; matter of fact, it was "Night of the Iguana" that put Vallarta on the map.
101.5	162.4	Turn left 5 blocks after bridge. Move right and after 2 blocks, turn right onto Insurgentes. Now after Hotel El Mesón de los Arcos at right, start winding up and thru residential area alongside Pacific. **GAS**, at right. Periférico (loop) at left around PV.
103.5	165.6	Pass El Set Restaurant – great food in Mexican atmosphere. Then fabulous Hotel Camino Real at right. To get there, turn off left and slow just ahead for tope.

IF TO: Barra de Navidad, Manzanillo, start Pto Vallarta - Manzanillo Log (not included in this book).

End of Log 11

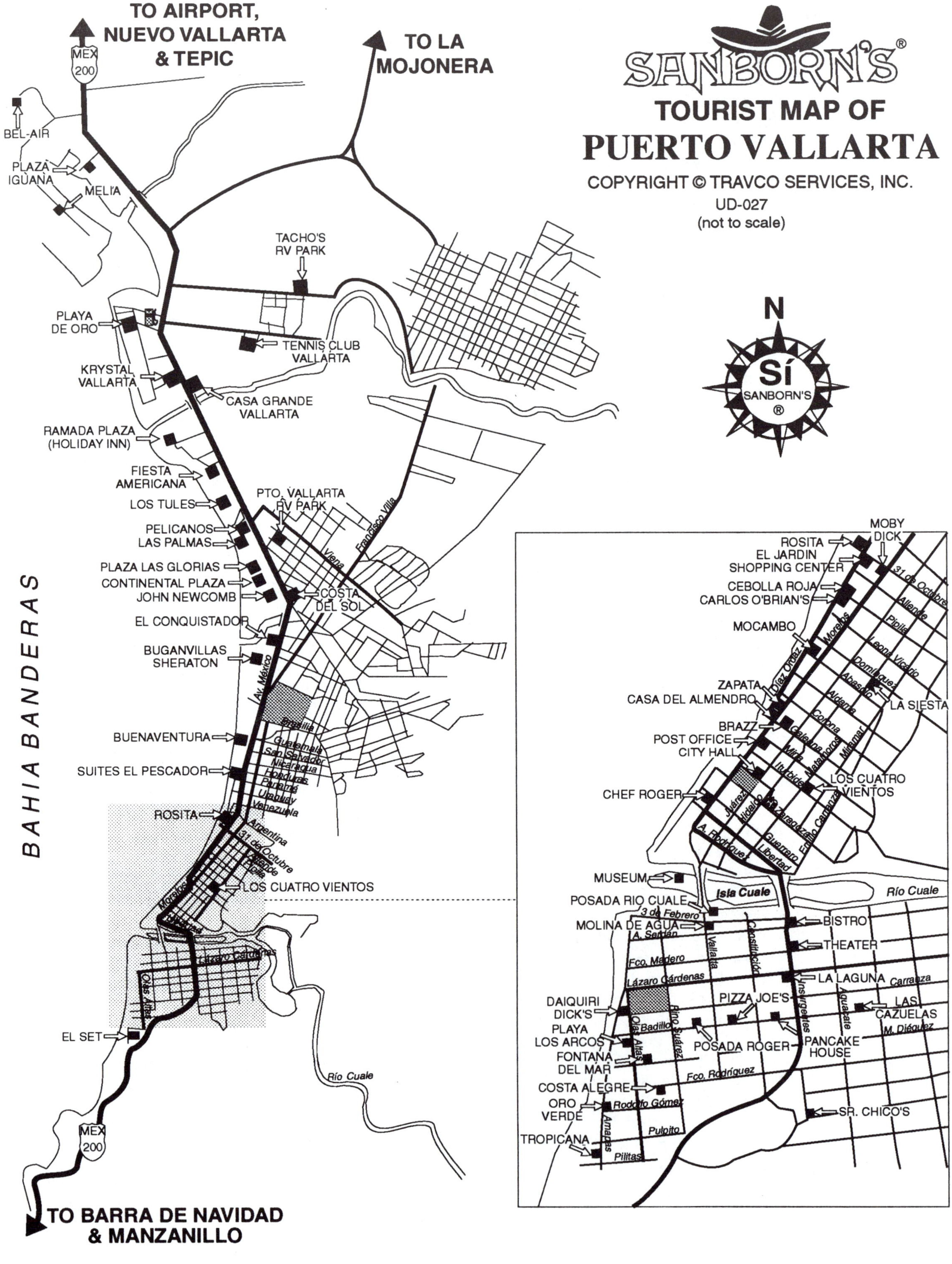

TO AIRPORT, NUEVO VALLARTA & TEPIC
MEX 200
TO LA MOJONERA
BEL-AIR
PLAZA IGUANA
MELIA
TACHO'S RV PARK
PLAYA DE ORO
TENNIS CLUB VALLARTA
KRYSTAL VALLARTA
CASA GRANDE VALLARTA
RAMADA PLAZA (HOLIDAY INN)
FIESTA AMERICANA
LOS TULES
PTO. VALLARTA RV PARK
Francisco Villa
Viena
PELICANOS
LAS PALMAS
PLAZA LAS GLORIAS
CONTINENTAL PLAZA
JOHN NEWCOMB
COSTA DEL SOL
EL CONQUISTADOR
BUGANVILLAS SHERATON
Av. México
Brasilia
Guatemala
San Salvador
Nicaragua
Honduras
Panamá
Uruguay
Venezuela
BUENAVENTURA
SUITES EL PESCADOR
ROSITA
Argentina
31 de Octubre
Aquiles
Morelos
Lázaro Cárdenas
LOS CUATRO VIENTOS
Olas Altas
EL SET
Río Cuale
BAHIA BANDERAS
MEX 200
TO BARRA DE NAVIDAD & MANZANILLO

SANBORN'S
TOURIST MAP OF
PUERTO VALLARTA
COPYRIGHT © TRAVCO SERVICES, INC.
UD-027
(not to scale)
N
SÍ
SANBORN'S

MOBY DICK
ROSITA
EL JARDIN
SHOPPING CENTER
31 de Octubre
CEBOLLA ROJA
CARLOS O'BRIAN'S
Allende
Pipila
MOCAMBO
Morelos
Leona Vicario
Domínguez
Díaz Ortaz
Aldama
Anacito
ZAPATA
CASA DEL ALMENDRO
Colonia
Matamoros
Miramar
LA SIESTA
BRAZZ
POST OFFICE
CITY HALL
Galeana
Mina
Iturbide
LOS CUATRO VIENTOS
CHEF ROGER
Juárez
Hidalgo
Morelos
Zaragoza
Corona
A. Rodríguez
Guerrero
Libertad
MUSEUM
Isla Cuale
Río Cuale
POSADA RIO CUALE
3 de Febrero
MOLINA DE AGUA
I.A. Serdán
BISTRO
THEATER
Vallarta
Constitución
Fco. Madero
Lázaro Cárdenas
LA LAGUNA
Carranza
DAIQUIRI DICK'S
PIZZA JOE'S
Insurgentes
Aguacate
LAS CAZUELAS
M. Diéguez
PLAYA LOS ARCOS
Olas Altas
Pino Suárez
POSADA ROGER
PANCAKE HOUSE
FONTANA DEL MAR
Fco. Rodríguez
COSTA ALEGRE
ORO VERDE
Rodolfo Gómez
Amapas
Pulpito
SR. CHICO'S
TROPICANA
Pilitas

LOG 12   *START:* **Tepic, Nay**   *END:* **Guadalajara, Jal**

147.3 MI or 235.7 KM
DRIVE TIME 4 – 5 1/2 HOURS
SCENIC RATING – 3

MI	KM	
0.0	0.0	Here at junction with Hwy #200, proceed ahead on Hwy #15.
0.6	1.0	Under railroad overpass. Just past overpass is side road (left) to downtown Tepic.
1.8	2.9	Los Sauces suburb on left. Left here to KOA RV Park. Paradise motel and **GAS**, left.
2.8	4.5	Over Río Mololoa (also known as Río de Tepic). Under over pass. KM 1.
3.1	5.0	Straight ahead is old congested Hwy #15 thru town. Take Right FORK.
6.2	9.9	Thru village of San Cayetano. Pass side road (right) to Pantanal.
9.3	14.9	Pass El Refugio at right. Mechanic to left.
14.3	22.9	Pass little town of La Labor over to right. **KM 200**.
18.8	30.1	Pass side road (left) to Santa María del Oro & La Laguna, with neat motel and trailer park Koala.

Koala Bungalows and trailer park is 52 KM SE from Tepic and 20 KM from Tepic/Guadalajara Hwy on Laguna de Santa Maria near Crater Lake (730 M above sea level & 2 KM in diameter). High entrance. 15 spaces with all hookups. Showers. Swimming. Boat ramp. Boating. Fishing. Ph: 2-3772 or 4-0509 (in Tepic).

MI	KM	
25.8	41.3	Pass village of El Ocotillo. Altitude 4,250 ft.
26.1	41.8	Careful now! Here's the turnoff for Puerto Vallarta.

IF TO: Puerto Vallarta take "PUERTO VALLARTA CUOTA & COMPOSTELA CUOTA" slot. Start Chapalilla – Compostela Special (page 74).

MI	KM	
27.1	43.4	Come to junction with toll road Free road stay in right lane. For toll road, veer to left at confusing circle and stop sign. Then turn left and ahead. Follow stub log below.

Toll Road to Guadalajara

MI	KM	
27.2	43.5	Having turned left onto toll road proceed ahead.
29.0	46.4	Wind up. Leave lush farmland and enter drier, poorer soil, mountain sides.
32.0	51.2	For Guadalajara, curve sharply to right straight goes back to Tepic). Come to toll house and pay toll (cars, $24, extra axle, $12). Now begin 4-lane.
38.0	60.8	Over bridge over gully of black lava rock down below and over mountain side.
45.0	72.0	Pass exit (right) to Jala and Ahuacatlán. Then ahead thru dry, treeless mountains with a few cactus.
49.0	78.4	Mirador pull-off with a view of the town of Ixtlán del Río.
52.0	83.2	Pass exit (right) to Ixtlán del Río.
57.0	91.2	Under overpass of Hwy #15 free road. **GAS** across over to left (inaccessible from this side).
58.0	92.8	Over puente Ocote. Ocote is a strip of pine wood, dripping with sap, used as a catalyst to start a fire.
59.0	94.4	Pass monument dedicating this toll road. Cross state line. Leave state of Nayarit and enter state of Jalisco. Also come to a new TIME ZONE – leave Mountain Standard Time and start Central Standard Time, so set your watches and dash clock AHEAD one hour. Mountains are now covered with deciduous trees.
63.0	100.8	Slow and curve over puente Platamar.
69.0	110.8	Come to toll house and pay toll (cars $51). 24-hour emergency medical service, cafeteria and clean restrooms.
81.0	129.6	Town of Magdalena over to left with pretty church dome.
83.0	132.0	Pass exit (right) to Magdalena. Sign says, Guadalajara, 75 km.
88.0	140.8	Down over puente Gorgorrones.
91.0	145.6	Over puente Tequila. Sorry folks, that doesn't mean that tequila flows in the stream below. Sign says, Guadalajara, 57 km.
96.0	153.6	To the right are fields of Blue Agave, the plant from which the finest tequilas are distilled. The Guadalajara area produces most of Mexico's tequila.
99.0	158.4	Come to last toll house (cars $44, extra axle, 22). There's a snack shop & restrooms. Then a mechanic shop.
101.0	161.6	Pass exit (right) to Ameca and now toll road joins free road. It's 4-lane but slow down. Join free road log at mile 124.3.

End Toll Road

MI	KM	
30.0	48.0	**GAS**, left. Then thru Chapalilla. Emergency Motel La Cumbre & Restaurant at left. Pass village of El Torreón on right. **KM 175**.
33.3	53.3	Into little town of Santa Isabel. Pass a sugar mill on left.
36.8	58.9	Pass side road (right) to Estación Tetitlán & Balneario Acatique Springs.

IF TO: Springs – Turn left at Balneario sign just beyond school. Over bumpy railroad tracks, 3/4 mile on right. Fresh water not hot. Large pools. Balneario Acatique. Proprietor J. Trinidad Dueñas A., a former taxi driver in Tijuana and former owner of a KFC in Phoenix. Space for self-contained RV's and trailers. Nice flat parking. They'll run a water hose for you. Very nice folks and a nice restful place.

37.3	59.7	Uzeta off to right. **KM 167**.
38.8	62.1	Parador Turístico to left. **KM 160**. In 3 miles, you're in for a treat!

Now here's Something Special – Have you ever wondered what it's like on another planet? Well, here's your chance to be a space man (and space lady) and land on Mars or Jupiter or somewhere. Now you go thru a short mile of the famous LAVA-BEDS-OF-CEBORUCO caused by the eruption of Ceboruco volcano in 1885. Sort of eerie, no? Like something out of this world – but bear in mind that it's against the law to pick up the little green one-eyed men or to stop and swipe lava samples.

42.3	67.7	Settlement of Copales.
45.3	74.5	Altitude 3,200 ft. Alongside railroad at right. **GAS**, right and town of Ahuacatlán over to right. There's a road to a nearby volcano. You can drive within 2 km of top, then walk. It's an active volcano. **KM 152**.
47.3	75.7	Pass side road (left) to Jala. From now on you'll spot patches of maguey (pronounced "muy-gay", the cactus from which the juice that is distilled into tequila is derived). Railroad runs along right side of road.
48.3	77.3	Pass side road (right) to Amequita and La Ciénega (The Swamp).
49.5	79.2	Over narrow bridge over railroad. Note at the left where the train comes out of the tunnel.
50.3	80.5	Note railroad tunnel ahead at left. Thru village of Mexpan. Straw weaving furniture etc.

When it rains, this road has invisible puddles that will give you an unpleasant surprise. Please slow down.

52.3	83.7	Ixtlán del Río's railroad station at left. Highway patrol station. 3,400 feet. **GAS**, left. Slow thru town of Ixtlán del Río (population 15,000). Ixtlán International airport. School on left. Then questionable hotel Calle Real to right. Motel-restaurant Santa Rita to right. Looks like the nicest in town. Topes. Careful for crosswalk for children in front of church. Hotel-restaurant Colón, left as you leave town. It's OK by me. Clean restrooms, good food. If it's late (or if you're frazzled by the drive), consider staying here. **KM 138**.
53.8	86.1	Up high on yonder mountain ahead you'll see the famed huge statue of CRISTO REY or "Christ the King." There's a side road up to it but don't tackle it – it's in very poor shape and we can't recommend it.
55.0	88.0	To left is IXTLÁN Archeological RUINS, on which very little is known (except that they are post-Classic, 900 A.D. and later). If you wish to drive over tracks and into compound, hop to it. (Admission is charged and zone is open from 9 AM – 4 PM daily.) Slow now. Railroad crossing.
57.3	91.7	Hotel Hacienda, left.
58.0	92.8	La Sidia restaurant to right. Spa Casida, for home folks. **KM 134**.
59.8	95.7	Village of Ranchos de Arriba off to left with church that stands out. Toll road crosses to left. **KM 129**.
62.5	100.0	For free road VEER LEFT. Toll road veer right. "Plan de Barrancas", Altitude 4,000 ft. Under over pass. Emergency telephone on right. **KM 117**. Magnificent view to left. Over railroad bridge.
63.3	101.3	Come to state line – leave state of Nayarit (pronounced "nye-a-reet") and enter state of Jalisco. Also come to a new TIME ZONE – leave Mountain Standard Time and start Central Standard Time, so set your watches and dash clock AHEAD one hour. Top. Cross bridge over the railroad. Careful for rocks on road. No foolin'.
65.8	105.3	Downhill view of El Zapote to left.
74.5	119.2	Santo Tomás to right. Under bridge and thru cut rock.
80.7	129.1	Hostotipaquillo to left.
82.0	131.2	Village of La Quemada, right.
87.1	139.4	**GAS**, left. Sometimes kids directing traffic around town on unofficial bypass. Take it.
91.3	146.1	TURN LEFT at stop sign and proceed on down thru town of Magdalena, an opal town. Plan on taking it easy through here. Congestion is amazing . After turn, you will see two Opal shops ahead. Airport, right. **GAS** at far end of town.

By the way, "La Única", the largest opal mine in the area, is located 7 miles from town atop Ocatera Mountain.

92.8	148.5	Quinta Minas hotel on South edge of town. Ph: 4-0560.

MI	KM	
96.5	154.4	Along in here you'll spot some jet-black rocky stuff called OBSIDIAN. You'll descend about 800 feet in the next 7 miles.
100.3	160.5	Climbing lane for oncoming traffic! Then down hill. CAREFUL! DANGEROUS, ALMOST HORSESHOE CURVE.
102.4	163.8	Down hill. CAREFUL! DANGEROUS, ALMOST HORSESHOE CURVE.
103.0	164.8	Village of Teresa down at left. If traffic's bad, don't try to hot-rod it around blind curves. **GAS**, right.
103.5	165.6	Nice panorama with deep Barranca de Santiago off to left. Burlap and carton factory on right.

If your windows are open, you'll know that you're coming into the famous Tequila-distilling town by the same name – TEQUILA (mostly off to right). Can you catch a whiff of the tequila smell in the air? On left just ahead is Mario's Restaurant and Tequila Shoppe – don't hesitate to stop for a coke or to buy a bottle of tequila. (Mario sells all kinds from Grade A on down at competitive prices.) If you'd like a tour of this interesting town, Mario will take you on one – he's on a first-name basis with just about everybody at the SAUZA and CUERVO tequila distilleries and speaks enough English to get by (see SPECIAL REPORT ON TEQUILA and map, pages 41 & 42). **GAS** at right. Curve left at the fountain (right fork to downtown). Leave Tequila.

109.0	174.4	Note brown cow keeled over by side of road. Careful for drunken cows here. They're such a problem that there's an organization to get them off the road – Udders Against Drunk Hoofers. *"Alto, Vea, Oiga"* means stop, look, listen. LOOK-&-LISTEN as you cross the railroad again.
111.5	178.4	Pass bullring on left. **GAS**, left & at far end. Skirt town of Amatitán, right. Pass cemetery, left.
116.8	186.9	Over fancy bridge. Careful for this railroad crossing! LOOK-&-LISTEN.
117.5	188.0	Sharp right curve. Little tequila distillery town of Arenal, right – note the wigwam-type grain silos.
119.6	191.4	Note the maguey ("muh-gay") growing on the hillsides hereabouts – it's the heart or core of the maguey cactus that they make tequila from.
121.5	194.4	Thru village of Santa Cruz del Astillero.
124.3	198.9	Slow a little for bumpy railroad crossing – Ameca branch line. Curve left (take left fork) past side road (right) to town of Ameca. This is where toll road joins the free road again.
125.3	200.5	Railroad crossing (LOOK-&-LISTEN). There may be a guy selling highway signs here! Now you see why folks (even us) get lost sometimes! **KM 25**.
125.5	200.8	Note deep arroyo (gulch) over to the right. Don't you agree that "arroyo" is a much prettier word than our English "gulch"?

IF TO: Río Caliente Spa, a vegetarian health spa, turn off to the right just ahead at town of Primavera and follow stub log below (see map). These folks frown on drop-in guests. Although they probably won't shoot you, it is best to call ahead and make a reservation, USA: 1-800-200-2927, Fax: (415) 615-0601.

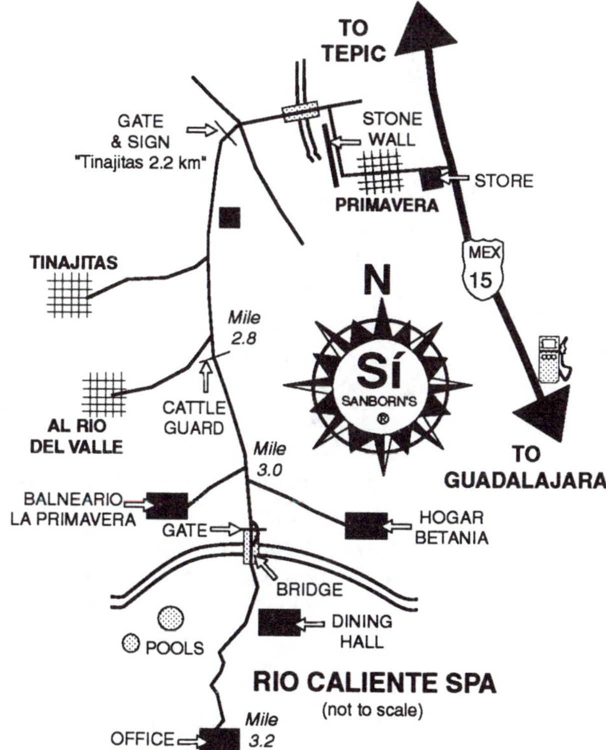

RÍO CALIENTE SPA

0.0	0.0	After right turn, go thru village of Primavera. When road dead ends, turn right. At "T," turn left and cross bridge. Continue straight at "Y" take middle fork with gate and sign that says "Las Tinajitas 2.2 km."
2.8	4.5	Come to another fork. Do not take right fork which goes to Al Río del Valle. Take the left fork. Go over cattle guard.
3.0	4.8	Pass road (right) to Balneario La Primavera and (left) to Hogar Betania. This is where nuns give mud baths and iridology readings.
3.1	5.0	Come to gate and a bridge over steamy river. If gate is locked don't despair. There is a little opening to left. Park and walk up hill to office. If you look respectable, they will let you in. Ask for Dr. Ricardo Heredia or Javier Contreras.
3.2	5.1	Cross bridge over steamy river into Río Caliente Spa.

END STUB LOG

MI	KM	
127.0	203.2	Wind past village of Primavera "Spring" (the season) in Spanish.
128.3	205.3	**GAS**, left. Careful for farm machinery. Thru village of La Venta del Astillero.
130.3	208.5	Hunting club of Jalisco, left.
131.5	210.4	Turnoff for botanical institute. Alongside the railroad. Slow a little for a sharp left-right "S" curve.
132.5	212.0	"Rancho Contento" at right – nice retirement condominium deal for Americans – has its own golf course.
134.7	215.5	Gamesa plant, left. Good cookies and crackers.
135.0	216.0	Still divided. Often cops here, so obey traffic laws. **GAS**, left. Pass side road left to Ocotán Air Force Base – also called "Zapopan" Air Force Base – one of Mexico's largest.
135.3	216.5	Intersection with Periférico. Stoplight. Straight. Hospital Dr. Angel Leano, left. Divided ends. Conasupo warehouses.

IF TO: Chapala, Morelia, Mexico City, etc., TURN RIGHT and pick up special Guadalajara Periférico – South Log at Mile 8.3 (not included in this book).

IF TO: Zacatecas, TURN LEFT and pick up special Guadalajara Periférico – North Log at mile 16.5 (not included in this book).

MI	KM	
136.0	217.6	Pass nice cemetery, right.
136.3	218.1	Traffic light. Nissan dealer, right. Overhead sign, "TRAILER-PARK-HACIENDA."
136.5	218.4	Corona Vallarta left. Right is to Trailer park, Hacienda. Protected right turn, but better turn ahead.
138.0	220.8	Chevy left. El Gallo Pope left. Divided begins again. Road widens. Car dealership, right. **GAS**, left. Hotel Nuevo Real Vallarta, left. Coca Cola dealer left.
139.3	222.9	Goodyear left. Left to U. Autónomo de Guadalajara. Banco Atlántico, left. Road widens. Interesting townhouses, left. Volks Vallarta, right. Farmacia Lite, right. Mayoral restaurant on left. Block sculpture in middle of street.
139.5	223.2	Pass electrical generating station, left. Pretty brick. Street changes name. Down & under overpass. Left lane for local traffic. Veer a little to right. Chrysler dealer on left.
139.7	223.5	Cross Av. Niño del Obrero.
139.9	223.8	General Tires on right. Tutankhamen bar & restaurant, left.
140.1	224.2	Hotel Malibu, way over to left.
140.5	224.8	Soccer field in middle of street!
140.8	225.3	Banco del Atlántico. Teléfonos de México, right.
140.9	225.4	"*Todo Fácil*" – a neat place like a Handy Dan or superstore for do-it-yourselfers, left. If you get a thrill from pushing a power saw or drilling stuff, you can probably find something in there to putter with. Of course, the "missus" might not like it, but you can always come back later. Renault dealer on right. Cross wide divided López Mateos.
141.4	226.2	**GAS**, left.
141.5	226.4	Ahead on wide divided Av. Cárdenas. Valencia restaurant and La Mansión a cabrito restaurant, left. Straight. Come to small glorieta. Go 3/4 around & veer left. Stop sign.
141.7	226.7	Under overpass. Road narrows. Left LANE DISAPPEARS!
142.0	227.2	Pass Farmer's market "Centro de Abastos", left.
142.5	228.0	MANZANILLO EXIT.
142.8	228.5	Pass Calzada del Sur exit.
143.8	230.1	Cárdenas is 3 lanes each way divided parkway. Left turn arrows DO NOT mean your lane dies – YET. It will in about 2 miles.
144.2	230.7	Pass LP gas tank & satellite dish vendor. Pass exit from Periférico. Should be in left lane for left turn. Turn Left.
144.9	231.8	4 lane divided street. Banco Nacional, right. PPG industries de México left. DANGEROUS INTERSECTION. Up, then cross RAILROAD CROSSING. LOOK & LISTEN.
145.3	232.5	Under RAILROAD CROSSING. TRAIN STATION Left.
145.5	232.8	Plaza, left. Market, right. Straight. Federal Express on right.
145.7	233.1	Left 3 lanes MUST go around glorieta. Railroad station dead ahead. Beautiful park, right. Follow signs for train. Pass Biblioteca Nacional. Right 2 lanes can turn right. (If you were going North, you could turn here with a protected right arrow.) Cross wide González Gallo. **GAS** right.

Right lane MUST turn right onto González Gallo – don't do that. You'll dead end into Curiel.

MI	KM	
146.3	234.1	Hotel 13,000 – not for you. STAY OUT OF RIGHT LANE. Airport, Bomberos signs. **GAS** right. Around little circle. Av. La Paz, left. **GAS** left. Cross divided 2-way Calz. Revolución. Next one-way left.

Sanborn's Special Reports

SPECIAL REPORT ON THE TOWN OF TEQUILA

TEQUILA, Founded in 1530 by Spanish Captain Cristóbal de Oñate, is quite a place! There are about 24 distilleries all busy turning out Mexico's number one liquor, tequila, which technically means the rock that cuts. Now, this doesn't refer to what it'll do when it hits the gullet — the town came first, then the drink. It got its name from the shiny black glass-like razor sharp obsidian that's found in the nearby hills.

Tequila liquor was first distilled here in 1600. The oldest and largest tequila distillery is called La Perseverancia (Endurance), operated continuously since 1875 by the Sauza family. Another old and large distillery is La Rojeña, operated continuously since 1888 by the Cuervo family. Both are very interesting plants so please feel free to visit them — tourist are most welcome. Across from the Sauza plant is the old Sauza family hacienda which was built in 1833 — you're also welcome to visit this fascinating old place. *Don't visit the distilleries between 1 and 2 PM — that's lunch and siesta time and almost everything shuts down tight.*

If you'd like a guide to show you the town and take you through the two main aforementioned tequila distilleries, we recommend Mario Sanchez who runs a restaurant and tequila shop on the highway. Mario speaks enough English to be helpful and will take you on a half to one hour tour. He knows the folks at each distillery and they sort of let him have the run of the place.

Tequila is made from the juice of the heart of the Agave cactus, better known as *maguey*. The heart is cooked and the juice is extracted from this pulp. It is then fermented, distilled, and bottled. Cuervo bottles its products at the distillery, whereas Sauza ships its tequila in big glass-lined tank trucks to Guadalajara where it is bottled at the big plant on the highway a few blocks toward town after the Camino Real Motel.

An interesting by-product of the tequila process are the shreds from the ground-up heart of the cactus. These brown shreds are purchased by Guadalajara brick makers who mix them with clay to produce a stronger brick.

There are two little emergency second-rate hotels in Tequila, Casa de Asistencia across the street from the Cuervo plant and Colonial on the main stem above the bus station.

There are a lot of smaller tequila factories located further through town. It seems as though too many of the old-time tequila distillery owners imbibed too freely their own products (sort of like the saying we had in our own Prohibition days that it was a no-account bootlegger who wouldn't drink his own hooch!) and so they all had big funerals and wealthy widows. Several of the distilleries are named for widows, like Vda. (abbreviation for *viuda* or widow) de Martínez and Vda. de Romero which would mean Widow of Martínez and Widow of Romero.

You'll have an enjoyable half hour or so here in TEQUILA — if you don't mind the smell.

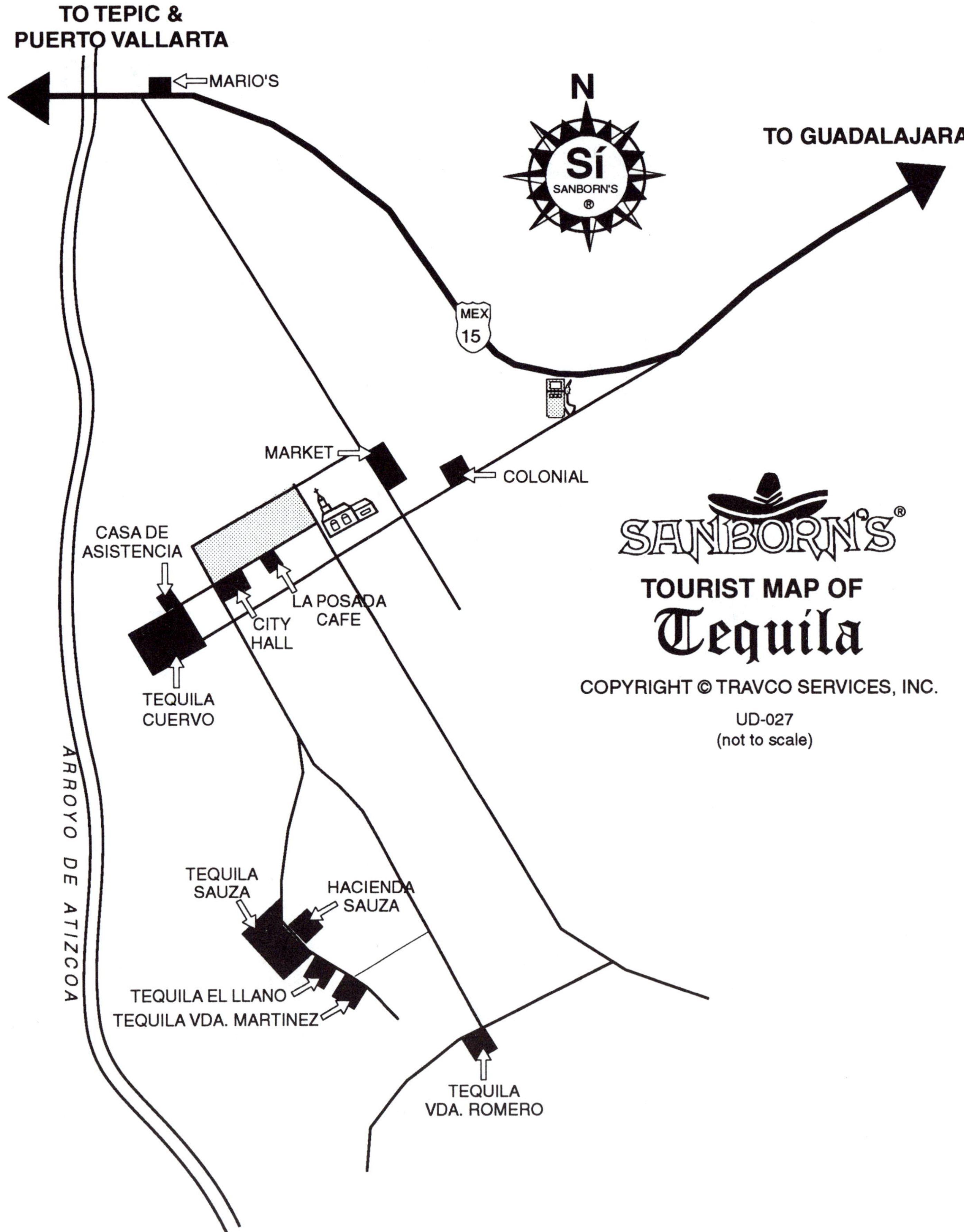

42
TO TEPIC &
PUERTO VALLARTA
MARIO'S
N
SÍ
SANBORN'S
®
TO GUADALAJARA
MEX
15
MARKET
COLONIAL
CASA DE
ASISTENCIA
LA POSADA
CAFE
CITY
HALL
SANBORN'S®
TOURIST MAP OF
Tequila
COPYRIGHT © TRAVCO SERVICES, INC.
UD-027
(not to scale)
TEQUILA
CUERVO
ARROYO DE ATIZCOA
TEQUILA
SAUZA
HACIENDA
SAUZA
TEQUILA EL LLANO
TEQUILA VDA. MARTINEZ
TEQUILA
VDA. ROMERO

MI   KM

146.5	234.4	Go around and straight ahead. Street left 2 way. Come to circle with Angel on top.
146.7	234.7	Streets crossing or dead-ending into Independencia will alternate one-way right, left. Cine Avenida, right. Pass Hotel Los Reyes, left.
146.9	235.0	Light. Cross Juárez left. Go under park. Left ONTO INDEPENDENCIA. 4 lanes each way.
147.0	235.2	MEXICO, SALTILLO, Right. Pizza Express, right. 1 lane.
147.3	235.7	Cross Carranza. Road widens. Stay left. Degollado Theatre to your left. Cross Pino Suárez left, Belén, right. Turn Left off Hidalgo, one-way, left. Parking lot, left. Cross Morelos, one-way your right. Ahead down Av Corona. Come to cathedral at your left.

IF TO: Mexico City via Morelia, turn right and start Guadalajara – Morelia Log; Via La Piedad, Irapuato-Querétaro, start Guadalajara – Querétaro Log (See *Mexico's Colonial Heart* book).

IF TO: San Luis Potosí direct, start Guadalajara – San Luis Potosí Log (not included in this book).

IF TO: Zacatecas & Saltillo, start Guadalajara — Zacatecas Log (not included in this book).

IF TO: Chapala & Ajijic, start Guadalajara —Jocotepec Log (See *Mexico's Colonial Heart* book).

IF TO: Manzanillo via Barra de Navidad, start Guadalajara — Barra de Navidad Log; Via Hwy #54 ("Corta"), start Guadalajara — Colima Log (not included in this book).

IF TO: Downtown, go 3/4 way around circle, take Zacatecas exit, immediately pull onto service road, and turn right at Calle Hidalgo which will take you straight to downtown. For accommodations see Guadalajara Eat & Stray (page 118)

End of Log 12

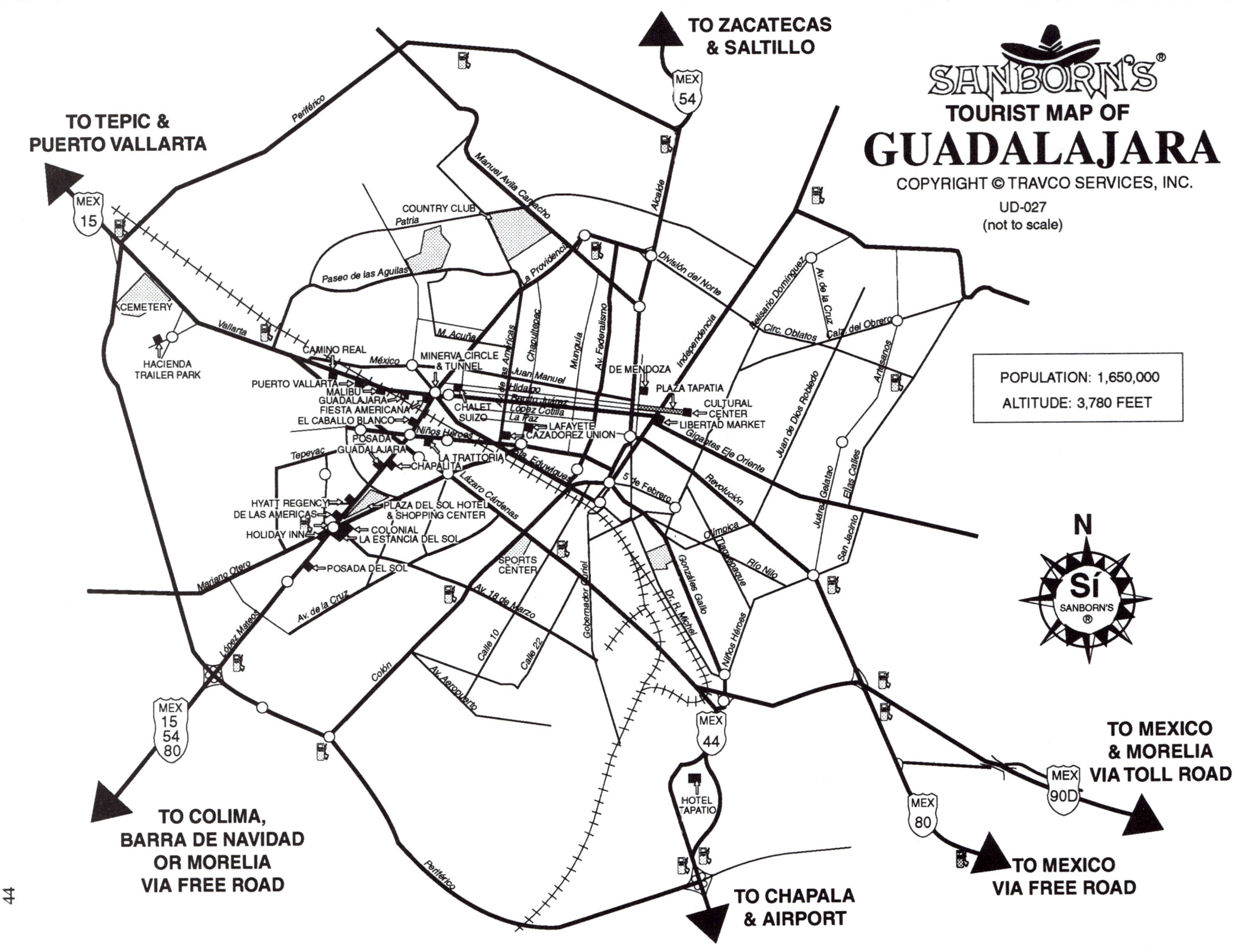

SANBORN'S
TOURIST MAP OF
GUADALAJARA
COPYRIGHT © TRAVCO SERVICES, INC.
UD-027
(not to scale)
POPULATION: 1,650,000
ALTITUDE: 3,780 FEET
N
SÍ
SANBORN'S
TO ZACATECAS & SALTILLO
TO TEPIC & PUERTO VALLARTA
TO COLIMA, BARRA DE NAVIDAD OR MORELIA VIA FREE ROAD
TO CHAPALA & AIRPORT
TO MEXICO VIA FREE ROAD
TO MEXICO & MORELIA VIA TOLL ROAD
MEX 15
MEX 54
MEX 44
MEX 80
MEX 90D
MEX 15 54 80
CEMETERY
HACIENDA TRAILER PARK
HOTEL TAPATIO
COUNTRY CLUB
Patria
Paseo de las Aguilas
CAMINO REAL
MINERVA CIRCLE & TUNNEL
PUERTO VALLARTA
GUADALAJARA
FIESTA AMERICANA
EL CABALLO BLANCO
COLONIAL
LA ESTANCIA DEL SOL
HYATT REGENCY
DE LAS AMERICAS
HOLIDAY INN
POSADA DEL SOL
PLAZA DEL SOL HOTEL & SHOPPING CENTER
SPORTS CENTER
POSADA GUADALAJARA
LA TRATTORIA
CHALET SUIZO
DE MENDOZA
PLAZA TAPATIA
CULTURAL CENTER
LIBERTAD MARKET
LAFAYETE
CAZADOREZ UNION
México
Niños Héroes
Manuel Avila Camacho
Hidalgo
López Cotilla
La Paz
Av. de las Américas
Chapultepec
La Providencia
Munguía
Av. Federalismo
Alcalde
Independencia
División del Norte
Belisario Domínguez
Av. de la Cruz
Periférico
López Mateos
Mariano Otero
Av. de la Cruz
Colón
Av. Aeropuerto
Av. 18 de Marzo
Calle 10
Calle 22
Lázaro Cárdenas
Gobernador Curiel
Gonzáles Gallo
Dr. R. Michel
Niños Héroes
Olímpica
Río Nilo
Revolución
Ramón Corona
Juan de Dios Robledo
Juárez Gelatao
San Jacinto
Elías Calles
Artesanos

SPECIAL A *START:* Hermosillo, Son *END:* Kino Bay, Son

73.0 MI or 116.8 KM
DRIVE TIME 1 1/2 — 2 HOURS
SCENIC RATING — 2

MI	KM	
0.0	0.0	Here in Hermosillo at the University of Sonora plaza, having turned off Hwy #15, proceed ahead on nice divided Luis Encias Blvd. Stick to middle lane — easier going. University campus at left.
0.2	0.3	Pass IMSS hospital, right.
0.3	0.5	Denny's at right. Sanborn's store & restaurant, left.
0.9	1.4	STAY IN LEFT 2 LANES, or you'll be forced to turn right. Then under pedestrian crossover.
1.0	1.6	Now down under overpass.
1.5	2.4	**GAS** at right.
1.6	2.6	Miyako Restaurant & Jardines — very nice Japanese restaurant.
2.0	3.2	Sports center at right and careful here at stoplight and junction with Periférico (bypass). Here's very good El Sahuaro **GAS** at right. This is where folks from the bypass stublog join us.
2.1	3.4	John Deere and Bancomer at right.
3.7	5.9	Cemetery to left.
4.2	6.7	Pass Mariscos Mateo, left.
4.5	7.2	Buho's Motel Suites (has jacuzzi) a motel del paso (sometimes won't rent to *gringos*), left.
5.5	8.8	Pass Hermosillo's airport at right.
6.5	10.4	Chinos Eventos Restaurant, left. KM 11.
7.0	11.2	Pass Casa Pedro Domecq winery at left (of Brandy Presidente fame). Then a short mile later pass Vinícola Vergel winery at right (makers of Viejo Vergel brandy).
8.6	13.8	Road narrows to 2 lanes.
12.8	20.5	University of Sonora experimental farm at left. There are quite a few flash-flood dips (*vados*) on this road, but you can take 'em easily and safely at 55-60 mph.
18.0	28.8	Road narrows to its regular width. Note grape vineyards thru here.
21.0	33.6	Pass side road (right) to Monte Carlo. A little later pass grape vineyards on right.
29.0	46.4	Pass roadside community of Costa Rica at right. Then cotton gin at left. Strange stand of tall sahuaro cactus at right.
33.0	52.8	Take RIGHT FORK. Left fork takes you to Guaymas. The road's good and it's only 54 miles to Hwy #15 plus another 24 miles to Guaymas. It's a time-saver and beats driving back thru Hermosillo, especially if you're heading to Guaymas on your return. If you take this shortcut, pick up Hermosillo — Guaymas Log at Mile 54.3 when you reach Hwy #15.
35.0	56.0	Lots of *ejidos* in this area. There's Ejido El Triunfo at right.
37.0	59.2	Cotton gin at left. Thru village of Miguel Alemán. Careful for topes. **GAS** at left. Then pass IMSS clinic at left. Palm oasis, left. Watch for topes.
39.3	62.9	Just about the longest chicken shed you've ever laid your eyes on at right — and there's another a mile or so ahead. Chickens are big business in these parts. Texans, note: I didn't say "Ranch" A là La Grange. The movie stared two of my favorites, Dolly Parton and Burt Reynolds.
41.5	66.4	Pass farm workers' campo of San Francisco at left. Veterano winery and vineyards at left.
42.8	68.5	Come to junction with road to Plan de Ayala.

IF TO: San Carlos and Guaymas, here to left is another shortcut. It's a great time saver. Start Kino Bay — Hwy #15 Shortcut Special (page 49).

MI	KM	
43.0	68.8	Thru community of Santa Isabel.
44.0	70.4	Pass side road (right) to La Choya and left to Sahuaripa.
46.5	74.4	Power plant at left and pass settlement of Orebalma at left.
48.0	76.8	Farm workers' campo of San Isidro at left. KM 79
54.0	86.4	Now for 5 more chicken sheds. Note fields of "nopal" cactus on right and then "saguaro."
64.0	102.4	Interesting Rancho Monte Cristo at left.
66.0	105.6	Pass side road (left) to Kino del Mar.

MI	KM	
67.3	107.7	Come now to El Desierto **GAS**. Ice plant at right. Stop sign and herd of goats out for a roadside ramble. Side road (left) goes to Islandia RV Park in OLD KINO, but remember that the action is all at NEW KINO. Continue ahead on highway to New Kino. Then Misión del Sol over to left.
68.0	108.8	Now alongside bay. This is the cleanliest beach in all of Mexico. Pass public camping area down at left. Then on right is Posada del Mar. For info on accommodations see Kino Bay Eat & Stray (page 79).
70.5	112.8	Posada Santa Gemma at left.
71.0	113.6	Saguaro RV Park at right.
72.5	116.0	Pingüino Restaurant and little Padre Kino plaza at right.
73.0	116.8	Come now to Motel/RV Park Kino Bay.

IF TO: Caverna del Seri Campground, continue ahead for half-mile to end of pavement.

End of Special A

SPECIAL B START: Kino Bay, Son END: Hermosillo, Son

UD-017

73.0 MI or 116.8 KM
DRIVE TIME 1 1/2 — 2 HOURS
SCENIC RATING — 2

MI	KM	
0.0	0.0	Starting here in Kino Bay at entrance to Kino Bay Motel/RV Park, continue ahead.
0.5	0.8	Pass Pingüino Restaurant and little Padre Kino plaza at left.
2.0	3.2	Pass Saguaro RV Park at left.
2.5	4.0	Pass Posada Santa German at right.
5.0	8.0	Pass Posada del Mar, left. Pass public camping area down at right. This is the cleanliest beach in all Mexico.
5.7	9.1	Pass Misión del Sol over to right. Pass side road (right) to Islandia RV Park in Old Kino, Ice plant at right, then El Desierto **GAS** station (accepts credit cards).
7.0	11.2	Pass side road (right) to Kino del Mar.
9.0	14.4	Interesting Rancho Monte Cristo at right.
27.3	43.7	Pass small new reservoir surrounded by newly planted trees and palapa stands, left.
29.5	47.2	Thru village of Santa Isabel.
29.8	47.7	Now come to junction with road to Plan de Ayala. Continue straight ahead. KM 69.

IF TO: Guaymas, turn right. This takes you through Plan de Ayala to Hwy 15 and on to Guaymas (You can also go straight and take next right if this road is in bad shape. All roads lead you to where you want to go — but be careful for turns). Start Kino Bay — Hwy #15 Shortcut Special (page 49).

IF TO: Hermosillo, straight ahead.

MI	KM	
33.7	53.9	Just about the longest chicken shed you've ever laid eyes on at left. Chickens are big business in these parts. Texans, note: I didn't say "Ranch" A là La Grange. The movie stared two of my favorites, Dolly Parton, Burt Reynolds was in it too.
36.0	57.6	Watch for topes. Palm oasis, right. Then IMSS clinic, right. Thru village of Miguel Alemán, **GAS** right. More topes. Then cotton gin at right.
40.0	64.0	Pass another road (right) that takes you to Hwy #15 and to Guaymas. The road's good and it's only 54 miles to Hwy #15 plus another 24 miles to Guaymas. It's a time-saver and beats driving back thru Hermosillo, especially if you're heading to Guaymas on your return. If you take this shortcut, pick up Hermosillo — Guaymas Log at Mile 54.3 when you reach Hwy #15.
44.0	70.4	Strange stand of tall sahuaro cactus at left. Then Cotton gin at right and past roadside community of Costa Rica, at left.
52.0	83.2	Pass side road (right) to Monte Carlo. Note grape vineyards through here.
60.2	96.3	Watch for flash flood dips (*vados*) on this road. University of Sonora experimental farm at right.
65.0	104.0	Pass Vinicola Vergel winery at left (makers of Viejo Vergel Brandy). Then a short mile later pass Casa Domecq winery (makers of famous Brandy Presidente) at right. Road widens.
66.5	106.4	Pass Chinos Eventos Restaurant, right.
67.5	108.0	Pass Hermosillo's airport, left.

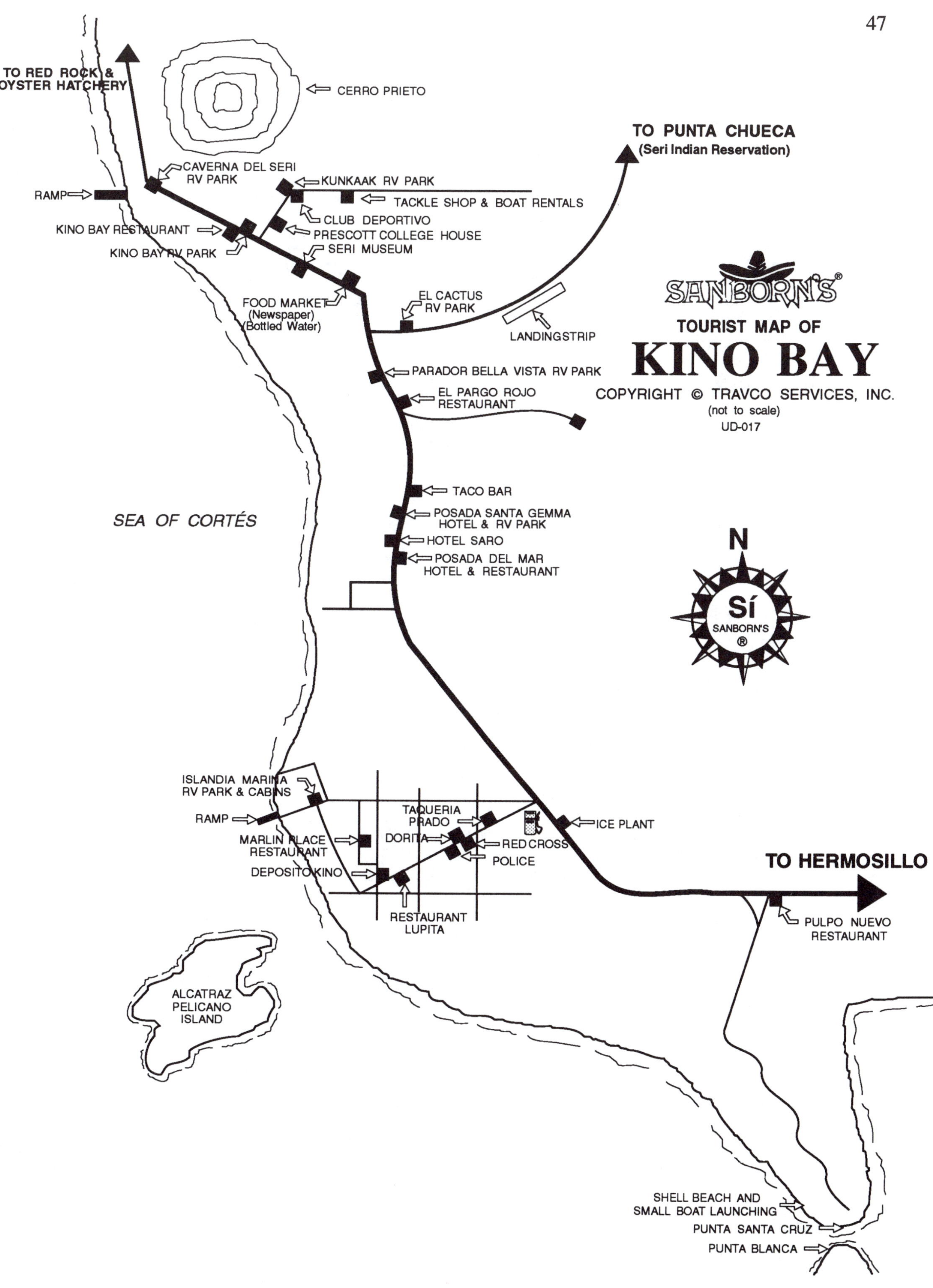

TO RED ROCK &
OYSTER HATCHERY
CERRO PRIETO
TO PUNTA CHUECA
(Seri Indian Reservation)
CAVERNA DEL SERI RV PARK
KUNKAAK RV PARK
TACKLE SHOP & BOAT RENTALS
RAMP
CLUB DEPORTIVO
KINO BAY RESTAURANT
PRESCOTT COLLEGE HOUSE
KINO BAY RV PARK
SERI MUSEUM
FOOD MARKET
(Newspaper)
(Bottled Water)
EL CACTUS RV PARK
LANDINGSTRIP
SANBORN'S
TOURIST MAP OF
KINO BAY
COPYRIGHT © TRAVCO SERVICES, INC.
(not to scale)
UD-017
PARADOR BELLA VISTA RV PARK
EL PARGO ROJO RESTAURANT
TACO BAR
POSADA SANTA GEMMA HOTEL & RV PARK
HOTEL SARO
POSADA DEL MAR HOTEL & RESTAURANT
SEA OF CORTÉS
N
Sí
SANBORN'S
®
ISLANDIA MARINA RV PARK & CABINS
TAQUERIA PRADO
ICE PLANT
RAMP
DORITA
MARLIN PLACE RESTAURANT
RED CROSS
POLICE
DEPOSITO KINO
TO HERMOSILLO
RESTAURANT LUPITA
PULPO NUEVO RESTAURANT
ALCATRAZ PELICANO ISLAND
SHELL BEACH AND SMALL BOAT LAUNCHING
PUNTA SANTA CRUZ
PUNTA BLANCA

MI	KM	
68.5	109.6	Buho's Motel Suites (has jacuzzi) a motel del paso (sometimes won't rent to gringos), right.
68.8	100.1	Pass Mariscos Mateo, right.
70.5	112.8	Bancomer and John Deere, left.
70.6	113.0	Here's very good El Saguaro **GAS** station, **GAS** and ice shop at left. Careful here at stoplight and junction with Periférico (bypass). Then sports center at left.

IF TO: Guaymas or Nogales via bypass around Hermosillo, turn right and start stublog below, otherwise jump down to mile 71.0.

Stub Log: Hermosillo bypass From Kino Bay Jct to Santa Ana Jct

0.0	0.0	Having turned right onto bypass, pass big dry cleaner at right.
0.3	0.5	Pass thatched marisco palapa, left.
0.7	1.1	Plaza Satélite, right, Then stoplight.
1.0	1.6	Another shopping center, right.
1.8	2.9	Another stoplight. Long distance fax office on right just past light.
2.2	3.5	Road goes over usually dry river and freeway to nowhere.
2.4	3.8	Amazing rock formation at right behind Las Palmas shopping center.
3.1	5.0	Under pedestrian overpass, then pass Calle Lázaro Cárdenas, right.
3.2	5.1	Cemento Campana, right. Then stoplight and **GAS** station, right.
3.4	5.4	Pass automatic transmission repair shop, left.
3.9	6.2	Pass Palo Verde business park, right.
4.3	6.9	Pass Plaza Sur shopping center (you can get slide film from photo stores only).
4.4	7.0	Come to junction with Hwy #15. Goodyear at left.

IF TO: Guaymas, turn right and pick up Hermosillo — Guaymas Log (page 12) at mile 3.3.

IF TO: Downtown, turn left.

4.6	7.4	Uniroyal at right.
5.2	8.3	**GAS** at right.
5.4	8.6	VEER LEFT at Santa Ana sign (straight ahead is to Yécora and Hwy 16 to Copper Canyon). Right is to Sahuaripa. Industrial park at right. Then pass street left to downtown Hermosillo. Ahead for you.
5.7	9.1	**GAS** at right. Cattle feed lot at right. Roll up your windows.
6.2	9.9	Prison at left. Then Lake Domínguez at right.
6.4	10.2	Careful thru school zone and over railroad tracks.
7.2	11.5	Railroad crossing. Curve right.
7.4	11.8	Cement plant to left.
8.0	12.8	Dangerous curve and over bridge. Railroad bridge overhead to right, then dangerous curve to left. CAREFUL.
8.4	13.4	Get in right lane. Left lane turns to the bus station.
8.7	13.9	Baseball field at right. Soccer field at left. Careful for school zone.
8.9	14.2	**GAS**, at right.
9.0	14.4	Veer right onto one-way street, "Las Vírgenes." Farmacia, left. AA (Spanish) *Buenos Amigos* at right (Alanon meetings — 4:30 till 6:00 PM, Mon & Wed).
9.4	15.0	Over railroad crossing. Curve right.
9.9	15.8	Look alive now! Pemex gasoline storage facilities at left and right. Ahead, to left, is highrise Fiesta Americana Hotel.
10.0	16.0	Firestone at right. Goodrich, left.
10.1	16.2	Come to junction with Hwy #15. Mobile and Chevy dealer at left. **GAS**, ahead at left.

IF TO: Nogales, turn RIGHT onto Hwy #15. Start Hermosillo - Santa Ana Log (page 147) at Mile 2.2.

IF TO: Downtown, turn Left.

End of Stub Log

71.0	113.6	Miyako Restaurant & Jardines – very nice Japanese restaurant.
71.2	113.9	**GAS** at left.
71.8	114.9	Under overpass. Then under pedestrian crossover.

MI	KM	
72.5	116.0	Sanborn's store and restaurant, right. Then Denny's at left.
72.7	116.3	Pass IMSS hospital, left.
73.0	116.8	University campus at right. Come to junction Hwy 15 at the University of Sonora Plaza.

IF TO: Nogales and Santa Ana, turn left and start Hermosillo - Santa Ana Log (page 147).

IF TO: Guaymas and points south, turn right and start Hermosillo - Guaymas Log (page 12).

End of Special B

SPECIAL C   *START:* **Kino Bay, Son**   *END:* **Jct Hwy #15**

UD-017

63.8 MI OR 102.1 KM
DRIVE TIME 1 – 1 1/4 HOURS
SCENIC RATING – 2

This log is a shortcut to go to San Carlos and Guaymas without going back to Hermosillo. Inquire locally as to the condition of this road before taking it.

0.0	0.0	Having turned onto road to Plan de Ayala, continue ahead.
2.7	4.3	Pass cornfields, left and right.
6.2	9.9	Pass campo La Tercera at right.
6.8	10.9	Pass orange groves on right.
7.2	11.5	Slow! *"Vados"* (dips) thru here.
18.2	29.1	Thru village of Plan de Ayala. Pass general store at left, then TURN LEFT at crossroads (If you pass this turn, road will end about 2 miles ahead). You're now heading east.
19.2	30.7	Road roughens.
23.3	37.3	Under power lines, just before electric generator station on right. Stop sign.
26.4	42.2	Watch for *"vados"* Then San Fernando and Lourdes to left.
28.5	45.6	TURN RIGHT, regular gas on left after turn.
37.8	60.5	Pass Puerto Arturo to right.
40.0	64.0	Deep vado.
44.7	71.5	Deeper vado.
46.2	73.9	Pass San Agustín and Colorado to right.
55.2	88.3	Very impressive view of desert with mountains at edges.
63.8	102.1	Come to junction with Hwy #15. Restaurant Los Arrieros at left across highway; strange looking shrine across highway. **GAS** at left on freeway.

IF TO: Guaymas or San Carlos, turn right and pick up Hermosillo - Guaymas Log (page 13) at mile 54.3

IF TO: Hermosillo, turn left and pick up Guaymas - Hermosillo Log (page 145) at mile 28.2

End of Special C

SPECIAL D   START: Jct Hwy #15   END: Kino Bay, Son

UD-017

63.8 MI or 102.1 KM
DRIVE TIME 1 – 1 1/4 HOURS
SCENIC RATING – 2

This log is a shortcut to Kino Bay without going to Hermosillo. Inquire locally as to the condition of this road before taking it.

MI	KM	
0.0	0.0	Starting here at junction with Hwy #15 and with **Restaurant Los Arrieros** behind you at your right, continue ahead on 2 lane road.
8.6	13.8	Very impressive view of desert with mountains at edges.
17.6	28.2	Pass **San Agustín** and **Colorado** to left.
19.1	30.6	Watch for deep "*vados*" ("dips").
23.8	38.1	Another "*Vado.*"
26.0	41.6	Pass **Puerto Arturo**, left.
35.3	56.5	Regular gas on right. TURN LEFT here.
37.4	59.8	Pass **San Fernando** and **Lourdes** to right. Then watch for "*vados.*"
40.5	64.8	Come to stop sign. Then under power lines just past Electric generator station. Road roughens.
45.6	73.0	Come to crossroads and TURN RIGHT. Then thru village of **Plan de Ayala**. Pass general store at right.
56.6	90.6	Slow! More "*vados*" thru here.
57.0	91.2	Pass orange grove on left.
57.6	92.2	Pass campo **La Tercera** at left.
61.1	97.8	Pass cornfields left and right.
63.8	102.1	Come to junction with road between Hermosillo and Kino bay.

IF TO: Kino Bay, turn left and pick up Hermosillo — Kino Bay Special (page 45) at mile 42.8.

IF TO: Hermosillo, turn right and pick up Kino bay – Hermosillo Special (page 46) at mile 29.8.

End of Special D

SPECIAL E   START: Hermosillo, Son   END: La Junta, Chih

UD-017

335.0 MI or 536.0 KM
DRIVE TIME 8 – 13 HOURS
SCENIC RATING – 3

NOTE: Watch for rocks on pavement along this route. And be sure to check your rearview mirror before attempting to pass.

0.0	0.0	Starting here in Hermosillo at junction with bypass, proceed ahead eastward on divided highway.
1.2	1.9	Pass new Hermosillo subdivision, right.
2.0	3.2	**GAS** at left. Better fill up to top here while you can. Sometimes gas is scarce on this route.
2.1	3.4	Pass Ford plant and industrial park, left.
3.0	4.8	T.I.F plant, left. Divided highway ends.
7.8	12.5	Over bumpy railroad crossing.
11.0	17.6	Majestic Cemento del Yaqui plant, right.
29.0	46.4	Over bridge and thru El Colorado. Two "topes." Pretty plaza with Bugambilias and palms, right. Then more topes.
46.0	73.6	Over puente San José Pimas. Road curves left and thru San José de Pimas. Topes. Green trees and pretty plaza to right.
51.0	81.6	Note mountains at left, that strange tilted top plateau affair.
74.0	118.4	Patty's restaurant at left – looks dead. Thru town of Tecoripa. Topes. Altitude 1,300 ft. Good turkey hunting here. **GAS** station, right, Nova only.

MI	KM	
81.0	129.6	Flat straight road. Enjoy!
88.0	140.8	Pass San Xavier, left. House with Tecate sign.
96.0	153.6	Going down now about 2,000 ft.
105.0	168.0	Cross El Yaqui bridge over Río Yaqui.
123.0	196.8	A variety of fowl thru here: Hawks, blue jays, roadrunners, etc.
135.0	216.0	Rough road. Thru town of Tepoca and over bridge.
136.0	217.6	Road has potholes. Watch for rocks on road.
139.0	222.4	Pass side road (left) to San Garipa.
140.0	224.0	Come to junction (right) with Hwy #117. Then pass town of San Nicolás on left.

IF TO: Esperanza, Cd. Obregón, turn left and start San Nicolás — Cd. Obregón Log (not included in this book).

IF TO: Chihuahua, straight ahead and continue this log.

MI	KM	
143.0	228.8	Cactus begin to disappear. Altitude 2,800 ft.
145.3	232.5	Come to crossroads. Santa Ana, left. Santa Rosa, right. Straight ahead for you.
158.0	252.8	Up very steep ascent. Come to summit. Altitude 6,000 ft.

REMEMBER: On downhill stretches, brake with your motor — not your brakes. A burning smell means you've used your brakes too much. If you can, pull over and let 'em cool for ten minutes or so. Also, turn off your overdrive on automatic transmissions (on some vehicles you push "off" button, on others, it's the "on" button, check owners manual).

MI	KM	
159.0	254.4	Magnificent mountains to left.
160.0	256.0	Pass big white house and restaurant on left.
167.1	267.4	Enter town of Yécora. Population 3,000. **GAS**, regular only, left. RV's can park at ball park across from **GAS** station. You'll find a restaurant and a grocery store. There is also Motel Las Brisas —MOD— (25 rooms, RV parking also). To get there, turn left into town, left at blue motel sign, right at blue Gasoline sign, left at next **GAS** sigh. Then straight till 3 blocks past medical and dental offices, then right at **GAS** sign.
180.0	288.0	Handsome steep rocks at left.
184.0	294.4	Pass farm buildings at left.
185.0	296.0	Start descent. Rock sculpture at right.
185.5	296.8	Down and over bridge. Then hairpin curve and up. More rock formations.
188.8	302.1	Descend again and cross bridge over river.
192.0	307.2	Ascend out of flatlands.
195.0	312.0	Wide open vistas to left.
195.3	312.5	Cow carcass to left, white skeleton with hide.
201.5	322.4	Thru village of Maycoba.
206.0	329.6	Over Kipor creek and thru village of Kipor.
209.7	335.5	Pass restaurant El Venadito, cute log cabin at left.
212.1	339.4	View of dramatic rock formations and thru red rock cuts.
212.3	339.7	Thru village of Arroyo Hondo. KM 245. Then steep climb.
213.1	341.0	Now another long climb.
218.0	348.8	Cross state line. Leave Sonora and enter Chihuahua. Also entering the Central time zone, so turn your clock forward an hour. Altitude 4,800 feet.
218.4	349.4	Begin a long ascent. Altitude 5,000 feet.
223.0	356.8	Thru red rock landscape with scrub trees. Curves and another ascent.
229.0	366.4	Thru lumbermill town of Yepachic. Tire repair shop and restaurant Los Pinos. Altitude: 5,500 feet.
231.6	370.6	Thru village of Piedras Azules. A botanist would have a field day here with all this plant variety.
236.3	378.1	Thru community of El Potrero.
237.6	380.2	Descend to bottom and up again.
239.1	382.6	Over bridge. Careful now on twisty turny climb.
249.0	398.4	Thru village of Pinos Altos.
253.2	405.1	Pass **GAS** station. KM 282.
255.2	408.3	Thru Bagüiriachic. Tire repair shop on left.
256.2	409.9	Pass doctor's office at left.
256.3	410.1	Come to junction (right) with road that leads to Basaseachic National Park Cascade fall 3 km). Hotel Alma

Rosa —ECON— very nice, but ask for the rooms in back, front rooms are basic. Restaurant. Overnight dry parking for RV's. Ph: (Chihuahua) 14-2-3698.

IF TO: Basaseachic National Park, turn right and follow stublog below. The parking lot is about 2 miles down the road. The falls are then a 20 minute up and down walk from there. However, you can't see much because you will be on the "back side" and will only be able to see the water go over the edge and not see it actually fall to the bottom. It's a beautifully scenic spot. Plans are being made to open up a new KOA Campground here.

IF TO: Creel, Cuauhtémoc, Chihuahua, continue straight ahead.

Stub Log: To Basaseachic Falls

MI	KM	
0.0	0.0	Having turned right. Start downhill.
1.9	3.0	Sign at left says "Divisaderos" straight on.
2.0	3.2	Camping zone (field), left.
2.5	4.0	Trail dead ends at big parking area.

End of Stub Log

257.1	411.4	Thru village of El Tocolote.
259.3	414.9	Pass state judicial police check point. Then pass side road (right) to San Juanito. It will be a great short cut to Creel when it is paved.
260.0	416.0	Thru nice little town — no name (Nemo?).
264.2	422.7	Thru village of Tonachic.
264.6	423.4	Pass Motel Villa Alpina at right.
265.6	425.0	Pass Tonachic airport at left. KM 261.
269.0	430.4	Thru village of El Perico (The Parrot).
269.8	431.7	Come to a summit. Altitude 7,300 feet.
276.0	441.6	Note colossal cliffs, caves ad rock formations to left.
277.0	443.2	Pretty rive down below at left.
279.7	447.5	Thru village of La Ahumada. Note that the roofs are wider than the houses, forming an overhang so you don't get wet while you open the front door.
280.7	449.1	Thru village of Agua Caliente. Checked out *ojo de agua* here — nothing doing (hole in farmer's yard).
281.8	450.9	Thru scattered community with no name. KM 235.
285.5	456.8	Careful for sharp curves right and left.
286.2	457.9	Over bridge and curve right.
292.0	467.2	Pass Cabaña Negra (Black Cabin), right.
293.0	468.8	Watch for unmarked topes. Then **GAS** at right.
293.4	469.4	Careful for topes (6 sets thru town) as you enter Tomochic. Watch for burro in middle of street.
301.4	482.2	Farm buildings at right. Then over bridge.
303.0	484.8	Careful on steep climb up hill. Top and down
305.0	488.0	Steep downgrade. Brake with your motor. Then pass Cieneguita (Little Swamp).
306.8	490.9	Over bridge and climb again. Altitude 6,500 feet.
308.2	493.1	Watch for "S" curves.
313.0	500.8	Come to another summit. Altitude 7,400 feet. Thru pine forest and down another downgrade.
321.6	514.6	Thru thick young apple orchards, right and left.
323.1	517.0	Pass Parrahuirachic to left.
323.9	518.2	Up long hill with double S curve.
324.7	519.5	Come to junction of Hwy #16 and #137. Four years ago this junction was marked by a tumbledown shack. Now it's replaced by two log cabins. Prosperity has struck!

IF TO: Creel, Batopilas, Divisadero, turn right and join Cuauhtémoc — Creel Special at mile 27.0 (page 53).

IF TO: Cuauhtémoc, Chihuahua, continue ahead.

325.2	520.3	Sharp curve left. Then over bridge.

MI	KM	
327.2	523.5	Slow for sharp curve left and up over hill.
334.2	534.7	Over bridge. KM 52.
335.0	536.0	Come to La Junta with Winn's Restaurant at left and **GAS**, left.

IF TO: Cuauhtémoc, Chihuahua, pick up Creel — Cuauhtémoc Special (page 59) at mile 68.4.

End of Special E

SPECIAL F *START:* Cuauhtémoc, Chih *END:* Creel, Chih

UD-017

92.0 MI or 147.2 KM
DRIVE TIME 3 — 3 1/2 HOURS
SCENIC RATING — 3

This is a beautiful scenic drive. There are several series of curves & lots of livestock .

Late breaking updates — Rv'ers: There is a gravel road from Creel to Divisadero. The Hotel LA MANSIÓN TARAHUMARA is our favorite spot. The owner is friendly and she will let RV's park there (if you want to drive the gravel road). Go about 3 1/2 miles past the first hotel, the Cabañas Divisadero (which is pricey). Maria's hotel is on the left. Be careful of the railroad track in front, as it's sometimes uneven. The road from Creel to Cd. Obregón or Hermosillo is open and an easy drive.

0.0	0.0	Starting at junction (left) with road to Buenaventura, proceed ahead on 2 lane road.
0.4	0.6	Pass huge LP gas plant at right. **GAS** at left. KM 108.
1.8	2.9	Pass big barn at right. That's the famous Copper Canyon railroad at right. You'll go thru pretty orchards. Careful for livestock & farm equipment!!
8.8	14.1	Local industry, Latin American Minerals (sulfur), at right.
10.8	17.3	Las Haciendas orchard, right (note fruit trees covered with hair nets). The Copper Canyon is 1 1/2 times as deep as the Grand Canyon & 4 times the area.
12.5	22.0	Rancho Las Glorias, left. Altitude 7,400 feet.
13.1	21.0	Thru village of Pedernales. Look at the old choo-choo, right! Then a straight stretch thru agricultural valley.
13.6	21.7	Log cabins & logging mills. That and orchards are the main industries around here.
18.6	29.8	Apple orchard, right. Although we say "the" Copper Canyon (*Barranca del Cobre*), there are actually 6 important canyons which form the network.
23.2	37.1	Pass Huerta Los Rosales at left. Careful for black spotted cow on road.
26.1	41.8	Careful! Crossroads sneak up on you! TURN LEFT (Hwy #16) beyond sign towards Basaseachic, Hermosillo or Tomochic. Straight goes to Madera on state Hwy #37. Don't go straight towards Matachic or Madera! You're now in La Junta. **GAS** at right, regular and diesel. Winn's restaurant next to **GAS** station at right.

IF TO: Hermosillo, Cd. Obregón, Basaseachic, start La Junta — Hermosillo Log (not included in this book).

26.9	43.0	Over bridge. The highway you're on has a name — *Gran Visión*.
27.6	44.2	Miñaca to right. Thru hills & over streams. Curves.
29.2	46.7	Thru cut. Down & up & over stream. KM 165.
31.5	50.4	Curve left and down. Creel, incidently, was named for a former governor who helped build the highway. Reminds you of Huey Long in Louisiana?
32.3	51.7	Settlement of Baquiachic, left. Be careful & watch for lumbering lumber trucks. Toot your horn when coming around a blind curve.
34.3	54.8	Sharp curve, right, then left. Birds commonly seen thru here are Roadrunners, ravens, Broadtail Blue Jays, Hawks and Grackles.
35.5	55.8	Cross railroad tracks. LOOK DOWN into canyon (if you're not driving!). Railroad now on left. KM 166.
36.0	57.6	Pay attention! At crossroads, TURN LEFT (South) for Creel towards San Juanito on Hwy #127. Straight goes to Hermosillo or Cd Obregón (Hwy #16) There may be a sign saying "Tomochic straight, 51 KM & Basaseachic 110 KM." There are log cabins at the crossroads. It's the only turnoff recently, so you probably won't miss it.
36.1	67.8	Having turned left at crossroads, there may be a sign saying "Creel 90 KM." KM 0.

54

MI	KM	
37.2	59.5	Rancho San Marcos to right. Panchera to left. Notice mountains ahead. That's where you're heading. Enjoy the next few miles of beautiful, peaceful scenery thru cattle country.
44.8	71.7	Sorry to break into your reverie, but sharp curves coming up. Left & down & over bridge & up. WHEW! Then begin pine and juniper forest. *Bienvenidos al Bosque* (welcome to the woods).
47.1	75.4	Nice picture spot with some room to pull off.

REMEMBER: On downhill stretches, brake with your motor — not your brakes. A burning smell means you've used your brakes too much. If you can, pull over and let 'em cool for ten minutes or so. Also, turn off your overdrive on automatic transmissions (on some vehicles you push the "off" button, on others, it's the "on" button, check owners manual).

MI	KM	
47.9	76.6	Nice view of Canyon. There are 85 railroad bridges in the canyon.
48.0	76.8	Sharp right, left, down, right. Then comes the curvy part. KM 19.
48.2	77.1	Over Arroyo "Ancho" (wide) & up. Two cows in middle of road.
48.8	78.1	Can this be the summit? Now down and more curves.
52.7	84.3	It's like you stepped back in time! Log cabins to the left of me, log cabins to the right. Nice mountain stream flowing alongside. Watch for goats crossing with black herd dog.
54.9	87.8	Down thru Cebollas ("Onions"). Watch for horses on road. KM 32.
57.4	91.8	Thru cut. Cross bridge over Río Alamillo and past El Alamito at right. The railroad was the dream of a young American engineer, Albert Kinsey Owens, who settled in Los Mochis, Sinaloa in 1872.
65.1	104.2	Thru Sehuerachic, altitude 8,000 feet! Okay, so it wasn't really the top back at mile 48.8 — but it sure felt like it. Aren't you glad you brought Sanborn's with you?
68.8	110.1	Pass lumber mill at left.
69.5	111.2	School at right. Then cross railroad tracks. Railroad became a reality in 1961, when Presidente Adolfo López Mateos inaugurated the "Chihuahua al Pacífico" railroad. Town of San Juanito (population 6,693). "Topes." Very rough railroad crossing.
70.3	112.5	Cobblestone begins. Bumpety-bumpety! Railroad now at left. Careful for logging trucks in town.
70.8	113.3	Very nice motel Posada del Cobre at right. Eight heated rooms. Restaurant attached. Long distance telephone at the drug store. "Super Nelson" store at right. Honest, I don't have family here. The proprietor named it for his son who was named after the singer, Willy Nelson.
71.0	113.6	There is **GAS** one block to right, to get there, turn right just before church.
71.4	114.2	You'll see railroad on your left. Pass Carta Blanca sign, barber shop (*peluqueria* or *barberia*), right. Turn RIGHT at stop sign (end of main street). There may be a sign saying "Creel & Basaseachic, to right." Don't worry, I thought I was lost, too, but it'll all make sense in a few minutes!
71.9	115.0	Crossroads! TURN LEFT to Creel — 36 KM. Basaseachic to right. Topes.
72.5	116.0	CAREFUL! SHARP CURVES! In winter, patchy ice as the sun doesn't hit the road until late in the day. Church at left. Two "topes." KM 77.
75.3	120.5	Over railroad crossing. Log storage at right.
79.8	127.7	Downhill. Brake with engine.
84.5	135.2	Downhill to valley and thru settlement of Chocquita & over bridge.
85.0	136.0	Now climb to 8,000 foot pass. Sharp curves. Watch for melting ice & snow in winter.
87.2	139.5	Down into town of Creel (population, 3,063). Topes. Pass Pensión Creel Bed and Breakfast.
90.0	144.0	Pass Hotel Nuevo Barrancas del Cobre at left. Then cross bridge and down.

IF TO: Downtown hotels, turn left onto Av. Cristo Rey. Go down steep hill to end. Turn right just before railroad tracks. Go 1/2 block, then cross tracks. CAREFUL, they're high & uneven! For accommodations see Creel & Copper Canyon Eat & Stray (page 102).

MI	KM	
90.8	145.3	Over railroad crossing. Then **GAS** at right.
92.0	147.2	Sign says Guachoci straight ahead 157 km. Then another sign: Batopilas 140 km (Hwy #129), Cusarare 22 km (Hwy #127), Basihuare 43 km (Hwy #127).

IF TO: Hotel Copper Canyon Lodge, straight ahead, 13.7 miles.

IF TO: Divisadero, turn right and start Creel — Divisadero Special (page 55).

IF TO: Batopilas, straight ahead and start Creel —Batopilas Special (page 57).

IF TO: Tejabán, turn right and start Creel — Tejabán Special (page 55).

End of Special F

SPECIAL G *START:* Creel, Chih   *END:* Divisadero, Chih

29.0 MI or 46.4 KM
DRIVE TIME 1 HOUR
SCENIC RATING — 4

This was not paved when we drove it, but was a good gravel road. It should not present any problems for most vehicles, unless you're really low hung.

MI	KM	
0.0	0.0	Starting here in Creel at junction with road to Batopilas.
0.2	0.3	Uphill and curve left.
0.6	1.0	Railroad tracks on right, road parallels track. Thru cornfields.
5.0	8.0	Curve down thru chalk-white rocks lining road surrounded by pine forests.
7.9	12.6	Take right fork and down long steep incline.
10.6	17.0	Up steep hill and thru sandstone cut walls .
12.0	19.2	Cross bumpy railroad.
13.0	20.8	Slow as you cross bumpy railroad again.
18.7	29.2	Another railroad crossing. Very rough road and uphill.
26.4	42.2	Enter town of Divisadero. Then hotel Cabañas Divisadero, right, in front of artisan market at left.
28.5	45.6	Long downhill. Then Motel Posada Barrancas —UPPER— (35 rooms Ph: (Los Mochis) 681-5-7040 Fax: 2-0046, lovely gardens) at right immediately after railroad crossing.
28.7	45.9	Thru community at right. Place to buy oil and auto parts.
29.0	46.4	Pass pretty church at right. Take very sharp left, uphill past railroad crossing to Hotel Mansión Tarahumara —MOD— (45 rooms, looks like castle or chalet up on hill. Family style dining. Feels more like a guest house than a hotel. Fireplace in big hall. Jacuzzi. Horseback riding. Tours. RV parking. Ph: (Chihuahua) 14-15-4721 Fax: 16-5444). Turn left into gate.

End of Special G

SPECIAL H   *START:* Creel, Chih   *END:* Tejabán, Chih

28.5 MI or 45.6 KM
DRIVE TIME 2 HOURS
SCENIC RATING — 4

The first 14 miles of this log is the same as to Batopilas. Two miles past the Copper Canyon Lodge exit, you turn right to go to Tejabán. This is a very rough drive suitable only for pickups and 4-wheel-drive vehicles. The hotel and views are spectacular.

MI	KM	
0.0	0.0	Starting at junction with road to Divisadero at right.
1.8	2.9	Pass side road (right) to Arecho and Urique canyon.
4.9	7.8	Pass side road (right) to Recohuata hot springs.
5.8	9.3	Sharp curves and down.
11.8	18.9	Pass side road (left) to Cusarare. Then curves. Exit to Copper Canyon Lodge is next dirt road to right.
12.1	19.4	CASCADA sign and road to Copper Canyon Lodge at right
14.0	22.4	Turn right onto dirt road. Straight is to Batopilas. Cross creek and curve left and up. Ford Cusarare river (more like a stream) and up, curving left.
14.7	23.5	Pass rock fountain at right. Road is straight for a while.
15.0	24.0	Road divides. Take right fork. Very bumpy.
17.0	27.2	First steep hill. Then down.
17.5	28.0	Pass log cabin at left. Then up. Altitude 8,000 feet.
18.5	29.6	Sometimes there are washouts here. Slow!
18.9	30.2	Really rough road and downhill.

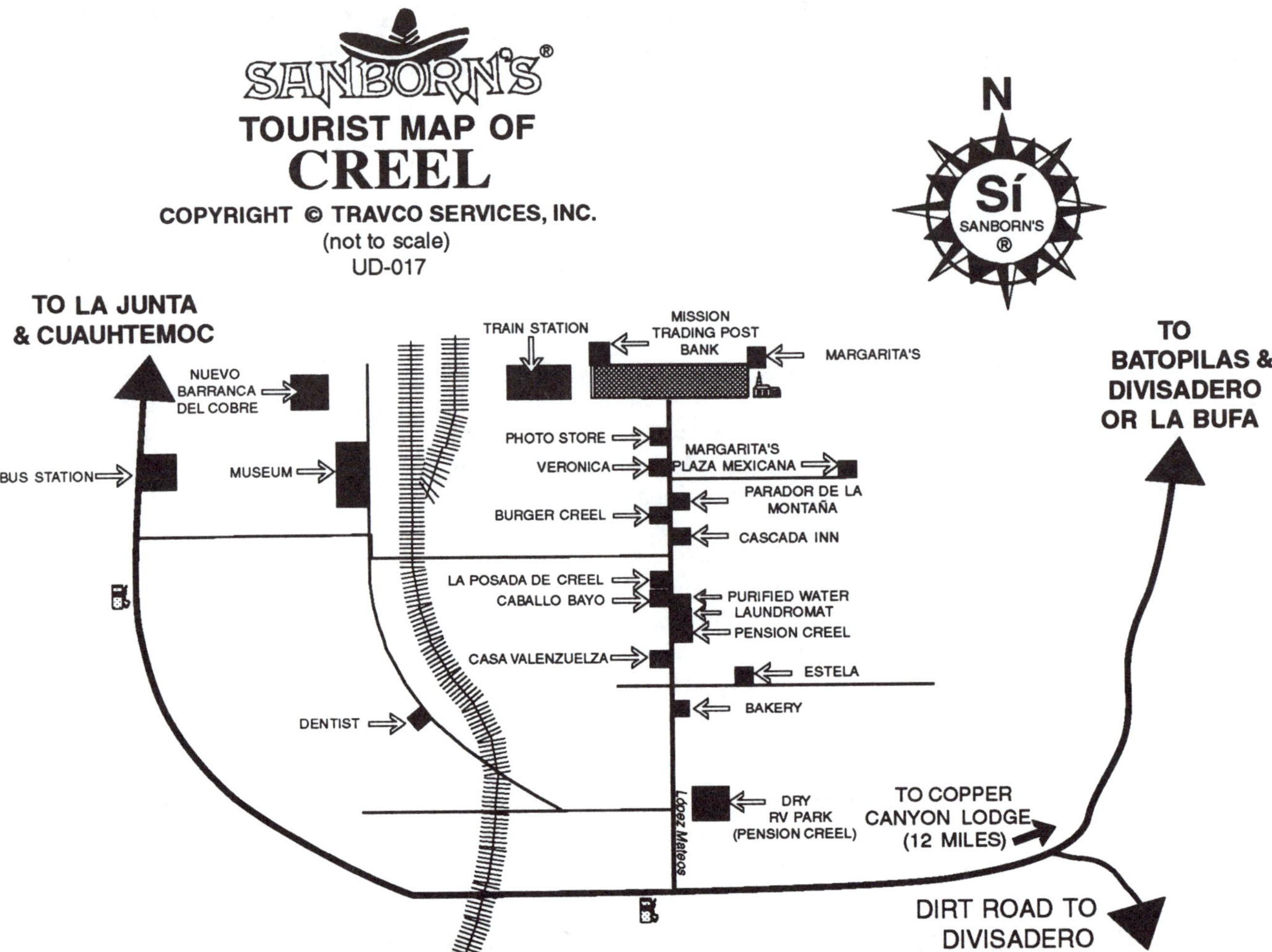

MI	KM	
19.2	30.7	Pass Tarahumara settlement and school, Bajío Largo, at left. Altitude 7800 feet. Then down and curve left. Take right fork and up.
20.2	32.3	Note cold water spring down to right.
20.5	32.8	Take right fork.
26.3	42.1	Take left fork. Now open rock area.
26.9	43.0	Rough white rock washing area.
27.0	43.2	Cross large landing strip. This area is La Mesa Colorada.
28.5	45.6	Come to Hotel Tejabán. Altitude 7,200 feet.

TEJABÁN — MOD — Isolated with stupendous view on the rim of canyon. Difficult to get to, you must have a vehicle with high clearance. 12 rooms with fireplaces and small tubs that have jacuzzi jets. Excellent Restaurant. Pool. 2 *casas* with tub jacuzzi. Own generating plant. Also has dormitory rooms with bunk bed space for 40 people. Altitude 7,200 feet. Great view.

Stub Log: Return to Creel

0.0	0.0	Having enjoyed your stay in El Tejabán, proceed ahead on road back to Creel. Take left fork.
1.9	3.0	Take right fork.
4.7	7.5	Sharp curves and up and up. Altitude 7,600 feet.
9.1	14.6	Curve right at settlement, heading east.
11.0	17.6	Take left fork.
13.7	21.9	Curve left and down.
14.5	23.2	Ford stream. Then turn left onto highway.

MI	KM	
16.3	26.1	Pass entrance (left) to Copper Canyon Lodge.
20.4	32.6	Pass side road (right) to Cusarare (2 km away). KM 112.
29.2	46.7	Pass beautiful lake, right. Picnic area with BBQ pits.
29.5	47.2	Camping area, right. Sites on lake, portapotties, showers, hiking trails (cost $10 per person).
32.2	51.5	Pass turnoff (left) to San Rafael and Divisadero.
32.9	52.6	Cross bridge over railroad tracks.
33.2	53.1	Enter Creel. **GAS** at right.

End of Special H

SPECIAL I *START:* Creel, Chih *END:* Batopilas, Chih

UD-017

85.0 MI or 136.0 KM
DRIVE TIME 13 HOURS
SCENIC RATING — 4

Mostly unpaved — it is not for any but the adventurous or foolhardy — pickup, suburban or 4-wheel drive needed. This road is practically vertical at many points and curvier than Dolly Parton. There's no **GAS**. There are no accommodations until Batopilas, so you may have to camp out. Still it is spectacular. An alternative is to take a local bus or let the Copper Canyon Lodge drive you and set you up on a package for the Hacienda Batopilas. The *New York Times* story of 7/5/95 about "Mexico" Mike was written here.

REMEMBER: On downhill stretches, brake with your motor — not your brakes. A burning smell means you've used your brakes too much. If you can, pull over and let 'em cool for ten minutes or so. Also turn off your overdrive on automatic transmissions (on some vehicles you push the "off" button; on others, it's the "on" button; check owner's manual).

0.0	0.0	Starting here in Creel with **GAS** station and Licores "RJ" at right.
0.3	0.5	Cross bridge over railroad tracks and down hill.
1.0	1.6	Pass turnoff to San Rafael and Divisadero.
1.4	2.2	Sign says: *No hay mañana, debe ser hoy mismo* (There is no tomorrow, it must be today).
4.1	6.6	Camping area, left. Sites on lake, portapotties, showers, hiking trails (costs $10 per person)
4.3	6.9	Pass beautiful lake. BBQ pits and picnic tables, left. Little girl selling woven belts and bags. Now road curves up hill till you reach the altitude of 8,000 feet. Then down.
8.3	13.3	Altitude 7,200 feet.
10.5	16.8	Over bridge and curve right.
13.5	21.6	Pass side road (left) to Cusarare (2 km away). KM 112.
13.7	21.9	Pass Copper Canyon Lodge, right, a short distance down road. Careful. Turnoff is next dirt road to right. Now begin a multitude of curves and exquisite scenery.
15.8	25.3	Pass road (right) to El Tejabán, an interesting side trip to the rim of the canyon.
24.3	38.9	Sharp right curve past "god" house on right.
26.2	41.9	Thru village of Basihuapa. Then uphill for a little while.
28.0	44.8	Hairpin turns. Very fancy scenery.
31.1	49.8	Downhill now.
31.8	50.9	Thru community of Humira. Altitude 6,000 ft. Then roadwork.
33.9	54.2	Pavement ends. Downhill on rough road.
36.1	57.8	Over bridge, then pass little shrine at left. KM 60.
42.8	68.5	At right is a large detailed map of area. Be sure to look at both sides of map at roadside.
44.6	71.4	Sign at right. Straight is road to Samachic and continues on to Hidalgo del Parral. Right is to Batopilas. SHARP RIGHT TURN.
46.4	74.2	Very sharp curve left and then up.
47.1	75.4	You're now on a red dirt road, very twisty, rough and steep, thru beautiful pine forest.
50.9	81.4	Very wide spot here in case you need to pull off.
51.7	82.7	You have achieved Basigochi. Elevation 7,500 feet.

MI	KM	
53.0	84.8	Thru woods with stream to left.
53.6	85.7	Go very slow — sharp deep curve to left thru magnificent pine and liveoak forest.
57.0	91.2	Wide pullout to right.
59.5	95.2	Another wide pullout to right. Then spectacular view.
59.9	95.8	Thru settlement of Kirare also spelled Quirare. Note shingle-roofed houses at right. Altitude 6,600 feet. School at left.
58.7	93.9	Over bridge and leave Kirare. Bank of century plants, right.

NOTE: From this point on you have very treacherous, steep, unpaved road and no turning around. So decide now. Watch for burros.

59.7	95.5	Steep descent beyond belief (and views as well). Break with motor and anything else you've got. Thru oak woodland.
60.0	96.0	Great photo opportunity. Altitude 6,000 feet. Then down thru narrow cut.
60.5	96.8	Flank of mountains in front of you is staggering. Altitude 5,000 ft. Serpentine road thru cuts and graffiti — *Dios los lleve* (May God carry you).
61.2	97.9	Careful for 180° turn.
63.3	101.3	Small pond to right (to admire only).
63.5	101.6	Tiny cemetery at left. Altitude 4,100 ft.
64.1	102.6	Above at right are large projecting rocks.
64.5	103.2	Over vado (ford).
65.7	105.1	Lookout for falling rocks. Hairpin bizarre curve.
65.9	105.4	Cross bridge. Altitude 3,100 feet.
66.3	106.1	Sign says La Bufa, but not much of a town. A one-handed Indian in corn patch on side of road is it. Careful over wooden bridge. KM 38.
67.9	108.6	Note cave up over at right.
68.3	109.3	Viewing pullout to right. See road on other side of canyon.
68.9	110.2	Little cemetery at right. Very pretty with mountains behind.
69.3	110.9	Slow for sharp right turn around tree
72.2	115.5	Thru cut. Altitude 3,000 feet.
72.9	116.6	Last steep descent. Altitude 2,500 ft.
73.0	116.8	Sign to M. Yerba Buena (Peppermint).
74.6	119.4	Over bridge. Altitude 2,200 feet.
77.9	124.6	A. de Santiago — thinning metropolis at left. Very desert scenery — tall cactus in bloom (late June).
80.1	128.2	Aqueduct at right on other side of river. Then another ford. Watch for bikes.
81.5	130.4	Cross white bridge to right and come into river town of Batopilas — a very pretty town.

WELCOME VISITORS — You are entering a hidden town of Mexico, full of history and friendly people. Founded in 1711. Population 500, Altitude 1,823 feet (556 meters), and subtropical climate. We hope you enjoy our hospitality, natural scenery, beautiful edifices and ecological environment. Please help keep the town clean. Don't run in the streets. If you drink don't drive.

85.0	136.0	Topes. Hotel Palmera at right — best inexpensive hotel in town. A short stretch farther is Hotel Chula Vista at right. Then the Hacienda Batopilas, one of the nicest in Mexico. Go to dead end and turn left. Hotel Mary, to right on Calle Juárez.

End of Special I

SPECIAL J *START:* **Batopilas, Chih**   *END:* **Creel, Chih**

UD-017

85.0 MI or 136.0 KM
DRIVE TIME 13 HOURS
SCENIC RATING — 4

0.0	0.0	Starting here in Batopilas take left fork up past Hotel Palmera, cross white bridge and curve left.
3.0	4.8	Downhill for a stretch.
3.4	5.4	Desert scenery — tall saguaro cactus in bloom (late June). Quite green in December.

MI	KM	
4.2	6.7	A. de Santiago, right. Altitude 2,000 feet.
4.5	7.2	Careful, if raining, for series of fords.
6.7	10.7	Steep downgrade. Then pullout at left. Note Kapok trees.
9.0	14.4	Turnoff to M. Yerba Buena (Peppermint). Begin steep ascent. Altitude 2,300 ft.
11.7	18.7	Thru cut and continue uphill. Altitude 3,000 feet. Then cave on right.
12.0	19.2	Slow over rough ford.
13.2	21.1	Pretty little cemetery to left.
14.7	23.5	Magnificent stucco-colored land formation, immediate left. Atop a small farm is a one-handed farmer. Historic town of La Bufa, 1/2 mile walk to right. Altitude 3,100 feet.
15.4	24.6	Over another ford.
15.9	25.4	Begin descent, cross wooden plank bridge. Altitude 3,000 ft. KM 38.
16.6	26.6	Cross another bridge and then begin major ascent.
18.7	29.9	Tiny cemetery at right. Altitude 4,100 ft.
21.1	33.8	Little homes at right. Sometimes little girls selling dolls in front. Pullout at right
21.7	34.7	Sharp curves thru cuts. Great photo opportunity.
22.5	36.0	Road straightens out — end of crisis.
23.7	37.9	Thru settlement of Kirare, also spelled Quirare. Altitude 6,100 feet.
24.5	39.2	Ilaka artisan store (stop if open) and school at right.
26.0	41.6	Thru magnificent forest. Sharp curve to right.
28.8	46.1	Slow curve right thru rough ford. Altitude 6,000 feet.
30.4	48.6	Thru town of Basigochi. Altitude 6,200 feet.
32.3	51.7	Slow around boulder in road. 7,100 feet.
33.3	53.3	Slow. Cross bridge then curve left uphill to 7,300 feet. Then downhill.
34.4	55.0	Very sharp curve right.
36.6	58.6	Pass side road (right) to Samachic which continues on to Hidalgo de Parral (Pancho Villa's home). TURN LEFT, then wind down hill.
39.7	63.5	Come to halfway point and Map of area on left. Road widens.
42.5	68.0	Notable downgrade for several miles.
44.6	71.4	Slow for series of crankcase crackers — very rough road.
49.8	79.7	Thru community of Humira. Altitude 6,000 ft. Begin uphill curvy road.
55.1	88.2	Hairpin turns. Then downhill. Very fancy scenery.
64.0	102.4	Pass side road (left) to El Tejabán.
66.2	105.9	Pass Copper Canyon Lodge at left, a short distance up road.
70.2	112.3	Pass side road (right) to Cusarare (2 km away). KM 112.
79.0	126.4	Pass beautiful lake, right. Picnic area with BBQ pits.
79.3	126.9	Camping area, right. Sites on lake, portapotties, showers, hiking trails (cost $10 per person).
82.0	131.2	Pass turnoff (left) to San Rafael and Divisadero.
82.7	132.3	Cross bridge over railroad tracks.
83.0	132.8	Enter Creel. Come to GAS station.

IF TO: Cuauhtémoc, start Creel — Cuauhtémoc Special.

End of Special J

SPECIAL K *START:* Creel, Chih *END:* Cuauhtémoc, Chih

UD-017

94.5 MI or 151.2 KM
DRIVE TIME 3 — 3 1/2 HOURS
SCENIC RATING — 3

This is called Gran Visión highway and is a beautiful scenic drive. There are several series of curves, lots of livestock and a few towns.

0.0	0.0	Starting here in Creel at junction to Divisadero and San Rafael, Turn left onto highway.
0.3	0.5	Exit at right goes into Creel but is a longer cobblestone route. Then up over bridge.

MI	KM	
1.9	3.0	Over railroad crossing. Then another road right into town. Topes. Hotel Nuevo Barrancas del Cobre. Also Pensión Creel Bed and Breakfast (see Creel Eat & Stray). KM 90.
3.8	6.1	Sharp Curves. Watch for melting snow and ice in winter.
7.0	11.2	Over bridge and thru settlement of Chocquita. Then wind uphill.
10.3	16.5	Topes. Over long bridge and more topes as you go thru Bocoyna. KM 77.
14.5	23.2	Pass side road (right) to Baharuchic (4 km away).
17.1	27.4	"Cuesta Prieta" Lumber yard at left. Slow over railroad crossing.
19.9	32.0	Estación San Juanito (population 6,933) turn to right. Straight on partly unpaved road goes to Basaseachic falls. Topes. Begin cobblestone road.
20.8	33.3	Come to stop sign. TURN LEFT to La Junta just before tracks. There is **GAS** one block to left; to get there turn left just past church. Super Nelson store at left. Named for owner's son Nelson named after a singer named "Nelson." Long distance and Fax for pay at left. Then very nice Hotel Posada del Cobre at left.
21.2	33.9	Over rough railroad crossing. Then curve left. KM 57.
21.4	34.2	Pass village of Tayalotes, right.
27.4	43.8	Thru Sehuerachic. Altitude 7,900 feet. Then KM 49.
34.4	55.0	Pass El Alamito to left. Then cross bridge over Río Alamillo.
36.2	57.9	Thru Cebollas ("Onions"). Watch for horses on road. Then KM 33.
37.6	60.2	Thru stretched out community of Rancho Blanco ("White Ranch"). KM 31.
39.3	62.9	It's like you stepped back in time! Log cabins to the left of me, log cabins to the right. Nice mountain stream flowing alongside. Watch for goats crossing with black herd dog.
43.8	70.1	Over Arroyo "Ancho" (wide) & up. Cows in middle of road. Careful on upcoming sharp curves.
44.9	71.8	Nice picture spot with some room to pull off.
56.0	89.6	Come to junction with Hwy #16.

IF TO: Hermosillo, Cd. Obregón, Turn left and start La Junta — Hermosillo Log at mile 10.3 (not included in this book). If you need **GAS** continue on to La Junta.

IF TO: La Junta, Cuauhtémoc, Chihuahua, turn right, cross bridge and continue this log.

60.0	96.0	Settlement of Baquiachic, right. Be careful & watch for lumbering lumber trucks.
64.4	103.0	Pass side road (left) to Miñaca. Toot your horn when coming around a blind curve.
65.9	105.4	Come to La Junta junction. **GAS** at left. Winn's Restaurant (truck stop) next to **GAS** station. Matachic and Madera to left. Cuauhtémoc TURN RIGHT.
66.6	106.6	Having turned right toward Cuauhtémoc, continue ahead thru cornfields.
68.8	110.1	Fruit orchard Huerta Los Rosales at right. Careful for black spotted cow on road.
78.3	125.3	Lumber yard at left. Apple packing plant at right. KM 147.
78.9	126.2	Thru village of Pedernales. Look at the old choo-choo, left!
79.5	127.2	Rancho Las Glorias, right. Altitude 7,400 feet.
81.9	131.0	Pass side road (right) to Santiago (11 km away). KM 129.
82.7	132.2	Dangerous curves. Slow!
83.2	133.1	Local industry, Latin American Minerals (sulfur), at left.
85.0	136.0	LP **GAS** at left.
91.2	145.9	**GAS** at right. Enter city of Cuauhtémoc (population 68,985). Búfalo Grill looks nice.
93.0	148.8	Begin one-way at bridge. Uniroyal, left. **GAS** at right. Come to stop light and TURN RIGHT.
93.1	149.0	Come to stop sign on Calle 16. Go two blocks and TURN LEFT at next stop sign onto López Rayón. Dólar store at left. Now two-way traffic.
93.3	149.3	AA meeting (Spanish) place on right.
93.9	150.2	Central Clinic at left. Argosa Pharmacy left. Then stoplight.
94.2	150.7	Mr. Burger restaurant, left. Goodyear, left. Then Equis Restaurant, downhill to left.
94.5	151.2	Come to stoplight at Calzada 16 de Septiembre, turn right. Chrysler/Dodge dealer at left. One block up is VW, right and Futurama on left.

IF TO: Chihuahua, start Cuauhtémoc — Chihuahua Log (not included in this book).

End of Special K

SPECIAL L *START:* Guaymas, Son *END:* San Carlos, Son

UD-017

7.9 MI or 12.6 KM
DRIVE TIME — 20 MINUTES
SCENIC RATING — 2

MI	KM	
0.0	0.0	Having turned west toward San Carlos continue ahead.
0.5	0.8	Camel humps of Teta de Cabra Mountains in distance.
4.8	7.7	Pass Hotel Posada San Carlos at right — little horses in the garden.
5.0	8.0	Condominios Triana, left
5.2	8.3	Hotel Fiesta San Carlos, left.
5.3	8.5	Tecali Trailer Park, right.
5.4	8.6	Neptuno Restaurant-Disco at left. Totonaca RV Park (w/laundry) at right,
5.5	8.8	La Roca Restaurant-Bar, left on beach.
5.6	9.0	Hacienda Tetakawi hotel & RV park (Best Western), right.
5.7	9.1	Pappa Tappas Restaurant, right.
5.9	9.4	Police station and Post Office, right. Laundry, left.
6.0	9.6	Rosa's Cantina Restaurant, left.
6.1	9.8	El Mar Dive Center, left. Terraza Restaurant, right.
6.3	10.1	Gary's boat trips, fishing and diving, left. Hotel Creston, left. Then a doctor's office, and **GAS**, right
6.5	10.4	Mar Rosa Suites, left. Then San Carlos Country Club, right.
6.7	10.7	Loma Bonita Condo Hotel, right.
6.9	11.0	Hotel La Posada de San Carlos driveway to left.
7.3	11.7	Veer left at circle. Right goes to San Carlos Plaza Hotel, and Club Med. Straight ahead to Marina.
7.6	12.2	Plaza Las Glorias, right. For info on accommodations see San Carlos Eat & Stray (page 82).

End of Special L

SPECIAL M *START:* Navojoa, Son *END:* Alamos, Son

UD-017

33.5 MI or 52.6 KM
DRIVE TIME 45 MIN — 1 1/2 HOURS
SCENIC RATING — 4

Driving over to Alamos is an absolute "must" — very worthwhile. If driving an RV, it's recommended that you put up at El Caracól RV park (9 miles before town, city bus stops at front gate) or at Dolisa RV park at entrance to town, as the streets of Alamos are just too, too narrow and are quite a chore (next to impossible) to negotiate with large vehicles.

0.0	0.0	Having turned off Hwy #15 here at Zarci Shopping Center in Navojoa at stoplight, proceed ahead and cross industrial railroad switch and then LOOK-&-LISTEN as you cross very, very bumpy double mainline railroad. Then over Francisco Sarabia (a famous pioneer Mexican aviator) bridge.
0.5	0.8	Past statue in middle of divided road. School at left. Then tuberculosis hospital, also at left.
1.0	1.6	Pass road (left) to airport. Regular **GAS**, right.
1.7	2.7	Basketball courts and ballfield, right. Mountains straight ahead in the distance.
2.5	4.0	That cluster of bright-green buildings over to left is Navojoa's red-light district, known as "la zona."
3.0	4.8	Large San Carlos 2 chicken farm at left. Then curve right and left and over bridge and up and right.
4.3	6.9	Pass Río Mayo Gun Club firing range at left.
9.0	14.4	Pass side road (left) up to top of Cerro Prieto (Dark Hill) where a microwave station is located. Curve left and around base of hill.
16.3	26.1	Lime Plant (Productos Calcareos) off to left.
17.8	28.5	Come now to side road (left) that goes to Presa (Dam) Ruiz Cortines, known locally as Presa Mocuzari — excellent bass fishing.

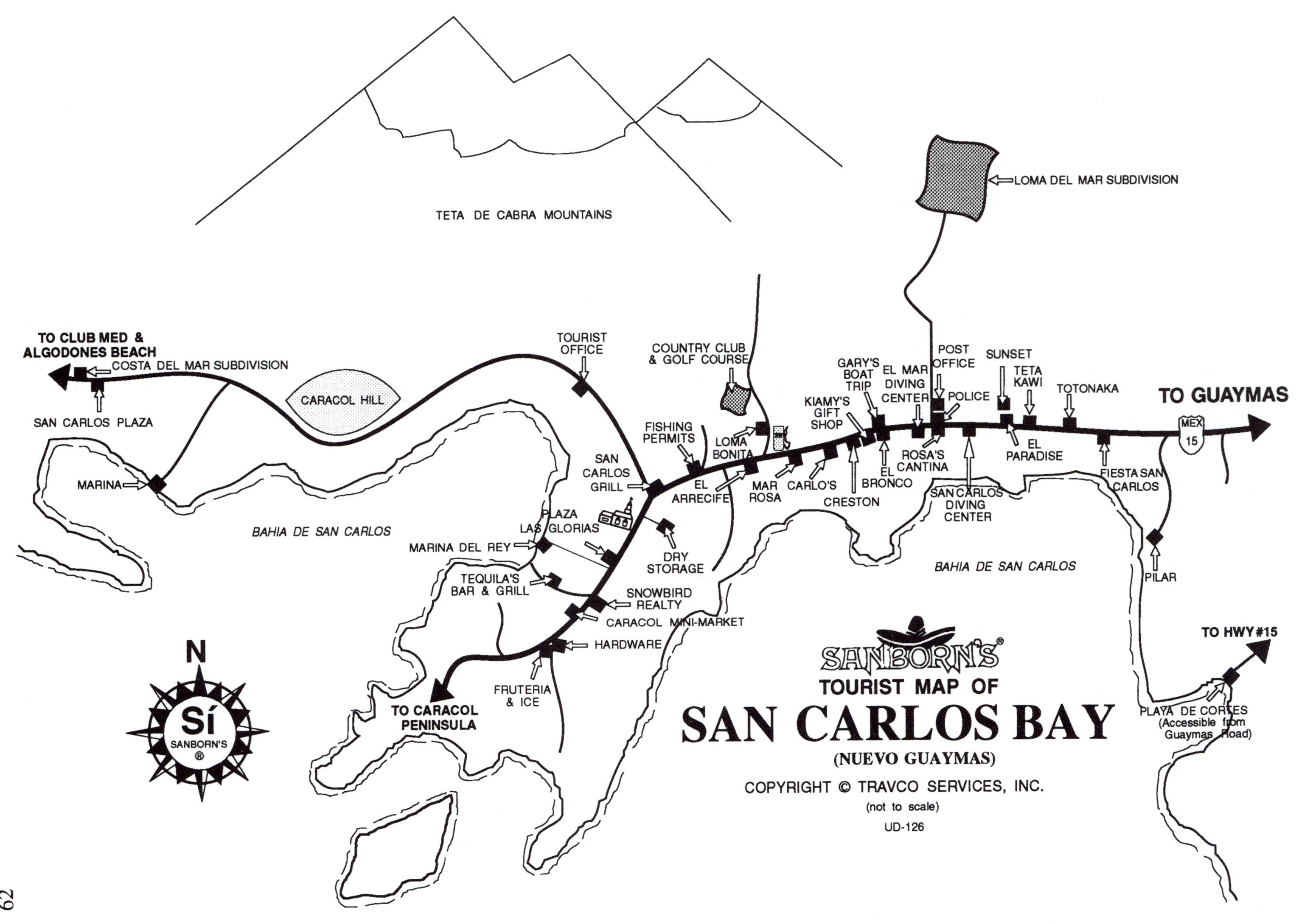
TETA DE CABRA MOUNTAINS
LOMA DEL MAR SUBDIVISION
TO CLUB MED & ALGODONES BEACH
COSTA DEL MAR SUBDIVISION
TOURIST OFFICE
COUNTRY CLUB & GOLF COURSE
POST OFFICE
SUNSET
GARY'S BOAT TRIP
EL MAR DIVING CENTER
POLICE
TETA KAWI
TOTONAKA
TO GUAYMAS
CARACOL HILL
SAN CARLOS PLAZA
FISHING PERMITS
KIAMY'S GIFT SHOP
MARINA
SAN CARLOS GRILL
LOMA BONITA
EL ARRECIFE
MAR ROSA
CARLO'S CRESTON
EL BRONCO
ROSA'S CANTINA
EL PARADISE
FIESTA SAN CARLOS
BAHIA DE SAN CARLOS
PLAZA LAS GLORIAS
MARINA DEL REY
DRY STORAGE
SAN CARLOS DIVING CENTER
BAHIA DE SAN CARLOS
PILAR
TEQUILA'S BAR & GRILL
SNOWBIRD REALTY
CARACOL MINI-MARKET
N
Sí
SANBORN'S
®
HARDWARE
FRUTERIA & ICE
TO CARACOL PENINSULA
SANBORN'S
TOURIST MAP OF
SAN CARLOS BAY
(NUEVO GUAYMAS)
COPYRIGHT © TRAVCO SERVICES, INC.
(not to scale)
UD-126
TO HWY #15
PLAYA DE CORTES
(Accessible from Guaymas Road)
MEX 15

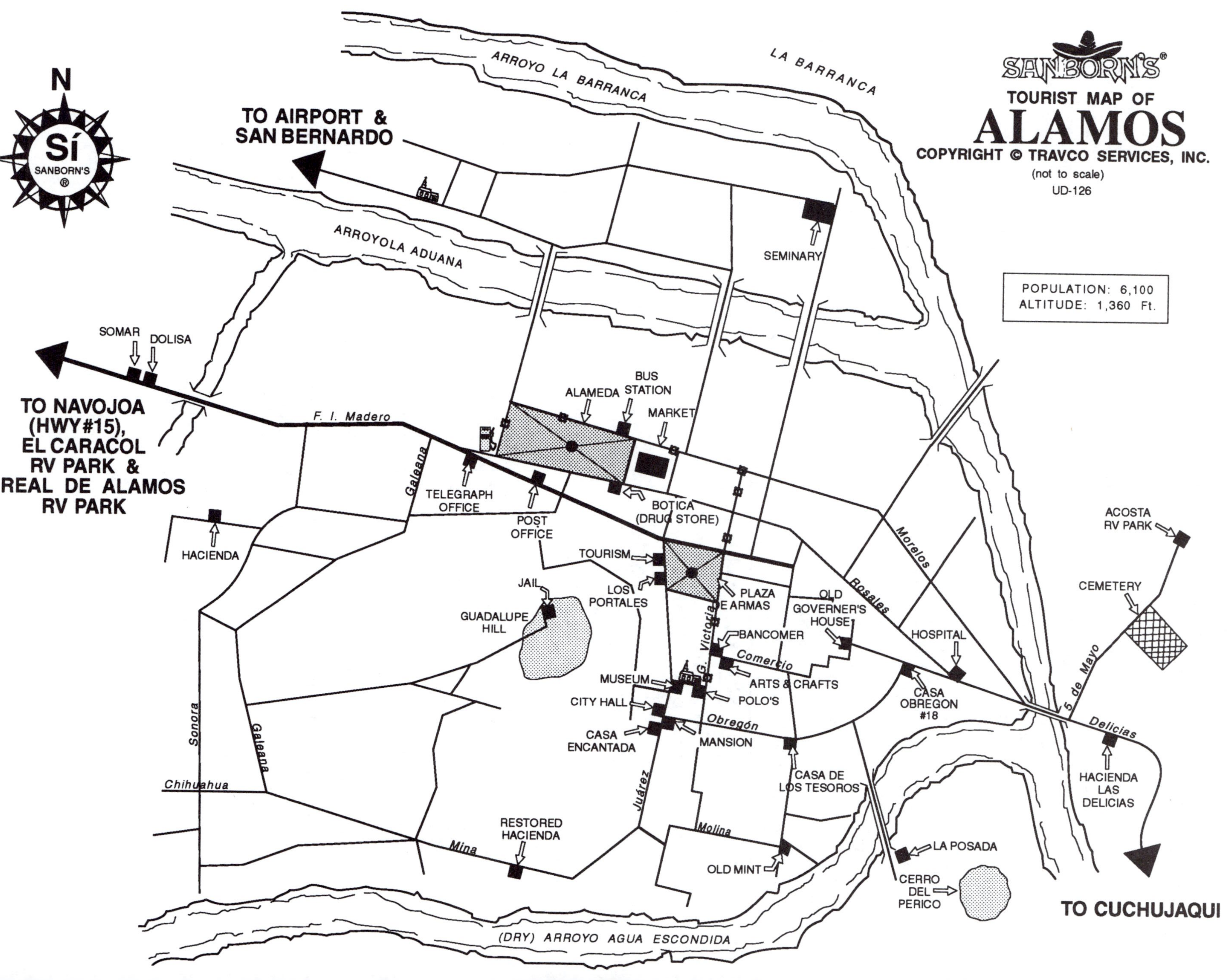

N
Sí
SANBORN'S
®
TO AIRPORT & SAN BERNARDO
ARROYO LA BARRANCA
LA BARRANCA
SANBORN'S
TOURIST MAP OF
ALAMOS
COPYRIGHT © TRAVCO SERVICES, INC.
(not to scale)
UD-126
ARROYOLA ADUANA
SEMINARY
POPULATION: 6,100
ALTITUDE: 1,360 Ft.
SOMAR
DOLISA
TO NAVOJOA (HWY #15), EL CARACOL RV PARK & REAL DE ALAMOS RV PARK
F. I. Madero
BUS STATION
ALAMEDA
MARKET
Galeana
TELEGRAPH OFFICE
POST OFFICE
BOTICA (DRUG STORE)
ACOSTA RV PARK
HACIENDA
TOURISM
Morelos
Rosales
CEMETERY
JAIL
LOS PORTALES
PLAZA DE ARMAS
OLD GOVERNER'S HOUSE
5 de Mayo
GUADALUPE HILL
Victoria
BANCOMER
HOSPITAL
Comercio
MUSEUM
ARTS & CRAFTS
CASA OBREGON #18
Delicias
CITY HALL
POLO'S
Sonora
Galeana
CASA ENCANTADA
MANSION
Obregón
Juárez
CASA DE LOS TESOROS
HACIENDA LAS DELICIAS
Chihuahua
RESTORED HACIENDA
Molina
Mina
OLD MINT
LA POSADA
CERRO DEL PERICO
TO CUCHUJAQUI
63
(DRY) ARROYO AGUA ESCONDIDA

MU	KM	
18.5	29.6	Pass school "La Argentina" and tiny community of Las Lomas. Then start up.
20.7	33.1	An "S" curve to right.
23.0	36.8	El Caracól (The Snail) RV Park at right with its excellent restaurant. That rugged peak at right is called "Cacharamba" (pierced ear in Yaqui, and it has, indeed, not visible from this side, a hole close to the top).
24.4	39.0	Horse rental sign at right. Road begins to climb and curve. KM 40.
27.5	44.0	Now thru village of Minas Nuevas (New Mines). Note a reopened silver mine off to right. School at right. Pass side road (right) to La Aduana, 3 KM, once a smelter where silver from Alamos was cast into ingots, today the site of an interesting religious pilgrimage taking place on November 20th which attracts the Mayo Indians living in the surrounding area.
31.5	50.4	There's another mine over to left, but it's a gypsum mine. Thru cut and over little Río La Aduana.
32.0	51.2	Real de Los Alamos RV Park (w/swimming pool) at right.
32.5	52.0	Shrine to San Bernardo, left; hospital sign, Red Cross, right. Still at left is Hotel Somar and then Dolisa Motel & RV park. Enter old, old town of Alamos.
33.0	52.8	Telegraph office at right. **GAS** at left. Benito Juárez bust in center. Traffic goes right, thru street lined with white stucco buildings.
33.0	53.3	Come to Plaza, TURN RIGHT. Hotel Los Portales at right. Cathedral at left.
33.4	53.4	Posada Casa Encantada at right. TURN LEFT to go to Hotel Mansión.
33.5	52.6	Hotel Casa de los Tesoros at right.

IF TO: Hotel La Posada, take first right, cross dry arroyo, and up little hill. Posada straight ahead at end of road. For info on accommodations, see Alamos Eat & Stray (page 88)

Stub Log: Return From Alamos To Navojoa

0.0	0.0	Starting at Casa Encantada go straight on street in front.
0.3	0.5	Curve with street gently to right.
0.4	0.6	With store gate in front of you, turn right.
0.5	0.8	Come to Sonora street. Turn left. Follow street between brick adobe walls.
0.8	1.3	Come to stop sign. Turn left and emerge onto road out, with Dolisa Motel at left.
5.5	8.8	Pass Minas Nuevas. KM 45.
6.4	10.2	Sharp curve to right, then left. Pass La Luna, right. KM 43.
10.0	16.0	Pass El Caracol RV Park, left.
14.3	22.9	Pass Escuela Argentina and tiny community of Las Lomas.
15.5	24.8	Pass side road (right) that goes to Presa (Dam) Ruiz Cortines.
29.5	47.2	Storage silos, left. Road curves left, over bridge, then right.
30.0	48.0	Granite and marble quarry, right.
32.5	52.0	**GAS** left, begin divided (by trees) 4-lane.
33.0	52.8	Statue of Benito Juárez in center. End divided.
33.3	53.3	Over bridge (Francisco Sarabia), then over double Railroad tracks.
33.5	53.6	Zarci shopping center, right and end of log.

IF TO: Los Mochis and points south, TURN LEFT and start Navojoa — Los Mochis Log (page 19).

IF TO: Guaymas and points north, TURN RIGHT and start Navojoa — Guaymas Log (page 141).

End of Special M

SPECIAL N *START:* Los Mochis, Sin *END:* El Fuerte, Sin

UD-017

47.8 MI or 76.5 KM
DRIVE TIME 1 — 2 HOURS

MI	KM	
0.0	0.0	Here at highway interchange into city of Los Mochis, take El Fuerte (Hwy #32) exit.
1.5	2.4	Spread out Ejido 5 de Mayo and soccer field at right.
6.4	10.1	Thru village of 2 de Abril with topes.
8.8	14.1	Little town of Mochicahui. Pass cemetery at right.
9.8	15.7	Nice mango orchard at right. Then thru Constancia with unmarked topes.
15.8	25.2	Continue straight at fork.
17.1	27.3	Curve left past cemetery at left.
19.0	30.4	Centuries-old alamos (cottonwood trees) lining highway. Over irrigation canal and thru Ejido Lázaro Cárdenas.
20.3	32.5	SLOW-LOOK-LISTEN as you cross bumpy mainline of Nogales-Guadalajara railroad. Big railroad station of El Sufragio at right.
21.1	33.8	Take RIGHT FORK. Left fork is to railroad town of San Blas.
22.3	35.7	Careful for low water crossing.
22.6	36.1	Careful (LOOK-&-LISTEN) as you cross railroad again. Big power plant at right. **GAS** at right.
24.3	38.8	Settlement of Cuesta Blanca at right and Río Fuerte meandering at left.
28.0	44.8	Settlement of Sibajahui. Curve left, then slow for vados.
36.6	58.6	LOOK-&-LISTEN as you cross Chihuahua-Pacífico railroad that runs thru famous Copper Canyon.
47.6	76.1	Social security clinic at left, and come to Av. Alvaro Obregón, cobblestone side road at left thru El Fuerte. **GAS** at left.
47.8	76.5	Pass side road (right) to El Fuerte's airport and on to railroad station. For info on accommodations see El Fuerte Eat & Stray (page 92)

End of Special N

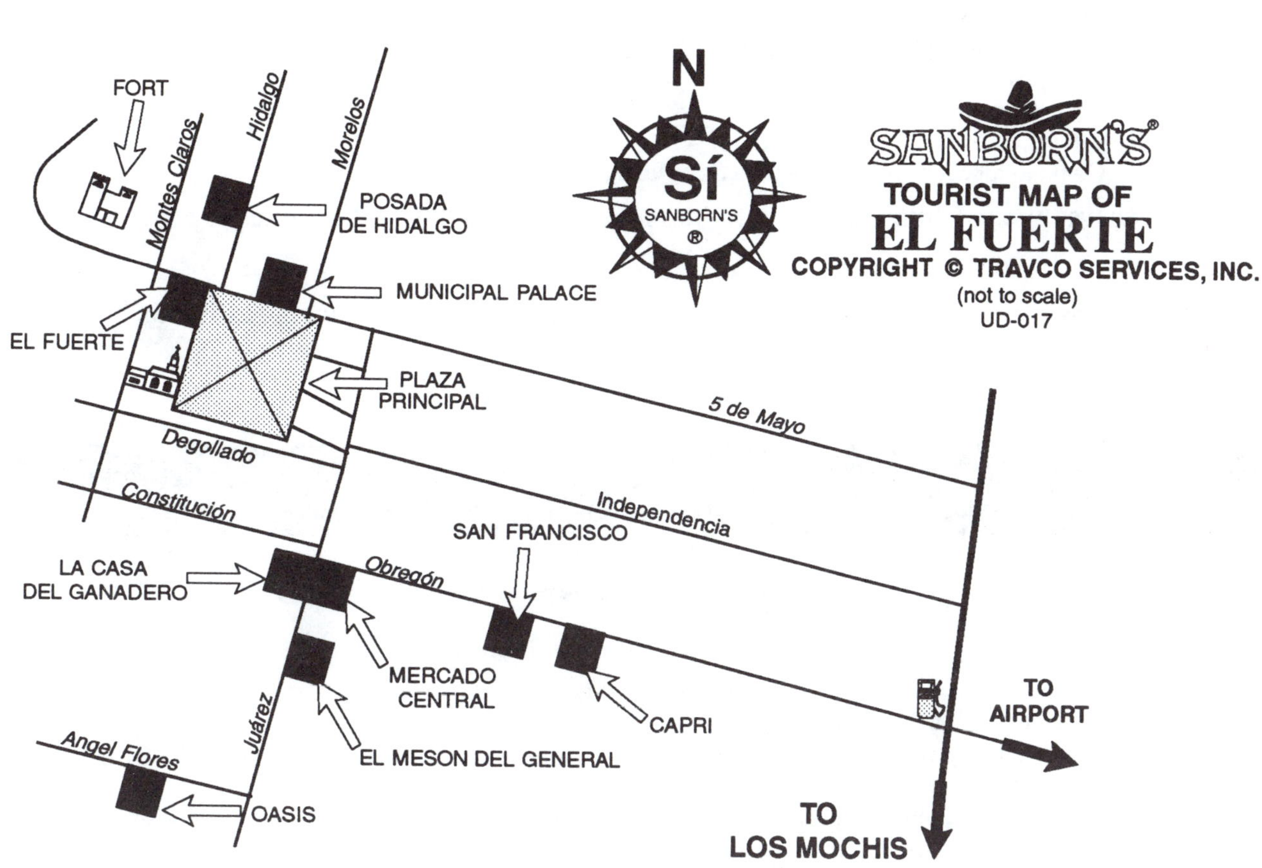

SPECIAL O *START:* Cd. Obregón, Son *END:* Sn Nicolás,

UD-017

100.4 MI or 160.6 KM
DRIVE TIME 2 — 2 1/2 HOURS
SCENIC RATING — 3

This is a great road in good condition with virtually no traffic and no garbage! And almost no crosses signifying accidents. It winds thru beautiful hills with various kinds of cacti, mesquite.

MI	KM	
0.0	0.0	Starting here in Esperanza, just north of Cd. Obregón, at junction with Hwy #15, pass golf course on right, then TURN RIGHT at sign to TESOPACO.
9.0	14.4	Pass sign to El Coyote to right.
10.0	16.0	Enter town of Los Hornos. Slow for topes. Base ball field on right.
11.0	17.6	Turn right at intersection at sign to TESOPACO.
12.5	20.0	Curve to right over bridge (dam).
21.3	34.1	Curve left.
33.3	53.3	Sharp curve right, then left and over Arroyo Santana.
35.0	56.0	Wide curve left then, right.
39.7	63.5	Curve left.
44.5	71.2	Passing thru hills into a pretty view of mountains.
47.2	75.5	Topes. Entering Rosario de Tesopaco. Colegio Juárez at left. **GAS** on left. Come to intersection. Turn left, following sign to Yécora, San Nicolás. Topes.
54.9	87.8	Pass side trail (right) to Paredones.
60.0	96.0	Start climbing.
61.5	98.4	Beautiful view to right, like a natural park. Begin descent.
64.3	102.9	Fabulous large painting on cliff and shrine, left.
69.6	111.4	Pass side road (left) to Nurí.
70.0	112.0	At left you see large white church in Nurí with stone "thumb" on top of mountain behind it.
76.2	121.9	Thru town of El Palmarito.
85.3	136.5	Thru town of Curea.
96.4	154.2	Cut thru red rock.
100.4	160.6	Come to junction with Hwy #16 at San Nicolás.

IF TO: Yécora, Creel, Chihuahua, turn right and join Hermosillo — La Junta Log (page 51) at mile 140.0.

IF TO: Hermosillo, turn left and join La Junta — Hermosillo Log (not included in this book) at mile 195.0.

End of Special O

SPECIAL P *START:* Hermosillo, Son　　　*END:* Douglas, Az

UD-017

229.5 MI or 367.2 KM
DRIVE TIME 5 — 5 1/2 HOURS
SCENIC RATING — 3

0.0	0.0	Here at junction with Hwy #15, proceed northeast.
1.8	2.9	Pass Restaurant Jardines San Pedro, right. Big Tecate sign. Come to junction. TURN RIGHT. Left is to Santa Ana via Hwy #15 free road.
2.4	3.8	Pass cemetery, left. Then curve right and over bumpy railroad crossing (Nogales — Guaymas line). **GAS** at left. Then thru San Pedro and down thru "vado" over Río San Miguel.
3.0	4.8	Curve to left. Note fruit stands at left.

MI	KM	
4.5	7.2	Thru little village of San Miguel de Horcasita.
15.3	24.5	Pass San Francisco del Batuc at right.
19.8	31.7	Pass village of Topahue with its technological and agricultural school at right.
22.3	35.7	Pass settlement of San José at right.
27.5	44.0	Note ruins at right. Then El Gavilán at right, an ideal spot for a picnic with its natural setting. Then cross bridge over Río Gavilán.
34.5	55.2	Pass side road (left) to San Rafael and (right) to Santa Rosalia. Then thru village of Las Lomas. Ice house and **GAS** at left. Then Cemetery at left and thru settlement of El Sauz at left.
39.5	63.2	Enter old town of Ures, founded in 1644 and once the capital of the state of Sonora from 1838-79. Park at left. **GAS**, also at left. Then social security clinic at right. Now curve right and leave Ures. Cemetery at right.
48.0	76.8	Pass village La Puerta del Sol at left. Then curve right and road gradually begins to climb.
51.0	81.6	Río Sonora at left. The mountain you're now traveling on is locally known as *El Monstruo de Plomo* (Lead Monster) and as also nicknamed "The Road of 700 Curves."
61.8	98.9	Thru village of Mazocahui (Indian for "The Hill of the Deer") which began as a ranch during the second half of the 17th century.
62.5	100.0	Slow now and TURN RIGHT. Follow Nacozari and Moctezuma signs. Straight ahead goes up to historical Arizpe (whose Indian name means "The Place of the Brave Ants") and on to copper mining town of Cananea.
68.0	108.8	Curve to left and on up. Then pass side road (right) to Mariscal.
72.0	115.2	Altitude now 3700 feet.
83.3	133.3	Pass side road (left) to Rancho El Calador.
98.5	157.6	Careful now for steep descent and several poorly banked curves.
100.3	160.5	Curve to left and over bridge. Note ancient Indian dwellings high in mesa (plateau) at right.
102.5	164.0	Cross bridge over Río Moctezuma. Now take LEFT FORK (right is to downtown Moctezuma). Skirt edge of Moctezuma, a town of 4,500 inhabitants founded in 1644 by the Jesuit Father Marcos Del Río.

While a sleeping pace seems to hover over the town, Moctezuma is an active agricultural center. It boasts an old plaza, where its early 18th-century church still preserves its original structure and colonial style. The town is also known for its leather industry which produces high-quality handmade embossed saddles. There are several leather shops in town. The best known is *Monturas La Industrial* a block from the Plaza and across from Hotel Martha, where you can see the artisans at work.

103.5	265.0	Merge with side road (right) coming out from Moctezuma and TURN LEFT. **GAS** at right. You are now on Sonora Hwy #12.
114.8	183.7	Thru Vado and then two more just ahead.
117.3	187.7	Pass side road (left) to Jecori.
121.0	193.6	Pass town of Cumpas at left, founded by the Jesuit Father Egido de Montefrío in 1643 as Misión de Nuestra Señora de la Asunción (Mission of Our Lady of the Assumption), There are 2 **GAS** stations in town.
121.8	194.9	Pass side road (right) to Cumpas' airport.
123.0	196.8	Pass village of Ojo de Agua at left. Then cemetery with centuries-old tombstones.
127.8	204.5	Thru El Valle.
130.0	208.0	Thru little village of Los Hoyos (The Holes).
135.3	216.5	Restaurant La Carretera at right.
140.5	224.8	Thru Bella Esperanza (Beautiful Hope) and over bridge. Cinder block factory at right. Slow for dangerous curve to left. Careful for rocks on road. Then into canyon with river at right and mountains to left.
150.3	240.5	Note piles of metal residue. Come to side road (right) to Nacozari de García, where one of Mexico's largest mines, "La Caridad", is located. There are a couple of strictly emergency hotels in town, the Andrade and Nacozari (by the way, "Nacozari" means, "bad prickly pear" in Indian language).

Once named Placeritos de Nacozari, this copper mining town changed its name to Nacozari de García in honor of its hero, Jesús Gracía. On November 7, 1907 at around 2 o'clock in the afternoon, siesta time, a gondola rail car loaded with dry hay caught fire at the railroad station located in the heart of town. The fire spread quickly and ignited two cars loaded with "Hércules" dynamite. Jesús García, a 26-year-old railroad engineer of the Moctezuma Copper Mine, realized the potential disaster and quickly jumped into Engine #501, backed it up, and coupled the two smoldering cars. At full steam he sped toward the outskirts of town and, minutes later, in an area where there were only a few scattered houses, the dynamite exploded, blowing the rail cars to pieces along with García's body. Thirteen people perished in the mishap, but García's heroism saved 5,000 lives. The United States declared him a "Hero of Humanity" and posthumously awarded him with the "American Royal Cross of Honor."

In the town plaza there is a replica of the famous Engine #501, immortalized in many "corridos" of folk songs.

MI	KM	
151.5	242.4	Merge with road at right from Nacozari. Then sports center for mine workers at right.
153.3	245.3	Slow for dangerous curve to right. There's another one about a mile ahead.
155.3	248.5	Over Agua Prieta-Nacozari main railroad line (LOOK-&-LISTEN).
158.0	252.8	LOOK-&-LISTEN as you cross railroad again.
164.8	263.7	Pass side road (right) to Nacozari's airport, La Caridad, and to Presa ("Dam") La Angostura, 34 miles from here on dirt road. The dam, built on the Río Bavispe, is famous for its catches of black bass, striped bass and catfish.
173.8	278.1	Settlement of La Pera at left. Then over vado and cross railroad once again.
176.5	282.4	Thru village of Turacachi.
180.8	289.3	Thru Esqueda, named after Enrique Esqueda, civil martyr of the revolution. Careful again as you cross railroad and curve right. Railroad station at right and over vado.
186.3	298.1	Curve right and over railroad (LOOK-&-LISTEN). Then curve left.
191.8	206.9	Slow now for vado.
193.3	309.3	Thru little town of Estación Fronteras, where Juan Bautista de Anza was born in 1734 — a soldier and explorer as well as founder of San Francisco, California and later governor of New Mexico Province.
197.3	315.7	Curve left and cross railroad line (LOOK-&-LISTEN). Slow for vado. Then thru Ejido 47.
208.5	333.6	Sharp right curve, railroad crossing (LOOK-&-LISTEN). Then over bridge and curve left.
213.3	341.3	Curve left and down long vado over Río Cabullona. Then thru village of Cabullona. Cross railroad again (LOOK-&-LISTEN). Custom inspection station at left — outbound motorists don't need to stop.
221.0	353.6	Pass side road (left) to Agua Prieta's airport and to lime plant (*planta de cal*).
225.3	360.5	Come now to "T" junction with Hwy #2. TURN RIGHT and ahead. Left is to copper mining town of Cananea and on to Imuris, 46 miles south of Nogales on Hwy #15.
226.0	361.6	Over a pair of bumpy railroad tracks and bridge.
226.8	362.9	SLOW now and TURN LEFT and head into Agua Prieta (population 70,000), which, incidentally, means "dark water." Ahead is to Janos and on to Chihuahua.
227.1	363.4	Pass Red Cross and **GAS** station left. Then ball park and big cemetery beyond on left.
227.3	363.7	Careful for stoplights. Continue straight ahead thru town.
227.5	364.0	Very nice Hotel Hacienda at left on corner (good dining room). Then TURN LEFT & ahead.
228.0	364.8	Come to stop-street. TURN RIGHT and proceed up to Mexican Customs official and turn in your tourist documents and head for U.S. Customs.

REMEMBER: Your vehicle permit is good for multiple entries into Mexico. However you MUST turn it in at the border BEFORE it expires. To turn in your papers, you'll have to park BEFORE you get to the bridge and walk into the customs building, unless there is a small building that says "BANJERCITO" or "HACIENDA"

228.1	365.0	Pull up to U.S. Customs and the officer will ask you questions regarding your nationality, etc. — and will probably ask you to unload your gear onto the table. Then ahead on wide two-way Pan American Street into very nice town of Douglas, Arizona.
229.3	366.9	In front of Cochise vocational college, TURN RIGHT onto Tenth Street past ultramodern city hall on right. Then Phelps-Dodge Mercantile department store on corner at left, which is a far cry from the old-time mining company stores of the past.

IF TO: Desert Inn or El Coronado Motel next door (or to Tombstone or Bisbee), turn left onto this Avenue "G" which is their main stem — motels are at far west end of town (refer to map page 4). Our Sanborn's Agent, Jones Associates Insurance Agency, is located at 533 10th St. Don't hesitate to stop in if you'd like to tell us about your trip.

IF TO: Lordsburg & IH-10, continue ahead.

End of Special P

SPECIAL Q   *START:* Imuris, Son   *END:* Douglas, Az

UD-017

104.0 MI or 166.4 KM
DRIVE TIME 2 — 3 HOURS
SCENIC RATING — 3

Note: If you were planning to head eastward (or northeastward) after you got to the border, like to New Mexico, Colorado, El Paso, etc., you'll find this Hwy #2 to Douglas, Arizona, quite a time-and-mileage saver with some mountainous winding and light traffic. It has some uphill and down hill mountainous winding, bur light traffic. It goes past the famous Mexican copper town of Cananea.

MI	KM	
0.0	0.0	In Imuris, at the top of the hill, take the right fork at the (#2) CANANEA sign.
2.0	3.2	Curve left and start easy winding stretch.
4.5	7.2	Down thru cut. Elevation 2,200 ft.
5.5	8.8	Pass side trail (left) to Rancho San Martin. Then start winding up thru mountains.
11.1	17.8	Top (4,400 feet). Now wind down.

REMEMBER: On downhill stretches, brake with your motor — not your brakes. A burning smell means you've used your brakes too much. If you can, pull over & let 'em cool for ten minutes or so.

24.0	38.4	Note newer church up at left next to ruins of old mission built by the great Padre Kino.
28.0	44.8	Pass village of San Antonio, then over bigger bridge and pass side road left to Santa Cruz up near Arizona border.
28.4	45.4	Pass customs inspection station for southbound traffic — Don't stop.
34.8	55.7	Cross bridge over Río Cuitaca and thru scattered village of Vicente Guerrero.
43.1	69.0	Top — 6,036 feet (or 1840 meters above sea level). Then down.
47.0	75.2	There's the Cananea copper mine over to right.
48.3	77.3	Pass road to the mine (no tours). Good view of the valley from here.
50.5	80.8	Sharp curve right at top and over railroad (LOOK-&-LISTEN). Pass OK **GAS** at left. Then take left fork — right fork would take you into Cananea. Volkswagen agency at left. Note monument at right in memory of the strikers killed in 1906 during a labor dispute.

If you have the time and wish to drive into Cananea, this is a nice little town with really nice folks. You can visit old jail, now a museum and just soak up the atmosphere. Take right fork above. Motel Zafari (into town 1 mile on left) —MOD— 36 A/C rooms, SATV. PH: (633) 2-1308, 2-1528, 2-1108 Fax: 2-3739.

51.5	82.4	Pass side road (right) down to old town of Arizpe. Past Motel Valle de Cobre —MOD— 38 rooms, CATV, pool, PH: (633) 2-2086 Fax: 2-3808. Also Motel and Restaurant Mesón, looks good, near Chrysler/Dodge dealership on left. Then some nice straight stretches.
63.3	101.3	Pass customs check (closed) at left. Then settlement of Ignacio Zaragoza to left.
67.1	107.4	Over pass (elevation 5,200 ft.). Then down hill on straight stretch.
73.3	117.3	Pass immigration check station at left (also not for you).
73.8	118.1	Pass Ejido Cuauhtémoc.

Cuauhtémoc (1502-1525) was the 11th & last Aztec Emperor. The son of Emperor Ahuizotl & princess Tilalcaptl, he was educated in the Calmecac school for nobles. Cortés made him a prisoner on Aug. 13, 1521 & had him killed by hanging him by his feet like a common criminal, on Feb. 28, 1525. He was 23. He was betrayed by Malinche, who acted as interpreter. To this day, a "Malinche" is a woman who cannot be trusted — that's the polite version.

76.5	122.4	Pass side road (left) that runs up to Naco, which is the Mexican border town opposite the American border town of Naco, approximately 12 miles from Bisbee.

If you would like to go to Bisbee and visit the Lavender Queen Pit Mine and on to famed old Wild West town of Tombstone, hop to it as the road is good blacktop all the way. The bed & breakfast Inn At Castle Rock in Bisbee is a "center for expanding consciousness", with *mucho* appeal for those on a journey of discovery. A new age, 60's kind of place.

91.3	146.1	There's Douglas and Agua Prieta ahead. The twin smoke stacks are at the big Phelps-Dodge copper smelter, which is the number one industry in these parts.

MI   KM

100.3	160.5	Pass junction right down to another copper town of Nacozari, 95 miles. This nice road (Sonora Hwy #12) takes you thru Nacozari, and Ures to Hermosillo where it connects with Hwy #15.
101.0	161.6	Over a pair of bumpy railroad tracks and bridge.
101.8	162.9	SLOW now and TURN LEFT and head into Agua Prieta (population 70,000), which, incidentally, means "dark water." Ahead is to Janos and on to Chihuahua.
102.1	163.4	Pass Red Cross and **GAS**, left Then ball park at left and big cemetery beyond, also on left.
102.5	164.0	Very nice Hotel Hacienda at left on corner (good dining room). Then TURN LEFT & ahead.
103.0	164.8	Come to stop-street. TURN RIGHT and proceed up to Mexican Customs official and turn in your tourist documents and head for U.S. Customs.

REMEMBER: Your vehicle permit is good for multiple entries into Mexico. However you MUST turn it in at the border BEFORE it expires. To turn in your papers, you'll have to park BEFORE you get to the bridge and walk into the customs building, unless there is a small building that says "BANJERCITO" or "HACIENDA."

103.1	165.0	Pull up to U.S. Customs and the officer will ask you questions regarding your nationality, etc. — and will probably ask you to unload your gear onto the table. Then ahead on wide two-way Pan American Street into very nice town of Douglas, Arizona.
104.3	166.9	In front of Cochise vocational college, TURN RIGHT onto Tenth Street past ultramodern city hall on right. Then Phelps-Dodge Mercantile department store on corner at left, which is a far cry from the old-time mining company stores of the past.

IF TO: Desert Inn or El Coronado Motel next door (or to Tombstone or Bisbee), turn left onto this Avenue "G" which is their main stem — motels are at far west end of town (refer to map).

Our Sanborn's Agent, Jones Associates Insurance Agency, is located at 533 10th St. Don't hesitate to stop in if you'd like to tell us about your trip.

Folks, it's been a real pleasure to get you to Mexico and back, all in one piece, and we hope you've had a marvelous time. Please come see us again next time you go South of the Border, Down Mexico Way. We'd like to hear from you about your trip — use the "Comments" sheet at the end of the log book. And do drive carefully the rest of the way home.

IF TO: Lordsburg & IH-10, continue ahead.

End of Special Q

SPECIAL R	START: Jct. Hwy #15	END: San Blas, Nay

UD-017

22.6 MILES or 36.2 KM
DRIVE TIME 30 MINUTES.
SCENIC RATING — 3

This special log will take you from Hwy #15 down to the ancient tropical Pacific port of San Blas, the starting point of the colonization expeditions of Coronado (military) and Padre Kino (religious — to Arizona) and Fray Junipero Serra (religious — to California). The road is good blacktop and you'll wind thru some beautiful tropical palm country. At the log's end the little old town is interesting, the beach is rather nice, and accommodations adequate. Don't hesitate to run down as you can see everything with time for a soft drink or lunch and still be back here at the junction in about 3.5 hours, or you might decide to stay the night or even longer — if you enjoy the peaceful atmosphere.

0.0	0.0	Having turned off Hwy #15 at San Blas junction, proceed west on blacktop Hwy #11. **GAS**, right. Then wind down easy-like.
2.5	4.0	Down and left thru Ejido Cinco de Mayo and over little Río Ciruelo (plum) and left and up and wind up steep mountain ahead.
6.0	9.6	Thru village of Navarrete. Then pass side road (right) to Sauta and La Presa (dam). And over little Río Navarrete and up and down on straight stretch. Careful for 4 sets of "topes" thru here.

MI	KM	
8.0	12.8	Pass side road right to Huaristemba.
8.3	13.3	Avocado and mango nursery at left. Then left thru El Palillo (the toothpick or little shack) and careful and down over low bridge over Río Palillo. Then left and up and wind.
10.7	17.1	Left and up on straight stretch. Village of Las Palmas at left. Maguey field at right.
11.6	18.6	Thru village of Guadalupe. Fields of papaya and mangos in this area.
13.0	20.8	Pass side road (left) to La Libertad. Then a short mile later, wind down.
16.0	25.6	Now wind down thru tropical forest of royal palms. Watch for cattle in road thru here.
17.5	28.0	Down and over little bridge and thru Singayta. Then more palms and jungles.
19.6	31.4	Come to shortcut to Puerto Vallarta. Now paved. Sign says: "Santa Cruz, Los Cocos, Matanchén" Matanchén Beach (2 miles), Playa Amor RV Park (8.8 miles, look for "papelia" tree at entrance, on right), Casa Mañana (9.7 miles), Sta. Cruz, Aticama, turn left here. Then bend left and thru marshes.
22.3	35.7	Cross bridge over Estuary El Conchal. This is embarkation point for long jungle boat trips. Careful for "topes" and ahead on divided for spell. Note old fort atop hill at left. Before you attempt to drive it, be aware it's a long, hard climb. Then up a little and into historic old San Blas.
22.3	35.6	Under welcome arch and ahead down main street (Juárez) with gas, left, town's only gas station. Street now becomes one-way. **GAS** available at dock next to ice house in port.
22.6	36.2	Come to main plaza, at right, and end of log. For info on accommodations see San Blas Eat & Stray (page 106).

IF TO: Suites San Blas, Posada Casa Morales, Los Cocos RV Park, and El Dorado Motel, turn left at end of plaza and follow map. Los Flamingos Hotel, Restaurant Torino's, etc., straight ahead.

End of Special R

SPECIAL S   *START:* Tepic, Nay   *END:* San Blas, Nay

UD-017

39.0 MI or 62.4 KM
DRIVE TIME 1 HOUR
SCENIC RATING – 3

Thanks to Bill & Joyce Holmberg of Aztec Custom RV Tours for logging this highway.

0.0	0.0	Starting here at Junction Hwy #15 at Miramar exit, proceed ahead due west. Go west, young man, go west!
1.1	1.8	El Ahuacate. Road winds somewhat. Altitude 3,200 feet.
2.6	4.2	Thru El Izote with topes. Note flower garden to right.
3.0	4.8	Thru Platanitos. Watch for school crossing.
5.0	8.0	Thru V. Carranza and more topes
7.3	11.7	Thru La Libertad.
9.5	15.2	Spectacular view to right.
10.1	16.2	Thru La Yerba. Topes with no signs, but easy to find.
11.8	18.9	Beautiful view of Pacific. All sorts of tropical fruits growing along the road.
14.9	23.8	Watch for brown horse in middle of the road.
15.4	24.6	Thru Jalcolotán with a long rather rough main drag – a busy place.
15.7	25.1	Sharp dip at intersection.
15.9	25.4	Plaza on right. Then topes.
16.2	25.9	Bend right. Watch for more topes. Then curve left and right and out of town.
21.8	34.9	Thru Tecuitata. Kind of wind through town. Watch for school crossings.
26.4	42.2	Road straightens out and heads for the coast.
27.1	43.4	Come to Hwy junction. Sign says San Blas, Los Cocos, Matanchén. TURN RIGHT. Straight is to Santa Cruz. Left is to Las Varas. Follow along coast. Note coconut palms and jungle foliage.
28.8	46.1	Careful for a couple of sharp curves.
29.1	46.6	Now you are next to water.
29.3	46.9	Motel Casa Mañana at right is real clean, and is owned by an Austrian couple. Opened in '93. 14 rooms. Small pool. No A/C.
29.7	47.5	Tire shop on right

MI	KM	
30.3	48.5	Playa Amor Trailer Park.
30.9	49.4	Thru Atacama with many little seafood restaurants on left that serve fine oyster & shrimp cocktails.
31.3	50.1	Leave town. Turn left.
32.0	51.2	Pass Rincón de Matanchén restaurant on left, then Oceanographic school on right.
35.3	56.5	Slow for big green iguana crossing road.
35.7	57.1	Gentle curve to left.
36.4	42.2	Leaving beach and curve left again.
36.8	58.9	Coming up on Matanchén and topes
36.9	59.0	Hard right and more topes.
37.1	59.4	Jungle boat docks on right.
39.0	62.4	Come to "T" intersection.

IF TO: San Blas, turn left and join San Blas Special at mile 20.5.

End of Special S

SPECIAL T   *START:* **Las Varas, Nay**   *END:* **Santa Cruz, Nay**

UD-017

25.4 MI or 40.6 KM
DRIVE TIME 1/2 HOUR
SCENIC RATING – 3

Thanks to Bill & Joyce Holmberg of Aztec Custom RV Tours for logging this highway.

MI	KM	
0.0	0.0	Turn left to Zaqualpan, one block north of Pemex in town of Las Varas. Follow divided street through town.
0.3	0.5	Pass school and divided ends. Take leave of Las Varas.
1.1	1.8	Sign advises to watch for livestock, also remember this is a farming area with lots of machinery on the road.
3.0	5.0	Narrow bridge without railings and a sharp right turn.
4.8	7.7	Bend left and enter town of Zaqualpan with topes.
5.1	8.2	Street divides but still has topes. Pemex on right, Nova and Diesel only. Then cobblestone starts. It's fairly rough so take it easy. After one block of cobblestone, turn left past plaza and continue straight on cobbles.
5.7	9.1	Cobblestones end. Go down hill, bend right across a narrow bridge and leave Zaqualpan.
7.0	11.2	Thru community of San Ysidro. Bend right and watch for topes.
7.6	12.2	Sharp left curve.
9.4	15.0	Curve right to San Blas at Ixtapa/San Blas sign.
10.0	16.0	Over Puente Las Jazmines, long right curved bridge and road winds for a bit.
11.4	18.2	Over Puente Arenoso, rather high crowned.
13.6	21.8	Over bridge with no name, also high crowned.
14.6	23.4	Watch for white horse in middle of road. Remember this is open range.
16.2	25.9	School zone and pretty village, Platanitos, to left and a great view of the Pacific Ocean.
18.0	28.8	Twin bridges and curve to left.
19.4	31.0	Top of summit with beautiful view of banana plantations, ocean, shrimp boats, palm trees, and mountains – a real tropical paradise.
20.3	32.5	Over no name bridge, somewhat rough.
21.4	34.2	Over Río Jolotemba bridge, the last one completed on this road.
23.1	37.0	Top another hill about 450 feet altitude and behold another spectacular view.
24.2	38.7	Bottom and sharp left curve then right curve and enter town of El Llano with 6 decorated BIG topes.
25.4	40.6	Cross Río El Llano and come to junction with Tepic, Santa Cruz highway.

IF TO: Tepic, turn right

IF TO: San Blas, turn Left toward Santa Cruz. Then turn right at intersection with sign to Los Cocos, Matanchen, San Blas. Ahead is Playa Amor Trailer Park on left. Join Tepic - San Blas Special at mile 27.1

End of SPECIAL T

SPECIAL U: *START:* Santa Cruz, Nay *END:* Las Varas, Nay

26.0 MI or 41.6 KM
DRIVE TIME 1/2 HOUR
SCENIC RATING –3

Thanks to Bill & Joyce Holmberg of Aztec Custom RV Tours for logging this highway.

MI	KM	
0.0	0.0	Start at corner of Tepic, Santa Cruz and Los Cocos, Matanchen road toward Tepic.
0.4	0.6	Come to intersection at right. Turn right to El Llano, Platanitos. Straight is to Santa Cruz.
0.7	1.1	Enter little town of El Llano with at least 6 big topes. After El Llano start winding through very pretty banana plantations. Uphill a little.
3.7	5.9	Top hill. Now start winding down.
4.2	6.7	Cross bridge over Río Jolotemba.
5.3	8.5	Over another bridge with no name.
6.3	10.2	Great view of the Pacific to right just before topping this little hill.
8.0	12.8	No name twin bridges.
8.2	13.1	Sharp left right curve right after twin bridges.
10.0	16.0	Leaving coast, heading inland through some mangrove swamps.
11.5	18.4	Tobacco fields onright.
14.5	23.2	Over Puente Arenoso with high crown.
16.0	25.6	Over Puente Jazmines a curved bridge with pretty view Then thru community of Ixtapa de la Concepción with repair shops and then bend left at junction and watch for traffic from right.
18.5	29.6	Pass village of San Ysidro.
18.7	29.9	Topes and pedestrian crossing.
19.0	30.4	Leave San Ysidro, bend left and cross a rather narrow bridge.
20.2	32.3	Curve left and enter Zaqualpan. Cross bridge and up into town. Cobblestones begin with topes too. Pass main square on left. It's very pretty with roses and Norfolk Island pines.
20.6	33.0	At end of plaza turn right, cobblestone for a block, then pavement starts and more topes.
20.9	33.4	Pemex on left – no Magna.
21.1	33.8	Bull ring on left.
22.8	36.5	Sharp left turn and cross narrow bridge.
23.4	37.4	Watch for big green combines on road. Seriously – lots of farming here with machinery on roads.
25.6	41.0	Entering outskirts of Las Varas. Pass bullring on right and street divides with topes.
26.0	41.6	Come to junction with highway #200.

IF TO: Tepic, turn left and join Pto. Vallarta - Tepic Log at mile 60.5 (page 131)

IF TO: Puerto Vallarta, turn right and join Tepic - Pto Vallarta Log at mile 41.8 (page 34). There's **GAS** one block to right.

End of Special U

SPECIAL V *START:* Compostela, Nay *End:* Chapalilla, Nay

UD-126

113.0 MI or 180.0 KM
DRIVING TIME: 2 HOURS
SCENIC RATING — 2

This log takes you on the toll road between Pto. Vallarta and Guadalajara that begins at the Compostela junction on the road between PV and Tepic.

MI	KM	
0.0	0.0	Turn right at Guadalajara Cuota Sign. Town of Compostela is off to left. Sign says, Guadalajara 213 km.
1.0	1.6	Pass an exit right to Mazatlán and Compostela. Ahead for you.
2.2	3.5	Come to toll house and pay toll (Cars $14, extra axle, $7). Then ahead on nice 2-lane road.
5.0	8.0	Slow for series of curves.
6.2	9.9	Pass exit (right) to Milpillas and continue winding.
10.0	16.0	Lo and behold a few lonely pine trees, but mostly cattle and corn.
11.0	17.6	Pass side road (left) to San Pedro Lagunillas. Then nice straight stretch. Note lake over to left.
14.0	22.4	Another side road (left) to San Pedro Lagunillas. Careful for slow-moving farm traffic.
16.0	25.6	Careful for sharp curves. A scenic photo pull-off. Then a sharp descent — brake with engine.
18.0	28.0	Community of Las Guásimas at right.
19.0	30.4	Striking view of green valley down to left.
21.0	33.6	Come to junction with Hwy #15. Tepic, straight. Guadalajara, veer right.

IF TO: Tepic, continue straight and join Guadalajara - Tepic Log at mile 97 (page 127).

IF TO: Guadalajara, veer right and join toll stub log of the Tepic - Guadalajara Log (page 37).

End Special V

SPECIAL W *START:* Chapalilla, Nay *END:* Compostela, Nay

UD-126

21.5 MI OR 34.0 KM
DRIVE TIME 1/2 HOUR
SCENIC RATING – 2

This is a toll shortcut highway for motorist traveling between Guadalajara and Puerto Vallarta or Rincón de Guayabitos, saving 35 miles over former route by way of Tepic. Don't hesitate to take this route – unless there's a reason why you prefer to go via Tepic, like maybe it's growing dark and you need a place to stay for the night. It's 97 miles from here to Puerto Vallarta, which we folks in the know refer to as "PV."

MI	KM	
0.0	0.0	Having turned left onto toll road proceed ahead on nice divided.
3.0	4.8	Pass exit (right) to Las Guásimas
8.0	12.8	Wind up past pretty Lake Lagunillas at right.
10.0	16.0	Bend left past exit right to San Pedro de las Lagunillas and under overpass.
15.0	24.0	Pass side road (left) to Milpillas.
18.5	29.6	Up over bridge over main line of Mexicali-Nogales-Guadalajara railroad line.
19.0	30.4	Slow as you come to toll house. Pay Toll.
20.0	32.0	**GAS**, at left. Also neat hole-in-the-wall restaurant. Take left after **GAS**, go 1/4 mile toward town. Just before pavement ends is white iron-fenced hacienda on right. "El Rincón del Montero" is there. Sign says "Mariscos." It's plain and for the adventurous. Inexpensive too.
21.5	34.4	Come now to junction with Hwy #200.

IF TO: Puerto Vallarta, turn left and join Tepic – Puerto Vallarta Log at mile 21.8 (page 34).

IF TO: Tepic, turn right and join Puerto Vallarta – Tepic Log at mile 81.5 (page 131).

End of Special W

SPECIAL X   *START:* Douglas, Az   *END:* Hermosillo, Son

229.3 MI or 366.9 KM
DRIVE TIME 5 TO 5 1/2 HOURS
SCENIC RATING— 3

The most interesting place to stay in Douglas is the historic old Hotel Gadsden with best restaurant in town. Motels are the Motel 6 and the Travelodge. If you wish to overnight in Agua Prieta and get an early start, there's the Hacienda Motor Inn. There are 2 RV parks. An hour away is Bisbee, AZ, an old mining town. The bed & breakfast Inn At Castle Rock is a "center for expanding consciousness," with mucho appeal for those on a journey of discovery. A New Age, 60's kind of place.

This highway is only a mile longer than the Douglas-Cananea-Imuris-Hermosillo route, but is much more scenic. Mostly desert and foothill country, there are a couple of winding stretches crossing the Sierras - 37 miles between Moctezuma and Mazocahui and 20 miles between Mazocahui and Ures which climbs over a mountain known as El Monstruo de Plomo (Lead Monster).

MI	KM	
0.0	0.0	Leave Jones Associates Insurance Agency (Sanborn's rep) on 10th street between "G" and "F" Ave. in Douglas, Arizona, heading West on 10th St. (Hwy #80).
0.1	0.2	Straight at light. Pass city hall at left.
0.3	4.5	After two long blocks, come to dead end. Cochise vocational college ahead. Turn **LEFT** onto wide two-way Pan American Ave. Ahead for about three-quarters of a mile.
1.0	1.6	Wave goodbye to U.S. Customs on your left (don't stop). Cross border (there's no river to cross here) on one-way bridge - you're now in Mexico.

Take far right slot and pull up to Mexican official and tell him you're going to Guadalajara or Guaymas or Kino or wherever you're going. He'll tell you to park diagonally just ahead at right. Then go into Mexican government building at right and head for the counter at MIGRACION (immigration) on right side of building where your tourist cards will be written (or those that you have will be validated). Then cut across the big room to ADUANA "BANJERCITO" where you'll get your car permit. They will put a decal on your windshield and you're free to be on your way.

Now back out of the diagonal parking spot and careful for incoming traffic. Then head straight down their main street. **GAS**, left on corner. You're now in Agua Prieta, Spanish for "dark water."

1.1	1.8	Slow for dip ("vado") and cross 3rd St. Straight ahead. Then **GAS** at left.
1.3	2.1	STRAIGHT 3 blocks. There'll be a fence on your left. STOP SIGN & church on left. Turn **LEFT** onto Sixth Street. Ahead and past plaza at left.
1.5	2.4	Straight for 2 BLOCKS. Stoplight. Turn **RIGHT** onto Sixth Avenue and straight on down.
2.0	3.2	Cemetery at right. Industrial park at left. Then ball park at right. Then **GAS**. Then Hotel Las Palmas.
2.8	4.5	Come now to junction Hwy 2 and turn right here for Cananea, Imuris, Nacozari, and Hermosillo. (Left here takes you to Janos and on to Chihuahua.)
3.5	5.6	CAREFUL! There are sometimes policemen here making sure you stop at ALTO sign. As we mention in our cover, you should always be careful at railroad tracks & watch the guy behind you, as not all people stop at them. Here, plan on stopping. Over two railroad tracks - line runs to Nacozari, another copper town.
4.3	6.9	Come now to junction with Sonora Hwy #12 and TURN LEFT to Hermosillo (thru Nacozari and Moctezuma). Straight ahead is to Cananea and on to Imuris, 46 miles south of Nogales on Hwy 15. Sign says "118 kilometers to Nacozari" or 73 miles.
7.5	12.5	Easy now for "vado" or dip.
9.0	14.4	Pass side road (right) to Agua Prieta's airport and to lime plant ("planta de cal").
16.3	26.1	Slow now and STOP for customs inspection. Then thru village of Cabullona and cross Agua Prieta-Nacozari railroad line (LOOK-&-LISTEN). Down long "vado" over Río Cabullona.
21.3	34.1	Slow for "curva peligrosa" (dangerous curve) to right. Then over bridge and cross railroad line again (LOOK-&-LISTEN). Curve to left.
32.5	52.0	Thru Ejido 47. Slow for "vado" and cross railroad line one more time (LOOK-&-LISTEN). Bend to right and out.

MI	KM	
36.0	57.6	Thru town of Estación Fronteras where Juan Bautista de Anza was born in 1734, a soldier; explorer; founder of San Francisco, California; later governor of New Mexico Province.
38.0	60.8	Slow for "vado."
42.5	68.0	Ejido Adolfo Ruiz Cortines at right, named after an ex-presidente (1952-1958).
43.5	69.6	Curve to right and over railroad (LOOK-&-LISTEN). Then curve left.
48.5	77.6	Thru Esqueda. Railroad station at left. Incidentally, this town was named after Enrique Esqueda, a civil martyr of the revolution. Curve left and over railroad (LOOK- &-LISTEN) and curve right and out.
53.5	85.6	Thru village of Turicachi.
55.0	88.0	Slow for right curve and then for a left, and another railroad crossing in-between (LOOK-&-LISTEN). Then over "vado." Settlement of La Pera at right. Río Nacozari at left.
57.8	92.5	Rancho El Vigia at right.
65.3	104.5	Pass side road (left) to Nacozari's airport of La Caridad and to Presa ("Dam") La Angostura, 34 miles from here. The dam, famous for its good catches of black bass, striped bass, and catfish, is built on Río Bavispe.
71.8	114.9	Slow for railroad crossing (LOOK-&-LISTEN).
74.0	118.4	Slow now for sharp curves ahead. . Then LOOK-&-LISTEN as you cross railroad again.
76.3	122.1	Thru rock cut and down.
78.3	125.3	Cemetery at left. Then thru long rock cut. Skirt edge of Nacozari de García, where one of Mexico's biggest copper mines, La Caridad, is located. Note mine workers' houses up at right. Pass side road (left) to Nacozari proper. There are a couple of strictly emergency hotels in town, the Andrade and the Nacozari. (Nacozari, by the way, means "bad prickly pear" in Indian language.) **GAS** in town.

Once named PLACERITOS DE NACOZARI, this copper mining town changed its name to NACOZARI DE GARCIA in honor of its hero, Jesus García. On November 7, 1907 at around 2 o'clock in the afternoon, siesta time, a gondola car loaded with dried hay caught fire at the railroad station located in the heart of town. The fire spread quickly and ignited two cars loaded with Hercules dynamite.

Jesús García, a 26-year old railroad engineer of the Moctezuma Copper Company, realized the potential disaster and quickly jumped in Engine 501, backed it up, and coupled the two cars. At full steam he sped away from town and a few minutes later in the outskirts of town where there were only a few scattered houses, the dynamite exploded, blowing the railroad cars to pieces along with García's body. Thirteen people perished in the mishap but García's heroism saved 5000 lives. The United States declared him a Hero of Humanity and posthumously awarded him the American Royal Cross of Honor. In the town's square there is a replica of famous Engine 501, immortalized in many corridos or folk songs.

79.5	127.2	Merge at left with road from Nacozari.
80.0	128.0	Note piles of metal residue. Río Nacozari at left.
88.3	141.3	Slow now for **dangerous right curve.** Then cinder block factory at left and over bridge. Thru village of Bella Esperanza.
94.8	151.7	Restaurant La Carretera at left.
96.8	154.9	Rancho La Noria at left.
99.3	158.9	Thru little village of Los Hoyos ("The Holes").
102.0	163.2	Thru El Valle.
106.3	170.1	Cemetery at right with centuries-old tombstones. Village of Ojo de Agua, also at right. Then thru rock cut.
108.5	173.6	Pass side road (left) to Cumpas airport.
109.3	174.9	Town of Cumpas at right, founded by Jesuit Father Egidio de Montefrío in 1643 as Misión de Nuestra Señora de la Asunción ("Mission of Our Lady of the Assumption"). There are 2 **GAS** stations in town.
112.5	180.0	Bend left and over vado and pass side road (right) to Jecori.
119.8	181.7	Thru left cut.
125.8	201.3	Slow now and **TURN RIGHT.** Straight ahead is to Moctezuma proper, and to **GAS.** Skirt edge of Moctezuma, founded in 1644 by the Jesuit Father Marcos del Río.

MOCTEZUMA is an active agricultural center. It boasts an old plaza, where its large 18th-century church still preserves its original colonial-style structure. The town is also renown for its leather industry which produces high-quality hand-made embossed saddles. There are several leather shops in town - and you can visit Monturas La Industrial and see the artisans at work, a block from the square and across from Hotel Martha.

126.3	202.1	Merge with side road (left) coming from Moctezuma, and out. Over Río Moctezuma.
128.3	205.3	Note ancient Indian dwellings at left high in mesa.

MI	KM	
129.8	207.7	Over another bridge and up.
135.5	216.8	You are now 3578 feet above sea level. **Careful for sharp curves ahead.**
140.0	224.0	Cafe Chuyen at left, a whistle truck stop.
147.0	235.2	Pass side road to Rancho El Calador, a little over a mile off to right.
151.0	241.6	Over bridge with Rancho El Rodeo at left.
158.5	253.6	Altitude now 3700 feet.
162.0	259.2	Pass side road (left) to Mariscal.
167.5	268.0	Come to "T" and TURN LEFT. Right takes you to historical Arizpe (which means "The Place of the Brave Ants" in Indian language) and to copper town of Cananea. Then thru village of Mazocahui (Indian for "The Hill of the Deer") which started as a ranch in the second half of the 17th century. There's **GAS** in village. That's Río Sonora at right whose bed was once the old road between here and Ures.
170.5	272.8	Over bridge La Junta and up, climbing a mountain locally known as "El Monstruo De Plomo" ("Lead Monster") or "Road of 700 Curves."
182.0	291.2	Village of La Puerta del Sol at right.
187.8	300.5	Thru San Pedro.
189.0	302.4	Cemetery at left. Then curve left and enter old town of Ures. Ures, founded in 1644, was once the capital of the state of Sonora from 1838-1879. Pass social security clinic at left. Then **GAS**, right. Pass park at right and take leave of Ures.
194.5	311.2	Little village of Las Lomas. **GAS** at right. Ice house at right. Pass side road (right) to San Rafael and (left) to Santa Rosalía.
202.1	323.4	Bridge over Río Gavilán. Then El Gavilán at left.
208.0	332.8	Settlement of San José at left.
210.8	337.3	Village of Topahue with its technological and agricultural school at left.
214.8	343.7	Pass San Francisco del Batuc at left.
225.5	360.8	Thru little village of San Miguel de Horcasita. Outside village note fruit stands.
227.0	363.2	Curve right and cross "vado" of Río San Miguel. Thru San Pedro with **GAS**, right. Then over railroad crossing (Nogales-Guaymas line).
229.3	366.9	Pass military university up at left, sort of a West Point. Come to junction Hwy #15.

IF TO: Hermosillo, TURN LEFT to Hermosillo and join Santa Ana — Hermosillo Log at mile 100.0 (page 9).

IF TO: Santa Ana, Nogales, and Mexicali turn right and join Hermosillo — Santa Ana Log at mile 7.2 (page 147).

End of Special X

Hermosillo

UD-017

Area Code — 62

HERMOSILLO is a nice town, its founding dating back to the beginning of the 18th century. Today it is the capital of the rich state of Sonora and has an official population of 500,000. It is a principal agricultural and industrial center as well as home of the University of Sonora.

The city offers many fine museums including the beautiful new *"Costumbrista"* (see map for location), converted from the old prison. *Cerro de la Campana* (Hill of the Bell) is also nearby. Of interest downtown is the cathedral and government palace (and mural in central patio) and their beautiful gardens, the plaza and its pretty kiosk, and many old picturesque mansions. Don't hesitate to stroll through downtown and along the town's boulevards shaded by huge Yucateco (Indian Laurels). These trees become the roosting place for literally thousands of birds at dusk. Quite a sight!

SLEEPING AROUND HERMOSILLO

ARAIZA INN — MOD — Blvd. Eusebio Kino #353 — 163 rooms with A/C. Restaurant. Snack bar. Pool. Tubs. Jacuzzi (control for Jacuzzi cool water is a front desk). Tennis. Golf. AE. **SAC.** Ph: 10-4541. Fax: 10-2717.

BUGAMBILIA HERMOSILLO — MOD — Blvd. E. Kino #712 — Good 108-unit A/C motel on north Hwy #15. Restaurant. Pool. Parking. AE, MC, VI. Ph: 14-5050. Fax: 14-5252. Mex: 91-800-62333.

CALINDA HERMOSILLO QUALITY INN — MOD — Av. Rosales #86 & Morelia — Highrise 12-story, 110-room A/C hotel in midtown just north of San Alberto. Rooftop gourmet restaurant. Coffee shop. Disco. Bar. Pool. Shops. Parking. AE, MC, VI. **SAC.** Ph: 17-2396. Fax: 17-2424.

EL ENCANTO — MOD — North Hwy #15 — 39-unit A/C motel. No restaurant. Pool. Parking. MC, VI. Ph: 14-4730.

FIESTA AMERICANA — UPPER — Blvd. E. Kino #389 — Highrise 225-room A/C motel at north end of town on Hwy #15 just south of Kino Circle. Restaurants. Bar. Disco. Pool. Shops. Parking. AE, MC, VI. Ph: 59-6000, 59-6011. Fax: 59-6060.

GÁNDARA — MOD — Blvd. Kino #1000 — 150-room A/C motor hotel on north Hwy #15. Restaurant. Coffee shop. Bar. Pool. Parking. AE, MC, VI. Ph: 14-4414, 14-4623. Fax: 14-4241. Mex: 91-800-62-344

HOLIDAY INN HERMOSILLO — UPPER — Blvd. Kino & Ramón Corral. Restaurant & Cafeteria. Lobby bar. Pool. AE, MC, VI. Ph: 14-4570 Fax: 14-6473. US: 1-800-HOLIDAY Mex: 91-800-00999.

KINO — ECON — Pino Suárez #151 Sur — 112-room, 4-story downtown A/C hotel. Restaurant. Parking. **SAC.** AE, MC, VI. Ph: 12-4599 or 13-3151. Fax: 13-3852.

LA SIESTA — ECON — 26-unit A/C motel on north Hwy #15, Blvd. Kino &1 de Mayo. Good restaurant. Parking. MC, VI. Ph: 14-3989 Fax: 14-3043.

PITIC VALLE GRANDE — MOD — Blvd. Kino & R. Corral — Good 144-unit, 2-story A/C motor inn out on north Hwy #15 across street from Norotel Bugambilia. Supper club. Coffee shop. Lobby bar, live entertainment. Pool. Parking. AE, MC, VI. Ph: 14-4570. Fax: 16-6473.

SAN ALBERTO — MOD — Serdán & Rosales — Big 174-room, 4-story A/C hotel in midtown (basic, some complaints). Restaurant. Coffee shop. Ladies bar. Pool. Gift shop. Beauty and barber shops. Bookstore. Parking. AE, MC, VI. Ph: 13-1840, 12-6314, 13-3736. Fax: 13-1897.

EATING HERMOSILLO

BLOCKY'O CLUB — MOD — Off Blvd. Rodríguez — Nice restaurant and club. Good Sonoran beef and Mexican dishes plus salad bar. Disco Friday and Saturday till dawn. Open noon till midnight daily for dining. AE, MC, VI.

EL PALOMINO — MOD — Blvd. Transversal at corner of Calle Bahía — Steakhouse in east part of town. Features wide variety of beef cuts.

HENRY'S — MOD — Very good restaurant converted from old home on Hwy #15 at far north end across from and beyond Bugambilia Valle Grande. Extremely varied menu. Children's menu. Tounge Española — great. Charbroiled steaks a specialty. Seafood. Salads. Open 1 PM till midnight. Mon. - Fri. 1 PM till 5 PM Sat. Ph: 14-7393.

JO-WAH — MOD — Rosales Street — Chinese restaurant on south Hwy #15. Open noon till midnight.

LA SIESTA — MOD — Specializes in huge 2 lb. steaks. Located in hotel of same name.

MANNIX — MOD — Blvd. Kino — Popular short-order restaurant just south of Chevrolet agency.

MERENDERO LA HUERTA — MOD — (Eating Place in the Orchard) — Calle 11 #136 Ote. — Seafood restaurant.

MIYAKO — MOD — Carr. Bahía Kino KM 4 — Japanese restaurant out on road to Kino Bay, established by a wealthy local business man who imported chefs from Japan. Surrounded an acre of formal Japanese gardens. Service from counter or from private rooms where you sit Japanese style.

RODEO — MOD — Blvd. Morelos and Av. Deanza — Cafe with open-air patio. Specialties include *carne asada* "Sonora" style and chicken. Open noon till midnight.

XOCHIMILCO — MOD — Calle Obregón #5 — Package special all parts of cows. Villa de Seris. Ph: 3-3489

VILLA FIESTA — MOD — Blvd. Rodríguez & Yañez #33 — Typical gourmet. Ph: 12-1840.

VARIOUS SERVICES:

KODAK LAB — Plutarco Calles & Manuel González #42

FOTOCOLOR DE HERMOSILLO — Calle Serdán #30 Pte.

LAVANDERIA AUTOMATICA — Sonora & Yañez and Juárez and Periférico Norte. Ph: 14-1543

LAVANDERIA REFORMA — Between Aguascalients & Tlaxcala. Ph: 15-5295.

END HERMOSILLO EAT & STRAY

Kino Bay

UD-017

Area Code — 624

KINO BAY (Bahía Kino) is divided into two areas — Old (Viejo) Kino southwest of El Desierto gas station and New (Nuevo) Kino where most of the accommodations are located. The area has an easygoing and relaxed atmosphere with excellent sunny weather year 'round, especially during winter when the area fills with long-term tourists. It offers fishing, diving, crabbing, clamming, and beachcombing — as well as a very interesting nearby Seri Indian settlement.

The Seri Indians, numbering approximately 500, live primarily in Desemboque (also known as Desemboque del Seri and not to be confused with El Desemboque situated farther north on the coast west of Caborca) and in Punta Chueca on the desert coast of Sonora. The Seris are known for their physical strength and power and have firmly resisted all attempts by the Mexican government to integrate them into today's society. They still preserve something of their pre-Hispanic religion, worshiping such gods as the god of the Center of the Earth (represented as a mole), the god of the Hills, and the god of the Seas. Their main festivals are held in May when the "caguama", or giant turtle, arrives on the shores to nest and in July for the gathering of the pitahaya fruits. (The "pitahaya" is a tall and very spiny cactus with purple flowers and bears an edible scarlet fruit.) On both occasions the tribe gathers to celebrate and feast on the giant turtle and pitahaya honey. The celebration continues with dancing and singing until dawn.

The Seri women weave heart-shaped baskets called *coritas* made from a fiber of the torote plant, which they strip off with their teeth and with the aid of a deer bone awl and natural dye, they make baskets valued by tourists and collectors alike. The men make a living from fishing and handicrafts, especially their carvings of animals made from *palo fierro* (ironwood). However, ironwood is be coming scarce, so the Indian craft may soon become a thing of the past. Some of these carvings are works of art and are often considered collectors' items. A smaller female industry, bringing in quick cash is that of making shell jewelry. Shell necklaces of intricate design are inexpensive and attractive to tourist.

Punta Chueca, 16 miles from Motel Kino Bay, is the closest of the two Seri villages and can be reached via a dirt road. However, a trip to Desemboque, a rather depressive place 65 miles north of Kino, should be attempted only with a truck or four-wheel drive vehicle. This once self sufficient tribe, its life, history and culture may be seen and studied at the Seri Museum on Mar de Cortés.

Also of interest (especially to nature lovers) is Isla Tiburón. Tiburón is Mexico's largest island and is approximately 29 miles long and 15 miles wide, while its highest point is 4,000 feet. It is a wildlife refuge, rich in plant and animal life, and belongs to the Seri Indians, but due to its ecological importance, the Mexican government has placed the island "off limits" to the Seris. Incidentally, *tiburón* is Spanish for shark. Arrangements for a boat and a guide can be made at the Prescott College House. Call Tadd at 2-0044. Prescott College has an abundance of additional information available.

So, you'll agree that Kino Bay is no Acapulco, Mazatlán, or Puerto Vallarta, but for those who like to get away from it all, this is the place to be.

FISHING — All season fishing from Bahía Kino is one of the major lures to the area. Bottom fishing around nearby rocky points is an experience even a novice may enjoy, especially when reeling in a sea bass or a yellowtail. Launching permits and fishing licenses may be obtained from the Club Deportivo, ask for Tony.

EMERGENCIES — Club Deportivo's Rescue One is a group of volunteers who can help in just about any kind of emergency, providing monitoring services and information on CB Channel 4 or VHF Channel 06. If someone's lost, or needs assistance at sea or on land, they can mobilize aircraft & seacraft to handle it. The Sanborn's sombrero is off to them! Contact them at club, which is across from Kunkaak RV park. (About 1/4 mile off beach, by landing strip.)

There is a resident doctor at the clinic in Old Kino 24 hours a day for emergencies. Besides that there are three other doctors: Raul Figueroa Canizales, located behind the Farmacia Aquario; José Luis González located at Topolabampo and Padre Kino Blvd; and Jorge Grijalva on Altata street; All in Old Kino. Drs. González and Grijalva speak English.

SAFETY — The narrow channel between Isla Tiburón and the mainland is subject to changing winds, strong currents and shifting sandbars. It's no wonder that area is known in Spanish as *El Infiernillo* (Little Hell). Ocean conditions may change rapidly, especially during the summer months. Diving and snorkeling around rocky areas north of Kino Bay can be worthwhile, but not spectacular. Sediments cloud the water. Swimming at Kino Bay's beach is relatively safe. At times there are strong currents and beware of the small clear-blue stinging man-of-war Stingray fish (or Jellyfish). If you see them, especially at incoming tide, stay out of the water.

ECOLOGY — The ecological system of the Gulf of California has been deteriorating due to overfishing by large fishing trawlers. In June, 1993, President Salinas de Gortari declared two large areas at the northern Gulf as biosphere reserve. In the most northern area, from San Felipe north to Santa Clara, no fishing or oil drilling will be allowed. In the Second area from San Felipe to Puerto Peñasco, shrimp nets will not be allowed and the size of gill nets will be restricted. These measures will be strictly enforced in order to protect the Totoaba, Vaquita and other species from extinction.

AA — ENGLISH — Wed. 7:00 PM, Club Deportivo and Saturdays at 7:00 PM in the recreation room at the El Saguaro Trailer Park. Both are "Open" meetings (that is, anyone can attend). For additional information, call 2-0141. Alanon has just started meetings at the Club Deportivo on Thursday at 1:00 PM (high season).

VISITOR'S GUIDEBOOK — An excellent handy guide for Kino Bay and vicinity is called *Your Place in the Sun* by Joan Stenberg and Gloria J. McDonagh, published by Kino Publications, Apdo. #135, Bahía de Kino, Sonora.

SLEEPING AROUND OLD KINO

RV PARK & CABINS — **ISLANDIA MARINA** — **ECON-MOD** — Nice folks! **ON** the fishing beach. Follow signs through town. Office at gate. 73 space RV park and 8 cabins on beach, (old, but well-maintained now, value). All hookups. Showers. Restrooms. 8 kitchenettes with 2 beds & 3 cots. Boat ramp and storage. Fish cleaning. 20 AMPS. Pets OK. Ph: 2-0081.

EATING OLD KINO

MARLIN PLACE — MOD — Clean, reasonably priced restaurant near Islandia Marina. Seafood specialties. Very good food and service. George, a singing waiter.
DORITA — In front of police station. Serve breakfast and lunch. Open 7:00 AM till 3:00 PM
EL PULPO NUEVO — In town. Seafood specialties.
TAQUERIA PRADO — ECON — Great tacos on road into town across from park. Open late.

SLEEPING AROUND NEW KINO

KINO BAY — MOD — 18-unit, 2 story A/C motel at north end. Good deal. Small restaurant. 8 kitchenettes. Boat rentals. MC. VI. Ph: 2-0049 or (62) 14-1492 in Hermosillo.
POSADA DEL MAR — MOD — Good value. 48-unit, 2 story A/C motel across from beach. Restaurant. Pool. AE. MC. VI. Ph: 2-0155 or (62) 18-1221 in Hermosillo.
POSADA SANTA GEMA — UPPER — Pricey 14-unit A/C apartment motel. Two bedroom split-level units with bath, kitchen, and fireplace. MC. VI. Ph: 2-0024, 2-0002 or 2-0026.
SARO — MOD — 16 rooms. Simple but very neat. On beach. Laundry. SATV. Betty and Saro, owners. Saro is an interesting character, speaks English, Italian and Spanish. Ph: (62) 42-0007.

EATING NEW KINO

EL PARGO ROJO — UPPER — Nice seafood & steak place on Av. del Mar 1426. Across from beach. Green Angels hang out here sometimes. Open 10-12, 7 days. AE, MC, VI. Ph: 2-0205
KINO BAY — MOD — Only place for breakfast. On Beach. Mexican food. Nice atmosphere. Ph: 2-0049 Open 8 AM till 10 PM
VILLAS DEL MAR NAUTILUS CLUB — UPPER — international cuisine and seafood. Closed Tuesday.

CAMPING, PARKING AND PLUGGING IN

CAVERNA DEL SERI — UPPER — Small 30 spaces on beach at far north end on paved road. All hookups. 14 spaces with patios & shade. Potable water. Restrooms. SATV. Store. Laundry service. Ice. Apartments. English. Boat ramp. 30 AMPS. Club house. Ph: 8-3180 or (62) 14-7134 in Hermosillo.
EL CACTUS — MOD — 33-space park a half-mile off main street on sand road. All hookups. Concrete pads. Showers. Restrooms. Fenced. Some small covered patios. Pool. Laundry service. Pets OK on leash. SATV. Free launching service. Ph: 6-1643 or 4-7032.
KINO BAY — UPPER — Very good 200-space facility in conjunction with motel. All hookups. Shady pull-thrus. Showers. Restrooms. Rec hall. Restaurant. Palapas. Laundry. Dump station. Store. Shaded concrete patios. Boat ramp, dock and rentals. Ice. Bungalows. Fishing supplies and cleaning. English. Ph: 2-0049 or (62) 15-3197 in Hermosillo. 30 AMPS. Apdo. 857-83000, Hermosillo, Son.
KUNKAAK — UPPER — 54 large space with patio and all hookups. Across from Club Deportivo. Potable water. Restrooms. Showers. Rec hall. Laundry — coin. Fish cleaning area. Fishing. Boat launch 0.5 miles away. 30 AMPS. Ph: 2-0209 or 2-0088. Hermosillo: (62) 17-4474, 17-0683 Ph & Fax: 17-4453.
PARADOR BELLA VISTA — UPPER — 18 spaces with all hookups. Concrete pads. Restrooms. Showers. Laundry — coin. 6.5 KM from entrance to Kino Bay, past Posada Santa Gemma. English spoken. Owner Sr. Lorenzo Penelli & his wife, María are very nice hosts. Children welcome. Pets OK. 20 AMPS. 2 furnished bungalows. P.O. Box NR 27. Ph: 2-0139.
POSADA SANTA GEMMA — MOD — Small 14-space park next to motel. All hookups. Restrooms. Showers. Palapa covered patios. Boat ramp. On beach. Store. Grills. 20 AMPS. Ana María, manager. English spoken. MC. VI. Ph: 2-0024, 2-0002 or 2-0001.
SARO — MOD-UPPER — 7 spaces with all hookups. First park on main road to town. Across from hotel by same name. Opposite beach. Owner speaks Italian, English, Spanish. Laundry. SATV. 30 AMPS. Boat access. Beach. Rec hall. Nice management. Ph: 2-0007. Saro is an interesting character, speaks English, Italian and Spanish.

Ya'll have a great time here — y'hear!

END KINO BAY EAT & STRAY

San Carlos

UD-017

Area Code — 622

SAN CARLOS (or Nuevo Guaymas, its official name) is a unique resort community nestled between the beaches of the Sea of Cortés and the Bacochibampo Mountains. It was developed as an alternative to the more crowded Mexican vacation spots such as Puerto Vallarta and Acapulco and offers a wide variety of outdoor activities and attracts those looking for a different kind of vacation.

Rafael Caballero, a developer from Nogales, Sonora, is the man behind the San Carlos boom. Having camped near Guaymas as a Boy Scout, he returned as a very young man to buy 17 miles of beachfront along Bacochibampo Bay (Bay of the Sea Serpents) and a 45,000-acre spread. But anticipating land problems, he formed his own *ejido* and ceded some 28,000 acres, including more than four miles of beachfront, to the government for future settlers. The rest was his, free from pressure felt by resort developers all the way to Acapulco.

Today San Carlos is a community with scenic shorelines and calm waters, hotels, motels, condominium apartments, RV facilities, a gas station, a police station (*comisaría de policía*) which is the only authority in San Carlos, fire department, potable tap water, and several well-stocked mini-markets.

The San Carlos country club facilities include a contemporary clubhouse with open terraces looking out onto the bay, a restaurant and lounge, a tennis and golf pro shop, men's and women's dressing rooms, a sauna and, a temperature-controlled, freshwater swimming pool. The tennis center is the pride of the country club. There are 13 Laykold courts all lighted for night use, including an amphitheater exhibition court. And there is an 18-hole, 6,617-yard golf course, designed by Roy Dye, overlooking the sea and small islands rising on the horizon.

San Carlos is famous for its deep-sea fishing. One will find not only an abundance, but a bewildering variety of game fish in the Sea of Cortés. Summer offers the most spectacular fishing (the annual San Carlos International Deep-Sea Fishing Tournament is held in September) but the weather following May is sometimes oppressively hot. The big runs of marlin and sailfish come in the spring, between April and June, but there is game fishing to satisfy the soul of the average angler during fall and winter months, such as roosterfish, trigger fish, sea bass, barracuda, grouper, red snapper, cabrilla, sea trout, yellowtail, dolphin, Pacific whitefish, sierra, giant ray, totuava, and corvina among others.

Water sports are excellent here. The beach by most of the hotels is somewhat gravelly with coarse sand. As you go out toward Algodones, though, there are miles of uncrowded, sandy beaches for swimming, strolling, snorkeling, and startling blue water for diving. Skin diving gear is sold and rented at a very good shop adjoining the Creston Motel.

The Marina San Carlos (Ph: 6-1062) is one of the largest, in Mexico with 400 slips for boats from 14-50 feet long. Water, power, concrete ramp, and tractor service are available for larger slips. Fishing craft and power boats can be rented, fishing gear can be purchased or rented, or pleasure cruises around the bay area are available. For those wanting to leave their boat in dry storage here, contact the super nice people, Tere & Eddie Grossman at the Marina San Carlos Dry Storage. They will help you with the paperwork. Ph: 6-1062.

Activities in San Carlos are not confined to fishing, swimming, golf, and tennis. One can also hunt from September through March or go horseback riding along the beaches or in the almost barren desert among giant stands of Saguaro cacti. Or one can climb the Cerro del Vigia, a 2000-foot mountain whose summit is reached by a winding and steep dirt road. A few miles north around the bend from San Carlos Bay is Playa de los Algodones (Los Algodones Beach) where Mike Nichols filmed Catch 22. Little is left of the original sets, but you can imagine them if you are familiar with the movie — unless you are just a young whippersnapper. In that case, just enjoy the white sand dunes and beach.

San Carlos, where the bare mountains in the background rise to 2,000 feet reflecting themselves in the warm, smooth waters of the harbor, is designed not just as a vacation retreat but also as one of Mexico's retirement communities. In the winter months one will see campers, trailers, and automobiles with license plates from almost every state in the Union. In fact, trailer spaces will be hard to find in winter, but are easy to find and less expensive in nearby Guaymas.

Some will find San Carlos a comfortable introduction to Mexico because it is small, well organized and much English is spoken. Others will find it too Americanized for their taste. If that describes you, check out Guaymas, which has a more "Mexican" flavor.

If you are just passing through, consider the Guaymas RV parks. They cost about half as much and are not crowded at all. It will take you about 1/2 hour to drive to them.

SLEEPING AROUND SAN CARLOS

CRESTON — MOD — Very good 24-unit A/C motel on beach. Pool. Shuffleboard. Parking. Pets OK. MC, VI. Phone 6-0020. Excellent value. Good comments from readers.

FIESTA SAN CARLOS — MOD — Carr. San Carlos KM 8 — Nice 33-unit, 3-story A/C motor hotel on beach. It resembles a modern Mayan temple when viewed from the beach. Dining room. Circular pool. Parking. MC, VI. Ph & Fax: 6-0229.

HACIENDA TETA KAWI — MOD — Best Western. Very nice 22 Rooms as well as 4 suites with refrigerator. Pool. AE, MC, VI. Ph: 6-0220 Fax: 6-0248.

LOMA BONITA — UPPER — At entrance to Country club and shopping center. Great place for families. 69 - 2 bedroom apartments. Pool. Water slides. Jacuzzi. Tennis. Parking. AE, MC, VI. Ph & Fax: 6-1413. US: 1-888-790-0366.

PLAZA LAS GLORIAS —UPPER — 87 Deluxe suites (8 with jacuzzi). Tubs. Very nice. Gym. Tennis. AE, MC, VI. 6-1021 to 29 Fax: 6-1034. US: 1-800-211-5111 Mex: 91-800-90229

POSADA DEL DESIERTO — MOD — 7 Apartments on Bajada del Corredor s/n close to the Marina, kitchen, also rents 2 houses Ph & Fax: 6-0467.

SAN CARLOS PLAZA — UPPER — Playas Los Algodones — 173 room hotel. 3 restaurants. Snack bar. Bars. Pool. Night club. Cold water jacuzzi (has to be turned on by staff). Tennis. Health center. Water sports. Horseback riding. Car rental. Boutiques. Ph: 7-0777, 7-0778 7-0779. Fax: 7-0098. US: 1-800-854-2320, Mex: 91-800-6-4368.

SUITES MAR ROSA — MOD — On left just before Country Club going into town. 6 A/C units. Kitchenettes. Some queen-size beds, some twin. Ph: 60250 Fax: 2-1117.

VILLA SUNSET — Furnished apartments with kitchenette behind El Paradise Restaurant. Ph: 6-0304

EATING SAN CARLOS

CARLO'S COMIDA CASERA — ECON — Mexican food, set menu. Open 7 AM till 9 PM. Very friendly. Homey atmosphere. No booze. No credit cards.

CARAMBA'S GRILL — MOD — Av. Serdán #664 — Next to supermarket. Same owner (Alejandro Maksabedian R.) as fritter restaurant. Good food and service. PH: 2-9606. Thanks to B &A Abraham, Sun Lakes, Az.

EL ARRECIFE — MOD — On the main street thru town #156-1 across from the country club. Small, casual & friendly. Some say they have the best seafood in town. Open Noon till 11 PM. Closed Wednesday. MC, VI. Ph: 6-1344.

EL BRONCO — UPPER — Across from Gary's. Specialties are steaks, bone marrow soup, pork loin and seafood (not on menu, ask). The best grilled lobster I ever had. Open 5 PM till 11 PM. Closed Monday. Sat & Sun, open 1 PM till 10 PM. Ph: 6-1230.

EL PARADISE — MOD — Seafood restaurant (across from Creston) serving excellent selection of shellfish (as well as various seafood). Open 11:30 AM till 10 PM daily. MC, VI.

NORSA — MOD — Excellent. A true family Mexican restaurant run by a wonderful Noriega family. Off the main highway going into town, turn right across from Fiesta San Carlos. Clean, neat & friendly. Good food, lunch and dinner. (Larry Kaminski, Steamboat Springs CO., customer recommended.)

PAPPAS TAPPAS — MOD — Arizona decor. Beef and seafood. Bar. Weekly buffet specials "All you can eat" Open 4:00 PM till 11 PM. MC, VI. Ph: 6-0707

ROSA'S CANTINA — ECON — Carr. San Carlos — CABRITO (though I didn't try it — please let me know how it is —MM)! Steak, enchiladas. Casual place, popular with younger folks. Bulletin board for buying, selling, renting or local events. Open 6:30 PM till 1:30 AM daily. MC, VI. Good value. Ph: 6-1000.

SAN CARLOS GRILL — UPPER — Varied menu. Chicken, fish, steak, crepes. Live music. Trendy. Open 7 days, 1 PM till 11 PM. MC, VI. Ph: 6-5009.

TEQUILA'S BAR & GRILL — ECON — Great place for breakfast, lunch or early dinner. Fresh toasted whole wheat bread, eggs, sandwiches, smoked bacon, seafood, Mexican dishes. Outside tables with view of Yacht harbor. Across from Lanchas de Pesca de Ostión St. Open 7:00 AM till 11:00 PM Mon, Thurs, & Sun; till 2:00 AM with live music, Tue, Fri & Sat. Good value. MC, VI (with 5% service charge). Ph: 6-0545.

CAMPING, PARKING AND PLUGGING IN

TETA-KAWI — Across street from the largest San Carlos Beach. Very nice 132 space facility. All hookups. Pull-thru slots. 20 AMPS. Showers. Jacuzzi. Toilets. Self-service laundry. Fish-cleaning room. Concrete patios (some covered). Refreshments. 4 furnished apartments. Mailing address: Apdo. Postal # 71. Ph: 6-0220 Fax: 6-0248.

TOTONAKA — UPPER — 140 space park next to Teta-Kawi. All hookups. 30 AMPS. Showers. Restrooms. Rec-hall. 2 laundries — coin. Restaurant. Bar. Concrete patios. Beach across street. 25 furnished apartments, some with kitchens. SATV. Phone, mail service. Ph: 6-0323, 6-0481, 6-0531 Fax: 6-0523.

OTHER SERVICES

AMBULANCE — CUERPO DE RESCATE across from Pemex station, between Venus & Del Gary streets.

FISHING BOATS are available at the Marina San Carlos in a variety of sizes as well as a diesel or gas-operated, fully equipped party boat.

GIFT SHOP — KIAMY'S — next to Creston. Good selection. Open 9 AM till 6 PM. AE, MC, VI. Ph: 6-0400

PHYSICIAN — Dr. Manuel Andueza Quiros. Plaza La Mar #4. Ph: 6-0129 Fax: 6-0097. Home: 1-1081.

REAL ESTATE — SNOWBIRD REALTY can do 2 or 3 year financing. Ph: 6-0551

SCUBA DIVING gear is available at San Carlos Diving Center on Del Gary St. (next door to Creston Motel) PH: 6-0049 and at Posada de San Carlos Hotel.

KAYAKING & HIKING — A 4-hour trip to Nacapuli Canyon or a visit to the Arches and natural aquarium are available at the Sonora Sports Center. Ph: 6-0929. Ask for Vince or Carl.

ENGLISH AA — Church of San Carlos (near KM 12) 8:15 PM Tues.

YOGA CENTER CAMINITO — Call Los Ranchitos: 6-0222.

ENGLISH CATHOLIC MASS - 4:00 PM Saturday.

NONDENOMINATIONAL CHURCH SERVICE — Inquire locally.

Ya'll have a nice time here!

END SAN CARLOS EAT & STRAY

Guaymas

UD-017

Area Code — 622

SLEEPING AROUND GUAYMAS

ARMIDA — ECON — Excellent value! On Blvd. García López. 125-unit A/C hotel on Hwy 15 in town practically at junction with main stem. One jacuzzi suite. Restaurant. Bar. Pool surrounded by two-century-old Yucateco trees. Boutique. Parking. **SAC** 20% discount. AE, MC, VI. Ph: 4-3035 Fax: 2-0044.

FLAMINGOS — ECON — North Hwy #15 — 55-unit surprisingly nice motel. Some A/C. Good beds. Restaurant. Bar. Pool. Parking. MC. VI. **SAC** 20% discount. Ph: 1-0961. Fax: 1-2061.

IMPALA — ECON — Calle 21 #40 — 46-room, 3-story A/C downtown hotel. Restaurant. On-street parking. Ph: 2-6500, Fax: 4-0923.

LAS   PLAYITAS — MOD — Carr. Varadero Nacional KM 6 (see stub log to RV parks — it's by the naval base, it's worth the drive) — 30 A/C cottages on Las Playitas Peninsula in conjunction with RV facility of same name. 7 bungalows. Popular restaurant. Boat ramp. Parking. **SAC** 20% discount. MC. VI. Ph: 2-2727 or 2-2753.

LEO'S   INN — ECON — VALUE! Bacochibampo Bay — Small 15 A/C rooms. Beachfront inn in Colonia Miramar. Very pretty grounds No restaurant (but Venenos next door). Parking. Ph: 1-0104, 2-1337, 2-9490. (Turn west just before De Cortés. It's about a mile on left, just before beach. Popular with Europeans).

PLAYA DE CORTÉS — MOD — Bacochibampo Bay — Excellent colonial atmosphere with oil paintings and tropical gardens. Famous 132-unit, 3-story A/C hotel, originally built by Southern-Pacific Railroad. 3 elegant dining rooms. Pool. Tennis. Boat ramp. Boutique. Parking. 8 bungalows. AE, MC, VI. Ph: 1-0142, Fax: 1-0135. US: 1-800-782-7608. RV park.

SANTA RITA — ECON — Serdán & Calle 9 — Budget, 3 story A/C downtown, 1 block off main street, across from Rest. Del Río. Parking. VI. MC. Ph: 2-6463, 2-6465, Fax: 2-8100.

EATING GUAYMAS

BIBLIO CAFE — ECON — Av. Serdán — Typical restaurant between Calles 13 & 14. Mexican food, seafood.

DEL MAR — UPPER — Av. Serdán and Calle 17 — Very good downtown restaurant. Excellent seafood and prime cuts from Sonora. Terrific seafood cocktails and clam and fish soups. Open 12:30 PM till 11:30 PM daily. AE, MC, VI. Ph: 4-0225.

HELADOS   BING — ECON — On Serdán just east of 5th — Ice-cream, sundaes & more!

LAS PLAYITAS — MOD — VALUE — Very good restaurant in conjunction with RV park of same name on road to naval base around Guaymas Bay. Superb seafood. Open daily. MC, VI. Ph: 1-5227.

MEXICO — ECON-MOD — Hwy #15 — "Typical" eatery, 1/8 mile East of Flamingos. *Al fresco* dining. Owned by same folks as in Hermosillo. The adventurous can order the *Paquete*, which contains ALL parts of cow. The conventional can stick with ribs & steaks. Ph: 2-7810.

PLAYA DE CORTÉS — MOD — At hotel of same name. Really good food at reasonable prices. Dive on patio overlooking bay. Elegant dining room. Romantic.

READER RECOMMENDATION — at the Club Deportivo Miramar, on the right 1/2-way to Playa de Cortés Hotel. Nice "white tablecloth" place. Thanks to G. Quist.

CAMPING, PARKING AND PLUGGING IN

BAHIA — MOD — On Playitas Peninsula — 80 space park. All hookups. 20 AMPS. Apartments. Restrooms. Showers. Patios. Rec. hall. Boat ramp. Ph: 1-5030.

LAS PLAYITAS — ECON — 100 space park on road to naval base around Guaymas Bay a mile or so beyond La Bahía. All hookups. 20 AMPS. Showers. Restrooms. Rec. hall. Pier. Cement pads. Pool. Restaurant. Bar. Patios. Boat ramp. Owner Josephina Borboa personable, English-speaking & helpful. Restaurant has special on Thursday. 12 kitchenette Apartments-motel. Pets OK. **SAC** 10% discount. Ph: 1-5196 Fax: 1-5227.

PLAYAS DE CORTÉS — MOD — Bacochibampo Bay — Very nice. By hotel with same name. 55 spaces, all hookups. Use of hotel facilities. Hunting fishing arranged. PO Box 66. 30 AMPS. Restrooms. Showers. Restaurant. Bar. SATV in bar. Pool. Tennis. Laundry service. Beach. Boat ramp and storage. AE, MC, VI. **SAC**. Ph: 1-0142, 1-1224, 1-1121, 1-1047, 1-0148. Fax: 1-0135. US: 1-800-782-7608.

HELPFUL INFORMATION

AA & OTHER 12 STEP PROGRAMS — See Other Services in San Carlos Eat & Stray or list in front of log for all Mexico.

MECHANIC — TETO'S — Family-run business with prompt competent service, some English and a fair price at Calle 9 #278 Sur. Ph: 2-1605.

TOURISM OFFICE AND INFORMATION — Now on Av. Serdán #441. Ph: (622) 2-1097; 1-800-4-SONORA (in U.S.)

BOATS — In town on waterfront across from city hall, Playa de Cortés Hotel, or Las Playitas RV Park.

LA CASONA SHELL SHOP — Across from cathedral plaza on 24th Street. Nice collection of sea shells and nice jewelry. Rents videos. English spoken. Ph: (622) 2-0199.

END GUAYMAS EAT & STRAY!

Ciudad Obregón

UD-017

Area Code — 64

CIUDAD OBREGÓN was named for General Alvaro Obregón who (with an assist from a chap named Pancho Villa) helped Carranza defeat Huerta in the 1913 revolution — and then had to whip Villa (for his boss, Carranza) at Celaya, where Obregón lost an arm. Later, he fell out with Carranza and defeated him, and became *presidente* (1920). Eight years later, when he was reelected (after he changed the rules to permit a second term) he was assassinated. Obregón came from these parts, so they renamed this nice town in his honor.

A big dam was built up on the Yaqui River some 30-odd miles northeast of town and with irrigation they've made this fertile Yaqui valley into a fabulous producer of cotton and vegetables, which accounts for all the gins, fertilizer factories, insecticide plants and vegetable sheds hereabouts — it's just about the boomingest town on the West Coast, with a population of about 300,000.

If you have a generous and compassionate heart and would like to visit an orphanage, you can visit *Hogar de Refugio Infantil Villa Juárez.* To get there go about 3 miles south of town (mile 83.5 on our log), turn right onto side road to Villa Juárez, go 26 miles on paved road, turn right for another mile, then turn left following signs to the orphanage. Bob Mason, the director, welcomes visitors. They are able to accommodate motor homes, trailers etc. and have a crude dumping station as well as electrical hookups.

SLEEPING AROUND CD. OBREGÓN

COSTA DE ORO — MOD — M. Alemán & Allende #201 — 2-story, 103 room a/c motel on highway (Miguel Alemán) thru town. Restaurant. Disco. Bar. Pool. Parking. AE, MC, VI. Ph: 14-1775. Fax: 13-3475.

HOLIDAY INN — MOD-UPPER — Miguel Alemán & Tetabiate — 2 story, 132 room a/c motor inn on north end on highway thru town. Attractive dining room. Coffee shop. Pool. Parking. AE, MC, VI. **SAC.** Ph: 14-0940. Fax: 13-4194.

SAN JORGE — Mod — Miguel Alemán #929 — Older 60 room a/c motel on north end. Small restaurant. Bar. Pool. Parking. Ph: 14-4353. Fax: 14-0110

VALLE DEL YAQUI — MOD — M. Alemán & Cájeme — Nice 84 room, 2 story a/c motel inn on north end on Hwy #15. Coffee shop. Bar. Club (best in town). Pool. Parking. AE, MC, VI. Ph: 14-1300 or 14-8389.

There are two new hotels in town recommended by reader Jim Kerchevac of Tucson, AZ, you might check out: Obregón Plaza and Imperial

EATING CD. OBREGÓN

EL CORTIJO — MOD — Calle 5 de Febrero — Nice restaurant just 2 blocks west of Hwy #15 thru town. Cabrito and paella are specialties.

MR. STEAK — MOD — Miguel Alemán & Mayo — Pleasant Western-style rustic restaurant just south of Norotel Nainiri Valle Grande. Specializes in *carne al carbón* (charcoal-broiled meats). Mr. Bar a part of the establishment. Open for lunch and dinner. Ph: 13-3570.

CAMPING, PARKING 'N PLUGGING IN

If you have a generous and compassionate heart and would like to visit an orphanage, you will find Hogar de Refugio Infantil Villa Juárez by turning right onto side road to Villa Juárez, go 26 miles on paved road, turn right for another mile, then turn left following signs to the orphanage. Bob Mason, the director, welcomes visitors. They are able to accommodate motor homes, trailers etc. and have a crude dumping station as well as electrical hookups.

END CD. OBREGÓN EAT & STRAY

Navojoa

Area Code — 642

NAVOJOA, the center of a major cotton and wheat-producing area, lies on the left bank of the Río Mayo. Originally a settlement known as "Navojoa" inhabited by the Mayo Indians, it was discovered in 1620 by the Jesuit missionary P. Diego de La Cruz and renamed "Navojoa."

With the building of the railroad station at the turn of this century, white families moved in and the town began to flourish; but in 1915 a terrible flood virtually wiped out the city and a new town was then rebuilt on higher ground. Today Navojoa boasts a population of 100,000 and is a rapidly growing city surrounded by agricultural wealth.

Navojoa is also the largest center of the Mayo Indians, a tribe related to the once potent Yaqui tribe. The Mayos fought long and hard for their liberty and tribal land, but today are almost entirely integrated, having turned to farming. They are slowly losing their identity although they still retain some old beliefs and rituals. A reenactment of these rituals highlights religious festivities during Easter Week and on June 23-24 when the Indians honor St. John the Baptist. Most memorable are the *danza del venado* (deer dance) and the *matachines* (masquerade and coyote dances).

Navojoa is the departure point to colonial Alamos and to Presa (dam) Mocuzari, famous for its bass fishing and duck hunting. On the south side of Navojoa, a paved road southwest connects to Huatabampo 23 miles away on the Mayo delta where ex-Presidente Alvaro Obregón is buried. Another 12 miles away is the little village of Huatabampito with a beautiful, unspoiled sandy beach that runs for 13-odd miles. The waters are mild and the beach is so wide and firm that small airplanes often use it for a landing strip.

SLEEPING AROUND NAVOJOA

COLONIAL — MOD — 24 room A/C motel at south end of town. Restaurant-bar. Club (*mariachis* on TH & F). Parking. Ph: 2-1919.

DEL RÍO — MOD — Pesquería #228 — Very nice 68 room A/C motel just beyond Alameda. Restaurant. Bar. Pool. SATV. Tennis. 5 Kitchenettes. Parking. RV park on north end. **SAC.** AE, MC, VI. Ph: 2-0331, 2-5601, 2-5402. Fax: 2-5751.

EL MAYO — ECON — Motel recommended by Ken Heins, Ralph and Jeane Gladfelter and several other customers. A good deal. One block off main highway at Otero and Jiménez. Bungalows with carports, nice, clean, comfortable and quiet. Ph: 2-0099, 2-6828 Fax: 2-6515.

EL RANCHO — MOD — Carr. Internacional KM 1788 — 66 room A/C ranch-style motel at far north end. Restaurant. Bar. Pool. Disco (F-Sat till wee hours of morning, making sleep impossible). Parking. MC, VI. Ph & Fax: 2-0004 or 2-0310.

FENIX — ECON — Hidalgo & Angel Flores #365 — Economy hotel. MC, VI. Ph: 2-2623.

MONTE CARLO — ECON — Corner of Independencia & Angel Flores — Good enough hotel. Ceiling fans. TV. Bar. Parking. MC, VI.

POSADA REAL — MOD — 154 room hotel. Continental breakfast free. A/C, nice but cold. Pool. TV. Parking. AE, MC, VI. Ph: 2-2179.

EATING NAVOJOA

EL GRANERO — MOD — Corner of Serdán & Zaragosa — Restaurant specializing in beef. MC, VI. Open daily.

LAS BRASAS — Fine steak house on main street next to Danesa ice cream parlor. Bar. AE, MC, VI.

MARLIN'S — Good restaurant on main street thru town. Specializes in seafood dishes.

QUINTA EL ASADERO — Very good restaurant (town's best) 1 KM south of Del Río on left. Specializes in charbroiled meats. Open noon till midnight daily. AE, MC, VI.

CAMPING, PARKING & PLUGGIN' IN

ALAMEDA — UPPER — North side on left bank of Río Mayo — Very good 100-space park. Reported run down and near closing. All hookups. 20 amps. Showers. Restrooms. Laundry service. Grilles. Store. Concrete pads set in grove of mango trees, full of fruit in early July. Ph: 2-5533, 2-1414.

END NAVOJOA EAT & STRAY

Alamos

UD-017

Area Code — 642

Congratulations! You've chosen to stay at one of the jewels of the west coast of Mexico. This town was going to be destroyed in the early part of the century when some of the rich and powerful business leaders were convinced to buy property here. Then Hollywood types came. Sometimes money and power can be used for the greater good. Thank you. You know who you are.

ALAMOS (cottonwood trees) is an interesting old town, sort of a national park like Taxco and the construction of buildings with modern architecture is not allowed. The town is one of the oldest in North America — Coronado's army camped here in 1530. Alamos once had a gold-silver-lead mine population of 40,000 but the mines played out some 70 years ago and the town was soon on its downswing. However, *Norteamericanos* have discovered this quaint place and quite a few have moved here and rebuilt the magnificent ruins, some of which are open to the public.

HOUSE TOURS — Check at your hotel. 10 AM Saturday, October 1 till May 1. They meet at the Museum. Money goes to Alamos Scholarship Fund. For special tours for group of 10 or more during the week contact Dolores Parker at 8-0348 or write her at Calle Juárez #25, Alamo, Sonora, Mexico 85760. Some guides offer tours but they can't get into houses, so be careful.

Incidentally, Alamos is where the Mexican jumping beans come from. It isn't a bean at all, but a little three-section nut with a tiny worm in each section, and it's the movement of the worm that makes the "bean" jump. There's a man in Alamos, Señor Joaquín Hernández, who is the jumping bean "king" and he buys up all the beans from natives who gather them and then ships 'em in drums to the States and all over the world. The beans "come on" in midsummer and keep hopping till late September when the worm apparently becomes just too pooped to hop anymore (can't blame him) so he burrows his way out and curls up and dies.

You'll enjoy old Alamos — don't hesitate to run over and stay the night. Incidentally, if no accommodations are available, it's only 33 miles to Navojoa.

AA — Ask for José Luis at the bar of Casa de los Tesoros. He's the bartender. How's that for a cosmic joke? There are several Spanish AA groups in town, Grupo 1 de Septiembre on Calle Morelos and Grupo Arroyo next to the arroyo.

SLEEPING AROUND ALAMOS

CASA DE LOS TESOROS ("House of Treasures") — UPPER — Value! While it is not cheap it is much less than the other quality hotels in town and includes breakfast, and it's the only one that takes credit cards. The atmosphere is equal to the others though not as chic-chic as Casa Encantada. You get more for your money here. Obregón #10 1 1/2 blocks from Plaza. 14 A/C rooms, and ceiling fans, converted from an 18th-century convent. Restaurant. Pool. One room with tub. Good water pressure in showers. Fireplaces. Parking. Interesting painting of St. Thomas in dining room hanging over the fireplace. AE, MC, VI. Apdo. 12, Alamos, Son., Mexico. Ph: 8-0010. Fax: 8-0400.

CASA ENCANTADA — UPPER — The most expensive hotel in town. I guess if you want atmosphere you've got to pay for it. It's a really charming but expensive bed & breakfast located at Juárez #20, a nice Antilysin style mansion built over 250 years ago. The owners are very friendly & accommodating. 10 rooms, suites or casitas decorated in a very chic fashion. Pool. No credit cards. Ph: 8-0482, 8-0221.

CASA OBREGÓN #18 — MOD — Value! 3 suites (more like apartments, 2 with tubs, 1 with full kitchen. You won't believe the place. Great courtyard. Enclosed parking. Monthly discounts. Often full. Less expensive than others in neighborhood. Owner speaks English. No credit cards but accept personal checks. No phone.

DOLISA — ECON — **VALUE!** Reasonable prices. Comfy 8-unit motel at Madero #72 on highway just before town (WITHIN WALKING DISTANCE TO CENTRO). Owner a nice man who really tries to make you comfortable. For those on a budget, you can't do better. No restaurant. Most rooms a/c; others with ceiling fans. Fireplaces. Coin operated laundry. Water purifying plant. Parking. Ph: 8-0131.

LOS PORTALES ("Covered Walks") — MOD — Older hotel. 9 rooms on Juárez #6 at Alamos' main plaza. No A/C; ceiling fans only. No restaurant. Fireplaces. Parking. Bar. Pleasant courtyard. Formerly private house of mine owner. Apdo. 31, Alamos, Son., Mexico. Ph: 8-0211.

MANSIÓN — UPPER — I've tried real hard to like this place. Some rooms are good enough and others are plain. I think it's overpriced. Obregón #2, down from Tesoros. 12 rooms. Ceiling fans & fireplaces. No credit cards. Ph: 8-0221.

POSADA — MOD — Good Value! Less expensive than many and nice enough. A remodeled old mansion on Prol. 2 de Abril. Good ambience and food. 9 rooms, one with tub. A/C and ceiling fans. Rooms are designed for families. Some have a loft bedroom and three beds. 3 kitchenettes. Secure parking. The manager, Ramón Quintana, knew Dan Sanborn. Ph: 8-0045 In Tucson, (520) 327-4683.

POLO ACOSTA — MOD — 6 rooms in conjunction with RV park on east side of town beyond cemetery. Restaurant which prepares food by reservation only. Pool. Hunting and fishing available. Parking. Ph: 8-0246 or 8-0077.

SOMAR — ECON — 16 room hotel on Madero #110 at entrance to town. No restaurant. Parking. Pleasant courtyard. Ph: 8-0195. The unusual feature of this hotel is the beds whose bases are made of *tucuruguari*, a mixture of slaked lime, calcium, oxide, and sand.

EATING ALAMOS

CASA DE LOS TESOROS — UPPER — Lovely dining area in courtyard. Sonoran specialties, and international cuisine.

EL CARACOL — MOD — Restaurant on a hilltop in conjunction with RV park of same name, 9 miles west of town. International and Mexican food. Live music on Sunday afternoons. Open noon till 9 PM; closed Mondays.

LA BARRANCA — ECON — Tacos and tortas. Across the barranca up on hill (inquire locally how to get there).

LAS PALMERAS — MOD — On plaza. Good breakfasts.

LOS SABINOS — UPPER — Across arroyo at end of Calle Obregón. Follow signs. Very good food and best prices.

POLO'S — MOD — Downtown seafood restaurant located behind church. American and Mexican food. Specialty is Mexican plate.

SIETE MARES — MOD — Between Casa de los Tesoros & Mansión. An unbelievable place — an old mansion with huge marble columns, lush gardens and fountain. They serve seafood (from 7 seas). You might think you're in Italy, Greece or Spain. Open 10 AM till 10 PM. Owner, Antonio Del Pardo.

CAMPING, PARKING AND PLUGGING IN

DOLISA — UPPER — West side — 50 space facility on highway, within walking distance to town. (Just before the road forks). Owner really cares about the place and it shows. 25 spaces with all hookups; 25 with water and electricity. Pull-thrus. Patios. Bungalows/Apartments. Restrooms. Showers. Security. Dump station. Coin operated laundry. Water purifying plant. Pets on leash OK. Tenting permitted. Friendly. Ph: 8-0131.

EL CARACOL — MOD — West of town, KM 37 — Big 65-space park on highway 9 miles west of town. All hookups. 30 amps Showers. Restrooms. Laundromat. Pool. Fishing. Restaurant (see above). Drive-thru spaces. Pets on leash OK. Ice. Laundry service. Dump station. Friendly. Good Sam-10% disc. SATV. Ph: 8-0117

ACOSTA — UPPER — East side — Older 18-space trailer "rancho" on far east side of town beyond cemetery.

Get to it by the river, not thru town, very pretty. All hookups. 30 amps. Patios. Restrooms. Rec hall palapa. Pool. Horses. Hunting and fishing. Restaurant. SAT TV. Lodge/Bungalows. Pets on leash OK. Friendly. Good Sam Club. Ph: 8-0246.

REAL DE LOS ALAMOS — UPPER — 51-space park on right 11/2 miles before town. Full hookups. Potable water. 30 AMP. Restrooms. Concrete pads. Pool. Laundry. Hot showers. BBQ areas. Special Caravan rates. Carlos Salazar Rodríguez, Manager. (Thanks to F. Eugene Rush Colorado.) Ph: 8-0008.

END ALAMOS EAT & STRAY

Los Mochis

UD-017

Area Code — 68

LOS MOCHIS is rather interesting and offers good accommodations and excellent seafood (only 14 miles from the Sea of Cortés). One of Mexico's most up-and-coming agricultural towns, Los Mochis houses one of the largest sugar refineries on the West Coast in addition to its cotton and vegetable production. Strangely enough Los Mochis was founded in 1893 by an American family, the Johnstons, who came from Virginia to build a sugar refinery — and they laid out the town, building the first church, the lighthouse atop Cerro de la Memoria (Memory Hill), and later an airport. Mr. Johnston died in Hong Kong in 1938 and the family later moved back to the States. The sugar refinery is now owned by Mexican interests.

Mr. Johnston hired very capable Americans to help him run the sugar mill. Among these was Dr. Chapman, the medical doctor for the sugar company and American colony. Following Mr. Johnston's death, Dr. Chapman stayed on and built the Motel Chapman.

Even before the Johnstons founded Los Mochis, there was a Utopian colony established by Albert Kinsey Owen in 1872, the man who conceived the railroad over the Sierras. There are still descendants of these Utopian colonists in and around Los Mochis.

Los Mochis sorta grows on you — it did on me. It's pleasant and clean and prosperous. 'Course, I had to hang around while my VW van was being fixed. Just to give you an idea of the ingenuity of Mexican mechanics, a fellow there **rebuilt** my water pump! Yep, he couldn't get the part, so we went to the *Bomba del Oro* (no foolin'), where another fellow rebuilt that sucker. There's a great taco chain, whose name I don't remember, that sells some pretty good eats. The mall on the north end of town by the old sugar mill is pretty up-to-date. Folks here are real friendly, kinda like Texans. Give Mochis a try, you'll like it. By the way, it doesn't mean "mosquito" as some folks will tell you.

FISHING — Freshwater largemouth black bass fishing is available only 55 miles from Los Mochis at either Presa (dam) Miguel Hidalgo or Domínguez near the picturesque colonial town of El Fuerte (see EL FUERTE SPECIAL). Deep-sea fishing (grouper, yellowtail, roosterfish, and cabrilla, year 'round; dolphin, sailfish, and marlin, June-September) is available from Topolobampo, only 14 miles from Los Mochis.

HUNTING — Los Mochis boasts a very good hunting season from November 1st to February 15th. Duck, speckled geese, quail, and white-tailed dove are plentiful. Hunting arrangements can be made through your hotel or RV park.

FERRY — "Topo" is a typical Mexican fishing village with its fleet of shrimpers and freezing plant, and it's also where the Baja car-passenger ferry operates. 6 weekly departures to La Paz, Baja California Sur: Mon thru Sat at 10 AM. The "Baja Express", a passenger only hydrofoil/catamaran deal will zip people across the bay. (When it works.) Check for schedules — it changes a lot.

MECHANIC — A good one who specializes in VW's is Taller García, Blvd. Jiquilpan #640 (between B. Domínguez and 20 de Noviembre) near the university.

SLEEPING AROUND LOS MOCHIS

COLINAS — MOD — Carr. Internacional & Gaxiola — Good 5-story, 121-room air-con motor inn & RV park atop hill south on Hwy #15 interchange. Restaurant. Coffee shop. Bar-club. 2 pools. Tennis. Parking. AE, MC, VI. Ph: 11-8111, 11-8222 Fax: 11-8181.

CORINTIOS — MOD — Obregón #580 Pte. Very nice, quiet 2-story 49-room hotel. Jacuzzi. Gym. Secure parking. AE, MC, VI. Ph: 18-2224, 18-2300 Fax: 18-2277. Mex: 91-800-69030. **SAC.**

EL DORADO — MOD — Leyva #525 Nte. and Ing. Valdez — 93-room, 3-story air-con hotel plus 50-unit, 2-story motel. Cafeteria. Nice restaurant. Bar. Pool. Playground. Secure parking. **SAC.** AE, MC, VI. Ph: 15-1111, 15-1582 Fax: 12-0179. Mex: 91-800-69009.

PLAZA INN — UPPER — An attractive and quiet Balderama hotel on corner of Leyva and Cárdenas — 125 units. 2 restaurants. Lobby bar. Pool. Parking. Ph: 18-1042, 18-1044 Fax: 18-1043 US: 1-800-862-9026.

POSADA REAL — MOD — Calles Leyva & Buelna — 35 A/C room economy hotel on north end of town. Some English TV. Coffee shop. Parking in front. Ph: 12-2179 Ph & Fax: 12-2363.

SANTA ANITA — UPPER — Corner of Leyva and Hidalgo — 5-story, 133-room downtown hotel. Town's largest. Dining room. Bar. Club. SATV. Travel agency. Parking. AE, DIN, MC, VI. Ph: 18-7046, 18-7184. Mexico City: 5-510-3398. Fax: 12-0046.

VILLA CAHITA — MOD — Corner of Leyva and Ramírez — Remarkably nice 4-story, 66-unit hotel. Parking. No credit cards. Ph & Fax: 12-1200.

EATING LOS MOCHIS

EL BUCANERO — ECON — Allende & Alfonso Cano, Inexpensive eatery. Surprisingly good sea food. Recommended by locals.

EL FARALLÓN (The Rocky Island) — MOD — Corner of Obregón and Flores — Nautical decor (fish nets, seashells, & murals depicting Sea of Cortés). Excellent seafood (the best in town) cocktails and dishes. Open 7 days, 8 AM till 10 PM. AE, MC, VI. Ph: 2-1273, 2-1428.

EL QUEMADO — MOD — Blvd. Macario Gaxiola #372 Sur, Topolobampo Hwy 3 block northeast of Obregón. Sometimes Cabrito, Carne asada, steaks. Down home place with thatched roof. Very popular with locals. Quesadillas on wheat tortillas are huge. MC, VI. Open 7 AM till 11 PM. PH: 15-1833.

ESPAÑA — MOD — On Obregón #525 Pte. Spanish cuisine. Very nice atmosphere. It has a waterfall and aquarium. Open 10 AM till 11 PM. AE, MC, VI. Ph: 12-2221, 12-2335.

LA PARRILLA DORADA — MOD — Leyva #222 Sur — Attractive restaurant converted from old home. Serving Swiss cuisine as well as menudo and other Mexican dishes and Charbroiled steaks. Open 7 AM till midnight. Ph: 12-2603.

PALACIO CHINO — On Blvd. Rosales #350. Ph: 18-1914.

PLAZA INN — On corner of Leyva and Cárdenas. Good food and a swinging place, great for young people who like to party.

SANTA ANITA — MOD — Located in Hotel Santa Anita. It's the only late-night place to eat downtown. Quiet Good. Langostino Pango (fish), steaks, chicken. Serves Peña Fiel agua mineral. Open 6 AM till 11:30 PM. Ph: 18-7046.

TACOS LOS FEOS — Callejón Sinaloa & Gabriel Leyva — A taco lover's delight. Tacos al pastor, carne asada, and tripita.

CAMPING, PARKING AND PLUGGING IN

COLONIAS — MOD — South end near bullring — 67 spaces (EWS). ENGLISH. Shower, toilets laundry. 30 AMP. PH: 11-8111 or 18-8222 Fax: 11-8181.

COPPER CANYON RV PARK — MOD — 1/2 mile off freeway. 120 spaces with all hookups. Mail address: Apdo. Postal #1201 Los Mochis 81200, Sin. Personal checks accepted. **SAC.** Ph: 12-6817 Fax: 12-0046.

LOS MOCHIS — MOD — 120-pull-thru-space park at north entrance to town. All hookups. Showers. Toilets. Rec. hall. Laundry. Brick patios. Security. Restaurant (seasonal). Pets OK. Convenient to town. Ph: 12-1388 or 12-6817.

RÍO FUERTE — ECON-MOD — Nice 58 pull-thru-space riverside facility just off Hwy #15, 10 miles north of town, 400 yards south of the overpass and just before the bridge. All hookups. Showers. Toilets. Rec. Hall. Laundry. Store. Heated pool (soon to be, it was not ready when I was there). Security. Pets OK. Ph: 15-6465 Fax: 12-6146. Mailing address is: Vicente Guerrero #440 Nte, Los Mochis, Sinaloa.

END LOS MOCHIS EAT & STRAY

El Fuerte

UD-017

Area Code — 689

EL FUERTE, accessible by a nice paved road, is a quaint colonial town still undiscovered by tourists. Originally named "El Fuerte de Montes Claros", the town was founded in 1564 by the Spanish conquistador Francisco de Ibarra and soon became the most important military post of the Spaniards in their conquest of Northwestern Mexico and California. El Fuerte, meaning "fort", was a stronghold of fortification built to protect the soldiers and settlers from the continuous fierce raids by the Yaqui, Mayo and other Indian tribes. The Yaqui tribe lives on the north side of river and the Mayo tribe on the south side. The settlement eventually flourished and for three centuries it was the principal commercial and farming center and the major trading post for silver miners as well as gold seekers. At one time there were more than 400 mines in the area. In 1855 it even became the state capital for a short period.

Today, El Fuerte has retained its old Mexican character and atmosphere — cobblestone streets, old houses with "*portales*" (arches), patios filled with beautiful tropical foliage, wrought-iron windows and doors, an ancient plaza with its ornate kiosk, a century-old church (with a cactus growing on its steeple), and much more. Of particular interest when in the area is a visit to the Ocolome Jesuit Mission and to the old Mayo Indian village where ancestral customs still prevail.

El Fuerte is a paradise for fishermen and hunters. Fishing at nearby Domínguez and Hidalgo Lakes is great. Black bass and catfish are plentiful and both "*presas*" (dams) are only a 30-minute drive from downtown El Fuerte. For the hunter there are duck, mourning and whitewing dove, and blue pigeon. It's not uncommon to shoot the daily limit of ducks and to catch the daily limit of bass the same day along the banks of Domínguez Lake.

Remember, you can take the train through to the copper canyon from here. We recommend you do that instead of going all the way to Los Mochis. You save three hours.

SLEEPING AROUND EL FUERTE

EL FUERTE — MOD — Very friendly place with 25 rooms and nice courtyard in old mansion. Excellent restaurant with fantastic meals. No credit cards. They can arrange tours and train tickets Owner, Robert Brand used to own La Paloma in Nuevo León state. Ph: 3-0226
OASIS — ECON — Angel Flores s/n. 10-room budget hotel run by nice elderly lady. Small rooms.
HIDALGO LODGE — Lupi Nieblas & Tom Jenkins, Nice lodge for hunting/fishing. 24 units. A/C. Ph: (706) 813-0657 in El Fuerte, Box 11. In U.S. P.O. Box 3036, Burbank, CA 91504, Ph: (213) 388-4157. Thanks to Ingrid Bautista for her help.
POSADA DE HIDALGO — MOD — Hidalgo #101, Centro Histórico de la Ciudad — Nice 37-room hotel a half-block from main square, once the largest and most beautiful colonial mansion in El Fuerte. Restaurant. Bar. Disco. Filtered pool. Street parking (with security). AE, MC, VI. (This hotel has been declared a historical landmark as it's where Presidente Venustiano Carranza slept in room 7 in September, 1913.) Ph & Fax: 3-0242 in El Fuerte, or 12-0046 in Los Mochis, or 14-16-5950 in Chihuahua. A Balderama hotel. A disco is next door.
SAN FRANCISCO — MOD — Av. Obregón #201 — OK 18-room hotel centered around a flowered patio on the cobblestone street into town. Restaurant. Bar. MC, VI. Ph: 3-0055.

*Rio Vista - on the hill & the river - 10 rooms
Reasonable rates - Mexican castle - owner - Charlie
take Dominguez Lodge - reasonable - also Hunting Lodge -
owners ... Trinidad*

EATING EL FUERTE

CAPRI — ECON — Next to San Francisco hotel. Open 7 AM till 11 PM. On Mondays, 8 AM till 4 PM. MC, VI.

✦**EL MESON DEL GENERAL** — MOD — Benito Juárez #202, one block towards highway from square. Seafood, steaks. Locally popular. MC, VI.

LA PALOMA — Restaurant in Posada de Hidalgo. Romantic, overlooking flower garden. Has crayfish soup, black bass (Lobina), panela asada — grilled goat cheese.

✦**PASEO DE LAS AVES** — Go 2 blocks past main plaza, then look for sign saying to turn left. Follow signs. It's on the river and has swings for kids. Specializes in Lobina. Open 9 AM till 11 PM. MC, VI. Ph: 3-0986.

END EL FUERTE EAT & STRAY!

Culiacán

UD-017

Area Code — 67

SLEEPING AROUND CULIACÁN

COLONIAL — ECON — Madero #730 Pte. — 47-room, 3-story a/c hotel. Restaurant. Parking. Pets OK. Ph: 12-8500.

DEL VALLE — MOD — Blvd. Solano #180 Ote. — 3-story, 42-room a/c motel on boulevard thru town. Restaurant. Beauty shop. Pharmacy. Ice machines. Parking. Small pets OK. AE, MC, VI. Ph: 13-9020, 13-9120, 13-9080, or 13-9170. This hotel is being renovated.

EJECUTIVO — UPPER — Corner of Obregón and Madero — Very good 6-story, 229-room a/c downtown hotel. Cafeteria. Restaurant. Bars. Pool. Servibars. Tennis. Gift shop. Solarium. Parking. AE, MC, VI. Ph: 13-9300, 13-9301 or 13-9310.

LOS CAMINOS — MOD-UPPER — South end of Solano Boulevard — Remodeled 51-room, 2-story a/c motel thru town. Restaurant. Bar. Pool. Night security. Parking. AE, MC, VI. Ph: 15-3300.

SALVADOR — ECON — Solano Boulevard — 40-room, 7-story a/c hotel thru town practically across from bus station. No restaurant. On-street parking. MC, VI. Ph: 3-7462.

SAN LUIS — MOD — Av. de las Palmas #1 — 45-unit a/c motel atop hill ("Lomas de Culiacán") on the south end of Obregón next to Basilica of Guadalupe Church. Rooftop dining room. Pool. Parking. AE, MC, VI. Ph: 13-1600, 13-1400, 13-1500 or 16-7010. Fax: 15-0815.

TRES RÍOS — MOD — KM 1423 Carr. Internacional — Good, recommended by readers, as not fancy, but good, 68-unit a/c motor inn at north end. Pleasant restaurant. Bar. Pool. Parking. AE, MC, VI. Ph: 15-4040, 15-4140, 15-4540, 15-4340 or 15-4440. Fax: 16-4435.

VALLE BONITO — MOD — Corner of Solano and Carranza — 40-room, 3-story a/c motel. Restaurant. Servibars. Parking. Small pets OK. AE, MC, VI. 13-9320 or 13-9220

EATING CULIACÁN

EL CHAPARRAL LOMITA — UPPER — Obregón #1244 Sur — Nice restaurant on far west end of Obregón just below San Luis. Specializes in steaks.

LA TAVOLA — MOD — Popular restaurant across from Plaza Ley, almost behind bus station. Pizza and Spaghetti a la Bolognesa plus draft beer.

TRES RÍOS — MOD-UPPER — Recommended restaurant in hotel of same name. Thanks to R. Heller of Green Valley AZ.

CAMPING, PARKING AND PLUGGING IN

TRES RÍOS — UPPER — North of town on Hwy #15 — Good 18-space park in conjunction with motel at north end. All hookups. 20 amps. Restrooms. Showers. Pool. Laundry service. Several patios. Restaurant. Boat ramp. Ice. Disco. TV lounge. Tennis. AE, MC, VI. Ph: 12-3030.

LOS CASCABELES — MOD — 13 miles south of town on Hwy #15, KM 1401 and 3.5 miles on Hwy #19 toward Costa Rica City. 20 acres with surrounding fence. Cabins. Boats. Restaurant. Pool. Store. Sport field. Phones. Hunting & fishing nearby. Ph: 13-6418 or 13-6822.

END CULIACÁN EAT & STRAY

Mazatlán

UD-017

Area Code — 69

WHAT'S HAPPENIN' IN MAZATLÁN

Altitude: 16 feet. Population: 500,000. Least crowded — Aug-Sept. Rainiest — July-Aug. Coolest — Jan-Feb. MAZATLÁN, meaning "Land of Deer" in Nahuatl, is on the same latitude as Honolulu and has an average temperature of 80° F. It's Mexico's largest Pacific coast seaport, a major vacation resort city and the closest one to the USA.

Spaniards officially founded the city in 1513 at the foot of Cerro de la Nevería. Here they loaded the Spanish galleons with gold and silver from nearby gold and silver mines for transport back to Spain — that is, if they managed to survive the storms and outwit the English privateers. It later became known as the Athens of the West and was finally incorporated in 1806.

Today, Mazatlán is a thriving seaport on the international trade routes and the center of one of the largest fishing industries in Mexico. More than 37 million pounds of shrimp are processed yearly and tons are frozen daily and shipped to the USA. Tourism has developed quickly into the second largest industry behind fishing. Mazatlán currently has more than 140 hotels and 8,500 hotel rooms and more are to come as new hotels are built and others expand.

Nicknamed the "Pearl of the Pacific", it's many folks' favorite spot. Like Acapulco, you can go there with a dollar in your pocket or a hundred — & have a good time. My favorite thing is to get away from the "Golden Zone" & walk along the "Olas Altas" promenade. Here's where the first "beachfront" hotels were. If you want an area where peddlers & condo salesmen don't besiege you, this is the place. The 17 KM boulevard is the 2nd longest beachside promenade in Latin America.

The area is infested with timeshare sales people. Many have "tourist information" kiosks. They are there to make an appointment for a "free" breakfast. Use your own judgement. Also people who ask "Are you enjoying your vacation?" are also sales people.

AQUARIUM — One of the largest in Latin America, it's off Av. Reforma, near Av. De los Deportes.

INTERESTING FOOD — It's the last place, south or east, where you'll find Toni-Col, a vanilla soft drink made in Rosario, Sin. Jericalla — a desert like flan without syrup, covered with chocolate. Good clean seafood place off malecón heading toward town center on bus route, Calle Nelson, only a stall at corner "Tonito's" clean and cheap. Thanks to Juliet McLaren, Vancouver BC.

If you want to save money, look for places that have a *"Comida Corrida"*, which is the traditional Mexican lunch. The menu will be set & you'll get maybe 2 choices of main courses, beans or rice, soup, a salad & maybe coffee or tea. Another way is to drink (eat?) a *"licuado"* for breakfast. They're fresh fruits (papaya, melón, mango, banana etc.) blended before your eyes with milk, sugar (or honey — *"miel de abeja"*). You can add wheat germ — *"trigo"*, oatmeal — *"avena"*, nuts or whatever they've got. It's quick, & cheap — a dollar or two for enough to fill you up. You'll find a good *licuado* stand (the only one that's open late at night) downtown, near the market, on Juárez, across from a bank. Make sure you specify *"con leche"* (with milk) instead of water. You'll find 'em everywhere in Mexico. Of course, papaya and many fruit juices are useful to "loosen one up" and banana is good as a "stopper", so make sure you order the right one. Also for some folks (like me) milk works like papaya — got it?

FISHING — Mazatlán enjoys a reputation as an outstanding deep-sea fishing port and is known as the billfish capital of the world. Several world records have been set here. Striped marlin abound from December thru April and sailfish from May thru November. There are several reliable fishing outfits in Mazatlán. BILL HEIMPEL'S STAR FLEET is one of the best. He has 5 boats — 2 / 34 feet (2 fishing chairs; maximum 4 persons); 38 feet & 40 feet (3 fishing chairs; maximum 5 persons); and 43 feet (4 or 5 fishing chairs). His boats meet U.S. Coast Guard standards, are equipped with life preservers, and are quite comfortable. The crews know their stuff. Cost is $70.00 per person to secure a back booth. 4 or 5 people and $240 to $300 to rent the whole boat. They'll fix you a box lunch (tuna or ham & cheese sandwiches) for a small fee. The fishing license is $7.00. Even Mikey can catch fish with them. For reservations call 82-3878 or 82-2665 Fax: 82-5155.

The Avis fleet is also very good with modern boats and safety equipment. They have 10 boats 2 - 28 feet, 3 - 31 feet, 2 - 33 feet, 2 - 36 feet, 1 - 45 feet. Cost: 28 feet - $290; 31-33 feet - $325; 36 feet - $375; 45 feet - $430. Fishing license $7.00. Will pick up at hotel at 6:30 AM. Ph: 16-3468. 1-800-525-1925, 1-800-634-3085.

For those willing to chance it, the El Dorado fleet certainly doesn't meet any safety standards, nor are their boats in good shape, but they are less expensive. They are single engine boats. Ph: 81-6204, 13-5820.

Another outfit is FLOTA FARO with a fleet of boats — 35 feet (2 fishing chairs); 35 feet (3 fishing chairs); and 42 feet (4 or 5 fishing chairs). Ph: 81-2824 or 82-4977 for reservations. Fishing trips are from 6:30 AM till 3 PM and include bait, tackle, and crew (fishing licenses extra). Beer and soft drinks are available on board. Remember that "catch & release" is the smart way to fish.

U.S. CONSULAR AGENT — Gerianne L. Nelson de Gallardo, Av. R. Laizo #202 adjacent to Hotel Playa Mazatlán. Open 9 AM till 12:30 PM Mon-Thurs, 10:30 AM till 2:30 PM, Fri. Ph: 16-5889. After hours call 91-62-17-2375.

SHOPPING — For dresses, shirts, rugs, etc., an easygoing place is *"EL GENERAL."* Market Bugambillas, Sabalo & Costa Azul #14 (in the Gold Zone). Owner Arturo Castro G. is a nice guy, speaks English & not pushy.

ARTS & CRAFTS CENTER — A block north of Playa Mazatlán on Las Gaviotas, is worth a visit to see artisans from several parts of Mexico work at their crafts. Large selection of gifts. Open from 9 AM till 6 PM, 7 days. THE DESIGNER'S BAZAAR, TEQUILA TREE, and CASA PACÍFICA (in the "Golden Zone") feature interesting clothes, leather goods, crafts, and jewelry.

SIGHTSEEING — The MAZATLÁN FIESTA CRUISE (3 hours) departs daily at 10:30 am from north end of main docks and features Mexico's largest fishing fleet, Seal Islands, La Paz Ferry, beaches from offshore, French Cannon, second-highest natural lighthouse in the world, and more. As with most of these deals, lots of booze and music. The **CITY TOUR** (2 1/2 hours) departs daily at 9:30 AM and at 2:30 PM and features the basilica, municipal palace, Fisherman's Monument, Spanish fort, residential areas, market, etc. The **COUNTRY TOUR** features a visit to some rural villages back in the foothills including Concordia (leather goods and furniture) and Copala and Rosario (old silver-mining towns). **LOS CHIVOS ISLAND TOUR** departures are daily at 11 AM, 1 PM, and 3 PM from Restaurant La Palapa (short distance up beach from Mazatlán) and next to Suites Las Flores by amphibious truck *La Barca de Oro.* To book any of the tours mentioned above, contact Agencia de Viajes ABZ (see INSURANCE).

BULLFIGHTS — Nov.-Apr. on Sun. Bullring on Blvd. Rafael Buelna. Buy tickets there, at El Camerón Motel or a travel agency. Ph: 84-1666.

SEA LIONS — Oct-May. Hire a boat to take you to the island where they winter.

PULMONIAS (Pneumonias?) — Open-air three-wheeled carts with only a canopy found all over town. They carry 3 persons and their fares are cheaper than taxi — and they're *mucho* fun!

ICE BOX HILL *Cerro de la Nevería* — So named because many years ago the ice brought from San Francisco by ship was stored in the two tunnels. In the very early days (during the 16th and 17th centuries) this "hill" was used as a lookout for pirate ships. Perhaps the most interesting part in history played by this "hill" was during the revolution in 1914 when Mazatlán became the second city in the world to be bombed by an airplane (first was Tripoli, Libya). General Carranza's forces sent an old biplane to bomb the lookout fort atop Ice Box Hill. The story has been told that the pilot overflew the target and the bombardier, overcome by airsickness, lost his grasp on the bomb and it fell into the streets below killing two civilians and injuring several others. We've heard that this crude bomb was dynamite and pieces of old iron packed in pigskin. How true? *¿Quién sabe?* There's a science-fiction book with this event as a setting.

CARNIVAL — This is Mazatlán's main event, held during Mardi Gras (but really starts the preceding Friday and peaks the Sunday before). It's a mixture of New Orleans and Río de Janero with parades, coronation parties, street dances, floats, fireworks, and costumed merrymakers. There is no sleep during those days and reservations must be made for hotels at least 6 months in advance. SPECIAL EVENTS (Besides Carnival) — May 1-10 — Rosario holds "Spring Festival", during which typical dishes & folklore shows are enjoyed. Sept. 4-10 — Escuinapa celebrates the "Feria del Mango & Mazatlán celebrates the "Week of Commerce." Every store in Mazatlán develops a different event or promotion.

STATE TOURISM OFFICE — Paseo Olas Altas #1300 1st floor Banamex Bldg. Ph: 85-0983, 85-1220, 85-1847.

MONEY EXCHANGE — La Farga at Sabalo # 508 in the Gold Zone, also sells stamps and has long distance phone and fax service Ph: 69-14-2199, 13-1560. Open 8 AM till 8 PM week days Sat & Sun 10 AM — 3 PM. Near El Cid, Holiday Inn & other hotels there are several. Aquilles Serdán, A. Serdán #1225, Centro. Ph: 82-2688. The Shrimp Bucket, Olas Altas.

CRESTON LIGHTHOUSE — On hilltop near fishing fleet harbor, reportedly the second highest lighthouse in the world (515 feet above sea level) — and quite a hike to the top!

CLIFF DIVERS — Local divers leap from rock cliffs near tourist office. Times vary, so check with tourist office for details.

FERRY TERMINAL — Located on Calle Carnaval (Prol. Muelles Fiscales). Be sure to book passage for both your passengers and vehicle when you arrive in Mazatlán. Regulations, phones, schedules change so refer to "HOW 'BOUT THEM FERRIES?." Our Mazatlán agent can make reservations for you.

FRIENDS OF BILL W. — (ENGLISH) — El Cid Country Club (clubhouse, across from the hotel). M.W.F. 8:00 PM.

LAUNDRY — EL SABALO — In Gold Zone at Sabalo #1666 across from Sr. Frog. Ph: 14-2634.

NEARBY ATTRACTIONS — TEACAPAN is only 56 miles south on Hwy #15, then 26 miles west, a little off the beaten track. Go there if you have a spirit of adventure and you are tired of the party atmosphere of Mazatlán. Naturalists will enjoy the place and the (so far) unspoiled beaches. You can fish, go birding and loaf. Wildlife includes white & pink heron and pichihuila and deer. This is a small town with friendly folks and beautiful scenery. There are two good hotels: In town is Hotel Denisse, which is small (5 rooms) & inexpensive; farther out is the Rancho Los Angeles with the best restaurant in town, perhaps in Mexico. It is for a more affluent crowd with private bungalows and a swimming pool. The only RV park is The Oregon, on the beach, near Sr. Wayne's restaurant.

COPALA is only 15 1/2 miles south on Hwy #15, then 27 miles east on Hwy 40. It's an old mining town and Daniel's restaurant is worth the trip. Daniel Garrison is the owner and was mentioned in the Nov. 1973 National Geographic article on the place. He's 60 and looks better than I. Well, I don't want to give you the wrong impression — he looks very good. He serves the best California-Tex-Mex-Arkansas style food in the world. His dad was born in Gravit Ark., but Daniel is Mexican. He lived in CA and came home, after working 15 years in the oil fields and realizing life in Mexico was better. Be sure to try his banana creme coconut pie.

SLEEPING AROUND MAZATLÁN

The oceanfront boulevard, which has most of the hotels, changes names several times, so don't become confused. Since Mazatlán is a popular resort with Mexicans, as well as Americans and Canadians, advance reservations are mandatory during the two weeks before and after Christmas and Easter. They're pretty smart from mid-December onward, too. If you don't make 'em, you'll still find a place to sleep, but you'll have to be flexible. Facilities are air-conditioned unless otherwise noted. Budget places (as anywhere) are located near the bus station, between the beach and downtown, and near the ferry terminal.

AMIGO PLAZA (Formerly, Las Brisas) — MOD — 53-room, 7-story hotel at Av. Del Mar #900 across from beach. Restaurant. Pool. Tennis. Parking. MC, VI. Ph: 83-0333, 83-6699 Fax: 83-7282.

AMMACZATLAN — MOD — Nice 3-story, 40-condo complex on beach at Sabalo Cerritos #576 at north end. One and two bedroom units. Pool. Parking. AE, DI, MC, VI. Ph: 14-1219.

AQUA MARINA — MOD — Rambling 100-unit, 2-story motel at Av. Del Mar #110. Restaurant. Bar. Pool. Parking. MC, VI. Ph: 81-7080 to 85 or 81-6909. Fax: 82-4624. Best Western.

AZTECA INN — MOD — Good Value! Av. Rodolfo T. Loaiza #307 — 74-room, 3-story motel across from

Playa Mazatlán. Noé at front desk speaks English and is helpful. Restaurant-bar. Pool. Jacuzzi. Parking. MC, VI. Ph: 13-4655, 13-4477 or 13-4425. MEX: 91-800-69770 Fax: 13-7476.

BALBOA TOWERS — UPPER — Delightful 52-unit hotel on Camarón Sabalo next to Balboa Club on beach. 30 rooms, 15 suites, and 11 master suites, all with kitchenettes. No restaurant. 2 pools with bar. Gym. Sauna. Travel agency. Curio shop. Parking. AE, MC, VI. Several customers have recommended it. "Every one there helpful, especially half owner Martin in restaurant." (Mr. & Mrs. Russell Heller) Ph: 13-7784, 13-7290, 13-7144, or 13-5558.

BELMAR — ECON — 200-room, 6 story old-time hotel near downtown on Olas Altas #166. Secure parking. Pool. Some rooms have good views. It's a little down at the heels but inexpensive. A sort of "faded grandeur" place. AE, MC, VI, Ph: 85-1111 AL 13, Fax: 81-3428.

BELTRÁN — ECON — Aquiles Serdán #2509 Nte. Backpacker hotel. 28 ceiling fanned rooms. Ph: 82-4654.

BUNGALOWS DE RUEDA - ECON — Sandy 6-apartment layout on north end. Pool. Parking. Pets OK. Ph: 82-5278.

BUNGALOWS MAR-SOL — MOD — Av. Camarón Sabalo #1001. Very clean, double & single beds with kitchenettes. Just beyond Posada la Misión. Real nice management. Parking for cars, MC, VI. (A. Verhulst, Grandview MO). Ph: 84-01-08.

CAMINO REAL — UPPER — Nice 170-room, 4-story beach hotel on north end up on knoll *"Punta del Sabalo."* 2 restaurants. 2 lounges. Club. Disco. Inviting pool. Tennis. Travel agency. Shopping arcade. Putting green. Masseuse. AE, MC, VI. Ph: 13-1111. US: 800-722-6466. Fax: 14-0311.

DOUBLE TREE (formerly CARAVELLE) — 128-room, 7-story beachfront hotel on Camarón Sabalo. Restaurant. Bar. Tennis. Parking. AE, MC, VI. Ph: 13-0200, 130377, 13,0288. Fax: 16-6261. US: 1-800-222-TREE MEX: 1-800-69559.

COSTA BRAVA — UPPER — Lovely 164-condo complex on Camarón Sabalo Cerritos next to Paraíso Mar. One- and two-bedroom units. Restaurant. Bar. Club. Nice pool. Tennis. Parking. AE, MC, VI. Ph: 83-6444.

COSTA DE ORO — MOD — 292 room, 4-story motel on Camarón Sabalo on beach. Beautiful grounds across from noisy disco. Restaurant. Bars. Pool. 3 Tennis courts. Shopping arcade. Travel agency. Curio shop. Parking. AE, MC, VI. Ph: 13-5344, 13-2005, 13-5800, or 13-5344. Fax: 14-4209. US: 800-342-2431. Mex: 91-800-69-666.

DAMY'S BUNGALOWS — ECON — 28-unit, 3-story motel on Av. Del Mar #1200 at Camarón Glorieta. 19 kitchenettes. Some A/C. Pool. Parking. Pets OK. Ph: 83-4700, 83-4766.

DAYS INN (POSADA DE DON PELAYO) — MOD — 160 unit, 10 story hotel at Av. Del Mar #111 across from beach. Restaurant. Bar. Club. Pool. Tennis. Car rental agency. Travel agency. Parking. AE, MC, VI. Ph: 83-1888 or 83-2233. Fax: 84-0799.

DE CIMA — ECON-MOD — Big 4-story, 140-room hotel on Av. Del Mar. Some quieter rooms. Restaurant. Cafeteria. Club. Pool. Tennis. Book Shop. Curio shop. Tunnel from hotel to beach. Parking. AE, MC, VI. Ph: 85-1855. Fax: 82-7311.

DEL SOL — ECON-MOD — 20 rooms, 12 kitchenettes at Av. Del Mar #800. Bar. Pool. Parking. AE, MC, VI. Ph: 85-1103 or 85-2603. A Sanborn's Agent.

EL QUIJOTE INN — UPPER — On beach at corner of Av. Camarón Sabalo & Tiburón. 67 rooms, kitchenettes. Pool. SATV. Restaurant. Bar. SATV. Jacuzzi. AE, MC, VI. Ph: 14-3621, 14-3609 or 14-1134. Fax: 14-3344.

FIESTA INN — UPPER — Lovely new hotel with beach on Av. Camarón Sabalo #1927. 117 rooms. 2 pools. Ph: 89-0100 Fax: 89-0150.

HACIENDA — MOD — 95-room, 9-story air-con hotel on corner Av. Del Mar & Flamingos. Pool. Restaurant. Bar. Parking. AE, MC, VI. Ph: 82-7000 Fax: 85-1579.

HOLIDAY INN — UPPER — 204-room, 6-floor beach front hotel on Camarón Sabalo #696. 3 restaurants. Bar. Disco. 2 pools. Tennis. Tobacco shop. Boutiques. Barber & beauty shops. Drug store. Parking. AE, MC, VI. Ph: 13-2222 Fax: 14-1287. US: 800-465-4329 Mex: 91-800-00-999.

INN AT MAZATLÁN — UPPER — Located at Camarón Sabalo #6291. 142 rooms. Ph: 13-5166, 13-5354, Fax: 83-4782.

ISLAS DEL SOL — MOD-UPPER — Good 75-unit, 19-story condo-hotel tower on Camarón Sabalo on beach next to Holiday Inn. 2-bedroom units. Restaurant. Bar. Pool. Parking. Use of Holiday Inn's facilities. AE, MC, VI. Ph: 13-0088, 13-0199, 13-0044, 13-0066, 13-0022, Fax: 13-5666.

JACARANDAS — ECON — Av del Mar across from noisy disco. 160 rooms, kitchenettes. Restaurant. Bar. 2 pools. Tennis courts. Ocean view. Parking. AE, MC, VI. Ph: 84-1177, 84-1277, Fax: 84-1077.

LA CASA CONTENTA — MOD — 8 one-bedroom kitchenettes on Playa Gaviotas just north of Playa Mazatlán. 5 A/C units. Pool. Parking. MC, VI. Ph: 13-4976, 13-9986

LA MARINA YACHT CLUB — MOD-UPPER — Av. Sabalos Cerritos. 103 rooms, kitchenettes. 2 tennis courts. SATV. AE, MC, VI. Ph: 83-0000.

LA SIESTA — ECON-MOD — 54-room, 2-story hotel at Olas Altas 11 Sur. A/C and ceiling fans in some rooms. Quiet with views. Shrimp Bucket Restaurant. Bar. No pool. Shops. Parking. AE, MC, VI. Ph: 81-2640 Fax: 13-7476 (Azteca Inn - same owner).

LAS PALMAS — MOD — 78-room, 2-story hotel at Camarón Sabalo north of Camarón Glorieta. Restaurant. Bar. Pool. Parking. AE, MC, VI. Ph: 13-4255, 13-4366, 13-4969 Fax: 14-3477 Mex: 91-800-69777.

LOS ARCOS — MOD — 20-apartment, 2-story beachfront motel on Playa Las Gaviotas beyond Playa Mazatlán. 1 & 2 bedroom kitchenette units. Pool. Parking. Ph: 83-5066.

LOS SABALOS — UPPER — Luxurious 185-room, 8-story beachfront hotel on Playa Las Gaviotas between Playa del Rey and Playa Mazatlán, on Rodolfo T. Loaiza #100. Some rooms are noisy from a nearby disco. Check first. Dignified. Restaurant. SATV. Bar. Club. Pool. Tennis. (Access to jacuzzi, sauna, steambath at health club in front of hotel — for a fee). Parking. AE, MC, VI. Ph: 83-5333, 83-5409. Fax: 83-8156. US: 800-528-8760. Mex: 91-800-69-700.

MARLEY — MOD — 16-kitchenette, 2-story beachfront motel on Playa Las Gaviotas. One and two-bedroom units. Pool. Parking. Ph: 13-5533.

MILÁN — ECON — J.M. Canizales Pte. #717 — A popular backpacker's place. 24 rooms, some with A/C. Ph: 81-3588.

OCÉANO PALACE — UPPER — 200-room, 6-story hotel on beach just beyond Holiday Inn on Camarón Sabalo. Restaurant-bar. Roxy Disco. 2 pools. Tennis. Shopping arcade. Travel agency. Parking. AE, MC, VI. Ph: 13-0666, 13-0777, 13-6605, 13-0688 or 13-0755. US: 800-352-7690. Fax: 13-9666. Mex: 91-800-69678

PARAÍSO DEL MAR — UPPER — 153-unit, 10-story condo-hotel on Av. Sabalo Cerritos next to Costa Brava on beach. Restaurant. Bar. Club. Pool. Billiards. Tennis. Bowling. Shops. Parking. AE, MC, VI. Ph: 83-6444.

PARAÍSO MAZATLÁN — MOD — 25-suite, 2 story complex at Calle del Calamar and Atún. 1-2-3-bedroom suites and houses plus a penthouse. Pool. Tennis. Rec hall. Parking. MC, VI. Ph: 83-8786 or 83-8767. Budget.

PLAYA MAR — ECON — 60 unit, 4 story hotel at Av. Del Mar #139 across from beach. 25 kitchenettes. Disco. Pool. On street parking. MC, VI. Ph: 14-0617.

PLAYA MAZATLÁN — UPPER — Av. Rodolfo T. Loaiza #202 — Good 425-room, 5 story beachfront hotel on Playa Las Gaviotas. Many restaurants and bars. Pool. Shopping arcade. Parking. AE, MC, VI. Ph: 13-4444, 13-1120 Fax: 14-0366 US: 800-762-5816. Mex: 91-800-69567.

PLAZA GAVIOTAS — UPPER — 66-room, 3 story motel across from Playa Mazatlán on Playa Las Gaviotas, Bugambillas #100. Restaurant. Bar. Pool. Boutiques. Parking. AE, MC, VI. Ph: 13-4322, 13-54233, 13-4754,134496, Fax: 13-6685.

POSADA COLONIAL — ECON — Older 18 unit motel at Alemán #11, about a half-mile from ferry terminal. Some A/C. Parking. AE, MC, VI. Ph: 13-1888. Budget.

POSADA LA MISIÓN — ECON — 96 unit, 2 story hotel on Camarón Sabalo across from beach. 54 kitchenettes. Restaurant. Bar. Pool. Parking. MC, VI. Ph: 13-2444 or 13-2533.

POSADA SANTA FE — MOD — 3 story, 28 unit beachfront apartment-motel on north beach. Pool. Parking. Ph: 83-5444.

PUEBLO BONITO — UPPER — On beach at Av. Camarón Sabalo #2121 — 245 rooms, kitchenettes, SATV. 3 restaurants. Bar. Pool. A/C. AE, MC, VI. Ph: 14-3700. Fax: 14-1723. US: 800-262-4500.

PUESTA DEL SOL — MOD — 50-room, 6 story hotel on beach on Camarón Sabalo adjacent to El Cid. Restaurant. Bar. Pool. Parking. AE, MC, VI. Ph: 13-5522, 13-5411, 13-5433 or 13-5544. Fax: 14-3381. Mex: 91-800-69-977

RIVIERA MAZATLÁN (formerly the ARISTOS, the PLAYA DEL REY) — UPPER — 258-room, 4-story hotel at Camarón Sabalo #51 on beach. Restaurant. Bar. Club. Pool. Jacuzzi. Tobacco shop. Car rental. Travel agency. Shopping arcade. Parking. AE, MC, VI. Ph: 83-4822, 83-4772. Fax: 84-4532. Mex: 91-800-69555

SANDS/LAS ARENAS — ECON — 67-room, Fairly quiet 3 story hotel on Av. Del Mar #191 across from beach next door to disco. Restaurant. Bar. Pool. Parking. AE, MC, VI. Ph: 82-0600, 82-0800, 82-1015, 82-0000. Fax: 82-1025. **SAC** 40% discount.

SAN JUAN — ECON — 56-room, 4 story hotel on Camarón Sabalo just north of El Cid. Restaurant. Bar. Pool. Parking. MC, VI. Ph: 83-5821.

SOLAMAR INN — MOD — 40-room, 4 story condo-hotel across from beach at Camarón Sabalo #1942 next to Las Brisas. Restaurant. Bar. 2 pools. Parking. AE, MC, VI. Ph: 83-6666.

SUITES CARIBE — MOD — 122-suite, 12 story condo-hotel on Loaiza next to Las Brisas. Pool. On-grounds parking. AE, MC, VI. Ph: 81-7288.

SUITES LAS FLORES — MOD — On beach, 119-kitchenette, 12 story hotel near arts-and-crafts center on Loaiza. Restaurant. Bar. Pool. Tennis. Parking. AE, MC, VI. Ph: 13-5100, 13-5122, 135011. US: 800-452-0627. CA: 800-252-0327. Fax: 14-3422.

SUITES LINDA MAR — MOD — 12-suite, 3 story hotel at Playa Las Gaviotas #222 on beach. Kitchenettes. Pool. Parking. AE, MC, VI. Ph: 83-5533.

SUITES LOS ARROYOS — MOD — 38-room, 4 story hotel at Camarón Sabalo #308. Restaurant. Pool. Tobacco shop. Travel agency. Parking. MC, VI. Ph: 13-4277.

SUITES MARCO — ECON — 12-kitchenette, 2-story layout on Av. Del Mar #1234. Pool. Parking. Ph: 83-5998.

SUITES TECALI — ECON — 14-kitchenette, 3-story complex at Gabriel Ruiz #3 in El Dorado Subdivision. Pool. Parking. MC, VI. Budget. Ph: 14-7754 Fax: 14-7755

TROPICANA — MOD — 140-room, 10-story hotel at Loaiza #17 across from Los Sabalos. Restaurant. Bar. Pool. Tubs. Parking. AE, MC, VI. Ph: 83-8000 Fax: 83-8233 MEX: 91-800-69600.

VIDALMAR — MOD — 14-suite, 3-story hotel at Av. Las Palmas #15 between downtown and north beach. Pool. No parking. Ph: 81-2190, 81-2197, 81-2820.

VILLA DEL MAR — ECON — A. Serdán #1506 Nte., near 21 de Marzo. 26 ceiling-fanned rooms. Parking. Rocking chairs in lobby. Simple, clean. Budget. Ph: 81-3426 Fax: 81-1952.

EATING MAZATLÁN

ALELUYA'S — MOD — Camerón Sabalo #406 open-air & enclosed restaurant just down from Panamá Restaurant. Mexican food, seafood. Party atmosphere. Open 11 AM till Midnight. Ph: 13-2040.

CASA DEL COUNTRY — MOD — On Camerón Sabalo in front of Hotel El Quijote Inn. A lively place with loud music and dancing. Great for kids. Serves seafood, cabrito al horno and lots of drinks. Like Carlos 'n Charlie but with more class. Ph: 16-5300.

CASA LOMA — MOD — Nice restaurant at Las Gaviotas #104. Secluded dining room plus informal outside patio. Variety of international dishes. Poached fish with 3 wine sauces is the specialty. Reservations suggested. Open Oct. — Apr. Hours: 12 Noon till 10 PM. AE, MC, VI. Ph: 13-5398.

COPA DE LECHE — ECON — Next to Belmar Hotel in Olas Altas. An open-air restaurant on Malecón. Popular with backpackers. Seafood and Mexican food. Open 7 AM till 11 PM. MC, VI. Ph: 83-5753

DONEY — MOD — ATMOSPHERE — Av. Mariano Escobedo 610. Downtown. Very good restaurant east of cathedral. All types of Mexican food including seafood and steaks — also **cabrito!** But only at lunch and only sometimes. Comida Corida! French bean soup, alubias. (It's an Italian name & it's like a little bit of Rome, with strolling violin, accordion & base trios.) Open noon till midnight. Popular with locals & tourists alike, having served Mazatlán since 1959. AE, MC, VI. Ph: 81-2651, 81-5441.

DONK 'N DONAS — ECON — #171 Guillermo Nelson, corner L. Valles — Donuts, coffee & tortas.

ERNIE'S TOMATOES — MOD — At Adolfo T. Loiasa 1/2 block from Azteca Inn. A lively place with a little bit of everything including loud music and a big screen TV. Pizza, ribs, seafood and Mexican food. Open Noon till Midnight. AE, MC, VI. Ph: 14-2474, 16-5426.

EL PARADOR ESPAÑOL — UPPER — Spanish restaurant next to El Cid on Camarón Sabalo #714. Specialty is paella. Open 7 AM till 11 PM. MC, VI. Ph: 13-0767, 14-6611.

EL PARAJE — ECON — Great inexpensive food and friendly atmosphere. Wednesday Bingo and a Jazz band some nights. American Legion rents it the first and third Wednesday of month. Quite a social gathering place. All you can eat for a low price. Blvd. Camarón Sabalo between Luna Palace and Océano. Pool table and CATV. Open 7 AM till 11 PM. MC, VI, AE. Ph: 16-1301. Meme & Mary Lou, owners, speak English.

EL PATIO — UPPER — Good, tropical-style restaurant across from Océano Palace. Lobster, steak, and Mexican specialties. Strolling musicians. Good margaritas and excellent wine selection. Open 11 AM till midnight daily. AE, MC, VI. Ph: 81-7301, 82-1709.

EL SHRIMP BUCKET — UPPER — Well-known seafood restaurant at Olas Altas #11 in La Siesta, the original restaurant of the Anderson chain. Marimba band. Open 7 AM till 11 PM. AE, MC, VI. Ph: 81-6350 or 82-8019.

FISHERMAN — MOD — (Quite a bit less expensive that others in the neighborhood) Av. Afredo T Loiaza #212 next to Las Flores Hotel. My favorite restaurant in the city with a wide variety of seafood including lobster, oysters, marlin, and rudolphi as well as BBQ ribs and steak. It has the quietest, most elegant atmosphere on the strip. A white tablecloth kind of place. They make a special *ensalada verde* at your table. Open 7 AM till 10:30 PM. AE. MC, VI. Ph: 13-5100.

GRILL LARIOS — ECON-MOD — Rodolfo T. Loaiza #413. Mexican food. Casual. MC, VI. Ph: 84-1767.

HARLEY'S — ECON — Av. Las Garzas #8. Everything charbroiled, botanas, hamburgers, salads. Owner owns a Harley. Open 12 Noon till 1 AM Ph: 16-5414.

JADE — MOD — #412 Morelos — Chinese, Cantonese food. Closed Monday. Noon till 10 PM.

LA MANZANA — MOD — Vegetarian restaurant at Belisario Domínguez #1809 and corner of Calle 21 de Marzo, Ph: 82-6143. Another is also located at Av. Del Mar between Gral. Pesquefra and Flamingos. Open for lunch only, 11 AM till 2 PM.

LOS ARCOS — MOD — Tropical open-air restaurant on Del Mar. Seafood fresh from ocean. Open noon till 10 PM. AE, MC, VI. Ph: 13-9577, 14-0999.

MAMUCA'S - MOD-UPPER — Simón Bolívar #404 — Popular downtown seafood restaurant a block off waterfront. A real down home seafood place, no frills, great food. It's like a New Orleans seafood restaurant and since 1961 is known as "Rey de Mariscos." Features Parillada de Mariscos plus "seafood explosion", a variety tray, and seafood dishes such as Paela, Langostinos (craw fish). Open 10 AM till 10 PM. MC, VI. Ph: 81-3490.

MR. "A's" —UPPER — Across from Costa de Oro. One half block off Camarón Sabalo. White table cloths, elegant & with soft music. Excellent.

MIKIKO — UPPER — In the golden zone by Banamex. Japanese food & drinks. Sushi, teppan yaki, sake & beer. AE, MC, VI. Ph: 81-6590.

PANAMÁ — MOD — On Camarón Sabalo next to Guadalajara Grill and across from Lobster Trap. Popular breakfast & lunch place and pastelería. Omlettes & nopales, tacos, submarine sandwiches, sopes, BBQ, Licuados, fehuccine Alfredo and a nice variety of fruit drinks, cakes and breads. No smoking. Open 7 AM till 11 PM. MC, VI. Ph: 13-6977

PARAÍSO 3 ISLAS — MOD — Rodolfo T. Loaiza, on the beach across from Seashell City and next to Las Cabañas shopping center. Seafood. Great lobster Casual. 8 AM till 11 PM, MC, VI. Ph: 14-2812.

PEDRO'S FISH & CHIPS — ECON — Open air restaurant on Camarón Sabalo next to Cavanderia. Breakfast specials on Mexican food. "El Sabalo" seafood. Open 9 AM till midnight.

ROCAMAR — ECON — Av. Del Mar next to Pizza Hut across from beach. Seafood with daily lunch specials. Open daily. Ph: 81-6008. Also at Av. Del Mar & Isla de Lobos. Ph: 81-0023

SR. FROG — UPPER — Popular disco/restaurant on Del Mar Between Hotel Del Sol and Suites Caribe. Popular with "party-hearty" crowd. Decent food, especially ribs and Oysters Madrazo. Excellent drinks. Open noon till midnight daily. AE, MC, VI. Ph: 85-1110 or 82-1925.

SHRIMP FACTORY — MOD — On Adolfo T. Loaiza, near North Beach on east side of Playa Las Gaviotas just north of Azteca Inn about 100 yards. Seafood, shrimp and lobster. Open 11 AM till 11 PM. MC, VI. Ph: 16-5318.

SUPER TACOS LA CARRETA — ECON — #325 Av. Gutiérrez Nájera — next to electrical store. Look for **neon pig** sign.

TONITO'S — ECON — Good, clean, cheap seafood place off Malecón heading toward the town center on bus routes at Calle Nelson. Only stall at corner.

TONY'S PLAZA — UPPER — Nice restaurant in Plaza Las Gaviotas. Another is located on the beach at Plaza Bonita next to Océano Palace. Good international cuisine and excellent service. Open noon till 4 PM and 6 PM till midnight. MC, VI. Ph: 83-4233.

CAMPING, PARKING AND PLUGGING IN

HOLIDAY RV PARK (formerly PLAYA ESCONDIDA) — MOD-UPPER — Tropical 232 space park out on far north end beyond Camino Real. Showers. Toilets. Saltwater pool. Rec hall. Store in office. 15 amps. Concrete patios. Pets OK on leash. Ph & Fax: 88-0077.

LA POSTA — MOD-UPPER — Nice place. It's a 210 space park just east of Camarón Glorieta (on bypass road to Hwy #15). All hookups. Showers. Toilets. Pool. 3 rec halls. Shuffleboard. Concrete patios. Car and boat rentals. Convenience truck (beer, sodas, vegetables, ice, etc.) daily. Beach near by. Pets OK on leash. Ph: 83-5310.

LAS PALMAS — UPPER — 66 space park at Camarón Sabalo #333. All hookups. Noisy from nearby clubs. Unconcerned management. Some rodent problems. Apartments. Showers. Toilets. Rec hall. Pool. Beach 11 KM. Pets OK on leash. Ph: 13-6424.

MAR ROSA — MOD-UPPER — 65 small spaces at north end next to Holiday Inn on beach. All hookups. New showers & toilets. Night security. Patios. Rec. area. Some pull-thrus. Small store. Pets OK on leash. Permanents have ocean fans (16 lots). Ph & Fax: 13-6187.

MARAVILLAS — MOD — 34 space park on secluded beach at far north end of town Between DIF and Quinta del Mar on Cerritos beach. Some spaces a little difficult for big rigs. All hookups. Showers. Toilets. Rec hall. Concrete patios. Pets OK. No phone.

POINT SOUTH MAZATLÁN TRAILER PARK — MOD — Value! In Zona Dorada on Camarón Sabalo #109 across the street from Hotel Riviera and Hotel Sabalos and next door to Los Venados Restaurant and Casa de Cambio. 50 spaces with full hookups. 30 Amp electricity. Cement patios. Baths. Hot showers. Beach nearby. Often full with caravans. English spoken. Emergency medical service. Full security parking. Ph: (69) 83-2157 Fax: 84-1833 US: 1-800-421-1394 US Fax: (909) 924-3838.

SAN BARTOLO — MOD — 46 space north end park off Camarón Sabalo across from beach. All hookups. Showers. Toilets. 15 amps. Rec. area. Friendly place. Ph & Fax: 13-5755.

OTHER

AA — 333 Sabalo, Suite 6, across from Guadalajara Grill in shopping center next to Las Palmas T.P. Mon, Wed, & Fri from 6:30 till 7:30 PM; (Nov-Mar) Sun, 10-11 AM. Contact Barbara R. 16-1568 or Ed. L. 14-0174. Also Spanish meeting daily, 8:00 to 9:30 PM and 8:30-10:00 AM, Wed-Sat.

ABZ TRAVEL AGENCY — Located at Hotel del Sol on Av. Del Mar #800. Ph: 81-7442. Open 8 AM till 12 Noon, Mon-Fri.

CLÍNICA LOMAS — Fracc. Lomas de Mazatlán, Buena Nevada #130. Dr Juan José Porras MD. speaks English. Ph: 16-5555. 83-3523, Fax: 86-3162 Cel. 90-69-191779.

SHARP HOSPITAL — Located at corner of Av. Buelna and Doctor Kumate. Excellent, totally new first class facility for major or minor operations or plastic surgery.

DENTIST — Roberto Cooper, speaks English. Across from Balboa Club.

END MAZATLÁN EAT & STRAY!

Creel & the Copper Canyon

UD-017

Area Code — 145

CREEL'S a great place to relax and return to a QUIET, unhurried life. Set against the backdrop of imposing mountains, you know you're in a special place. Like Alamos, Son; Bisbee, AZ; Real de Catorce, SLP; or Palenque, CHI, it attracts a special type of searcher. More for visionaries, or those whose life-vision has become limited than excitement seekers. This is a place where you can find yourself by losing yourself. Let the Canyon work its magic on you. You'll be glad you came. You can walk around town in less than an hour. Remember, though, that you're at 7,000 feet. Take it easy. Some spots listed below you can drive to & others you'll have to take a tour. As in the US, please lock your car & don't leave any valuables in it before heading off. Your hotel can arrange a tour for you. Here's a list of some of the spectacular things to see.

BASASEACHIC FALLS — 900 feet of cascading waterfall! A day trip.

BATOPILAS — Old mysterious mining town below La Bufa. Semitropical vegetation.

CUSARARE WATERFALL — Out by the Copper Canyon Lodge, you can walk from there in a hour each way. It's a couple of miles by dirt path.

EL TEJABÁN — Perhaps the best view of the canyon — pretty remote. Allow a day to get there & back.

LA BUFA — Mysterious site of Spanish mine. One story has silver the size of basketballs coming out of here. Some stories have hordes of silver hidden by the Tarahumara Indians in special places. Steep descent from 7,000 to about 2,500 feet.

RECOHUATA HOT SPRINGS — 2 to 3 hours steep strenuous hike (see Pensión Creel).

VALLEY OF THE GODS — Wind, rain, sun & climate have carved some magnificent expressions in the rocks.

CHRIS HALL — A good tour guide. He speaks English, French, Italian and Spanish. A great guy. He can be found at Burger Creel or at Margarita's (use her fax #) or call Presidio Information Center 1-800-597-4168 in Presidio, TX.

SLEEPING AROUND CREEL

CASA VALENZUELA — ECON — Least expensive in town. Rooms with bath in private house across from Abarrotes LaCombe

CASCADA INN — MOD — Next to Parador. 32 Rooms. Good beds. Heaters. Steak house restaurant. Parking. Indoor pool. Ph: 6-0151 Fax: 6-0253.

COPPER CANYON LODGE — MOD — 12 miles south of town beyond lake. 29 rooms. Old-world atmosphere. Rustic. Wood-burning stoves & kerosine lanterns. Fireplace in lobby. Fine restaurant. First lodge in Creel, restored by Skip McWilliams, open since 1965. Popular with hikers & Europeans. Reservations advised through travel agent in Chihuahua, Ph: 14-12-8893. US Reservations: 1-800-776-3942 He also owns inn at Batopilas. A great experience. My friends, Carl Franz and Lorena Havens are often guides there.

KORACHI — ECON — Francisco Villa #116 next to bus station — 20 rooms (12 with bath). There are also 14 cabañas in back with wood stoves and large private baths. Ph: 6-0207.

LA POSADA DE CREEL — MOD — Av. López Mateos #25, on left as you go into town. 21 units, some with private bath. Ph & Fax: 6-0142.

MARGARITA'S — ECON — Very nice 17 Cabañas, 3 bedroom and various layouts, 1 suite and 1 cabañita. With breakfast and dinner. Ph & Fax: 6-0245. Good guide — Chris Hall.

MARGARITA'S CASA MEXICANA — ECON — Hostel-like (Casa de Huéspedes) Calle Chapultepec s/n All with breakfast and dinner. BBQ and great atmosphere. For backpackers and those on a budget Ph & Fax: 6-0045

NUEVO BARRANCAS DEL COBRE — MOD — Very nice hotel in town, behind train depot — 22 heated and carpeted rooms. Very good management. Lots of hot water. MC, VI. Ph: 6-0022.

PARADOR DE LA MONTAÑA — MOD — Av. López Mateos #44 — In town, just across tracks & 1 block right (South) past station on left side of street — 36 rooms, 3 Jr. suites, 1 Presidential suite, which sleeps 8 with kitchen. Can house 125 people. Restaurant. Bar. Tours. Gift shop. House doctor. Very nice. Phones in room. Second oldest lodge in Creel, open since 1971. The cast for the movies "Altered States" and "Wolf Lake" stayed here while shooting them. Ph: 6-0075 or 6-0085. Chihuahua: (14) 10-4580. Fax: 15-3468. Eugenio Cuesta, owner.

PENSION CREEL — MOD — Bed & Breakfast on Av. López Mateos #61. Cabins with 3 bedrooms, bath and kitchen. Wood stove in rooms 11-room stone house with public bathrooms. Secure parking. Laundry. Restaurant. RV Parking — Five spaces with EWS and concrete pad, dry camping space for caravans. English and French spoken. Reasonable tours: Day trips with transportation and overnight camping (optional) — Arareco Lake & Cusarare falls, Recohuata hot springs, Urique Canyon, La Bufa, Batopilas (2 days — 175 mile trip), Basaseachic falls, Tejabán, Guacaivo. Ph: 6-0071 Fax: 6-0200

EATING CREEL

Both the Copper Canyon Lodge & the Parador have good restaurants with varied menus.

BURGER CREEL — Opposite Parador. Quesadillas, burritos and great burgers. Open 9 AM till 11 PM.

EL CABALLO BAYO — MOD — Nice restaurant and bar next door to La Posada de Creel. Varied menu Open 2 PM till 10 PM. Ph: 6-0136.

ESTELA — ECON — Very nice little place. Home cooking, guisado and good soups. Cook — Manela. Open 7 AM till 9 PM.

LUPITA — ECON — Across from Parador 1/2 block toward town, same side as train station. Great Mexican food. Neat. Clean. Comfy with old fashioned jukebox.

CAMPING, PARKING & PLUGGIN' IN

PARADOR DE LA MONTAÑA — MOD — In connection with hotel. Accepts RV's in secured parking area. NO HOOKUPS, but owner will let you use facilities if not full. Can arrange for tours & rail trips. English. Friendly. Ph: 6-0075 or 6-0085.

PENSION CREEL — MOD — In connection with hotel at Av. López Mateos #61. RV dry camping for caravans. Five spaces with EWS and concrete pad. 8 dirt pads. Tours available. English & French spoken. Ph: 6-0071 Fax: 6-0200.

BEYOND CREEL

EL TEJABÁN

TEJABÁN — MOD — Isolated with stupendous view on the rim of canyon. Difficult to get to, you must have a vehicle with high clearance. 12 rooms with fireplaces and small tubs that have jacuzzi jets. Excellent Restaurant, where you'll undoubtedly eat as it's too much trouble to go back to town. Pool. 2 casas with tub jacuzzi. Own generating plant. Also has dormitory rooms with bunk bed space for 40 people. Altitude 7,200 feet.

DIVISADERO:

CABAÑAS DIVISADERO BARRANCAS — UPPER — The first hotel you come to. You pay for the fact that they are on the canyon rim. 52 rooms. Meals included in price. In Chihuahua: Apdo. Postal #661 C.P. 31238 MC, VI. Chihuahua Ph: (14) 12-3330, 15-5136, OR 15-1199 Fax: (14) 15-6575.

LA MANSIÓN TARAHUMARA — UPPER — 15 cabins. Restaurant. Bar. Ph: (14) 15-4721 Fax: 16-5666 in Chihuahua. Go about 3 1/2 miles past the Cabañas Divisadero, it is the second hotel you'll see (the first is the Misión). It is on hill to the left. Owner María Barriga is very friendly and knowledgeable and a good friend of Sanborn's, one of my favorite people in Mexico. *RV's can park here! There is even a honeymoon suite! Be careful for railroad crossing at entrance to her place. Sometimes they are uneven. Customer Sally Cook of Granada Hill, CA. said — "Marvelous."*

MISIÒN — UPPER — 30 rooms. Very nice place with good restaurant. Reservations thru Santa Anita hotel in Los Mochis. Ph: (681) 5-7046. In Chihuahua: 14-16-5950.

PARAÍSO DEL OSO — UPPER — 15 rooms with bath. Rustic hotel at the foot of a toothy mountain with a natural rock profile of a bear. Offers a Urique Canyon trip by four-wheel drive vehicle.

POSADA BARRANCAS MIRADOR — MOD-UPPER — An extension of Rancho Posada Barrancas. 30 rooms and 2 suites. Fantastic fireplace view of Canyon. Restaurant. Bar. Gift shop. Soft beds. Dining room. Group rates. Reservations thru Santa Anita in Los Mochis. Ph: (681) 8-7046 Fax: (681) 2-0046. In Chihuahua: (14) 16-5950 or 16-6589.

RANCHO DEL OSO CAMPGROUND — 5 km north of Cerocahui. Buried cave and archeological sites. Owned by Doug.

RANCHO POSADA BARRANCAS — MOD-UPPER — A Balderama hotel. 35 rooms. Wood-burning fireplaces. Garden, vineyard and orchard. Reservations thru Santa Anita in Los Mochis. Ph: (681) 8-7046 Fax: (681) 2-0046. In Chihuahua: (14) 16-5950 or 16-6589.

BATOPILAS:

SLEEPING AROUND BATOPILAS

HACIENDA BATOPILAS — UPPER — Staying at this luxury resort is like stepping back into another century. The old-world furnishings, oriental rugs, feather beds. Ceiling fans, and lush gardens make you feel like you are in a turn-of-the century hacienda, which is the desired effect. You'll be served gourmet meals to boot. The sitting room might remind those who know of a bordello (of course, I wouldn't know), with its oil paintings and furnishings. The ceiling is painted with cherubs and churches like in a cathedral. Tubs. Tours. It's pricey, and you must stay for three days. Make reservations in the U.S. at 1-800-776-3942. If you didn't plan ahead, try making a reservation at the Copper Canyon Lodge back in Creel, since all guests originate from there. Price includes transportation from Creel to Batopilas and you might as well take advantage of it and save the wear and tear on you vehicle. The owner, Skip McWilliams promised a small discount to SAC members. Reservations in Chihuahua. Ph: 14-1582. Ph: & Fax: 14-1505.

CASA BUSTILLOS — ECON — On the plaza, sort of,. Look left for "Indian Curios" sign. 4 rooms, rather Spartan, but with hot water and gardens. River behind sounds nice. No screens on doors. Popular with the backpackers. Owner has a washing machine.

MARY — ECON — On Calle Juárez, across from the church. Many long term guests. Well run. 12 rooms, two stories. Nice garden courtyard. Hot water.

BATOPILAS — ECON — On road into town. Good water pressure. Ceiling fans. Public bathrooms. Primitive.

PALMERA — ECON — The first hotel as you enter town. 6 rooms. My favorite. The best of the economy hotels. It's clean, the owner is nice and the place is spic 'n span. Nice restaurant.

CHULA VISTA — ECON — On road into town. 8 room. Common bathroom. Spartan, but will do in a pinch..

EATING BATOPILAS

Hotels Palmera, Mary and Casa Bustillos have restaurants. Food is mainly tacos, enchiladas, guisados and chicken. Guests at the Riverside Lodge, have excellent meals, but if you aren't a guest, you can't eat there. You can make deals with individuals to cook for you in their homes. You can also make deals to rent rooms.

DOÑA MICA'S — This isn't really a restaurant, you eat on the lady's front porch. Mica's been serving guests for 25 years. To get there, walk past the basketball court to the dead end, turn right, then walk a long block. Her house is on the right, just before the walkway goes uphill and narrows. Look for a house with a big porch. There are two tabes with plastic covers over colorful tablecloths and little wooden chairs. You can't just drop in. You have to go by in the morning and tell you want to eat. She has to buy the food for you for the next day for breakfast, lunch or dinner. Although she has electricity, like gourmet cooks the world over, she doesn't trust it for cooking and uses her gas stove. She says she doesn't have much money, but is rich in friendship. Eating there is like making a new friend or grandmother.

GENERAL INFO

Things to do here include visiting the Shepherd mansion, now in ruins, hiking the many trails and visiting the old cathedral at Satevó. Some guidebooks refer to this as a lost cathedral, but it was never lost. It's on the royal road to Alamos, so its location was never a mystery. It has been neglected, though. To get there, go to the end of town (to the left of the plaza), turn left to the river. This is a steep embankment, so be careful. Follow the only road around until you see the cathedral on your left. It will take about 45 minutes. Ask for the key at the first house on the left. There are very old drawings and an air of decay inside. It's worth a visit.

END OF CREEL EAT & STRAY

Tepic

UD-017

Area Code — 32

SLEEPING AROUND TEPIC

BUGAMVILLAS – UPPER – Very nice 50-room hotel at Av. Insurgentes and Libramiento Pte. Family restaurant. Pool. CATV. Suites with jacuzzi. Ph & Fax: 18-0225.
CORITA – MOD – 34-room, 3-story hotel on Hwy #15 one block south of sports center. Restaurant-bar. Pool. Disco. Enclosed parking. MC, VI. Ph: 12-0477.
DEL SOL – MOD – 25-unit motel a few blocks south of Hwy #15-200 junction. No a/c. Small restaurant. Enclosed parking. Pets OK. MC, VI. Ph: 12-2828.
FRAY JUNIPERO SERRA – MOD – Lerdo #23 Pte. – Good 5-story, 85-room downtown hotel across from main plaza (on south corner). Some a/c. Restaurant. Bar. Parking. AE, MC, VI. Best hotel in town. Ph: 12-2525. Fax: 12-2051.
LOS PINOS – MOD – Comfy little 17-kitchenette motel and RV park a couple miles south on Hwy #200 next to Linda Vista. Pool. Parking. Pets OK. Ph: 13-1232.
SAN JORGE – MOD – Lerdo #124 – 3-story, 39-room downtown hotel, a couple of blocks back of main plaza. Restaurant. Parking. MC, VI. Ph: 12-1755 or 12-1709.
SANTA FE – MOD – Calzada de la Cruz #385 – 2-story, 36-room hotel a block off Hwy #200, across from normal school. No a/c. Restaurant. Parking. Ph: 13-1966.
SIERRA DE ALICIA – MOD – Av. Mexico #180 Pte. – Fair 3-story, 60-room hotel a block before main plaza. No a/c. No restaurant. Parking. Pets OK. SAC. AE, MC, VI. Ph: 12-1040. Fax: 12-1309.
VILLA LAS ROSAS – MOD – Insurgentes #100 Pte. – 30-room motel, old Hwy #15 thru town. Restaurant. Bar. Enclosed parking. MC, VI. Ph: 13-1800 or 13-1857.

EATING TEPIC

BEACHCOMBER – MOD – Insurgentes & Durango – Thatched-roof restaurant on Hwy #15 across from Loma Park. Delicious carne asada and seafood. MC, VI.
FONDA HUICOT – MOD – Colonial restaurant on Hwy #200 (toward Puerto Vallarta). Serves basic Mexican food, but menu includes some American dishes. MC, VI.
FU SENG – Cantonese food and take out, in historic building 1 1/2 blocks from plaza. Ph: 12-0010
INTERNACIONAL (ROBERTO'S) – MOD – Militar & Insurgentes – Good restaurant a half-block from La Loma across from north side of Loma Park. International cuisine. Excellent food and service. Open 1 PM till 1 AM. MC, VI. Ph: 12-2717.
LA TERRAZA – MOD – Insurgentes Pte. #98 – Restaurant-soda fountain (Hwy #15 thru town) across from park. Specialties include Pollo Asado (grilled chicken). Newsstand with U.S. publications. Open 7 AM till 11 PM. MC, VI.
LOS MOLCAJETES – MOD – Calle Mexico – Popular place serving Mexican and American food (main street into downtown) a block from state capitol.
TIN JAO – MOD – In front of Loma park at Paseo de la Loma #199-A. Unpretentious Chinese food. Shank fin soup very good. Open 1 PM till 11 PM. Owner speaks English, Spanish and Taiwanese. No credit cards. Ph: 14-0944

CAMPING, PARKING & PLUGGIN' IN

KAMPAMENTO KOA – UPPER – 87-space park about 3.5 miles east of town and about a half-mile off Hwy #15 down cobblestone road just beyond Lázaro Cárdenas tobacco plant ("Planta Despitadora Lázaro Cárdenas"). 34 spaces with all hookups; 31 with electrical & water only; 12 tent spaces. Laundry. Showers. Restrooms. Pool. Dump stations. Rec hall. Store. Ice. Ph: 13-2699. Fax: 13-3113.

KOALA BUNGALOWS & T.P. – MOD – 52 KM Southeast of Tepic and 20 KM from Tepic/Guadalajara Highway on Laguna de Santa Maria. Near crater lake. 730 M above sea level and 2 KM in diameter. 65 spaces with electricity and water. Camping. Boat ramp. Swimming. Boating. Fishing.

LOS PINOS – UPPER – From south bypass, follow road to city for 2 KM. Located on left. 24-space RV park with all hookups. Showers. Toilets. Concrete pads. Store 1/2-km. Ph: 12-2427.

End of Tepic Eat & Stray.

San Blas

UD-017

Area Code — 328

SAN BLAS used to be an important port for Spanish fleet & had galleons unloading from the Far East regularly. Now it's popular with surfers, birders and laid-back gringos. Matanchen beach is delightful, though Playa Borrego at the end of town is more easily accessed.

TOURIST OFFICE – next to McDonald's. Fishing licenses – Pesca office beyond Las Brisas.

NEARBY ATTRACTIONS

LOS COCOS BEACH – between Aticama & Santa Cruz. Very nice. "Police" permanently stationed in small building in front of restaurant La Manzanilla. Will help with car problems!

Two places nearby are of particular interest to Mexico-philes. Closest is Santiago Ixcuintla, home of the Huichol Center for Cultural Survival. From the junction with Hwy #15 & San Blas turnoff, it's 14 miles north, then west 8 KM. If you have an interest in these native peoples' way of life, or would like to learn some of their unique beadwork or weaving techniques, you should check it out. Their eye-socket popping beadwork is prized by collectors everywhere. You've seen (or will see) some of it in Pto. Vallarta. If you're truly interested, call Susana Eger Valadez (323) 5-1171. If she can, she'll arrange a class for you. Since this is also a medical center for the Huichol people, she discourages drop-ins, but if you have an honest interest in learning, helping with the hospital, or buying a lot of Huichol artwork, you couldn't ask for a better opportunity. If you got this Travelog from a friend (yes, we know ya'll photocopy 'em, but please, buy your insurance from us next time so we can afford to keep producing these guides!), or are back in the States or Canada, you can order a color catalog of the Huichol works for sale from: Huichol Center, P.O. Box 1430, Cottonwood, AZ 86326. PH: (602) 634-3946.

The other is Mexcaltitán, the "Venice of Mexico" and traditional home of the Aztecs. It was here that Aztec priests saw a snake in a cactus, which directed them to build the great city of Mexico. Turnoff is 23.7 miles north of the San Blas jct. with Hwy #15. Annual "Feria de Mexicanidad" celebrates the event in Tepic, Nay., Nov. 16 – Dec 2.

LOCAL EXCURSIONS

JUNGLE BOAT TRIP #1 – departs from next to the bridge over Río San Cristóbal as you enter town. It takes about 3 hours and goes down the river for a short way and then up La Tobara Tributary to beautiful La Tobara Springs with amazingly clear water. Take your swim suit as the boat stops for an hour there. Refreshments are available.

JUNGLE BOAT TRIP #2 – is shorter than #1 (1.5 hours) because the boat is boarded farther up Río Tobara where the gravel road to Matanchen beach crosses the river.

JUNGLE BOAT TRIP #3 – leaves from the same place as #2, but goes to jungle zoo – crocodile farm – same price as #2.

BIRD TRIPS – San Blas is renowned among bird watchers! More than 300 species of birds can be seen here. They come in groups just for the birding. Manuel works with Audubon groups and will take you out. Ask at the Las Brisas hotel. While you're there, a great book on the feathered friends who visit the area is for sale – Finding Birds in San Blas. It's reasonably priced and excellent.

FISHING – Great! Get a guide and go river or deep-sea fishing. Just make sure you both agree on a price before you set out (always a good idea anywhere). Also, check the boat to make sure they have enough safety features for your liking. Call Pipla 5-0362 or ask for Tony Aguayo or Tony P. at the docks or Las Brisas.

AA – English. M–W–F 6 PM 9:30 Sun. Comes and goes. Check at restaurant McDonald's to see if any are going on..

JEJENES – Well, folks, we'd be remiss in our responsibility to you if we failed to tell you about the reason why San Blas has been saved from becoming a Cancún or Ixtapa. It's the home of a pestiferous little gnat called a "jejene", pronounced "he-he-nee." These nasty little gnats are most prevalent during the summer months, but they can show up at any time – early morning, late evening, night. Methinks they take a siesta at midday. They're a sort of sand fly and are quite tiny, but they bite BIG. Don't worry, they won't really hurt you, and they're quite democratic, biting locals and tourists alike. A citronella candle might help (it does wonders with mosquitoes) and a bug-bomb can slay a jillion of 'em at just one "psssst."

FAX – If you need to get in touch with your broker or other psychic, inquire at Farmacia Económica, 1 block from the plaza on Calle Batallón, toward beach. PH: (321) 5-0111.

PAVED SHORTCUT TO PUERTO VALLARTA – Take the road to Santa Cruz, Plátanos, Zacualpan and Las Varas. It's a beautiful drive and saves lots of time. In Santa Cruz start our new log, Las Varas South Special. Check locally on road conditions, as heavy rains can wash it out.

We hope you have a most enjoyable time here in old San Blas.

SAN BLAS isn't Puerto Vallarta or Mazatlán. There's no "Gold Zone." That's why some folks love it. If a rustic, off-the-beaten-track place is your cup of tea, then you'll drink your fill in old San Blas. If discos or glitz are for you; San Blas isn't.

SLEEPING AROUND SAN BLAS

BUCANERO – ECON – Juárez #75 – 2-story, 33 room emergency-economy hotel converted from old warehouse mansion on main street a long block beyond plaza. Restaurant. Very loud, in-&-out bar. Parking. Pets OK. MC, VI. Ph: 5-0101.

LAS BRISAS – MOD – Paredes S/N – The nicest place in town! 42-rooms. All A/C; some ceiling fans. Breakfast included. Very nice restaurant-bar. SATV. Pool. One & two-bedroom kitchenette. Enclosed parking. Pets OK. Fishing & tours arranged. Birdwatchers' headquarters. English, French, German spoken. Nice book & souvenir shop with unique items. AE, MC, VI. Ph: 5-0112. Fax: 5-0308.

LOS FLAMINGOS – ECON – Calle Juárez #163 – 2-story, 24-room emergency-economy hotel converted from German consulate on main street a block beyond Bucanero (and like the Bucanero, has seen better days). Some A/C; mostly ceiling fans. No restaurant. Parking. Pets OK. Ph: 5-0448.

MARINO INN – ECON – Av. Heróica Batallón de San Blas – 54-room air-con hotel across from Centro de Salud on road thru town. Restaurant. Disco. Pool. Parking. MC, VI. Ph: 9-1321 or 5-0340.

POSADA DEL REY – MOD – Folks, some customers have complained about security here, so use your own judgement. Simple, clean 12-room motel. No A/C; ceiling fans only. Restaurant/bar serves snacks. English spoken. Pool. Parking. MC, VI. Ph: 5-0123.

SUITES SAN BLAS – MOD – Fracc. Palmar De Los Cocos, 3 miles – 3-story, 23-unit hotel (17 one-bedroom and 6 two-bedroom kitchenette suites at south end of town. No air-con; ceiling fans only. No restaurant. Pool. Playground. Disco. On-street parking. Monthly rates. AE, MC, VI. Ph: 5-0047 or 5-0505.

EATING SAN BLAS

EL DELFIN – UPPER – At Las Brisas Hotel. Elegant white tablecloth place. A/C. Fish fillet with oyster & pecan sauce or oysters, mushrooms and shrimp. English spoken. Be sure to ask if food is prepared with alcohol, as some of their sauces are.

LA HACIENDA – MOD – Calle Juárez #33 – Across street & down a few doors from bank. Charming decor. Wonderful carnitas (deep fried pork)! Can buy by kilo or 1/2.

LA FAMILIA – MOD – Batallón #18 – Very attractive authentic Mexican-style restaurant housed in an old restored colonial home in town. Domingo Gutiérrez is your gracious host, an educated man who once studied to be a vet. Hand painted menus by Rafael Gutiérrez, (his father) whose paintings adorn the wall. They are for sale. Try pescado or shrimp quetenque. Soothing dinner music. Open 5 PM till 10 PM daily; closed Sunday. Ph: 5-2058.

McDONALD'S – MOD – Calle Juárez #36 – (Not the golden arches type) Good restaurant a block west of main plaza. Good Mexican-style beef filets, fish filets, broiled lobster, shrimp, tacos, and enchiladas. Reasonable prices. Local gathering spot for local gringos, including Friends of Bill W. Open 7 AM till 10 PM daily. Ph: 5-0432

ROSY'S – MOD – Typical & clean family restaurant. Mexican food, including sopes, enchiladas, tacos, tostadas. On plaza, near church.

TONY'S INN LA ISLA – MOD – Paredes Sur – Small, decorated with nets & shells, restaurant with excellent shrimp, fish, lobster, and steak. Open from 2 till 10 PM daily. Ph: 5-0407.

TORINO'S – MOD – Town's largest restaurant located downtown a block beyond plaza across from Bucanero, on main stem. Open 8 AM till 10 PM daily. MC, VI. Seasonal.

SLEEPING AROUND IN LOS COCOS

CASA MAÑANA – MOD – 9.7 miles south of junction of "Santa Cruz – Aticama" highway and San Blas road (same as Playa Amor T.P.). 7 rooms, 2 bungalows. Nice views. Owned by nice German fellow.

EATING LOS COCOS BEACH

SOUTH COCOS – MOD – Good seafood, hamburgers – "*estillo* USA." Open 9-1, 5-9.

CAMPING, PARKING & PLUGGING IN!

LOS COCOS – ECON-MOD – 100-space park off main stem near beach. All hookups. Pull thrus. Showers. Restrooms. SATV in bar. Laundry service. Rec hall. Bar. Boat ramp, nearby. 20 amps. Pets OK. Nice place. Ph: 5-0055.

PLAYA AMOR – MOD – Between San Blas & Santa Cruz – Highly recommended! 40-space facility on beach. 25 with all hookups. 15 with electricity and water. 30 amps. Showers – hot water. Toilets. Security wall and guard. English spoken. Fishing. Hiking. Boat ramp. Laundry service. Rooftop patio rec hall. Just before San Blas, take left to Alicama/Santa Cruz, go 6 miles south on paved road. On right. Look for "papelia" tree at entrance.

End of San Blas Eat & Stray!

Rincón de Guayabitos

UD-017

Area Code — 327

SLEEPING AROUND RINCÓN DE GUAYABITOS

COSTA ALEGRE — 72 room, 2 story beachfront motel on Tabachines. 19 kitchenettes. Some a/c. Pool. Parking.

DIANA BUNGALOWS — 19 bungalow, 2 story motel a half-block away from beach on Av. Del Sol Nuevo. Restaurant. Pool. Parking. Pets OK.

EL DELFIN BUNGALOWS — 14 bungalow, 2 story motel on Ceibas near beach. Pool. Parking. Pets OK.

EL RINCONCITO — 10 bungalow, 2 story beachfront motel on Ceibas. Restaurant. Bar. Club. Pool. Parking.

Reservations suggested. Pets OK.

FIESTA MAR — Nice 24 room, 2 story a/c hotel two blocks from beach. Restaurant. Bar. Enclosed parking. MC, VI. Ph: 21-3535 in Guadalajara.

LAS HACIENDAS — 19 room kitchenette motel on Laureles on beach. Pool. Parking. Pets OK.

MARIA TERESA — 15 kitchenette complex a block from beach. No restaurant. Parking. Small pets OK.

PEÑA MAR — 86 room a/c hotel on north entrance to town near beach. Restaurant. Piano bar. Disco. Pools. Tennis. Parking. Ph: 14-9871 in Guadalajara.

PLAYA DE ORO — NEW HOTEL UNDER CONSTRUCTION ON BEACH.

POSADA DEL SOL — 10 bungalow, 3 room complex on Del Sol Nuevo near beach. Restaurant. Pool. Parking. 4 RV spaces.

QUINTA TERE — 7 kitchenette, 2 story complex in residential area on beach. No restaurant. Pool. Parking. Pets OK.

SAN CARLOS — 32 bungalow, 27 room, 2 story complex on Laureles on beach. Restaurant. Bar. Pool. Parking. Pets OK. Ph: 7-0025 in Compostela, NAY.

EATING RINCÓN DE GUAYABITOS & VICINITY

BEACHCOMBER — Rustic beachfront restaurant near Tropico Cabañas. Seafood specialties.

ROBERTO'S — Another rustic beachfront restaurant specializing in seafood, of course.

VILLANUEVA'S — Seafood restaurant in conjunction with RV park of same name.

CAMPING, PARKING & PLUGGIN' IN

DELIA — 16 space facility across from Paraíso del Pescador. All hookups. Showers. Toilets. Laundromat. Coffee shop. Grocery. Curio store. LP gas. Ice. Pets OK.

EL CARACOL — 22 space facility in Lo de Marcos on beach. All hookups. Dump station. Showers. Toilets. Concrete patios. Pets OK. 5 bungalows with kitchenette.

EL DORADO — Nice 21 space facility set in an acre of tropical flowers and coconut palms on beach. All hookups. Showers. Toilets. Boat ramp. Pets OK.

EL FLAMINGO — 20 space facility north of El Dorado on beach. Showers. Toilets. Pets OK.

EL NUMBER UNO — 20 space facility on beach next to Roberto's. Showers. Toilets. "Plazita" with benches and tables. Ice. Refreshments and beer. Pets OK. Ph: 25-7627 in Guadalajara.

LA PEÑITA — 200 space facility in La Peñita 2.3 miles north of Rincón de Guayabitos and 0.3 miles west. Some with all hookups; others with electricity and water only. Showers. Toilets. Pool. Laundromat. Brick patios. Cooking area. Ice. Refreshments. Palapas. Pets OK.

MARY'S — 13 space facility next to Motel Russell. All hookups. Toilets. Pets OK.

PARAÍSO DEL PESCADOR — 90 space facility among fruit trees on beach. All hookups. Showers. Toilets. Fish cleaning station. Pets OK.

POSADA DEL SOL — SEE ABOVE.

RUSSELL — 11 space facility 2.3 miles north of Rincón de Guayabitos in La Peñita. Shower. Toilet. Concrete patios. Laundry service. Ice. Refreshments. Pets OK.

SAYULA — 10 space facility 1.5 miles off highway on serene, secluded beach. 10 spaces with hookups. Space for 40 more. Showers. Toilets. Concrete patios. Dump station. Pets OK. Not recommended for large RV's as access road is very bad.

TROPICO CABAÑA — 30 space facility next to Villanueva's on beach. All hookups. Showers. Toilets. BBQ pit. Rec room. Pets OK.

VILLANUEVA'S — 30 space facility on beach. Showers. Toilets. Restaurant. Pets OK. Ph: 11 in La Peñita, NAY.

End of Rincón de Guayabitos Eat & Stray.

Puerto Vallarta

UD-017

Area Code — 322

PUERTO VALLARTA is a medium-sized town that blends into the countryside and climbs the mountainside overlooking the Pacific. It's a very popular winter resort (December 1 – May 5), especially during holidays (both U.S. and Mexican. If you plan to be in "Vallarta" then, advance reservations are pretty smart. In summer, there are lots of discounted deals.

Known as the "Poor Man's Riviera" in the early '60's, "Vallarta" offered a certain charm. It was serene, and only a handful of fisherman and vacationers visited regularly. Later it became a popular spot to "get away from it all." Many well-heeled Americans built vacation homes on the Río Cuale, an area known today as "Gringo Gulch." The Hollywood set discovered it thanks to Elizabeth Taylor and Richard Burton, who built houses across the street from each other. They had a catwalk built between them so they could "visit" whenever they wanted. I guess it was so Liz wouldn't be known as a streetwalker. John Huston also loved the place (and anything that didn't move). See Mr. Huston's statue with the text of Humphrey Bogart's eulogy. It's on the island.

In those days only DC-6 props flew into and out of the area utilizing a small ramshackle old terminal held together by bailing wire and hope. With the completion of Highway #200 south from Tepic in the late 70's, however, "Vallarta" was discovered and has since become an increasingly popular resort with Europeans and Canadians as well as with Americans. Today, Vallarta is perhaps a bit too tourist-oriented for some, but there's still a lot of the old charm if you stay out of the "Golden Zone." The surrounding countryside and beaches are breathtakingly beautiful.

SANBORN'S AGENT

CLEMENTE CELIS – Calle Rocallosa #379 (corner Ecuador & Rocallosa). Ph: 2-2364. PLEASE DO NOT CALL MR. CELIS AT HIS OTHER JOB. Call him and he will come to you. If you want to visit him: Turn east at Sheraton. Go 5 blocks on Americas, left a Ecuador (Lion's Club school). Go 1 block, then left 1/2 block. IGNORE ANYTHING THAT SAYS TO CALL HIM ANYWHERE ELSE.

GALLERIES

GALERIA UNO – Moreles 561. Established in 1971 and consistently features the finest Mexican artists. Open 10 AM till 8 PM. Ph: 2-0908 or 2-4559.

GALERIA OLINALA – Lázaro Cárdenas # 274 in south end of town between Vallarta and Constitución. Owner Nancy Erickson possesses a wealth of information about origins and symbolisms of Indian Tribal art and has the widest range of ceremonial and combat masks representative of most Indian groups. Open daily 10 AM – 2 PM and 5 PM – 9 PM. Ph: 2-4995.

GALERIA MUVIERI – At 177 Libertad 2 blocks south of main plaza. Specializes in Mexican tribal art of the Huichol and Cora tribes. Open daily 10 AM – 2 PM and 4 PM till 8 PM. Ph: 3-2695

GALERIA PACÍFICO – Insurgentes #109 (second floor). Open Mon – Sat. 10 AM till 9 PM. Ph: 2-1982

GALERIA RAC – Lázaro Cárdenas 286. Gallery featuring paintings, collage, ceramics and masks. Rita Zanoni Burns, famed master ceramicist/sculptor from Oklahoma and Bowie, Texas, is an exhibitor at the gallery. Ms. Zanoni can be reached by calling 322-2-5984 in Puerto Vallarta.

GALERIA VALLARTA – Juárez 263. Ph: 322 2-0290. Gene & Barbara Peters, owners, are very hospitable and knowledgeable and will help you make an intelligent purchase. They like to encourage young artists. They're from Texas. Stop in and visit them. Open Mon – Sat 9:30 AM till 8 PM. Sun. 10 AM till 3 PM.

SIGHTSEEING

LUIS GUTIÉRREZ – Ph: 249-39 or 255-35. Tours with bilingual guides. A very good fellow. Recommended.

JACK'S WATER TAXI – Round trips from Los Muertos pier to Mismaloya, Boca de Tomatlán, Las Animas, Quimixto, Las Caletas and Yelapa (great waterfall!) every day.

Bike Mex Adventures – Mountain biking adventures for the active traveler. Equipment provided. Bilingual guides. Call 3-16-80.

HORSEBACK RIDING – Rancho Ojo de Agua, 4-8240 or 4-0607; Rancho 1 Charro, 4-0114.

MILLER TRAVEL SERVICE – In Sheraton – Bus sightseeing tours. Professionals. Recommended. YATES YELAPA, S.A. – Four different cruises. Contact Servicios Mexicanos Turísticos S.A., Av. Juárez No. 174 Despacho No. 104 & 105. Ph: 2 0026 or 2 1003. Departures daily from the marina pier 9:30 AM. Music, dancing & lots of drinking. Sundeck.

GENERAL INFO

LAVANDERIA DE CINE BAHIA – 357 Francisco Madero. Open 8 AM till 2 PM, 4 M till 8 PM M–F, 8 AM till 4 PM Sat. Other location next to Junto Rest Place Van Dome. English spoken.

RICARDO LEÓN, DVM – Venustiano Carranza No. 254. Ph: 235-64 and 235-84. Full service hospital for cats & dogs, cages, vaccinations, etc.

POST OFFICE LOCATIONS – Main office 2nd block north of main plaza; on Malecón – Paseo Díaz Ordaz; At airport, north of town; and on Columbia, 2 blocks south of Hidalgo Park.

SHOPPING CENTERS – Plaza Marina, just south of airport at north end of town. Plaza Caracol across from Fiesta Americana. Villa Vallarta, on Hwy to airport at 2nd stoplight north of bypass around town.

SPANISH LANGUAGE CLASSES – The University of Guadalajara has set up an extension of its very successful program at the main campus in Guadalajara. The Puerto Vallarta center is conveniently located downtown at Jesús Langarica #200 (about 2 blocks fro the Malecón McDonald's) in the penthouse suite. For more info call Lic. Carlos de la Torre at 3-0043, Fax: 2-4419

FOR THE INNER PERSON

FIRST BAPTIST CHURCH – Argentina 181, next to Hidalgo Park. Sunday "All English Service", 10 AM. All faiths welcome.

12 STEP PROGRAMS IN ENGLISH

CHAPALA, JAL. – AJIIC AREA. Sun – Jocotepec, call David (376) 3-0280. Mon – Little Chapel, 4 PM. TUES. – Río Zula #1, WED – ACOA, Hidalgo #63, Ajiic, AL-ANON, Río Zula #1, 4 PM. THUR – Río Zula #1, 4 PM. FRI – No. SAT – AL-ANON, Río Zula #1, 9:30 AM

MEXICO D.F. – Call 540-6057, or 596-5119, Anita, 568-5104, Jane, 373-9008, Mary, 540-2637 for info. MON – Río Danubio #39, Upstairs, Col. Cuauhtémoc, 2:00 PM, St. Patrick's Church., Calle Bondojito #248, Col. Las Americas, Tacubaya 8:00 PM. WED – Union Church, 1870 Reforma (way out beyond Chapultepec) 8:00 PM, THUR – Río Danubio #39 Upstairs, 8:00 PM. FRI – Union Church, 1870 Reforma (way out beyond Chapultepec) 8:00 PM. SAT – Río Danubio #39, 4:00 PM, Lutheran Church, Palmas 1910, 600 PM. SUN – Río Danubio #39 Upstairs, 6:00 PM & Lutheran Church, Palmas #1910, side door, 6:00 PM.

GUADALAJARA, JAL. – Clubhouse, Filadelfia #2015 (off López Mateos & Las Americas, near Brazz restaurant). Mon, Wed 7:30 PM. Call Dick 31-2553, Linda 33-2155 or Bill 32-4047 for info.

OAXACA, OAX – Inquire at English library or leave note in P.O. Box 414 at main post office. 802 Crespo, near Hotel Victoria across from kindergarten.

PTO. VALLARTA, JAL – EDIFICIO CINE BAHIA (in old section of town, across the Río Cuale) at 181 Insurgentes (near Madero), 2nd floor, RM. # 208. Daily, 6:30 PM. Mon-Sat, 9:00 AM, Sun, 11:30 AM. Most meetings are nonsmoking. There's an 8:00 smoking meeting some nights. N.A. Tues-Thur-Sat, 5:00 PM. O.A., Tues, 8:00 PM. Alanon, Mon., 5:00 PM.

SAN BLAS, NAY. – Check at restaurant McDonald's for times. Ph: (321) 5-0338.

YELAPA, JAL. – Wed, Sat, 3:00 PM, Domingo's on beach.

ZIHUATANEJO/IXTAPA, GRO. – Cafe Kapi-Kopi, Calle Pedro Ascencio #12. FRI, 11 AM. Ph: (743) 4-3767. Many thanks to Sanborn's Hotel & Restaurant Reviewers, Charles & Millicent Saunders, who can be reached at (011-52)-(322) 2-0879. In an emergency, they may be able to assist you.

PHYSICIANS

V.D. CAMACHO, M.D. – General Practitioner – 1 block from City Hall, 437-2 Juárez – Ph: 2-1854.
AGUSTIN FERNANDEZ – Orthopaedic Surgery & Traumatology – Ph: 2-6894 or 2-6923 (Emergency calls through radio 2-4448, operator of Hotel Plaza Vallarta) – Postgraduate training in Switzerland.
MÓNICA GÓMEZ – Ophthalmologist – Allende 190 – Ph: 2-2316 – Treatment for diseases of the eyes and contact lenses & fitting. English spoken.
ÓPTICA ITALIA – Ph: 2-1431 – Glasses & contact lenses. Eye tests by a licensed optometrist. DR. JORGE TREJO – Specialist in Cardiology & Internal Medicine – Ph: 2-6894 or 2-6923 (Emergency calls through radio 2-4448, operator of Hotel Plaza Vallarta) – Postgraduate training in Baltimore, Johns Hopkins University Hospital.
Most of the hotels here have SATV, so we didn't specify. Also, rates vary a lot here from winter (high season) to summer (low season). Many hotels will give you a better rate if you just ask, depending on how good business is.
Thanks to A. Corelis for her help in updating this area.

SLEEPING AROUND PUERTO VALLARTA

BEL AIR – LUXURY – UPPER – Marina Vallarta, north of town near airport. Pelícanos 311 Marina Vallarta, Puerto Vallarta 48300, Mexico. One of the nicest hotels in Mexico. Mikey's favorite. Member of the Small Luxury Hotels & Resorts Assn. 67 rooms – all suites. The Grand Class suites have jacuzzis in room. 25 villas, with private small pools. This is a class place, with statuary, handcarved and painted furniture from Michoacán done up in pastels. You'll probably have a hard time finding the TV! Classical music in lobby and halls. First-class restaurant. Reservations suggested, especially on weekends. Golf and tennis privileges with other hotels. No swimming pool, or public jacuzzi, but use of another hotel's facilities. AE, MC, VI. Ph: 1-0800. RESERVATIONS: 91-800-36-015. GUAD: (36) 52-0000. USA 1-800-362-9170. FAX: 1-0801.
BUENAVENTURA – MOD – 210-room, 4-story A/C hotel at Av. México #1301 near waterfront boulevard on beach. Restaurant. Lobby Bar. Club. Pool. Tennis at nearby club. Shops. Travel agency. Car rental. Laundromat. Sauna. Parking. AE, MC, VI. Good buy. Ph: 2-3737 or 2-3742 Fax: 4-6400.
BUGANVILLAS SHERATON – UPPER – KM 1 Paseo de las Palmas, CP 48300, Puerto Vallarta, Jalisco, Mexico. Luxurious 501 rooms. 169 suites. 14 story (actually 6 towers) A/C Beach-front hotel. 4 restaurants. 5 bars. Club. Disco. Lovely pool. Shops. Boutiques. Travel agency. Car renta. Laundromat. Water sports. Tennis. Parking. AE, MC, VI. Ph: 3-0404. US: 800-325-3535.
CALINDA PLAZA LAS GLORIAS QUALITY INN – UPPER – 243-room, 4-story A/C hotel on beach on Av. De las Garzas. 2 restaurants. 3 bars. Pool. Travel agency. Car rental. Sauna. Tennis. Golf nearby. Children's activities. Water sports. Parking. AE, MC, VI. Ph: 2-2224.
CAMINO REAL – UPPER – Terrific 10-story A/C hotel a mile south of town, KM 2.5 on Hwy 200 in beautiful tropical seaside setting on beach. Playa de las Estacas, P.O. Box 95, 48300. Their Royal Beach Club tower is luxurious. 87 rooms for those who can afford to be pampered. The 337 rooms in the rest of the hotel are pretty nice, too. Health club, aerobics, tennis, golf, sauna, steam room & two pools. Convention facilities. AE, MC, VI. Ph: 1-5000.
CONTINENTAL PLAZA RESORT – UPPER – 438 room, 4 story beach front hotel on Airport Boulevard. 4 restaurants. 2 bars. SATV. Club. Nice pool. Shopping arcade. Travel agency. Beauty shop. John Newcombe tennis club. Health club. Parking. AE, MC, VI. Ph: 4-0123.
COSTA ALEGRE – ECON – 30-room, 3-story budget hotel downtown at Fca. Rodríguez #168. No restaurant. Small pool. 1 block to beach. Parking. MC, VI. Ph: 2-4888 Fax: 2-0583.
COSTA DEL SOL – MOD – 88-room, 3-story A/C hotel on Paseo de las Palmas across from Plaza Vallarta. No restaurant. Parking. MC, VI. Ph: 2-2055.
COSTA FLAMINGOS – ECON-MOD – 113-room, 2 story A/C layout on Hwy #200 about 15 miles north of town on nice secluded beach. Restaurant. Bar. Pool. Tennis. Parking. MC, VI. Ph: (329) 8-0226 Fax: 8-0333.
COSTA VALLARTA BEACH CLUB – UPPER – Paseo de los Cocoteros, corner Paseo Cancún in Nueva Vallarta. Everything you'd expect at a resort like this. 1201 bedroom suites that sleep 8. Fancy, highrise sur-

roundings with tennis, club, bars, pools, TV's, golf, a marina for your yacht, horses for riding, sauna, child-care. Ph: 70515.

EL CONQUISTADOR VALLARTA CLUB – UPPER – 104-kitchenette, 2 story A/C hotel on north beach on Airport Boulevard. Restaurant. Bar. Pool. Travel agency. Parking. MC, VI. Ph: 2-2088 or 2-2764.

ELOISA – MOD – 150 room, 6 story (some) A/C hotel on Lázaro Cárdenas on south side near waterfront. Restaurant-bar. Pool. Parking. MC, VI. Ph: 2-0286 or 2-1500.

EL PRESIDENTE – UPPER – 120 deluxe suites overlooking bay at KM 8.5 south on Hwy #200. 2 restaurants. Bar. Pool. Tennis. Gym. Ph: (329) 3-0507 Fax: (329) 3-0116.

ENCINO – ECON – One block south of Insurgentes Bridge. 4 story, 40 room inexpensive but nice place. Elevator. Phones. Rooftop restaurant. If you like blue and coral decor, you'll like this place. Rooftop pool. No parking, but on street parking appears OK. MC, VI.

FIESTA AMERICANA CONDESA – UPPER – Beautiful 291 deluxe rooms, with 33 junior suites on 12th floor, A/C hotel on beach at Los Tules, KM 2.5 Paseo de las Palmas. 4 restaurants. 4 bars. Olympic pool. 5 night lit tennis courts. 3 Km jogging track. Shopping arcade. Car rental. Travel agency. Beauty shop. Parking. AE, MC, VI. Ph: 4-2010 Fax: 4-2108 US: 1-800-FIESTA-1

FONTANA DEL MAR – MOD – 45-room, 5-story A/C hotel on dead end at Manuel Diéguez #171. Pool. Parking. AE, MC, VI. Ph: 2-1712 or 2-0712 Fax: 2-0583

GARZA BLANCA (White Heron) – UPPER – LUXURY layout 4.5 miles south of town on beautiful secluded beach near Mismaloya. Nice, tropical 57 unit and villa A/C. Open-air restaurant. Natural pool at nearby waterfall. Private pools with villas. Tennis. Putting green. 9-hole, par-3 golf course. Parking. AE, MC, VI. Ph: 2-1023.

KRYSTAL VALLARTA – UPPER – Terrific 500 room, 3 story A/C hotel north of town on airport boulevard on beautiful section of beach. 6 restaurants (including 24-hour coffee shop). 6 bars (some with live entertainment). 2 pools. All villas with private pools. Tennis. Horses. Shopping arcade. Travel agency. Art gallery. Beauty shop. Water sports. Parking. AE, MC, VI. Ph: 4-1041 Fax: 4-0222. A village in itself!

LAGUNITA (YELAPA) – Tropical 23-unit cottage-style layout 17 miles south of town at Yelapa reached only by boat. Open-air restaurant. Contact Miller Travel Service at 2-1197.

LA SIESTA – 24-unit, 2-story hotel at corner of Domínguez and Matamoros in town. Restaurant. Bar. Club. Small pool. Nice view of town. Parking. MC, VI.

LAS FERMAS – MOD-UPPER – Tropical 153-room, 5-story A/C layout on north beach off Airport Boulevard. Restaurant. Bars. Pool. Travel agency. Boutiques. Car rental. Parking. MC, VI. Ph: 2-0543 or 2-0650.

LOS CUATROS VIENTOS ("Four Winds") – MOD – Plenty of character, but lots of stairs at this 13-unit inn high at Matamoros 529 (3 blocks east of lighthouse). Open-air patio dining at Chez Elena Restaurant. Small pool. Parking. Ph: 2-0161.

LOS TULES – UPPER – Very good 450 unit, 4 story A/C layout at north end on airport boulevard. Some suites with full kitchen. Poolside restaurant. Pools. Travel agency. Car rental. Laundromat. Sauna. Mini-super. Beauty shop. Tennis. Water sports. Parking. AE, MC, VI. Ph: 2-2990.

MELIA – Marina Vallarta – UPPER – Located at Paseo de la Marina Sur. One of the Spanish chain of grand hotels. I like these hotels, they aren't cheap, but they usually offer good value for your money. 403 rooms, all ocean view. Tennis, squash, volleyball. Rooms have safes. Health club. 2 Pools. 2 restaurants. Convention center. Was dedicated by the King of Spain, Dec. 1989. At the same time all the city streets were improved. AE, MC, VI. Ph: 1-0200, 1-0126, 1-0715. FAX 1-0118. Western US/CANADA: 800-888-5515, Eastern US 800-336-3542, FAX: 305-854-0660.

MOLINO DE AGUA – MOD – After you go over bridge over Río Cuale, it's IMMEDIATELY on your right. To park, take 1st street to right after bridge. P.O. Box 54. Parking is secured behind gate. Beachside restaurant. "Mexico Mike" likes this place very much. It has one of the best JACUZZIS I've seen. Heated, huge. Enclosed by a stone wall, it's absolutely QUIET! 29 bungalows, 8 seafront apartments, 4 suites and 12 junior suites. Bar. Pool. Laundromat. Lovely gardens. Parking. MC, VI. Ph: 2-1957, 2-1927. Reservations in U.S. Ph: US: 1-800-826-9408, CA: 2-800-423-5512.

ORO VERDE – MOD – 162 room, 8 story A/C hotel on Calle Rodolfo Gómez #111, Playa del Sol in heart of old "Vallarta." Restaurant. Bar. Pool. Boutique. Travel agency. Car rental. Parking. AE, MC, VI. Ph: 2-3050.

PELÍCANOS – MOD – 186-room A/C hotel next to Playa Las Palmas north of town. 15 bungalows. Restaurant. Bar. Beachside restaurant-bar. Disco. Pool. On-street parking. AE, MC, VI. Ph: 4-1010 Fax: 2-1915.

PLAYA CONCHAS CHINAS – MOD – 55 room, 5 story A/C hotel on Hwy 200 south of town. 2 restaurants. Bar. Pool. Boutique. Laundromat. Parking. AE, MC, VI. Ph: 2-0156.

PLAZA IGUANA – MOD – KM 7.5, Carr. Aeropuerto. In Marina Vallarta, on north side of town. 3-4 story, 100-room, peach-colored place that tries to blend into the natural scenery. Pool. Tennis. Golf. Yacht club access. Ph: 1-0880.

PLAYA DE ORO – MOD-UPPER – 392-room, 5-story A/C hotel on beach at far north end near airport at de las Garzas 1. Restaurants. Tahitian-style beachside bar. Pool. Tennis. Horses. Book and drug store. Shops. Travel agency. Car rental. Laundromat. Water sports. AE, MC, VI. Ph: 4-6868 US: 1-800-882.

PLAYA LOS ARCOS – MOD – 135 room, 4 story air-con hotel at Olas Altas #380 in town on beach. 10 master suites. Restaurants. Bar. Pool. Car rental. Gift shop. Water sports. Parking. AE, MC, VI. Ph: 2-0583.

PLAZA LAS GLORIAS – MOD – Located at Villa Vallarta Center KM 2.0 Carr. to Aeropuerto 48300. Marina & hotel – 320 rooms. 91 villas with kitchenettes. SATV & service bars. Restaurant. Bar. Golf course. Tennis club. Beach club. 2 Swimming pools surrounded by beautiful gardens and with view of the marina. Travel agency and car rental. Ph: 4-4444. US: 1-800-342 AMIGO USA. Mexico DF Ph: 514-3420 and 514-5240. GUAD: 52-1126 and 52-3818.

POSADA DEL ANGEL – ECON – 36-room, 2-story A/C hotel on airport boulevard 3 blocks from beach. Restaurant. Bar. Pool. Parking. AE, MC, VI. Ph: 2-1229 in Guadalajara.

POSADA RÍO CUALE – ECON-MOD – 25 room, 2 story A/C hotel in south part of town at Aquiles Serdán #242. Restaurant. Bar. Pool. Lots of character and nice rooms, with winding iron stars to rooms. Walking distance to beach. Parking. AE, MC, VI. Ph: 2-0450.

POSADA ROGER – ECON – Basilio Badillo #237. Upper budget price, favorite of many economy travellers. 52 rooms in two & a half stories. Some have ceiling fans, some A/C. Nice garden courtyard. Most rooms very pleasant, but some are a bit dark, so look first. "El Tucán" bar/restaurant downstairs. Pool on second story. MC, VI. Ph: 2-0836.

QUALTON – UPPER – KM 2.5 Paseo de las Palmas. 255 deluxe rooms. 8 master suites and 2 presidential suites with jacuzzi. Health club with first class facilities, including hydromassage, eucalyptus inhalation, herbal wraps, salt & mud treatment. Gymnasium decorated in pastels with mini-mirrors, & has every exercise machine imaginable. Ph: 4-4446.

RAMADA PLAZA – UPPER – 466-room, 17-story A/C hotel on beach at KM 3 Paseo de las Palmas. 2 restaurants. Piano bar. Club. Nice pool. Travel agency. Car rental. Laundromat. Golf nearby. Shopping arcade. Tennis. Water sports. Parking. AE, MC, VI. Ph: 4-1700.

ROSITA – ECON – Older 111 room hotel downtown. Restaurant. Pool. On-street parking. MC, VI. Ph: 2-0033 or 2-1033.

SIERRA RADISSON – UPPER – A 350-room all inclusive hotel at Paseo de los Cocoteros #19 in Nuevo Vallarta, Nayarit. 5 restaurants. Water sports. Fitness center. Ph: (329) 7-1300 Fax: (329) 7-0082.

SUITES EL PESCADOR – ECON – 42 unit, 4 story A/C layout downtown at corner of Paraguay and Uruguay. No restaurant. On-street parking. Use of Rosita's facilities. AE, MC, VI. Ph: 2-2169 or 2-1884.

VILLA DEL MAR/PALMAR – MOD – 315 room, 10-story A/C hotel at KM 3 Paseo de las Palmas a mile from airport at north end of town. Restaurants. Bar. 2 pools. Boutique. Travel agency. Beauty shop. Gym. Tennis. Sauna. Parking. MC, VI. Ph: 4-0635.

VILLA DEL ORO – UPPER – 135-room, 4 story A/C condo-hotel on beach on Airport Boulevard. Restaurant. Bar. Pool. Parking. AE, MC, VI. Ph: 2-3306.

VILLA TIZO – ECON-MOD – 23 unit, 2 story hotel situated high above road south of town. Very steep entry although you can park at road level on opposite side of curve and ride cable car up. No restaurant. Pool. Parking. Ph: 2-1570.

EATING PTO. VALLARTA

ARCHIE'S WOK – Francisco Rodríguez #130. Across from the Hotel Marsol. Regional Asian cuisine. Owner Cynthia Alpeuia really nice, mellow. Archie's Wok became legendary when he was chef for John Huston. His legacy lives on. "They did their own thing in their own time," to borrow a line from "Easy Rider." Excellent food, white tablecloth. New Age music and vibrations. Highly recommended. Ph: 2-0411.

BASKIN & ROBINS – 31 flavors – downtown on Paseo Díaz Ordaz just one block north of main plaza.
Best tamales in town – On the town side of the one-way North bridge, the lady on the left (as you're driving towards the Gold zone) has three flavors. About a buck a tamale. Good. One thousand stars.

BISTRO – Easygoing restaurant at Isla Cuale #16-A. Dine indoors or on outside patio. Sea food, meats, good salads, and soups. Open daily 9 AM till 12 AM; closed Sundays. AE, MC, VI.

BOGART'S – On Hwy 200 and in Hotel Krystal. Very pricey. International food. Unique Arabic atmosphere. More waiters than you can shake a stick at. Romantic dining. Open 5 PM till Midnight. Ph: 4-0202.

BRAZZ – Good, casual restaurant at corner of Morelos and Galeana another of the renowned Guadalajara chain. Excellent charcoal-grilled meats and fish. Good bar and *mariachi* music daily. Open noon till midnight. AE, MC, VI. Ph: 2-0324.

CAFE EUROPA – MOD – New European style cafe at Basilo Badillo # 252 Complete french pastry line. Open 9 AM till 10 PM. Ph: 3-1925.

CAFE DES ARTISTES – Guadalupe Sánchez #740. Serves gourmet cuisine in an artistic setting. Superb dishes prepared by award-winning Chef Thiery Blouet. Ph: 2-3228

CARLOS O'BRIAN'S – Bar-grill at Díaz Ordaz #786 on waterfront downtown. International cuisine. Open for lunch and dinner. AE, MC, VI. Plenty of atmosphere where there's never a dull moment! For the "party-hearty" crowd.

CASABLANCA – UPPER – Díaz Ordaz #570. EXPENSIVE. Among PV's fanciest restaurants. Specialties include lower star, Coquilles St. Jacques, Chateaubriand, and Mahi-Mahi. Excellent service. Popular bar. Upstairs dining overlooking ocean. Open 8 AM-4 PM; 5 PM-1 AM. AE, MC, VI. Ph: 2-1723.

CASA DEL ALMENDRO – International restaurant at Galeana #180 a half block off Díaz Ordaz. Specialties include shrimp scampi, almond lobster, and chicken dishes. Open 5 PM till midnight. AE, MC, VI. Ph: 2-4670.

CHEF ROGER – Agustín Rodríguez #267. "Fine food for simple prices," is what they advertise & deliver. Swiss and French cuisine. Chef Roger is Swiss and a Vallarta personality. English spoken. Open 6:30 PM till 1 AM. Closed Sundays. VI, MC. Ph: 2-5900.

CHEZ ELENA – Below the Hotel Cuatro Vientos at Matamoros #520. Courtyard dining by pool or inside, international and Mexican. Really elegant food, but not a stuffy atmosphere. Live musician, ballad singer, paid by the house, wanders around. "El Nido" (The Nest) rooftop bar a hefty climb, but worth it. Wonderful sunsets. Mikey lies it. Ph: 2-0161.

CHICO'S PARADISE – Remotely located restaurant about 12 miles south of town on Hwy #200 above Mismaloya Beach – Jungle atmosphere. Delicious spareribs and crawfish; coconut pie is a special treat. Open 11:00 AM till 11:30 PM. AE, MC, VI.

DAIQUIRI DICK'S – Olas Altas #314 and Basillo Badillo on Los Muertos beach. Open daily 9 AM till 10:30 PM. MC, VI. Ph: 2-0566.

DENNY'S – In Marina Vallarta – just south of airport at north end of town.

DOMINO'S PIZZA – 2 locations: Next to main plaza, downtown on Zaragoza by Los Arcos. – On Hwy to airport at Lucerne #101. Open daily 12 Noon till 2 AM. Home delivery. Ph: 4-1222 or 4-2222.

CUETOS – Marisquería, Brasilia 475. Dinners only, 7 days a week. Family owned and run by José & Irene Cueto. Serves only fish, but menu is enormous, every conceivable fish & seafood served every way. Large servings beautifully presented and reasonably priced. They serve FREE DRINKS and usually have at least one group of musicians to entertain the people while they wait. Linen tablecloths and napkins. Ph: 3-0363.

EL DORADO – Tropical open-air beachside restaurant at Amapas and Pulpito. Good for a snack as well as Mexican and seafood – "Old Vallarta" atmosphere. Open 8 AM till 7 PM. MC, VI.

EL SET – Mountainside restaurant overlooking bay near Camino Real. Top-notch seafood and broiled steaks. Pool. Open 4 PM-midnight. Don't miss this place whether for an afternoon drink or dinner. AE, MC, VI. Ph: 2-0302.

HOT ROD CAFE – On Hwy 200 North end of town, just South of Sheraton. Supreme Court of Rock'n'Roll. Cafe & bar has something for everyone. Town's tallest beers. For the "Party Hearty" crowd. For those who like to dance, be there about 10 PM. A party every night! Open 24 hours a day.

IL MANGIARE – Mexican-European-style restaurant (no foolin') at corner of Abasolo and Díaz Ordaz on waterfront. Romantic and elegant. International food with accent on Italian specialties. Open 5 PM till midnight. MC, VI.

KENTUCKY FRIED CHICKEN – At Juárez and Zaragoza on main plaza. No parking. No credit cards. Open daily 9:30 AM till 11 PM. Ph: 2-3813

LA CASA DE MARISCOS – B. Badillo, Pino Suárez PTO. Vallarta, Jalisco. Features good seafood at reasonable prices. Open 4 PM till 11 PM daily. Ph: 2-33-17.

LA CEBOLLA ROJA ("The Red Onion") – Popular restaurant-bar on waterfront at Díaz Ordaz #822 adjacent to Carlos O'Brian's. Seafood specialties plus soups, chicken and pork dishes, etc. Open 1 PM till 1 AM – MC, VI. Ph: 2-1087.

LA CHATA – Located on Paseo Díaz Ordaz #700. Traditional Mexican cooking. Live Marimba music. Open 8 AM till late evening.

LA FUENTE DEL PUENTE – Corner of Insurgentes and Agustín Rodríguez at foot of northbound bridge. Mexican and international food. Live music. Mariachis. Ph: 2-2987 or 2-1141.

LA HACIENDA – Elegant restaurant decorated in greenery at Aguacate #274. Specialties include snails, papillote of fish, Crepes St. Jacques, Lobster a la Hacienda, plus good salads. Open 6 PM till midnight. AE, MC, VI. Ph: 2-0590.

LA IGUANA MEXICAN FIESTA – Famous indoor-outdoor restaurant a couple of blocks South of Río Cuale at Lázaro Cárdenas #311. Used for semi-private *noche buenas*. Open 7 PM till 11 PM. Ph: 2-0105

LA JOYA DE MISMALOYA – Palapa-style restaurant off Hwy. #200 near Mismaloya. Seafood specialties including crab crepes au gratin, lobster, octopus, etc. Open 9 AM till 7 PM. AE, MC, VI. Nice view of Mismaloya Bay.

LA PERLA – International cuisine in the Camino Real – "Not cheap, but oh so nice," according to one patron. One of the best views. PH: 1-5000.

LAS CAZUELAS – Very good restaurant at Vaillo #479. Reservations suggested. Mexican and international cuisine including shrimp, roast pork, and other delicious entrees. Excellent service. Open 6:30 till 11 PM. Ph: 2-2498 or 2-1658.

LAS PALOMAS – Waterfront restaurant on corner of Díaz Ordaz and Aldama downtown. Good breakfasts as well as seafood and Mexican specialties. One of the most popular sunset watching spots in town. Find movers and shakers at early breakfast in back room. Open 8 till 11:30 PM. AE, MC, VI. Ph: 2-3675.

LE GOURMET – French restaurant at Serdán #284. French cuisine including lobster, shrimp, Steak Diane, many dishes prepared at your table. Live piano music. Open daily 6 PM till midnight. AE, MC, VI. Ph: 2-0914.

LOS ARBOLITOS – Lázaro Cárdenas #184 and the Río Cuale. Good seafood and Mexican food. Handmade tortillas and good mole. Reasonable prices. Ph: 2-4725.

KAMAKURA – UPPER – Elegant restaurant at the Kristal Hotel, serving excellent Japanese cuisine in high style. Open 6 PM till midnight. Ph: 4-0202.

McDONALD'S – At North end of Malecón, Paseo Díaz Ordaz at 31 Octubre. – In Marina Vallarta, just south of airport. Open 9 AM till 11 PM.

MR. FISH – Seafood restaurant on airport boulevard across from several major hotels. Open 12 noon till midnight. AE, MC, VI. Ph: 2-1962.

MOBY DICK – Seafood restaurant at Octubre #31 downtown a half block off main boulevard. Seafood (natch) served family style. Open noon till 1 AM. MC, VI. Ph: 2-0655.

MOCAMBO – Corner of Díaz Ordaz and Abasolo. Restaurant/grill/bar club at International cuisine including terrific prime rib and Italian sandwiches. Piano music. Open 7 AM till 12:30 AM. MC, VI.

PALACIO – 302 Lázaro Cárdenas, corner Constitución, across from "La Iguana." Chinese. Very good, especially the butterfly shrimp. Seafood. Open daily, 1:30 PM till midnight. VI, MC. Ph: 2-0580

PANCAKE HOUSE, THE – Basilio Badillo #289. This place is very simple, clean and fairly attractive. English is spoken. "The" breakfast place where local North Americans and tourist in the know catch up on "what's new" over a great cup of coffee and over 70 breakfast possibilities. What a choice! Very, very imaginative. Served with fruit, lots of good butter, jams, syrups, and portions are quite large. Open daily, 8 AM till 2 PM only. Ph: 2-6272.

PIETRO'S PIZZA – Italian restaurant at corner of Hidalgo and Zaragoza downtown. Try "Piatto del Giorno" (dish of the day). Open noon till midnight. MC, VI.

PIZZA HUT – Avenida de las Palmas at plaza Caracol, across from Fiesta Americana.

PIZZA JOE'S VILLA – Basilio Badillo #269. Moved up in the world. Couldn't have happened to two nicer

folks. Joe & Claire will treat you right at this authentic Italian place. Spaghetti, lasagna, pizza, etc. Courtyard or indoor dining. Classical music. Open 5 PM till 11 PM. A "Mexico Mike" favorite. Closed Mondays. Ph: 2-2477.
PUERTO NUEVO – Basillo Badillo #284. Probably the most famous seafood house in town. Open daily, 12 Noon till 11 PM. Ph: 2-6210.
RITO'S BACI – At Domínguez #181. Features handmade pizza dough and breads stuffed with Italian sausage. Also pasta favorites. Top service, reasonable prices. Ph: 2-6448
RODOLFO'S – F. Madero, #406. VALUE. Pozole Estillo Guerrero with onions (chili piquine on the side), avocado con chicharrón. Interesting photos of food on wall to tell you what you're ordering. Blue tablecloth restaurant.
SANTOS – Francisco Rodríguez #136. Across from the Mar Sol & next to Archie's Wok. White tablecloth on place-mat budget. Mexican food. Good value. Open 4 PM til 11 PM. Ph: 2-5670
SR. CHICO'S – Open-air restaurant at Pulpito #377 south of town. Chateaubriand, prime rib, sirloin, frog legs, red snapper, etc. Open 5 PM till midnight. MC, VI. Ph: 2-3570.
ZAPATA BAR & GRILL – Mexican-style restaurant at Díaz Ordaz #522. Live music nightly in Latin American atmosphere. Open 11 AM till 4 PM and 6 PM till 1 AM. AE, MC, VI. Ph: 2-4748.

DISCOS

FRIDAY LÓPEZ – In Fiesta Americana Hotel. Modern decor with two dance floors and live music. Open 10 PM till 2 AM. AE, MC, VI.
LA JUNGLA – In Camino Real Hotel. Footprints in neon light on ceiling. White-and-silver jungle growth. Open 9 PM till 3 AM. AE, MC, VI.

CAMPING, PARKING & PLUGGING IN.

PUERTO VALLARTA – Very good 70 space park out on north edge of town across road and down from Pelícanos. All hookups. Showers. Toilets. Laundromat. Pool a block away. Long-distance phone service. Ph: 2-2828.
TACHO'S – Very good 155 space facility out on north end across from marina. All hookups. Showers. Toilets. Laundromat. Brick pads. Bus service to town.

12 STEP PROGRAMS

ALANO CLUB – AA in English plus NA, OA, ALANON and CODA. Meetings: Mon- Sat at 9:00 AM and nightly at 6:30 PM. Located at Insurgentes #181 Room 208, at the Cine Bahía Theatre. For more information call Paul B. 2-6060 ext. 204; or Helen V. 2-5919.

OTHER SERVICES

BAY MEDICAL SERVICES – 24-hour bilingual service including patient evacuations, ambulance, X-rays, pharmacy, dentist, gynecologist and various specialists. Located at Km.1, Paseo de las Palmas #500. Ph: 2-2627, 2-5152, or 3-1600.
HOSPITAL MEDASIST VALLARTA – 24-hour, bilingual, private hospital with emergency room, laboratory, X-rays, and full staff of specialists. Located at Manuel Diéguez #360, near south side gas station. Ph: 3-0656, 3-0444, 3-0497, Fax: 2-3301.
CHIROPRACTORS – Dr. Paul J. Constante. California licensed. English spoken. Calle Jesús Langarica #200-22 Ph: 3-0081 Emergencies after 10 PM call 4-5420 or 4-5025 ext. 1216.
DENTIST – Dr. Martha Peña. General odontology. Francisco Madero #372 Ph: 2-0174.
HOLISTIC MEDICINE – Dr. Abel Jiménez M.D. Manuel Diéguez #322. Ph: 3-1505, or 2-3772.
MASSAGE – Stress reduction, pain relief, reflexology. Calle Amapas #114, just around the corner from Hotel Oro verde. Ph: 3-0132.
PSYCHOLOGICAL SERVICES – Psychotherapy. Abuse recovery. Colleen McDonald, M.S., MFCC or Lic. Miguel Angel Sosa Cravlota. Affiliated with CMQ Medical offices Ph: 2-5660 or 90-329-4-0078

End of Puerto Vallarta Eat & Stray!

Guadalajara

UD-017

Area Code — 3

DEGOLLADO THEATRE

East side of Plaza de la Liberación. Its facade is lined with 8E Corinthian columns, and below the frieze, which depicts the Nine Muses of Greek Mythology, are engraved these words: "The Rumors of Discord Shall Never Arrive." Named after the governor who ordered its construction in 1865, the Degollado Theatre is home of the Guadalajara Symphony Orchestra and the University of Guadalajara Folkloric Ballet. Concerts, plays, operas, and special performances are also presented in the theatre. Open 10-1 and 4-7. Ph: 613-1115.

LIBERTY MARKET ("Mercado Libertad")

Just east of downtown section at corner of Calz. Independencia and Av. Javier Mina. Guadalajara's largest market, also known as "Mercado San Juan de Dios" because San Juan de Dios River runs underneath, covers an area of 430,400 square feet and is open daily. Bargaining is the name of the game here (and be sure to hang on to your purse/wallet).

FLOWER MARKET (*Mercado de Flores*)

West side of Parque Agua Azul on Calz. Independencia around corner from Casa de Artesanías near Sheraton Hotel. This market is open from mid-morning to early evening and always offers an impressive display of colorful flowers. Bargaining is also customary here.

ZAPOPAN

Suburb of Guadalajara a couple of miles northwest of downtown on Calzada Avila Camacho (5 mi or 7.5 km). This is the location of the 17th-century Franciscan shrine where the Blessed Virgin of Zapopan is venerated. Famous throughout Mexico, the statue of the Guadalajara patroness is made of corn husks with a wooden carved face and hands. On October 12th a spectacular procession takes place ending at night with music, dancing, and fireworks. At the right of the shrine entrance is an interesting Huichol and Cora Indian Museum. Open daily 10 AM till 1:30 PM and 4 till 7 PM.

CABAÑAS ORPHANAGE ("Hospicio Cabañas")

Block behind Liberty Market at corner of Calle Hospicio and Av. Cabañas across from Plaza de Toros Progreso ("Progreso Bullring"). Founded in 1803 by Bishop Ruiz de Cabañas, the dwelling was an orphanage for 178 years but has now been converted to a cultural center called "Centro Cultural de las Americas" where artistic and cultural events are held. Resembling the more famous "Monastery de El Escorial" near Madrid, the center features 23 flower-filled patios and outstanding murals by Orozco, among them the "Conquest of Mexico", the "Four Horsemen of Apocalypse", and his masterpiece, the "Man of Fire." Small fee. Open Tues-Sat 10:15 AM till 6 PM, Sun 10:15 AM till 3 PM.

CATHEDRAL

Av. 16 de Septiembre downtown in center of four plazas which form a cross around the structure. Started on July 31, 1571, the cathedral's original twin towers were destroyed by an earthquake in 1848. It is a product of many architectural styles including Gothic, Corinthian, Ionic, Doric, Byzantine, and Mudejar, and displays fine paintings of Paez, Uriarte, Castro, and Cabrera, and in the sacristy is Murillo's finest work, the "Assumption of the Virgin." Closed Thurs & Sun at noon for confirmations.

GOVERNMENT PALACE

East side of Plaza de Armas. The building dates from 1643 and features some of Orozco's earlier murals including "Man and His Philosophies", "Progress in a Spiritual and Material World", and "The Ghost of Religion in Alliance With Militarism." In this building in 1810, Hidalgo decreed the abolition of slavery in Mexico. Free admission. Open 8 AM till 8 PM.

REGIONAL MUSEUM OF GUADALAJARA

North side of Plaza de la Liberación (behind cathedral) at Calles Corona and Hidalgo. Once a seminary, the museum now houses a display of regional arts and crafts, archaeological artifacts, and an excellent collection of European, colonial, and modern paintings. Small fee. Open 9 AM till 3:45 PM daily; closed Mondays.

ENGLISH AA

Go to any lengths way out in Sector Providencia. Filadelphia #2015. Near Av. de las Americas & López Mateos, corner of Filadelfia. Up from highrise office building, Torre Americas. Down side street from Brazz restaurant, across from the Roosevelt School. M, W 7:30 PM. Call Bill: (3) 663-1417 or Vick 625-2613. Spanish-AA M, TH 7 PM; Ph: 641-2935 or 623-1317.

CHAPALA, JAL – AJIJIC AREA – Sun, Jocotepec, call Bill (376) 5-2575. Mon – Little Chapel, 4 PM. Tues – Río Zula #1, Wed – ACOA, Hidalgo #63, Ajijic, ALANON, Río Zula #1, 4PM. Thurs – Río Zula #1, 4 PM. Sat – ALANON, Río Zula #1, 9:30 AM.

ATTENTION!

You may be approached by unscrupulous scalawags who claim to know more about Mexico auto/RV insurance than Sanborn's. They'll offer many spurious reasons for changing from a Sanborn's insurance policy to a one written through another company. DON'T BE FOOLED! WE'VE BEEN HERE SINCE 1948 TO SETTLE YOUR CLAIMS IN BOTH THE U.S. AND MEXICO. WE HAVE HUNDREDS OF ADJUSTERS THROUGH-OUT MEXICO. DO THEY?

We sell our insurers what we believe to be the best and most complete coverage for Mexico.

We recommend a policy never be canceled while in Mexico, leaving equipment uninsured because "that's what the other guy is doing." What you pay for with insurance is financial security as well as peace of mind – and in this day and age that's worth something. If you can't afford to lose it – insure it! If for some reason a Sanborn's policy must be canceled, the matter CANNOT be handled in Mexico. It must be mailed to the issuing office or to Sanborn's home office in McAllen, Texas.

Our Number One Priority is to provide our customers with adequate, sensible insurance protection along with the best service possible. Sanborn's has always been and will continue to be the strongest and most reliable Mexico auto insurance organization in existence.

WHEN YOU NEED INSURANCE.

If your policy is nearing expiration (or if you need info on Guadalajara and surrounding area), there is a Sanborn's agent in the vicinity: Martin Parker, Callejón Del Arroyo #200, Villa Nova, Ajijic, Jal. Apdo. Postal #575, Ajijic 45920 Jal. Ph: (333) 3-0720, 5-2381.

MECHANIC

European Car Service. Excellent, hard working and conscientious. Alberto Rivas C. Depto. Volkswagen, Prol. Alcalde 2144 Ph: 24-5612. English spoken. Jeep, Nissan (Datsun), VW, Chrysler, Chevrolet, & Ford.

SLEEPING AROUND GUADALAJARA

ARANZAZU – MOD – (part of Hoteles Vista chain) 540-room, 10-story twin-tower a/c hotel just off Av. 16 de Septiembre at Revolución #110. Restaurant. Cafeteria. Bars. Fancy clubs. 2 pools. Barber shop. Beauty shop. Travel agency. Tobacco shop. Parking. AE, MC, VI. Ph: 613-3232 Fax: 614-5445; Mex (91-800) 36133; US

120

800-882-8215.

CAMINO REAL – UPPER – Deluxe 244-room a/c hotel in west end of town at Av. Vallarta #5005. French restaurant. Coffee shop. Bar. Club. 5 heated pools. Tennis. Putting green. Travel agency. Car rental. Boutiques. Horses. Lovely grounds. Parking. AE, MC, VI. Ph: 647-8000 Fax: 647-6781; Mex. 91-800-90321; U.S. 800-228-3000.

CARLTON – UPPER – Very nice 222-room, 20-story a/c hotel near downtown on corner of 16 de Septiembre and Av. Niños Héroes. Restaurants plus elegant rooftop restaurant with live entertainment. Club. Bar. Pool. Boutiques. Parking. AE, MC, VI. Ph: 614-7272 Fax: 613-5539; U.S. 800-871-5278.

CHAPALITA – MOD – 79-room, 2-story a/c hotel at López Mateos #1617 across from Posada Guadalajara. Restaurant. Shakey's Pizza & Chicken Restaurant adjoining. Bar. Pool. Beauty shop. Parking. AE, MC, VI. Ph: 622-4484.

COLÓN – MOD – 6 story older hotel near downtown on Av. Revolución #12. A/C, servi-bars, TV, phones. Sometimes has specials. Ph: 613-3753.

DEL PARQUE – MOD – VALUE. 845 Av. Juárez. 77-room, 4-story a/c downtown hotel just west of Parque de la Revolución. Dining room. Parking. AE, MC, VI. Ph: 625-2800.

DE MENDOZA – MOD – Attractive 104-room, 5-story a/c hotel right in heart of town adjacent to Degollado Theater at Carranza 16. Restaurant. Bar. Pool. Travel agency. Parking. AE, MC, VI. Ph: 614-2621.

DON QUIJOTE PLAZA – MOD – Nice, reasonably-priced hideaway. Niños Héroes #91. 32 rooms (15 with tubs!) & 1 suite. TV. A/C. Carpets. Lobby bar that closes 9-10 PM. Parking 5 blocks away. Ph: 658-1299.

EL TAPATIO – UPPER – Overpriced 207-room a/c hilltop hotel out on Hwy #44 on road to Chapala. Restaurants. Bar. Disco. Club. Pool. Boutiques. Tennis. Putting Green. Playground. Horses. Bullring. Parking. Advertises a spa, but no facilities. AE, MC, VI. Ph: 635-6050 Fax: 635-6664; U.S. 800-431-2822.

EXELARIS HYATT REGENCY GUADALAJARA – UPPER – Beautiful 350-room, 14-story a/c hotel resembling a pyramid at Av. López Mateos #2500 across from Plaza del Sol shopping center. Several restaurants and bars. Club. Pool. Ice skating ring (only one in town). Physical fitness center. Spectacular atrium with panoramic elevators. Parking. AE, MC, VI. Ph: 678-1234 Fax: 622-9877; U.S. 800-233-1234 or 800-228-9000.

FENIX – MOD – 259-room, 12-story a/c downtown hotel at Corona #160 a block south of Juárez. Continental restaurant. Lobby bar. Disco. Pool. Boutiques. Travel agency. Car rental. Jewelry store. Boutiques. Parking. AE, MC, VI. Ph: 614-5714. Best Western Hotel.

FIESTA AMERICANA – UPPER – Terrific 396-room, 22-story a/c deluxe hotel overlooking Minerva Fountain. Restaurants. Bars. Disco. Clubs. Pool. Tennis. Shopping arcade. In-room movies. Travel agency. Car rental. Parking. AE, MC, VI. Ph: 625-4848 or 625-3434 Fax: 630-3725; U.S. 800-FIESTA-1; Mex. 91-800-36302.

FUTURA DEL SOL – MOD – 18-apartment complex complete with housekeeping facilities a block from Plaza del Sol. No restaurant. Parking. Weekly and monthly rates. Ph: 621-8566.

GUADALAJARA PLAZA – MOD – 170-room a/c motel at Giralda #200 near Plaza del Sol. 4 restaurants. Bars. Club. Pool. Tennis. Sauna. Green area. Security. Parking. AE, MC, VI. Ph: 647-5279.

HOLIDAY INN – UPPER – 305-room, 2-story (plus 9-story tower) motor inn on López Mateos just beyond Plaza del Sol shopping complex. Restaurants. Clubs. Disco. Pool. Curio shop. Tennis. Putting green. Beauty shop. Kennel. AE, MC, VI. Ph: 634-1034; U.S. 1-800-HOLIDAY.

ISABEL – MOD – 60-room motel at Montenegro #1572 a block off Enrique de León some 7 blocks south of Av. Vallarta from university corner. 10 kitchenettes. Restaurant. Pool. Parking. AE, MC, VI. Ph: 626-2630.

LA ESTANCIA DEL SOL – MOD – 2-story, 64-room motel on Mariano Otero #2407 just beyond Plaza del Sol. Some kitchenettes. Restaurant. Pool. Parking. MC, VI. Ph: 631-8025.

LAFAYETTE – UPPER – 181-room, quiet 17-story a/c hotel at Av. de la Paz #2055 known as "first hotel" because of its original works of art decorating rooms (no two alike) and public areas. Restaurant. Cafeteria. Bar. Pool. Shops. Parking. AE, MC, VI. Ph: 615-6750 Fax: 630-1112.

LAS CALANDRIAS – MOD – 18-kitchenette suite hotel 3 miles south on Hwy #15 and a half-block east on Calle Nebulosa. No restaurant. Parking. MC, VI. Ph: 621-0216.

LAS PERGOLAS – MOD – 200-room, 4-story a/c hotel at Av. Morelos #2244, 3 blocks east of Minerva Circle in nice residential area. Restaurant. Coffee shop. Bar. Pool. Boutique. Beauty shop. Barber shop. Parking. AE, MC, VI. Ph: 630-0629.

MALIBU – MOD – 180-room, 9-story a/c hotel at Av. Vallarta #3993. Restaurant. Bar. Pool. Boutique. Tennis.

Car rental. Beauty shop. Parking. AE, MC, VI. Ph: 621-7676.

NUEVA GALICIA – MOD – 95-room at Av. Corona #610 Ph: 614-8780 Fax: 613-9089.

POSADA DEL SOL – MOD – 54-room, 2-story motel at López Mateos #4205 across from Holiday Inn. Some kitchenettes. Restaurant. Bar. Pool. Parking. MC, VI. Ph: 631-5205, 631-5620, 631-5514 or 631-5133.

POSADA GUADALAJARA – MOD – 180-room, 8-story a/c hotel on López Mateos near railroad underpass not far from Minerva Circle. Restaurant. Bar. Club. Pool. Parking. Ph: 621-2022 or 621-2424.

POSADA SAN ISIDRO – MOD – 45-unit, 3-story motel out on Hwy #54 at San Isidro Golf Course subdivision development. Restaurant-bar. Pool. Golf. Tennis. Country club privileges. Parking. Weekly and monthly rates. AE, VI. Ph: 624-0622.

PUERTO VALLARTA – ECON – 32-room, 2-story motel at Vallarta #4003. Some a/c. No restaurant. Parking. Small pets OK. MC. Ph: 621-7361. Budget motel.

QUALITY INN CALINDA ROMA – MOD – Old-time 177-room, 4-story a/c downtown hotel on east end of Av. Juárez. Restaurants. Bar. Secretary service. NO SMOKING ROOMS! Telex service. Pool. Travel agency. Parking. AE, MC, VI. Ph: 614-8650.

QUINTA REAL – UPPER – On corner of López Mateos and México. Magnificent and romantic. Has jacuzzi suite. Parking (go 1 block toward Minerva and take first right). Ph: 615-0000 Fax: 813-1797; US: 1-800-445-4565.

RANCHO RÍO CALIENTE – MOD – 36-unit vegetarian hot springs health layout about 3 miles off Hwy #15 thru village of Primavera (follow winding road to its location alongside Río Caliente). Homegrown food. Pools (cool and hot). Steam and massage room. Yoga and meditation. Horseback riding. Hiking. Volleyball. No children under 15. American plan only. Charge for visiting and using facilities. Advance reservations suggested. USA: 1-800-200-2927. In Guadalajara call Elizabeth Hill 634-3890.

SAN FRANCISCO PLAZA – ECON – VALUE! Charming little place. 60 spacious rooms – 6 with tubs. Degollado #267 across from little plaza. Go 2 blocks toward Tapatia Plaza from Fenix or towards downtown from Aranzazu – which is where you'll park if you stay there. Just up from (& more reasonable than) Don Quixote. Courtyard with fountain (that shuts off at night – darn!) Restaurant – reasonable. Dark wood, polished tile, hanging plants. This could be a romantic place. AE, MC, VI. Ph: 613-8954, 613-8971 or 613-8966.

VISTA PLAZA DEL SOL – UPPER – Pricey. 352-room, 9-story a/c hotel on premises of Plaza del Sol shopping complex on Av. López Mateos. Restaurants. Bars (live music – noisy). Pool. Shops. Solarium. Car rental. Parking. AE, MC, VI. Ph: 616-7274.

BUDGET

If you really want to save pesos, look around the old bus or train stations. The usual caveats apply – look at your room, expect it to be fairly noisy (though you can say the same about any 1st class hotel with a disco) and count on your mattress being as old as you, and sagging even more. You'll often get large rooms and get to meet some nice folks, or you'll hate it. Water not always very hot & towels have seen better days. Some of the below are better than the run-of-the-mill ones, though. You may find a good cheap hotel to be a real bargain and a chance to meet younger European and Mexican tourists.

CONTINENTAL – ECON – OK. 450 Corona – corner with Libertad. 128-rooms, 7 floors, elevator, lobby. TV, no bar. Restaurant. Parking. Street noise, but no discos nearby. Ph: 614-1117.

NUEVO VALLARTA – ECON – 14-room, 2-story motel at Vallarta #3999 at corner with Degollado. No restaurant. Parking. MC. Budget motel.

POSADA REGIS – ECON – Charming little place (10 rooms) across the street from the Fenix. Corona 171. Old mansion carved into rooms. Bird-cages & tropical plants make the lobby a wonder. Big projection TV with movies each night. Little restaurant. Friendly staff. Owner speaks English. Does laundry for a reasonable price. No parking, but a reasonable lot next door. Hotel begins on 2nd floor. You must walk up a flight of steps. Ph: 613-3026.

GENOVA – ECON – 63-room, 6-story a/c hotel on Juárez between Molina and Degollado. Restaurant. Parking. AE, MC, VI. Ph: 613-7500 or 613-0403. Being remodeled.

POSADA ESPAÑA – ECON – BASIC. Small place, 12 rooms. Courtyard. Cheap. López Cotilla #594. Ph: 613-5377.

POSADA DE LA PLATA – ECON – BASIC. Small, 9 rooms. Inexpensive. López Cotilla #619. Ph: 614-9146.
UNIVERSO – MOD – VALUE. QUIET. 137-rooms, 7 stories at López Cotilla, corner with Degollado. TV. PH. Laundry. Elevators. OK restaurant. AE, VI, MC. Ph: 613-2815.

EATING GUADALAJARA

ACUARIUS – ECON – Priciliano Sánchez #416. Vegetarian fare. Good price & good food. Soyburgers Milanesa de Trigo. Fruit drinks. The most famous veggie place in town. Open 9:30 AM till 8 PM. Ph: 613-6277.

ALBATROS – MOD – Good open-air restaurant set in beautiful home on Av. de la Paz #1840, three blocks from Av. Chapultepec. Seafood specialty and international cuisine. Open noon till midnight. MC, VI. Ph: 625-9996 or 625-7723.

ARTHUR'S – MOD – Excellent English pub and steak house at Av. Chapultepec sur #507. Good steaks and ribs prepared to order, lobster, and lavish salad bar. Open for breakfast serving menudo on Saturday mornings. Beautiful bar in Victorian decor where you can enjoy a drink and a tortuga adobada. Terrific wine list. Open Monday-Saturday, 8 AM till 1 AM. AE, MC, VI. Ph: 626-0167 or 626-1505.

ASAHI – ECON – Av. de la Paz #2056 near Lafayette Hotel. Japanese food. Reasonable prices. Subdued atmosphere. Open daily 1:30 till 11 PM. MC, VI. Ph: 616-3203.

BRAZZ – MOD – Chain of 3 restaurants (Av. López Mateos #1195; López Mateos Sur #6022 (next to English AA, corner Filadelfia); and Av. 16 de Septiembre #720), each with different atmosphere but all specializing in grilled meats including New York steaks, rib eyes, and sirloin. Ph: 647-5050 or 647-9231; 641-4827.

CAPORALES – MOD – Mexican-style restaurant with regional Jalisco atmosphere at López Mateos Sur #5290 south of hotel area. Mexican cuisine with floor shows and mariachi music. Parking. Open 2 PM till 1 AM daily; Sun, 2-7 PM. AE, MC, VI. PH: 631-4543, 631-4596 or 631-4139.

CARNITAS URUAPAN – ECON – Colón #338 corner with Libertad. Tacos carnitas, gorditas – a good taco place. Open 10 AM to 7 PM

CASA de PAELLA – MOD – Since 1952. Spanish, Mexican, International. Nice place. Americas #930, across from Torre Américas. Jazz 9 PM – 1:30 AM. Ph: 641-5669, 641-6853.

CHALET SUIZO – MOD – Swiss-style restaurant at Hidalgo #1983 near Minerva Circle. Swiss and International dishes. Piano bar upstairs. Open 1 PM till 11 PM; closed Monday. AE, MC, VI. Ph: 615-7122.

CHE MARY – UPPER – Spanish restaurant at Av. Guadalupe #596 at corner of San Rafael, Colonia Chapalita. Open 1 PM till 12 Midnight daily. Ph: 621-2951 or 622-2505.

COLOMBO – MOD – Av. López Mateos #131 near Minerva. Good lunch buffet. Since 1957, good Italian food (chicken cacciatori, cannelloni) and pizza (also with anchovy). Can make strictly vegetarian dishes. Piano music at night. Open 1:30 till midnight; till ten, Sunday; closed Wednesday. Very friendly owner. Ph: 615-7900.

COPA DE LECHE – ECON – Downtown restaurant at Av. Juárez #414, a Guadalajara institution since 1932. International cuisine served in traditional and typical Tapatian (Guadalajara) atmosphere. Sidewalk cafe and balcony dining. Open daily 7 AM till midnight for breakfast, lunch, and dinner. AE, MC, VI. Ph: 614-5347 or 614-7976.

COPENHAGEN – MOD – Intimate, relaxing, and romantic restaurant on López Cotilla #750 corner of Mario Castellano in front of Parque Revolución. Soft jazz music (9 AM till 1 AM, 3:30 - 4:30 PM and 8 PM - 1 AM). International food with specialties such as paella, zarzuela, and pepper steaks. Open daily 1 PM till 1 AM. AE, MC, VI. PH: 625-2803. Jazz Club off Federalismo.

D'ELYS – MOD – 456 Corona. Sandwich shop and bargain eatery. Across from Hotel Continental. Mexican food, hamburgers, cheap breakfasts.

DON QUIJOTE – MOD – Hotel San Francisco Plaza, Degollado 267. Restaurant. Bar. Ph: 658-1299.

DURÁN DURÁN I – MOD – WACKY, FUNKY PLACE. Av. Vallarta #1543-A, Ph: 616-4095. Music and video bar. Incredible assortment of "stuff" hanging from ceiling. Tacos, steaks, hamburgers, drinks. Decent prices. Open 1 PM to 11:30 PM.

EL ABAJEÑO – MOD-UPPER – Typical Mexican restaurant at Av. López Mateos #4796, La Calma; serving Jaliscan specialties including delicious tacos, carnitas, chalupas, enchiladas. Open 8 AM till 11 PM daily. MC, VI. Ph: 631-30097. Also another at Av Vallarta #2802. Ph: 630-2113 or 630-0307

EL CHE – ECON – Argentine-style charcoal-beef restaurant at López Hidalgo #1798 specializing in El Churrasco.

South American guitars and vocalists. Open 1 PM till midnight. AE, MC, VI. Ph: 652-0325.

EL DELFIN SONRIENTE (The laughing dolphin) – ECON – Good seafood. Reasonable prices. Frog legs. Ceiling fans. Try *"Pachanga de Mariscos"* (Seafood party – octopus, squid, shrimp in soup). Family place. Av. Niños Héroes #2239. VI, MC. Ph: 616-0216, 616-7441.

EL GRULLO – MOD – NW corner Plaza del Sol. Vegetarian fare. A little pricier than others, but good. The fanciest in town.

EL MESON DE SANCHO PANZA – MOD – Marcos Castellanos #114. Spanish, Mexican, and international food. Open 1 PM till 9 PM TUES. - Sun, closed Mon. Ph: 625-2898 or 626-5886

EL OSTIÓN FELIZ (The Happy Oyster) – MOD – Seafood restaurant at Av. Las Américas #1301 serving a fresh, dazzling array of seafood, from cold platters to Alaskan catfish specialties. Also features good Mexican food. Indoor and outdoor dining rooms. Bar with large TV screen. Open noon till midnight daily. AE, MC, VI.

EL PARGO DEL PACÍFICO – MOD – Av. de la Paz #2140. Seafood. Popular. Ph: 626-7150 or 615-7465. Another on Federalismo #876. Ph: 610-5285.

GUADALAJARA GRILL – MOD – For young, boisterous, "party-hearty" types. Sponsors drinking contests. One of the Anderson chain, at López Mateos Sur #3771, near Plaza del Sol and Holiday Inn. Several dining rooms plus outdoor terrace. Spare ribs, chicken, meats, shrimp, and oysters. Homemade bread and biscuits (from outside oven). Open Monday-Saturday 1 PM till midnight; Sundays 1 PM till 5 PM.

KOPPEL HAUS – MOD – Av. America # 764 German food. Seafood. Mon- Fri 7 AM - 11 PM. Sat. 8 AM - 11 PM, Sun. 8 AM - 3 PM. Simple, could be intimate if TV not on. AE, MC, VI. Ph: 641-4563.

LA CHATA – ECON – Mexican food. López Mateos & Otero. Another by Zoo and train station. Ph: 632-1379 or 632-4532.

LA MISIÓN – MOD – Mexican restaurant housed in elegant mansion at Pedro Moreno #1125 in residential area. Good Mexican cuisine. Open noon till 1 AM daily. MC, VI. Ph: 626-1133.

LA PIANOLA – MOD – Mexican restaurant at Av. Mexico #3220 serving Mexican and International cuisine. Piano music. Open 8 AM till 1 AM daily. AE, VI. Ph: 647-7881. Another at Miguel de Cervantes Saavedra #86 630-2774.

LA TRATTORIA – MOD – Good Italian restaurant at Niños Héroes #3051 just off López Mateos (Hwy #15) featuring homemade pasta, spaghetti, lasagna, Veal Scallopini and Parmesan, salad bar, and more. AE, MC, VI. Ph: 622-4425.

LAS CALAS – MOD – Av. Tepeyac #1156, Chapalita. Ph: 647-0383 or 647-0270

LAS MARGARITAS – MOD – Moroccan-style restaurant and store featuring vegetarian cuisine at López Cotilla #1477 (corner Av. Chapultepec). Open 8 AM till 9:30 PM (8 PM Sunday). Ph: 616-8906.

LOS ITACATES – ECON – VALUE! Av. Chapultepec Nte. #110 Family restaurant. Nice refined decor, especially if you like blue. Cuisine mexicana. Open 8 AM - 11 PM M-F, 8 AM - 10 PM Sun. Ph: 625-1106.

LUSCHERLY – MOD – Duque de Rivas #5 corner of Morelos. Good Swiss food. Romantic atmosphere. Open Tues.–Sat 1:30 PM till Midnight, Sun 1:30 till 6 PM. Ph: 616-2988 or 615-0509.

NUEVO LEÓN – ECON – Inexpensive Mexican fast food. Specialty: Cabrito al Pastor. Independencia Sur #223 Ph: 617-2081, Av. Libertad #1586, Ph: 625-4700 or 625-7827. Another on Calz. Independencia sur #223 Ph: 617-2740 or 617-2081.

PILECA – MOD – Colonias #279 (near Lafayette Hotel) Vegetarian food, daily buffet 1 - 5:30 PM. Ph: 625-3544

PIPIOLO – ECON – Bargain food. Carne asada, Mexican fast food. Open 1 PM – 1 AM. All over town.

RECCO – MOD – Nice restaurants at Av. Libertad #1981 a half-block off Av. Chapultepec and at Circunvalación Providencia #1090. Italian cuisine as well as international including Chicken Cacciatore, lasagna, and shrimp Casamona. Open daily 1 PM till midnight. AE, MC, VI. Ph: 625-0724 and 641-4932.

SAINT MICHEL – MOD – Vallarta #1700 Crepes, sandwiches, capuchino. Intimate, romantic. Open 8 AM till Midnight.

SIROCCO – MOD – Fine restaurant at Libertad #1906 featuring seafood and steaks, including Lobster Thermidor and Filet New Orleans Style. Also offers sea grill. Open 1 PM till midnight daily. AE, MC, VI.

SUEHIRO – MOD – Excellent, authentic Japanese restaurant with bar and many dishes prepared at your table by Japanese chefs, at Av. de la Paz #1701. It's quite a kick ordering Japanese food in Spanish to a Japanese-

Mexican waitress in a kimono! Specialties include tepperiyaki and teriyaki, and shabu-shabu. Open 1:30 PM till 11 PM daily. AE, MC, VI. Ph: 626-0094 or 625-1880.
SUSHI NORI – Next to Quinta Real. Shushi bar with satsumi and a few other Japanese dishes like the Mexico Maki. Open 1:30 PM till midnight Mon – Sat and 1:30 till 11 PM, Sun. AE, MC, VI. For home delivery call 616-3135.

CAMPING, PARKING AND PLUGGIN' IN

GUADALAJARA – MOD – 210-space park at north end on Hwy #54. All hookups. Showers. Toilets. Pool. Laundromat. Tile patios. Rec hall. BBQ pits. Dump. Store. Daily activities. Ph: 623-1317 or 623-0869.
HACIENDA – MOD – 100-space facility out in west end of town. All hookups. Pool. Laundromat. Showers. Toilets. Rec hall. Daily activities seasonally.
SAN JOSE DEL TAJO – UPPER – 225-space restful wooded layout some 7 miles southwest of town on Hwy #15 to Morelia and then a half-mile off highway to right by cobblestone road. All hookups. Dump. Pool. Toilets. Showers. Coffee shop. Rec hall. Store. Daily activities. Several motel rooms and one-bedroom kitchenettes available on monthly basis. Ph: 622-2193 or 621-2902.

End of Guadalajara Eat & Stray

LOG 13 *START:* Guadalajara, Jal *END:* Tepic, Nay

143.3 MI OR 229.3 KM
DRIVE TIME 4 HOURS
SCENIC RATING – 3

MI	KM	
0.0	0.0	Starting with cathedral at your right, ahead down Av. Corona. Cross Morelos, one-way your left. Parking lot, right. Turn RIGHT onto Hidalgo, one-way, right. Cross Pino Suárez right, Belén, left, Degollado Theatre to your right. Narrows to 1 lane. Stay right. Cross Carranza.
0.3	0.5	1 lane. Pizza Express, left. MEXICO, SALTILLO, LEFT.
0.4	0.6	RIGHT ONTO INDEPENDENCIA. Go under park. 4 lanes each way. Cross Juárez right. Light.
0.6	1.0	Pass Hotel Los Reyes, right. Cine Avenida, left. Streets crossing or dead-ending into Independencia will alternate one-way left, right.
0.8	1.3	Come to circle with Angel on top. Street right 2 way. Go around and straight ahead.
1.0	1.6	Cross divided 2-way Calzada Revolución. Next 1-way right. Gas right. Av. La Paz, right. Around little circle. Gas left. Airport, Bomberos signs. STAY OUT OF LEFT LANE. Hotel 13,000 – not for you.
1.6	2.6	Gas left. Cross wide González Gallo. (If you were going North, you could turn here with a protected left arrow.) Left 2 lanes can turn left. Pass Biblioteca Nacional. Follow signs for train. Beautiful park left. Right 3 lanes MUST go around *glorieta*. LEFT lane MUST turn left onto González Gallo – don't do that. You'll dead end into Curiel. Railroad station dead ahead.
1.8	2.9	Federal Express on left. Straight. Market, left. Plaza, right. CALZ. GOV. CURIEL STRAIGHT.
2.0	3.2	TRAIN STATION, RIGHT.
2.4	3.8	Up, then over railroad crossing (LOOK & LISTEN). DANGEROUS INTERSECTION. PPG industries de Mexico right. Banco Nacional, left. 4 lane divided street. No dividing strip.
2.8	4.5	Get into right lane for right turn ahead.
3.1	5.0	Should be in right lane for right turn onto Lázaro Cárdenas. Turn RIGHT onto L. Cárdenas. Signs: Clínica IMSS, ZONA INDUSTRIAL SIGNS AHEAD. Pass LP gas tank & satellite dish vendor.
3.5	5.6	Cárdenas is 3 lanes each way divided parkway. Right turn arrows DO NOT mean your lane dies – YET. It will in about 2 miles.
4.5	7.2	Pass Av. Cruz del Sur exit (left).
5.3	8.5	Pass Farmer's market, *Centro de Abastos*, right.
5.6	9.0	Road narrows. RIGHT LANE DISAPPEARS! Under overpass.
5.8	9.3	Come to small glorieta at Av. Mariano Otero. Stop sign. Go 3/4 around & veer right. Straight. Valencia restaurant and La Mansión a *cabrito* restaurant, right. Ahead on wide divided Av. Cárdenas.
5.9	9.4	GAS, right.
6.4	10.2	Cross wide divided López Mateos. Renault dealer on left. *Todo Fácil* – a neat place like a Handy Dan or superstore for do-it-yourselfers, right. If you get a thrill from pushing a power saw or drilling stuff, you can probably find something in there to putter with. Of course, the "missus" might not like it, but you can always come back later.
6.5	10.4	Teléfonos de México, left. Banco del Atlántico.
6.8	10.9	Soccer field in middle of street!
7.0	11.2	Movie theater at right. GAS, left.
7.2	11.5	Hotel Malibu, way over to right.
7.4	11.8	Tutankhamen bar & rest, right. General Tires on left.
7.6	12.2	Cross Av. Del Niño Obrero.
7.8	12.5	Chrysler dealer on right. Veer a little to left. Right lane for local traffic. Nogales sign overhead. Down & under overpass. Street changes name to Av. Vallarta. Pretty brick. Pass electrical generating station, right.
8.0	12.8	Block sculpture in middle of street. Mayoral restaurant on right. Volks Vallarta, left. Road narrows. Interesting townhouses, right. Banco Atlántico, right. Right goes to Universidad Autónoma de Guadalajara, on Av. De la Patria. Goodyear right.
8.5	13.6	Coca Cola dealer right. Hotel Nuevo Real Vallarta, right. GAS, right. Car dealership, left. Road narrows – 2 lanes each way. No longer divided. El Gallo Pope right. Chevy right.
9.5	15.2	Left is to Trailer park, Hacienda. Protected left turn, but better turn ahead. Corona Vallarta right.
9.7	15.5	Protected left turn. Nissan dealer, left. Traffic light.

MI	KM	
10.7	17.1	Pass nice cemetery, left.
11.0	17.6	Conasupo warehouses. Road divides again. Hospital Dr. Angel Leano, right. Straight. Could take right here for Saltillo & Hwy #54. Straight for Nogales. Stoplight. Intersection with Periférico.
12.0	19.2	Pass side road (right) to Ocotán Air Force Base – also called "Zapopan" Air Force Base – one of Mexico's largest. **GAS,** right. Often cops here, so obey traffic laws. Still divided.
12.6	20.2	Gamesa plant, right. Good cookies and crackers. Divided 4 lanes.
14.0	22.4	"Rancho Contento" at left – nice retirement condominium deal for Americans – has its own golf course.
15.8	25.3	Slow a little for a sharp right-left "S" curve and alongside the railroad. Turnoff for botanical institute.
17.0	27.2	Hunting club of Jalisco, right.
17.4	27.8	Thru village of La Venta del Astillero. Careful for farm machinery. **GAS,** right.

IF TO: Río Caliente Spa, a vegetarian health spa, turn off to the left just ahead at town of Primavera and follow stub log below. These folks frown on drop-in guests. Although they probably won't shoot you, it is best to call ahead and make a reservation, USA: 1-800-200-2927, Fax: (415) 615-0601.

RÍO CALIENTE SPA

0.0	0.0	After left turn, go thru village of Primavera. When road dead ends, turn right. At "T", turn left and cross bridge. At "Y" take middle fork with gate and sign that says Las Tinajitas 2.2 km.
2.8	4.5	Come to a fork. Do not take right fork. It goes to Al Río del Valle. Take left fork, Go over cattle guard.
3.0	4.8	Pass road (right) to Balneario La Primavera and road (left) to Hogar Betania. This is where nuns give mud baths and iridology readings.
3.1	5.0	Come to gate. If gate is locked don't despair. There is a little opening to left. Park and walk up hill to office. If you look respectable, they will let you in. Ask for Dr. Ricardo Heredia or Javier Contreras.
3.2	5.1	Cross bridge over steamy river into Río Caliente Spa.

END STUB LOG

19.3	30.9	Wind past village of Primavera "Spring" (the season) in Spanish.
20.7	33.1	Cattle inspection station then roadside restaurant at right.
21.5	34.4	Grain silos at right.
21.8	34.9	Note deep arroyo (gulch) over to the left. Don't you agree that "arroyo" is a much prettier word than our English "gulch"?
22.0	35.2	Road narrows. There may be a guy selling highway signs here! Now you see why folks (even us) get lost sometimes! Then bumpy railroad crossing (LOOK-&-LISTEN). **KM 25.**
22.5	36.0	Curve right (take right fork) past side road (left) to town of Ameca. Come to junction with toll road to Tepic. For toll road veer left and up over overpass and follow stub log below. For free road stay in right lane. If you want to visit the town of Tequila take the free road.

Toll Road to Tepic

22.6	36.2	Having veered left onto overpass for toll road, proceed ahead on 4-lane.
24.0	38.4	Come to toll house and pay toll (Car, $44, extra axle, $22). There's a snack shop and restrooms.
27.0	43.2	To the left are fields of Blue Agave cactus, the plant from which the finest tequilas are distilled. The Guadalajara area produces most of Mexico's tequila.
32.0	51.2	Over puente Tequila. Sorry folks, that doesn't mean that tequila flows in the stream below.
35.0	56.0	Up over puente Gorgorrones.
40.0	64.0	Pass exit (right) to Magdalena.
42.0	67.2	Note town of Magdalena over to right with pretty church dome.

MI	KM	
54.0	86.4	Come to another toll house and pay toll (cars, $51). You'll find a 24-hour emergency medical service, cafeteria and clean restrooms here.
60.0	96.0	Slow and curve over puente Platamar.
64.0	102.4	Cross state line. Leave state of Jalisco and enter state of Nayarit. Also come to a new time zone. Leave Central Standard time and start Mountain Standard time. Turn you watch and dash clock back one hour. Then pass monument dedicating this toll road.
65.0	104.0	Over puente Ocote. Ocote is a strip of pine wood, dripping with sap, used by the farmers as a catalyst to start a fire.
66.0	105.6	GAS right. Then under overpass of Hwy #15 free road.
71.0	113.6	Pass exit (right) to Ixtlá del Río.
78.0	124.8	Pass exit (right) to Jala and Ahuacatlán.
85.0	136.0	Cross bridge over gully of black lava rock down below and over mountain side.
91.0	145.6	Come to last toll house and pay toll (cars, $24, extra axle, $12).
96.0	153.6	Come to junction with free road.
97.0	155.2	Now come to junction with turnoff to Pto. Vallarta.

IF TO: Pto. Vallarta, turn left and start Chapalilla - Compostela Special (page 74).

IF TO: Tepic, straight ahead on free road. Join free road log at mile 116.2.

End Toll Road

		Continuation of free road.
23.0	36.8	Slow a little for bumpy railroad crossing (LOOK-&-LISTEN) – Ameca branch line.
24.5	39.2	Thru village of Santa Cruz del Astillero.
27.3	43.7	Bumpy stretch begins.
27.7	44.3	Note the maguey ("muh-gay") growing on the hillsides hereabouts – it's the heart or core of the maguey cactus that they make tequila from.
29.0	46.4	Little tequila distillery town of Arenal (11,594 folks), left – note the wigwam-type grain silos. Sharp left curve.
30.5	48.8	CAREFUL. EVEN TRUCKS STOP FOR THIS railroad crossing! LOOK-&-LISTEN. Then over fancy bridge.
34.7	55.5	Tequila Orendain plant, right. Pass cemetery, right, and skirt town of Amatitán, left. GAS, right & at far end. Pass bullring on right. Clean restrooms at store beside gas.
37.3	59.7	*Alto, Vea, y Oiga* means stop, look, listen. LOOK-&-LISTEN as you cross the railroad again. Note brown cow keeled over by side of road. Careful for drunken cows here. They're such a problem that there's an organization to get them off the road – Udders Against Drunk Hoofers.
41.5	66.5	Burlap and carton factory on left. If your windows are open, you'll know that you're coming into the famous Tequila-distilling town by the same name – TEQUILA (mostly off to left). Curve right at the fountain (left fork to downtown). Gas at left. Can you catch a whiff of the tequila smell in the air? On right just ahead is Mario's Restaurant and Tequila Shoppe – don't hesitate to stop for a coke or to buy a bottle of tequila. (Mario sells all kinds from Grade A on down at competitive prices.) If you'd like a tour of this interesting town, Mario will take you on one – he's on a first-name basis with just about everybody at the SAUZA and CUERVO tequila distilleries and speaks enough English to get by (see SPECIAL REPORT ON TEQUILA and map, pages 41-42). After Mario's leave Tequila. Note small distillery over at right. Then nice panorama with deep Barranca de Santiago off to right.
42.0	67.2	GAS, left. Village of Teresa down at right. If traffic's bad, don't try to hotrod it around blind curves. Lottsa folks don't make it. Besides, I've done it, worked like _____ and been so frazzled that I had to stop for a *refresco* at the end. While I was sitting there, every truck & VW, I'd risked our lives to pass, rolled on by. Mt. McCreedy dead ahead.
44.9	71.8	**CAREFUL! DANGEROUS, ALMOST HORSESHOE CURVE.** Then up hill. KM 66.
47.0	75.2	**CAREFUL! DANGEROUS, ALMOST HORSESHOE CURVE.** Then up hill. Climbing lane!
50.8	81.3	You've climbed about 800 feet in the last 7 miles. Along here you'll spot some jet-black rocky stuff called OBSIDIAN.
54.3	86.9	Quinta Minas hotel, Ph: 4-0560. Plan on taking it easy through Magdalena, an opal town with a population of 11,021. Congestion is amazing. The reason is there's only one stop sign at the end of the square, so be patient. Across on right is the regional hospital. Altitude 4,200 ft. Opals de Magdalena store at right. TURN RIGHT at end of plaza at traffic light and proceed on up thru town.

By the way, *La Unica*, the largest opal mine in the area, is located 7 miles from town atop Ocatera Mountain.

MI	KM	
54.3	86.9	Curve right. Bank of Promex. Restaurant Evangelina.
54.8	87.7	GAS, at far end of town. Airport, left.
60.0	96.0	Come to cross roads, Hostotipaquillo to right.
62.8	100.5	Pretty little village of El Zapote down at right. Police check point. You've climbed another 600 feet!
65.4	104.6	Exit left for Tepic toll road. Veer right for free road. Veer left if you want to take the toll road.
72.0	115.2	Lavender and mauve colored mountains. Free S.O.S. phones positioned throughout.
73.7	117.9	Pull off point. Altitude 4,500 ft.
76.9	123.0	Top. And come to state line – leave state of Jalisco and enter state of Nayarit (pronounced "nye-a-reet"). Also come to a new TIME ZONE – leave Central Standard Time and start Mountain Standard Time, so set your watches and dash clock BACK one hour.
77.0	123.2	Pass monument on right. Longitude 22 degrees. Go under pedestrian bridge.
77.4	123.8	Pull-off on right.
78.1	125.0	Sharp decline. Veer left to Tepic. Topes. Dangerous intersection.
80.0	128.0	Cross bridge over the railroad.
82.0	131.2	Railroad village of Ranchos de Arriba off to right with church that stands out. Toll road crosses to right. **KM 129**.
85.0	136.0	Hotel Hacienda, right. Balneario Casida, for home folks.
85.7	137.1	La Sidia restaurant to left. **KM 134**.
86.0	137.6	Up high on yonder mountain ahead you'll see the famed huge statue of CRISTO REY or "Christ the King." There's a side road up to it but don't tackle it – it's in very poor shape and we can't recommend it.
87.0	139.2	Slow now. To right and just over railroad tracks are IXTLÁN Archeological Ruins, on which very little is known (except that they are post-Classic, 900 A.D. and later). If you wish to drive over tracks and into compound, hop to it, it's quite nice. (Admission is charged and zone is open from 9 AM – 4 PM daily.)
87.1	139.4	Truck stop to right. Hotel Vacancy Ixtlán to right.
88.0	140.8	Hotel restaurant Colón, right. It's OK by me. Clean restrooms, good food. If it's late (or if you're frazzled by the drive), consider staying here, because you're 110 hard miles from PV, and 47 easy ones from Tepic. Then stoplight. Slow thru town of Ixtlán del Río (population 24,064). GAS, at end of town on right. Altitude 3,400 feet.
90.0	144.0	Ixtlán del Río's railroad station at right. International airport to right.

When it rains, this road has invisible puddles that will give you an unpleasant surprise. Please slow down.

91.0	145.6	Thru village of Mexpán. Then note railroad tunnel ahead at right. Baskets & woven chairs for sale.
92.2	147.5	Over narrow bridge over railroad. Note at the right where the train comes out of the tunnel.
94.0	150.4	Pass side road (left) to Amequita and La Ciénega (The Swamp).
95.0	152.0	Pass side road (right) to Jala.
96.2	153.9	Pass town of Ahuacatlán over to left on railroad. There's a road to the volcano around here. You can drive within 2 km of top, then walk. It's an active volcano. GAS, left. Then alongside railroad at left. **KM 152**.
99.5	159.2	Settlement of Copales. In 3 miles, you're in for a treat!

Now here's Something Special – Have you ever wondered what it's like on another planet? Well, here's your chance to be a space man (and space lady) and land on Mars or Jupiter or somewhere. Now you go thru a short mile of the famous LAVA-BEDS-OF-CEBORUCO caused by the eruption of Ceboruco volcano in 1885. Sort of eerie, no? Like something out of this world – but bear in mind that it's against the law to pick up the little green one-eyed men or to stop and swipe lava samples.

101.0	161.6	Parador Turístico at right. **KM 161**.
105.0	168.0	Uzeta off to left. **KM 167**.
105.5	168.8	Pass side road (left) to Estación Tetitlán & Balneario Acatique Springs.

IF TO: Springs – Turn left at Balneario sign just beyond school. Over bumpy railroad tracks, 3/4 mile on right. Fresh water not hot. Large pools. Balneario Acatique. Proprietor J. Trinidad Dueñas A., a former taxi driver in Tijuana and former owner of a KFC in Phoenix. Space for self-contained RV's and trailers. Nice flat parking. They'll run a water hose for you. Very nice folks and a nice restful place.

109.0	174.4	Past a sugar mill on right. Then into little town of Santa Isabel. Pottery.
114.0	182.4	Past village of El Torreón on left. Emergency Motel La Cumbre & Restaurant at right. Then thru Chapalilla. GAS, right. **KM 175**.

MI	KM	
116.2	185.9	Careful now! Here's the turnoff for Puerto Vallarta on Hwy #200. You will climb 200 feet in the next few miles. Altitude 3,300 ft. KM 113.

IF TO: Puerto Vallarta take "PUERTO VALLARTA CUOTA & COMPOSTELA CUOTA" slot. Exit right, curve around and start Chapalilla - Compostela Special (page 74). THIS IS A FINE ROAD. There's **GAS** at end of toll road. Also neat hole-in-the-wall restaurant. Take right after **GAS**, go .25 miles toward town. Just before pavement ends is white iron-fenced hacienda on left. "El Rincón del Montero" is there. Sign says *Mariscos*. It's plain and for the adventurous. Inexpensive too.

116.5	185.6	Past village of El Ocotillo. Altitude 4,250 ft.
118.2	189.1	Rest stop. Altitude 3,800 ft.
121.6	194.6	Pass side road (right) to Santa María del Oro & La Laguna, with neat motel and trailer park Koala. Tepic straight ahead.

IF TO: Koala Bungalows and trailer park is 52 KM SE from Tepic and 20 KM from Tepic/Guadalajara Hwy on Laguna de Santa María near Crater Lake (730 M above sea level & 2 KM in diameter). High entrance. 15 spaces with all hookups. Showers. Swimming. Boat ramp. Boating. Fishing. Ph: 2-3772 or 4-0509 (in Tepic).

128.0	204.8	Pass little town of La Labor over to left. Mechanic. **KM 200**.
133.0	212.8	Pass El Refugio at left.
134.0	214.4	That's Tepic in distance ahead.
139.2	222.7	Pass side road (left) to Pantanal and thru village of San Cayetano. Slow for "topes."
140.2	224.3	Come now to nice divided bypass around Tepic. Take LEFT FORK. Under railroad overpass. Straight ahead is old congested Hwy #15 thru town.
141.0	225.6	Over Río Mololoa (also known as Río de Tepic).
141.3	226.1	**GAS,** right. A right here goes to KOA RV park. Paradise motel, nice. Ph: 4-0334.
142.7	228.3	Just before overpass, turn right for Puerto Vallarta or downtown Tepic. **KM 5**.
143.3	229.3	Come now to junction with Hwy #200.

IF TO: Downtown Tepic turn right (follow TEPIC CENTRO signs). For accommodations see Tepic Eat & Stray (page 105)

IF TO: Puerto Vallarta, turn right here and start Tepic – Puerto Vallarta Log (page 34).

IF TO: San Blas, Mazatlán, etc. continue straight ahead under double railroad overpass and start Tepic – Mazatlán Log (page 132).

You'll like Tepic, capital of the state of Nayarit, an interesting, colorful, and friendly town of 238,101. If you look closely you might get a glimpse of the Cora and Huichol Indians in their native costumes, especially on Sunday, Tepic's market day. Of interest are the cathedral, finished in 1750, with its two perfect Gothic bell towers, and the Regional Museum of Anthropology with its excellent collection of Indian crafts and archeological items.

End of log 13

LOG 14	*START:* **Pto Vallarta, Jal**	*END:* **Tepic, Nay**

UD-126

102.3 MI OR 163.7 KM
DRIVE TIME 3 1/2 — 4 HOURS
SCENIC RATING — 3

0.0	0.0	Starting here at the fabulous Hotel Camino Real at left, proceed on up Hwy #200, winding thru residential area alongside the Pacific. Then pass El Set Restaurant — great food in Mexican atmosphere.
1.5	2.4	GAS, at left. Periférico (loop) at left around PV.
1.8	2.9	Now pass Hotel El Mesón de los Arcos at left. Then *Supermercado* Gil at left on corner with Av. Lázaro Cárdenas. Then cine Bahía at right.

MI	KM	
2.0	3.2	Up over bridge over Río Cuale. Note houses up at right built up alongside river. That's famous "Gringo Gulch", a colony of expatriate Americans and plush homes. Actress Liz Taylor and Richard Burton used to have a house up there, as they were here when the film "Night of the Iguana" was made down at Mismaloya, 8 miles South of town; matter of fact, it was "Night of the Iguana" that put Vallarta on the map. On left, there's a park in the river with good restaurant, Hacienda del Sol, and an anthropological museum.
2.3	3.7	Bend right and pass *Mercado Municipal* (city market) at left. Go 2 blocks beyond market and turn right onto Juárez at Banco Industrial de Jalisco.
2.5	4.0	Aviación Mexicana offices at right. Then AeroMexico ticket office at left. Helados Bing (town's best ice cream parlor) at right, and Banamex at left on corner with Calle Zaragoza.
2.8	4.5	PV's main plaza and city hall at left. Then supermarket El Gallo Marinero at right. In next block is Las Margaritas, one of PV's best restaurants, and Vallarta Pharmacy on next corner.
3.3	5.3	Careful Now! Here at this wide cross-street (Calle 31 de Octubre), turn left. You can see Hotel Rosita down at right. Go one block and turn right onto Morelos, then straight.
3.5	5.6	Big GAS, station at left. Then after a couple of blocks, turn right and merge with Hwy #200. Then cross bridge over Arroyo Camarones and out.
4.0	6.4	Pass Sheraton Hotel at left. Sports field at right.
4.2	6.7	Careful at stoplight. *Libramiento* at right, a bypass around Vallarta. Then pass side road (right) to Puerto Vallarta RV Park.
4.5	7.2	Disco at left and side road (left) to Economical Hotel Los Pelícanos and Hotel Las Palmas.
4.8	7.7	Los Tules Resort and Fiesta Americana (outstanding), at left.
5.3	8.5	Highrise Ramada Inn at left. Then over Arroyo Pitallil and pass side street (left) to big Hotel Krystal and Hotel Playa de Oro, and Miller Travel Service, located across street from Hotel Krystal.
5.5	8.8	Car-passenger ferry and cruise ship terminal at left. Paved side road (right) to Tacho's RV Park.
6.3	10.1	Naval base ("Armada de Mexico") over at left. Cross bridge over part of Río Ameca delta.
6.5	10.4	Marina to left.
7.0	11.2	Las Iguanas Marina & Resort hotel at right. Then LP gas at right.
7.3	11.7	GAS, at right.
7.5	12.0	Puerto Vallarta's International airport at left.
9.8	15.7	Pass side road (right) to Las Juntas, 2 kilometers.
10.8	17.3	Pass Policía Federal de Caminos. Then up and over big, long toll bridge over Río Ameca. This is also state line — leave Jalisco and enter Nayarit. Likewise, this also marks a time zone — leave Mountain Time and enter Central Time. You lose an hour — set your watches and dashboard clock AHEAD an hour (you become an hour older).
11.8	18.9	Pass side road (left) to Jarretaderas.
12.5	20.0	Pass side road (left) to Nuevo Vallarta, an exclusive private and residential resort.
14.5	23.2	Pass side road (left) to San José del Valle, Valle Banderas, and San Juan de Abajo. Then thru settlement of Mezcales.
16.0	25.6	Nice Country Club de Golf Los Flamingos at left, open to public. Restaurant-bar. Pool. Pro shop. Sauna. Massage. Green fee. Electric cart fee. Caddie fee. GAS, on left.
17.5	28.0	Pass side road (left) to Hotel Flamingos and to Bucerias RV Park. 25 spaces with hookups, 30 more with electricity and water, showers, toilets, laundromat, rec room.
18.0	28.8	Costa Dorada at left, a very nice a/c 5-story, 15-apartment condominium (ocean-view rooms; piped-in music; pool; restaurant-bar; laundromat).
18.5	29.6	Over Río de Bucerias and thru seaside village of Bucerias.
19.5	31.2	Bungalows Vista del Bahía at left on beach. 8 nice kitchenettes. Pool. Pets OK. Portable fans only. 5 RV spaces, all hookups, shower, toilet. Bungalows Los Picos, also at left on beach. Complex of 6 buildings, each with two 3-bedroom, 2-bath apartments. Portable fans only. Pets OK.
20.5	32.8	Pass side road (left) to La Cruz de Huanacaxtle and to its nautical institute. There is also a Japanese resort Pinta Mitaketmar.
28.5	45.6	Tropical settlement of San Ignacio at left. Then curve right.
29.5	47.2	Pass side road (left) to Sayulita and Sayula RV Park on beach, 1.5 miles.
32.5	52.0	Settlement of San Francisco at left with its own hospital and vocational fishing school. Also Hotel Costa Azul Sport Resort. Adriana's Bed and Breakfast is one block from plaza. Banana plantations on both sides of road.
39.3	62.9	Pass side road (right) to Lo de Marcos and to nice El Caracol RV Park (22 spaces; all hookups; showers; toilets; concrete patios; beach).

MI	KM	
41.8	66.9	Thru settlement of Chula Vista.
44.0	70.4	Pass edge of village of El Monteón at left.
47.3	75.7	Pass side road (left) to Rincón de Guayabitos (see Eat & Stray, page 108), a popular resort development.
48.0	76.8	Over Río de Jaquey. Ice house a few blocks off to left. Then over Río La Peñita.
48.5	77.6	Slow for topes and into seaside brick-making village of La Peñita de Jaltemba (simply known as "La Peñita"). Pass divided boulevard to left to downtown La Peñita.

IF TO: Russell RV Park, go to end of boulevard and then a block North (or right).

49.3	78.9	Pass side trail left to La Peñita RV Park, a nice cliffside layout overlooking the Pacific. Then **GAS**, at left.
54.8	87.7	Over Río de la Lima. Then pass side road (left) to Lima de Abajo and Puesta de la Lima. Note tobacco-drying racks.
56.3	90.1	Pass side road (right) to El Capomo, 5 kilometers away.
60.3	96.5	Over Río Las Varas. Then pass side road (left) to Chacala — an old pirate hangout. This used to be magnificent jungle — but look at the price of progress.
60.5	96.8	**GAS**, at left. Now thru booming little tobacco town of Las Varas. Note red brick tobacco factory and Tabaco Mexicano office ahead on right. Side road (left) to Zacualpan.

IF TO: San Blas via Zacualpan and Santa Cruz, turn left and start Las Varas North Special and San Blas Special (page 70).

63.5	101.6	Over Río Viejo and careful for topes as you go thru little settlement of La Cuata (The Female Twin). Then over Río Las Piedras and thru village of Las Piedras (The Stones).
71.0	113.6	Thru village of Mesillas.
81.5	130.4	Come to junction right with toll road that cuts across East to Chapalilla on Hwy #15, a nice shortcut for motorists traveling between Puerto Vallarta and Guadalajara (or vice-versa). Then pass Autonomous University of Nayarit branch over at left.

IF TO: Guadalajara, turn right and start Compostela — Chapalilla Special (page 74).

82.8	132.5	Cross Río Compostela. Then gas at right.
83.3	133.3	Take LEFT FORK here and curve left thru cut for bypass around town of Compostela (10,000 population), biggest place between Tepic and "PV" with a couple of emergency hotels on plaza. Of interest here is the old church built with red *tezontle* (volcanic rock) in 1539.
87.5	140.0	Over bridge over Río Refilión. Then pass side road (right) to coffee-growing El Refilión.
93.5	149.6	Pass settlement of Emiliano Zapata over to right.
97.0	155.2	Thru settlement of El Testerazo, mostly at right.
100.0	160.0	Thru little town of Xalisco. Pretty plaza at left. Then **GAS** at left. Careful now as you come to junction with Periférico (Loop) and Hwy #15 around Tepic. For accommodations see Tepic Eat & Stray (page 105)

IF TO: Mazatlán, San Blas, Culiacán, etc. turn left (take Mazatlán exit) and start Tepic — Mazatlán Log.

IF TO: Guadalajara, turn right and start Tepic — Guadalajara Log (page 37).

IF TO: Tepic and to Linda Vista and Los Pinos RV Parks, La Loma Motel, Fray Junípero Serra Hotel, or excellent Roberto's International Restaurant, continue straight ahead.

End of Log 14

LOG 15   *START:* Tepic, Nay   *END:* Mazatlán, Sin

173.5 MI OR 277.6 KM
DRIVE TIME 4 1/2 – 5 HOURS
SCENIC RATING – 2

Some divided, mostly two lane. Heavy truck traffic. Stretches of poor surface.

MI	KM	
0.0	0.0	Here just North of the double railroad overpass, the highway from Pto. Vallarta joins the bypass, proceed ahead. Distributor de Radiadores Sanher at left. **KM 5**.
0.4	0.6	Thru rock cut. **KM 6**.
1.1	1.8	Cuauhtémoc suburb to left.
1.4	2.2	Cement block factory to right.
1.5	2.4	Colonia del Bosque to right. Curve left. **KM 8**.
2.5	4.0	Pass side road (right) to downtown Tepic.
3.7	5.9	School and suburb to right. Housing project to left. Following highlines. Mazatlán straight. Hotel Bugam Villas on right. GAS station (under construction) at left. **KM 12**.
4.2	6.7	Curve left under overpass. Right goes to Tepic.
4.4	7.0	Begin divided.
4.8	7.7	Free road exit at right. Toll road straight ahead.
7.4	11.8	Mazatlán *Libre*, straight. Mazatlán *cuota*, Hwy #15D, go straight. Libre exit right. 280 KM from Mazatlán. Altitude 3,000 ft.
9.0	14.4	Sharp downhill slope. Use your motor to break. KM 3. 3 miles. Toll booth now at 2,500 ft. Pay toll (car – $12; 2 (rear) axles – $24; extra axle – $6).
11.2	17.9	Summit at 2,600 ft. Community of Trapachillo.
16.3	26.1	Mazatlán, veer left. Tepic veer right. This is where the free highway intersects toll. 4 lanes.
16.9	27.0	Divided highway begins.
18.9	30.2	Pass Restaurant Amalia at right at TOME FANTA sign – cold cokes, package snacks, plus a zoo of sorts including jaguars, parrots, etc. Careful now! GAS, left and come to junction (left) with side road down to famed old-time seaside town of San Blas. If you have a couple of hours to spare, run down for a quick look-see at this tropical historic place. Friends of Bill W. sometimes in town. **KM 32**.

IF TO: San Blas, see SAN BLAS SPECIAL Log (page 70).

IF TO: Mazatlán, straight. 260 KM. Santiago 30 KM.

22.2	35.5	El Paraíso at left. Note big stand selling freshly squeezed fruit juices.
27.5	44.0	Pass side road (left) to tobacco town of Villa Hidalgo. Mazatlán straight, 240 KM.
28.0	44.8	Wind past another tobacco town of Valle de Lerma at right. Note tobacco fields thru here. Many Huichols make their living as field workers harvesting tobacco.
29.0	46.42	Estación Nanchi to right.
29.5	47.2	Cross Río Grande de Santiago on big steel bridge. This is a bad-acting river. Flooded in 1927 & 1992.
29.9	47.8	La Luz Del Mundo (The light of the world). A fancy new school to right just before you enter Del Capomal.
30.0	48.0	Pass side road (right) to Estación Yago on railroad.
30.5	48.8	Thru village of Capomal.
32.4	51.8	Pass side road (left) to Santiago Ixcuintla and on to Los Corchos (The Corks) on beach. GAS, in town. Mexcaltitán to right. Mazatlán straight.

If you're interested in the Huichol Indians' weaving and beadwork, this is the place where the Huichol Center for Cultural Survival and Traditional Arts is located. Susana Valadez, who helps organize things will be glad to arrange classes for interested groups. She runs a hospital and cultural center there, so please be considerate. She's not ready for troops of tourists to drop by and visit, but if you have a sincere interest, or a fledgling importer who wants to buy some really unique art, please call and make an appointment to see her. She's usually gone in late June-July. She'll put on demonstrations for tour groups also. The hotel Bugam Villas is the best, just on the outskirts of town. There is an OK hotel, Casino, in town, basic, but clean. You can call her at (323) 5-1171 Fax: 5-1006, or write: 20 de Noviembre #452, Santiago Ixcuintla, Nay.

When you get back, if you want to buy some of their art work, they have a US outlet: 801 2nd Ave., Suite 1400, Seattle, WA 98104 Ph: (206) 622-4067 Fax: (206) 622-0646. The Huichols are shy, artistic people who are becoming extinct due to TB & other diseases. They have a 50% infant mortality rate. IF you want to help with medical supplies or donations, they are tax-exempt: IRS # 95-3012063.

MI	KM	
35.6	57.0	Community of Heróico Batallón de San Blas up road, right.
40.6	65.0	Cross Río San Pedro and thru roadside market community of Peñitas. Careful for side road, left, to Tuxpan. **GAS**, right.
41.6	66.6	Come now to side road (left) to little island town of Mexcaltitán, Mexico's mini-Venice.

If you insist on visiting Mexcaltitán, go approximately 29 miles over a rough gravel road to a place called "El Embarcadero" where you'll park, then hire a dugout canoe for the 15-minute trip to the island town of about 3,500 inhabitants, many of whom have never left the island. This side-sortie is suggested only for the adventuresome as Mexcaltitan isn't ready yet for the normal course of tourist traffic but the shrimp is fresh, jumbo-size, and delicious.

MI	KM	
44.1	70.6	Banana Plantation on right.
44.8	71.7	Cross bridge over Río El Bejuco. Road bad for while after rains. Pass side road (left) to Chilapa. **KM 77**.
52.3	89.6	Railroad town of Rosamorada (Purple Rose), right. Cross Río Rosamorada. Railroad bridge, right.
53.2	85.1	GAS, left.
53.6	85.8	Couple of bridges and railroad at right. Truck stop of El Mil (1000) at left. Gas, left.
65.8	105.3	TOPES. TOPES. Be careful of people selling stuff on topes! Thru village of Tierra Generosa (Generous Land).
70.1	112.2	Abandoned kiddie park at right. Village of San Miguel, mostly to right.
77.1	123.4	Thru San Francisco and over Río Acaponeta.
78.5	125.6	Now slow for sharp curve and over narrow and very bumpy steel bridge. Pass side road (left) to Sayulita. Then right curve.
80.4	128.6	Then pass side road, right, to Acaponeta, founded in 1584 by the Franciscans (about 1.3 miles away where there's OK motel Cadenales at entrance to town). Then paved side road, left, to Tecuala and on to Novillero (22 miles), a rather solitary village on the Pacific coast with miles and miles of open beaches known as "Playas de Novillero." You'll find the accommodations somewhat inadequate and primitive – Margarita 2-story, 33-room hotel within walking distance of beach; ceiling fans, restaurant, covered parking and Bungalows Paraíso 12 kitchenette units on beach, space for few RV's with no hookups, tenting permitted. Hotel & Restaurant Miramar across street, a little more humble but nice
80.7	129.1	GAS, left.
81.2	129.9	Up and over bridge over railroad.
82.2	131.5	Inspección de Sanidad Fitopecuaria Y Forestal. No pigs allowed!
86.1	137.8	Over Río Cañas and cross state line – leave Nayarit and enter Sinaloa. Then curve left and stop at truck inspection, right. Thru village of La Concha.
90.1	144.2	Pass railroad village of Copales.
94.4	151.0	Careful for couple of sharp curves ahead. Community of Las Mulas (The Mules).
95.4	152.6	Now slow for sharp left curve. Up alongside mountain with salt marshes on left.
98.6	157.8	Thru village of Palmillas.
103.6	165.8	Big Ejido La Campaña, right. Pick up railroad on left.
110.5	176.8	Village of Tecualilla, off to left, behind trees.
112.5	180.0	Santa Anita fumigation station at left.
115.6	185.0	LP gas, right. Now thru 1.3-mile long mango grove. Chapel at left. **KM 195**.
116.9	187.0	Thru Escuinapa. Mall to right. Clean restrooms ($1 peso). Restaurants.
117.1	187.4	Follow one-way street thru town. GAS, to right on one-way the other way. Come to junction with road (left) to Teacapan.

IF TO: Teacapan, turn left,

TEACAPAN, Sinaloa is a little off the beaten track, 26 miles away, a sleepy tropical village with nice white beaches. This is a birder's paradise area. Efforts are underway to have the government declare it a sanctuary and park. And just for your info, Country/Western singer Loretta Lynn has a vacation home here. A great place to go if you have a spirit of adventure and you are tired of the party atmosphere of Mazatlán. Naturalists will enjoy the place and the (so far) unspoiled beaches. You can fish, go birding and loaf. Wildlife includes white & pink heron and pichihuila and deer. This is a small town with friendly folks and beautiful scenery. There are two good hotels:

134

In town on plaza is Hotel Denisse, which is small (5 rooms) & inexpensive; farther out is the Rancho Los Angeles (after 15.8 miles, turn right at mini-Super Los Angeles sign; use gate entrance to right of arch; enter and veer right, follow dirt road 1.5 miles to hotel) with the best restaurant (excellent Bar-B-Q fish) in town, perhaps in Mexico. It is for a more affluent crowd with private bungalows and a swimming pool. The only RV park is The Oregon, on the beach, near Señor Wayne's restaurant. Hotel Palmeras (under construction) will be a nice place once it's finished. Jejenes (no-see-ems, or sand fleas) do exist here but are not as bad as in San Blas. They only come out for about an hour in the morning and an hour at dusk. Also there are few mosquitos (the city sprays).

MI	KM	Back on one-way Hwy #15.
117.9	188.6	CAREFUL. Merge, right, with traffic onto Hwy #15. Over bridge and leave town of Escuinapa (population 60,000). Where protest took place.
119.0	190.4	Good enough Motel Virginia on right.
122.9	196.6	Cross South fork of Río Baluarte.
125.2	200.3	TOPES. Pass side road (left) to Chametla.
130.0	208.0	Over bumpy, long steel bridge over another fork of Río Baluarte.
131.0	209.6	Up past village of Chilillos. Past LP gas, right. Up, down and cross Río Baluarte on 1/2-mile-long bridge. GAS, right. Skirt town Rosario (population 47,497). Nice snack stands soft drinks etc. Ice house, left. Hotel Los Morales at left.
134.0	214.4	That's Mount Yauco dead ahead.
137.0	219.2	Thru settlement of Los Otates (The Bamboos), right. Over bridge.
141.0	225.6	Cross río and pass village of Las Higueras off to right. Side road (right) to Presa (dam) Las Higueras.
142.5	228.0	Then experimental fruit station. Village of Potrerillos down at left.
143.5	229.6	Thru Tablón #1.
144.4	231.0	Ejido El Tablón, mostly at left. On his deathbed, Casanova is reputed to have said, "Mamma ... Mamma."
146.1	233.8	Village of El Huajote, at left, with its baseball field.
149.0	238.4	Sometimes there's an immigration stop here.
157.0	251.2	Motel El Pino, right, OK. **GAS**, left.

IF TO: Hwy #40 to Durango, Torreón, Saltillo, Monterrey etc., turn right here. Start Mazatlán - Durango Log (not included in this book).

IF TO: Mazatlán, ahead on Hwy #15 for you.

157.5	252.0	Curve right and into town. Slow thru town of Villa Unión. SPEED 30 KM. TOPES.
158.5	253.6	Divided highway begins. **KM 271.**
158.8	254.1	Hotel El Kino, right. I ate there. OK. TOPES. Leave town. Cross Río Presidio.
161.3	258.1	Pass side road (right) to Mazatlán's airport. **KM 272.**
164.1	262.6	Large penitentiary, right. Speed limit 80 KM. Pass "el Zipi-Zape" veggie packers. **KM 275.**
164.4	263.0	GAS, left. **KM 279.**
165.9	265.4	Large thermoelectric power plant, left.
166.6	266.6	Colonia La Sirena, left. Salt flats, left.
168.1	269.0	Under overpass with sign "Bienvenidos A Mazatlán" (Welcome to Mazatlán). Up hill.
168.3	269.3	Golf course, right. Tractores de Occidente, right. Look alive! City traffic begins.
168.7	269.9	LP gas, right. Coke distributor at left. John Deere at right. Goodyear at left.
169.1	270.6	Curve right. Stoplight. GAS, left. Sign says "Culiacán straight. Mazatlán Centro, Playas and Ferry to left."

IF TO: Ferry, turn left here. Go this way only if planning to take the ferry. Otherwise continue straight.

169.7	271.5	Curve left and past school at right. Thru suburb of Rincón de Urias. Pass Café Marino plant right. Farmer's market (Central de Abastos), right.
169.9	271.8	Bimbo to the right.
170.2	272.3	Ezukadi tire distributor. **KM 209.**
170.7	273.1	Over bridge.
170.9	273.4	Pass multi-colored Colonia (subdivision) Lic. Mario A. Arroyo and cemetery at left.
171.1	273.8	Pass up motel Real, a motel del paso (rents by the hour), to left.
171.9	275.0	Corona distributor to left. Culiacán quota road curve right here. Playas left.
172.1	275.4	GAS, left. Road narrows here.
173.5	277.6	Culiacán toll road, right. Libre road, straight.

IF TO: Mazatlán, turn left. Follow "Playas" signs.

IF TO: Culiacán, straight. Follow Mazatlán - Culiacán Log. Having turned left off Hwy #15, (following Tepic, Aeropuerto signs) ahead on nice divided bypass around Mazatlán.

IF TO: North end RV parks, Hotel Camino Real, go 6.7 miles to sign "Mazatlán Playas", turn left, go to beach and turn right.

End of Log 15

LOG 16	*START:* Mazatlán, Sin	*END:* Culiacán, Sin

UD-126

135.4 MI or 216.6 KM
DRIVE TIME 3 — 3 1/2 HOURS
SCENIC RATING — 2

Note: This log also covers the toll road. The toll road is rather expensive. There are 2 toll booths, one at entrance just North of Mazatlán and the other at KM 122. Some say it's worth it (if you're in a hurry) saving at least an hour of driving time and is safer. Others feel like it's "highway robbery" since they can fill up twice for the cost of the toll and enjoy the more scenic free road. It's your choice. The free ("*Libre*") road is OK, but has old & slow-moving trucks.

Stub Log From Downtown to Hwy 15

MI	KM	
0.0	0.0	Starting at ocean blvd. with McDonald's on left and Hotel San Diego at right, proceed ahead.
0.1	0.2	La Posta Trailer Park at right. Then GAS, right (they take credit cards).
0.3	0.5	Sharp Hospital, right.
0.5	0.8	Gigante at left. Then bullring at left.
1.0	1.6	Come to intersection with stoplight. Turn left here for Hwy 15.
1.2	1.9	Stoplight and then up and over railroad tracks.
1.5	2.4	Pacific beer distributor at right and Motel Relax at left.. Come to junction with Hwy #15.

End stub from Downtown

0.0	0.0	At junction of bypass around Mazatlán and Hwy #15, proceed ahead (North). **GAS**, left. Restaurant La Palmita, right.
0.7	1.1	**GAS**, left. *Centro de Bodegas* at right. Then at right, *Ciudad de los Niños* ("boys' town" or "orphanage", not to be confused with the "red-light district"). Gamesa Plant right.
1.0	1.6	Luenaillo, left. **KM 2**.
1.3	2.1	Carta Blanca Agency at left. Federal Police Highway. Ph: 1-6355.
1.9	3.0	Come to junction with toll road. For accommodations, see Mazatlán Eat & Stray (page 94).

IF TO: Toll road, take first left after bridge and start stub log below.

IF TO: North end hotels, do not take the toll road.

IF TO: Free road, straight. Road narrows to 2 lanes.

MAZATLÁN - CULIACÁN TOLL ROAD

0.0	0.0	Cross over free road on nice divided toll road.
1.0	1.6	Pass police station at right.
4.5	7.2	Careful for traffic merging from right from the North end entrance to Mazatlán.
14.5	23.2	Over Río Quilete. You are now passing thru rolling hills and farm country.
17.2	27.5	Come to toll house and pay toll. Cars - $61, extra axle - $30, they accept AE, MC, VI. **KM 26**.
60.0	96.0	Pass exit (right) to La Cruz and Cueta. This is also the exit to take if you want to go to Cosalá.

Cosalá, founded in 1516, is a small Spanish colonial town with cobblestone roads and churches over 250 years old. There are two OK (two Mexican star) hotels and some restaurants. The Sabinal river feeds the *Vado Hondo* spa (not reviewed) with clear water. 20 KM North is Lake Comedero chock-full of largemouth bass. We stayed at the hotel Conde (hot water). Also a Museum of the History of Mining. The Balneario and waterfall are 8 KM off the highway on a dirt road. Do not attempt this road when it's been raining. It is 6.5 miles before town, on the left.

PRESA LÓPEZ PORTILLO (LAKE COMEDERO) — One of Mexico's two hottest lakes, Comedero was opened to fisherman only since in 1987. Comedero has fast become a legend in the number of fish caught per man per day. With catches from 100 to 200 bass per day common, it is easy to see why this remote lake has become a prime destination for the traveling angler. Turn East on the Cosalá turnoff to the town of Cosalá. (50 miles). The lake is 30 miles from town on a dirt road that winds up in the steep mountains to the village of Higueras de Urrea. The San Lorenzo river is the source of Lake Comedero and the lake is one of the prettiest in the northern hemisphere. Towering mountains surround the lake with lush subtropical jungle right up to the waters edge. Comedero's banks are lined with some brush and cover, however the lake is large and very open and it's also very, very deep. With depths approaching 300 feet in places, Comedero's fish tend to school up and suspend. Sometimes in water as deep as 60 feet. At present there's only one full time camp on the lake. Full packages are available as well as room and board. Contact: Ron Speeds S & W Tours, 1013 Country Lane, Malakoff, TX, 75148 (903) 489-1656.

MI	KM	
96.0	153.6	Pass exit (right) to Quila and El Dorado.
109.8	175.7	Come to second toll house and pay toll (Car - $63, extra axle - $31). GAS on left.
111.3	178.1	Exit to Culiacán and Costa Rica and Los Cascabeles. After exit, get in left lane for Culiacán. Curve up and around and rejoin Hwy #15 on still divided 4-lane.

There is a nice pastoral spot 4.1 miles West of here on highway #19. It's Los Cascabeles, on the lake of the same name. 20 fenced acres with 10 cabins, boats, pool, hunting and fishing. RV section (MOD) with 44 spaces, electricity and water. Dump station. Medical services. Palapa. BBQ pits. Security. Store. Self service laundry. Restaurant. FAX: (67) 13-6418 or in Culiacán (671) 3-6418, 3-6822.

114.0	182.4	Agricultural experimental school at right.
116.5	186.4	Villa Juárez, left and GAS, left.
117.9	188.6	LP gas on right just before village of El Quemadito.
121.1	193.8	To Guasave and Los Mochis, left. Veer left and follow Guasave sign. Right goes into Culiacán. Start Culiacán - Los Mochis Log (page 138).

END OF TOLL ROAD

2.9	4.6	Highway police station at left. Big mango grove at right.
4.1	6.6	Hilltop restaurant at right. **KM 7**.
6.0	9.6	Come to crossroads, left to El Habal and right to La Noria.

IF TO: Beach. Take side road (left) to Playa Cerritos and shortcut beach road to Mazatlán. (If heading to North beach hotels, RV parks, etc., go ahead & turn here. When you come to ocean, turn left and head toward town.)

IF TO: Culiacán, points North, straight.

9.9	15.8	Pass side road (right) to La Palma.
10.0	16.0	Pass side road (left) to El Potrero. Note bust of General Juan Carrazco at left.
10.4	16.6	Roadside food at left. **KM 16**.
14.7	23.5	Come now to TROPIC OF CANCER — note marker at left. Sorry, you'll have to reign in your libido from here on out.
15.5	24.8	Los Zapotes off to right and El Recreo off to left.
20.5	32.8	Over Río Quelite, then curve left past side road (left) to Mármol (marble). I've always wanted to go there. Wonder if there's any marble?
21.9	35.0	Pass side road (right) to El Quelite.
25.5	40.8	Straight stretch ends. Begin curves. El Moral off to right. Climbed 400 ft. at this point.

MI	KM	
37.6	60.2	Pull off for view watches to right.
37.9	60.6	Pass side road (right) to El Limón and more winding with sharp curves.
41.7	66.7	**GAS** right. Watch the kids here. Pass side road (right) to San Ignacio, 32 KM.

San Ignacio is a very picturesque town. Founded in 1582 and named after San Ignacio de Loyola. Painted palm trees line the road into town with a grand mauve entrance that, when you pass through it, opens to a bridge that crosses a rather large river.

MI	KM	
46.0	73.6	Pass side road (right) to Hacienda Piaxtla. Then settlement of Crucero de Piaxtla.
49.9	79.8	Village of Piaxtla off to right.
53.0	84.8	La Minita (The Little Mine) up at right. The mill here grinds ore brought in from Mexico's interior, separating zinc, copper, and lead.
56.0	89.6	Left and wind down. Pass so-so-restaurant-bus stop. Then slow for sharp left curve.
57.0	91.2	Cross Río Elota. Then pass side road, right, to nearby town of Elota.
65.5	104.8	Pass side road (left) to La Cruz. Red Cross. **KM 105.**
66.5	106.4	Pass side road (right) to picturesque ex-mining town of Cosalá, 33 miles, on Hwy #D-1.

Cosalá, founded in 1516, is a small Spanish colonial town with cobblestone roads and churches over 250 years old. There are two OK (two Mexican star) hotels and some restaurants. The Sabinal river feeds the *Vado Hondo* spa (not reviewed) with clear water. 20 KM North is Lake Comedero chock-full of largemouth bass. We stayed at the hotel Conde (hot water). Also a Museum of the History of Mining. The Balneario and waterfall are 8 KM off the highway on a dirt road. Do not attempt this road when it's been raining. It is 6.5 miles before town, on the left.

PRESA LÓPEZ PORTILLO (LAKE COMEDERO) — One of Mexico's two hottest lakes, Comedero was opened to fisherman only since in 1987. Comedero has fast become a legend in the number of fish caught per man per day. With catches from 100 to 200 bass per day common, it is easy to see why this remote lake has become a prime destination for the traveling angler. Turn East on the Cosalá turnoff to the town of Cosalá. (50 miles). The lake is 30 miles from town on a dirt road that winds up in the steep mountains to the village of Higueras de Urrea. The San Lorenzo river is the source of Lake Comedero and the lake is one of the prettiest in the northern hemisphere. Towering mountains surround the lake with lush subtropical jungle right up to the waters edge. Comedero's banks are lined with some brush and cover, however the lake is large and very open and it's also very, very deep. With depths approaching 300 feet in places, Comedero's fish tend to school up and suspend. Sometimes in water as deep as 60 feet. At present there's only one full time camp on the lake. Full packages are available as well as room and board. Contact: Ron Speeds S & W Tours, 1013 Country Lane, Malakoff, TX, 75148 (903) 489-1656.

MI	KM	
68.0	108.8	Thru Agua Nueva.
68.7	109.9	Cemetery at right.
69.5	111.2	Pass Glass House Resort hotel — MOD — 36 rooms, restaurant, pool, English spoken; looks brand new and very nice. **KM 112.** Curve left, then thru El Aguaje.
73.0	116.8	Thru El Espinal. "Topes." **KM 118.**
81.0	129.6	Thru settlement of El Avión. **KM 130.**
87.5	140.0	Pass side road (left) to Estación Abuya.
89.5	143.2	Pass village of Higueras de Abuya, then cross South fork of Río Obispo and curve left.
93.0	148.8	Pass side road (left) to Obispo (bishop).
95.7	153.1	Over North fork of Río Obispo and curve left. Thru village of Las Flores.
97.5	156.0	Pass side road (left) to Oso (bear).
102.7	164.3	Thru Tabala. Note ruins of ancient church at left with burial tombs. Cactus growing out of spiral on church. Then curve left and up over Río San Lorenzo. **KM 165.**
108.7	173.9	**GAS**, right. Cross a couple of bridges Río Salado, then up thru town of El Salado. Topes! Topes!
108.8	174.1	El Dorado to the left. Culiacán straight.
114.8	183.7	Thru San Fernando.
117.5	188.0	El Carrizal, and Sebu cattle ranch at left.
119.3	190.9	**GAS**, both sides of the road. Danesa 33 Ice cream Store. Restaurant Centro Recreativo Los Cascabeles. Turn at Costa Rica to the left to get to Los Cascabeles.

There is a nice pastoral spot 4.1 miles West of here on highway #19. It's Los Cascabeles, on the lake of the same name. 20 fenced acres with 10 cabins, boats, pool, hunting and fishing. RV section (MOD) with 44 spaces, electricity and water. Dump station. Medical services. Palapa. BBQ pits. Security. Store. Self service laundry. Restaurant. FAX: (67) 13-6418 or in Culiacán (671) 3-6418, 3-6822.

MI	KM	
120.0	192.0	Pass side road, left, to Costa Rica. Careful for slow-moving farm traffic. Seafood restaurant. This is where Toll road rejoins free road.

IF TO: Culiacán, Nogales, look alive! Junction with bypass coming up. The signs say "Los Mochis" or "Guasave Cuota." You'll turn left. Just don't get off onto the "Libre" route.

129.1	206.6	Come to junction with bypass around Culiacán. TURN LEFT to Guasave and Los Mochis. Culiacán (population: 602,100) is straight. For accommodations see Culiacán Eat & Stray (page 93).
130.1	208.2	Having turned left, pass little town of El Ranchito.
133.4	213.4	Motel Cabañas del Rey.
135.4	216.6	Guasave cuota (toll road) to left. **GAS**, right (Beware! Scam at this GAS station — guy will install weather stripping for 18 pesos a meter; it'll end up costing about $100.00 dollars. MM was taken in by this. A woman wouldn't have fallen for it). LP gas at right, 1 mile ahead.

IF TO: Los Mochis, Nogales, turn left and start Culiacán — Los Mochis Log.

End of Log 16

LOG 17　　*START:* Culiacán, Sin　　*END:* Los Mochis, Sin

UD-126

129.5 MI or 207.2 KM
DRIVE TIME 2 — 2 1/2 HOURS
SCENIC RATING — 1

0.0	0.0	Having turned left at junction with Culiacán bypass & Hwy #15 (the "Libre", or free road from downtown), proceed ahead on 4 lane divided This is one of the most fertile farming regions in Mexico, thanks to irrigation projects.
0.7	1.1	**GAS**, right. Restaurant on left and right. Toll road is called: "Autopista Benito Juárez." Come to toll house and pay toll (Car - $15, Extra axle - $8). Restrooms at right just past toll booth. Nursery at left.
7.0	11.2	Pass exits for San Pedro and La Curva on Hwy #280 to right. **KM 13.**
14.0	22.4	Under overpass.
16.3	26.1	Exit, right, to La Palma and Vitaruto a couple of miles over to right on Hwy #259. **KM 31.**
26.0	41.6	Over bridge, curve left — nice cattle farm over to right.
29.5	47.2	Pass Restaurant Mar de Cortés, left.
39.4	63.0	Restaurant El Bacatete, right.
40.0	64.0	Pass side road (left) to La Reforma and Zapatillo, Hwy #70. **GAS** to left. **KM 63.**
68.5	109.6	Pass side road (left) to Angostura and right to Guamúchil. There is a hot/cold spring 18 km away in Mocorito (turn left at cemetery before town). Come to toll house and pay toll (Car - $15, extra axle - $8). **KM 109.**
73.4	117.4	Thru underpass. Straight ahead. Careful for traffic merging from old two-lane "libre" highway. **KM 123.** Veer left to Guasave. KM 125. Las Brisas exit right. Still divided.
82.5	132.0	Palos Blancos, left. Then another toll booth (Car - $10, extra axle - $5).
92.8	148.5	Over Río Petatlán. Now thru edge of boom town of Guasave, founded in 1595 (population: 257,821). Shopping center to right.

GUASAVE has three hotels and a great mechanic, Taller Bojórquez (see map inset). The best hotel is El Sembrador at Guerrero & Zapata. It has 85 nice quiet rooms, 10 suites, restaurant, bar, parking and is very reasonably priced. SATV (English & weather channel, HBO, CNN, etc). Ph: (687) 2-4062, 2-3141, Fax: 2-3131.

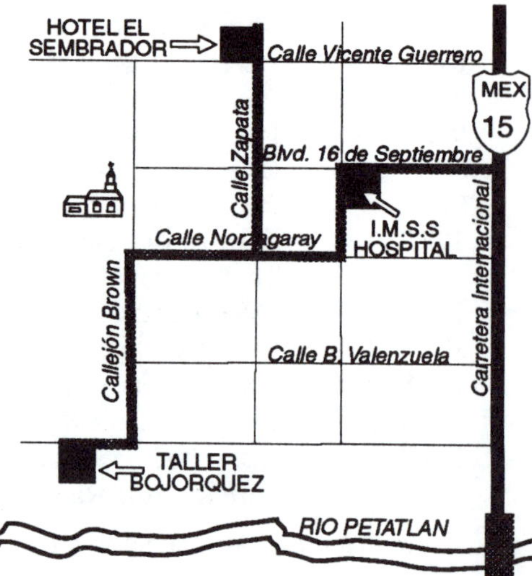

If you have a notion to go fishing at Lake Baccarito (Presa Díaz Ordaz) we recommend that you change your mind. There is no reason to go to that out-of-the-way lake. It has been gill-netted out and there have been assaults on the road.

MI	KM	
94.5	151.2	Pass ball park at left (Guasave belongs to the powerful Mexican Pacific League).
96.0	153.6	Pass Trébol Park Motel, right.
99.0	158.4	Right to Est. Naranjo. **GAS** on road to Est. Naranjo.
105.0	168.0	Pass side road (left) to Huitusi over on Bahía de San Ignacio. Do the Watusi!
105.1	168.2	Batamote to right. Pass LP gas to right.
110.6	177.0	Little town of Ruiz Cortines, at left, named for a past *presidente* of Mexico (1952-58).
111.5	178.4	**GAS**, on right. Unfriendly (WATCH 'EM!)
113.2	181.1	Cerro Cabezón, to left.
118.3	189.3	Government agricultural experiment school (Ciapan), right. **GAS**, left. Big town of Juan José Ríos (the largest ejido in Mexico) at left. **KM 186.**
120.0	192.0	Curve left past Ejido *Las Vacas* (The Cows) at left. Cross Río Estero. Heading due West.
124.0	198.4	Pass entrance to industrial park at left. Then rice factory at left. Northrup-King seed plant, left. (*Arroz* is rice in Spanish, *Algodón* means cotton and *algodonera* means cotton gin.)
127.5	204.0	Up and over Chihuahua-Pacífico Railroad overpass which is the same line that goes up into the Sierra Madres thru scenic Copper Canyon. Sanborn's logs the road. You can drive from Cd. Obregón or Hermosillo to Creel on the other side. And no, you can't put your rig on it. Curve left around hill.
128.5	205.6	Note tomato packing sheds thru here. Mountain at left is called *Cerro de la Memoria*. Turnoff, right, is to nice Hotel Colinas & RV Park, right, on hilltop (67 spaces EWS, 30 AMP, PH: (681) 2-0101, 2-0134)). It was formerly a Holiday Inn. *Lienzo del Charro* arena at left where the Mexican *charro* (cowboy) performs in the rodeo, usually on Sunday. **GAS**, left.
129.5	207.2	Careful now! Go under two overpasses. Come to junction with El Fuerte Hwy & Los Mochis. **GAS**, right (Watch 'em).

IF TO: Los Mochis or Topolobampo, take right lane (follow LOS MOCHIS signs) and then left and up and over highway. For accommodations see Los Mochis Eat & Stray (page 90).

IF TO: Navojoa or Cd. Obregón, straight ahead, under overpass. Start Los Mochis — Navojoa Log.

IF TO: El Fuerte and Domínguez and Hidalgo Lakes, exit right & start Los Mochis — El Fuerte Special (page 68).

The twin lakes of Hidalgo and Domínguez are about 40 miles NE of the Pacific coast town of Los Mochis via a paved road, a few miles from the town of El Fuerte. The two lakes are about 5 miles apart. They have some of the best fishing South of the border. See El Fuerte Eat & Stray (page 92).

Incidentally, the Chihuahua-Pacific (Copper Canyon) Railroad passes near El Fuerte — you might wish to combine a little fishing with this very scenic train ride through the Sierra Madre Occidental.

End of Log 17

LOG 18 START: Los Mochis, Sin END: Navojoa, Son

UD-126

98.0 MI OR 156.8 KM
DRIVE TIME — 2 HOURS
SCENIC RATING — 2
Divided toll highway thru fertile farming country.

MI	KM	
0.0	0.0	Here at Los Mochis interchange, proceed ahead. **GAS**, right but watch 'em.
7.0	11.2	Cavalry's 18th regiment barracks at left. If you go through on leave day, don't be alarmed. There'll be hundreds of soldiers hitchhiking.
9.9	15.8	Now thru edge of little town of San Miguel Zapotitlán. **KM 16. GAS**, right — sometimes they try to charge more for it, so watch 'em.

RV'ers take note: the exit to El Fuerte RV Park is 0.3 miles ahead. Get in left lane. Turn left at next left.

MI	KM	
10.2	16.3	Over Río Fuerte. Then just past overpass, Higuera Zaragoza turn off to left and El Fuerte RV park to left.
12.6	20.2	Prepare to pay Toll at "caseta puente San Miguel." Cars — $14, extra axle — $7. **KM 20.** Going North. Start uphill. Begin rolling hills.
16.3	26.0	Begin series of S curves.
18.2	29.1	Now pass very large Ejido A.G. Calderón, right.

By the way, an *ejido* is a government-sponsored community agriculture project — you'll pass many of these on your Mexico motor trip. They usually have fancy names, like famous revolutionary heroes, ex-presidentes or historical dates. There are about 30,000 *ejidos* throughout Mexico. The concept of some land for every Mexican was one of the tenets of the Revolutionary struggle in Mexico. The ejido system has been eliminated in modern times, but the names and signs live on.

MI	KM	
23.0	36.8	Big Ejido Los Natochis at right.
26.7	42.7	Vast ejido of Chihuahuita at right.
32.2	51.5	Restaurant La Posta, right. **KM 52.**
33.4	53.4	El Fuerte to right and Choix turnoff.
38.0	60.8	Ejido El Carrizo at left, headquarters town for irrigation district of huge El Fuerte irrigation project. Red Cross. **GAS**, left. KM 55. CAREFUL — THERE'S A SHARP DROP FROM THE HWY TO THE SHOULDER.
39.0	62.4	Big Ejido Talamantes at left. Pass side road (right) to San Francisco microwave tower.
39.5	63.2	Ejido Dolores Hidalgo at right. Cemetery at left.
40.2	64.3	Truck agricultural inspection station on left for South bound vehicles only.
42.0	67.2	Thru Desengaño ("Disillusion"). Slow for vibrators.
43.1	69.0	Come now to state line, leave the state of Sinaloa, which is pretty lengthy — 397 miles. Enter the state of Sonora, the longest state in Mexico. It's 433 miles from here to Nogales; and if you go by way of San Luis Río Colorado, you'll be in Sonora for the next 665 miles. There is a very thorough drug inspection checkpoint here. Allow for a 20 minute delay. Pass thru Agricultural, Immigration inspection. **GAS**, right, diesel. Watch for monster topes.
46.0	73.6	Thru village of Estación Don. ("Don" is pronounced "Doan", sort of like Doan's back pills, except it's pronounced crisper.)
51.5	82.4	Ejido Manuel Caudillo at left. There are a jillion ejidos thru here. Roll up your windows thru here, it's very earthy country. **KM 72.**
58.0	92.8	Big Ejido Francisco Sarabia at left. Bumpy railroad crossing! Then huge Conasupo farmers' co-op at right. **GAS**, left — nice, clean restrooms, diesel. **KM 93.**
59.0	94.4	Railroad station community of Estación Luis at right. Then pass side road, right, to Ejido Tierra y Libertad (Land and Liberty).

"Tierra y Libertad" was Emiliano Zapata's cry as he seized and burned the haciendas in his home state of Morelos and divided the land among his white-clad Indian followers, paving the way for Article 27 of the Mexican Constitution, upon which all subsequent land reform laws have been based.

MI	KM	
63.0	100.8	Mexico's always attracted dreamers & visionaries, for instance Albert Kinsey Owens, who founded an American colony in Los Mochis. He wanted to grow sugar cane & build a railroad to the U.S. in 1872 and build a utopian community. **KM 100.**

MI	KM	
67.7	108.3	Truck stop restaurant Carmelita, right.
71.7	114.7	Pass side road (left) to Masiaca, 6 miles and right to Las Bocas, 7.5 miles, a beach resort on the Sea of Cortés.
77.0	123.2	Toll road straight. **KM 128**. Turn left here for free road to Navojoa via Huatabampo.
78.0	124.8	At right is Ejido Luis Echeverría, named after one of Mexico's ex-presidentes (1970-1976). Then pass side road left (free road) to Huatabampo "Willow Tree in the Water", a nice little city located in a large, prosperous irrigated district 28 km away. Four miles South of that town is Huatabampito, a little resort on the Gulf of California with miles and miles of inviting sandy beach.
79.0	126.4	Slow for toll booth. Stop and pay toll (car - $32, extra axle no charge — trailers are the same price as cars in this state only). No restrooms here.
85.5	136.8	Curve left thru Ejido Bacabachi and school at left. Then cemetery off to right.
88.0	140.8	Rest area El Abajeno at left, popular with truck drivers. Then small shrine at left. **KM 140.**

By the way, these shrines are places where someone died in an accident. The families often visit them and put flowers on them on saints' days and birthdays. Also during the week of the "Day of the Dead" (*Día de los Muertos*), just after Halloween, you'll see them covered with flowers.

89.3	142.9	Pass Restaurant Santa Ana, left.
90.0	144.0	Pass granja El Milagro, left. Railroad tracts follow road at right.
92.8	148.5	Pass airfield at right.
95.5	152.8	Pass **GAS**, left (watch 'em). Speed limit slows to 40 KPH. Electrical generating station to left. Tres Estrellas at right. Cotton gin.
96.0	153.6	Free road from Los Mochis joins highway here at left. **KM 153**.
96.7	154.7	Pass thru an industrial zone with Tecate Brewery to right. Then Pemex industrial to right.
97.7	156.3	Enter city of Navojoa. **KM 155**. Motel Colonial on left. Over railroad tracks. Social security hospital (ISSTE) on left. Curve left. Big flour mill (Conasupo) also on left.
98.0	156.8	Pass **GAS**, right. Motel El Mayo (Ph: 2-6828) on right. Tips' restaurant, right. On left, Goodrich, VW dealer & Chrysler/Dodge (I highly recommend this Dodge dealer — He helped me out). Come to junction (right) with side road to Alamos and stoplight. For accommodations, see Navojoa Eat & Stray (page 87).

IF TO: Guaymas via toll road, proceed ahead and start Navojoa — Guaymas Log.

IF TO: Guaymas via free road, turn left and start Navojoa - Guaymas Free Road Stub Log .

IF TO: Alamos, turn right and start Navojoa — Alamos Special (page 61).

End of Log 18

LOG 19	*START:* **Navojoa, Son**	*END:* **Guaymas, Son**

UD-126

121.5 MI OR 194.4 KM
DRIVE TIME 2 — 2 1/2 HOURS
SENIC RATING — 3

Easy flat drive on divided toll highway. Fertile farming country and glimpses of Pacific Ocean.

0.0	0.0	Here at junction with highway from Alamos, proceed ahead. At left is Goodrich. At right is MZ supermarket (good fast-food carry-out counter). General tire on right. Stoplight. Pass Nissan dealer left.
0.3	0.5	Stoplight. Big auto parts and Telemex office on right. Another stoplight. Pass side road (left) to San Ignacio and Tetanchopo.
0.6	1.0	Firestone on left and Uniroyal on right.
0.9	1.4	Town of Tesia to the right. ISSTE clinic on right. Restaurant Pekin to left. Ph: 2-8556. General tire on left. Chevy right. Nissan left. Goodyear right. 2 Smiling elephants at left. Restaurant/bar Los Coporales on right. **GAS**, right.
1.5	2.4	Then Asadero Restaurant (tasty *carne asada*), right. (Friends of Bill W. in town - Spanish only - Tel: 2-5953. AA at Pesqueíra #105 Nte.) Straight on thru on nice wide main street. Very good **GAS**, right. This has SELF-SERVICE lanes! What's Mexico coming to? Neat little coffee shop, Alamos, next door with packaged ice, etc. If bypass completed around town, follow signs. If you want to go through town, feel free. Leave Navojoa

(Population: 122,390), a clean agricultural boom town and birthplace of LA Dodgers' pitcher, Fernando Valenzuela.

Navojoa means "place among the tunas" in Mayo Indian, tuna being a prickly pear.

IF TO: Alameda RV Park, exit left immediately before bridge.

MI	KM	
1.6	2.6	Restaurant Los Arcos on left. Motel Del Río on left. Then turn left into RV Alameda just before bridge.
2.4	3.8	Then thru little community of Guaymitas. Motel Rancho down at left. Begin divided highway again. Left lane is for Navojoa free road, also Villa Juárez. Straight for toll road. If you choose to take the free road, begin the following stub log. Otherwise jump down to continuation of log (mile 7.3). Free road is OK. It takes 15 minutes longer. KM 1.

Stub Log: Navojoa - Guaymas Free Road

0.0	0.0	Having veered turned onto free road, continue ahead.
4.6	7.4	Pass village of Became Nuevo to right.
7.0	11.2	Pass sign that says "Ejido 7 Leguas."
10.4	16.6	Pass side road (left) to Buaysiacobe. KM 20.
13.5	21.6	"Topes" and pass farm equipment yard, right. Then thru Agua Blanca and more topes. **KM 24.**
14.0	22.4	Over canal at KM 26. Then pass village of Bacobampo and Calle 26 at left.
15.6	25.0	Come to junction. TURN RIGHT for Cd. Obregón, straight is to Villa Juárez. **KM 28.**
21.5	34.4	Texaco sign, right. "Topes" and more "topes." Then thru village of Jecopaco, store with phone.
28.8	46.1	**GAS**, right.
29.6	47.4	Goodyear, right.
31.5	50.4	Come to junction with Hwy #15 toll and resume continuation of log at mile 25.0.

End of Stub Log

7.3	11.7	Straight for toll.
9.0	14.4	Pass side road (left) to Villa Juárez, 30 km. (18 miles).

If you have a generous and compassionate heart and would like to visit an orphanage, you will find Hogar de Refugio Infantil Villa Juárez by turning left onto side road to Villa Juárez, go 26 miles on paved road, turn right for another mile, then turn left following signs to the orphanage. Bob Mason, the director, welcomes visitors. They are able to accommodate motor homes, trailers etc. and have a crude dumping station as well as electrical hookups.

10.7	17.1	Cotton community of Sibolibampo.
23.6	37.8	Toll booth. Stop and pay toll ($32). **KM 196.**
25.0	40.0	Pass another exit (left) for Villa Juárez.
29.1	46.5	Pass enormous statue to the Virgin of Guadalupe at left. **Turnoff to it is just past KM 203.**
31.5	50.4	Ejido Francisco Villa way over to left.
32.7	52.3	Pass side road (left) to airport.
37.5	60.0	**GAS**, left but watch 'em. **KM 210.**
38.0	60.8	Pass another side road (left) to Villa Juárez. Conasupo to left. Bumpy railroad crossing. At stoplight, straight ahead. General tire mobile on right. DHC left. Veer right at waterfall. Stoplight. Onto Ave. Alemán. KM 220.
38.9	62.2	Petroleum tanks on right. **KM 219.**
39.5	63.2	Cayenne Fertilizer plant, right. Come to junction (left) with free road to Guaymas here at Cd Obregón. If you decide to take free road, turn left and ahead on narrow 2 lane road, but you're on your own.
40.0	64.0	Welcome to the prosperous town of Cd. (abbreviation for *ciudad* "city") Obregón, Industrial park, left. SLOW-LOOK-&-LISTEN at railroad. Plenty of cotton and grain-related industries here. Then big Gamesa (Galletas Mexicana, S.A.), right, one of Mexico's largest cookie producers — sort of like Nabisco in the States. Coca-Cola bottling plant, left. **KM 222.**

Cd. Obregón is the agricultural heart of the Yaqui Valley (known as the Bread Basket of Mexico) with a population of 450,000. This was formerly called Cájeme after the famous chief of the Yaqui Indians, but the name was later changed in honor of Presidente Obregón. His family was originally of Irish lineage.

40.2	64.3	Ley shopping center, right.

MI	KM	
40.8	65.3	To avoid town take next right for bypass. At Guaymas - Cuota sign, make an immediate right. Ahead of you is a **GAS** station.
41.0	65.6	Having made an immediate right (before **GAS** station) at Guaymas - Cuota sign, proceed ahead on one-way stretch that takes you thru an industrial section of town.
41.2	65.9	Pass grain silos on right and tall MUNSA 3-tower grain Silo on left.
41.7	66.7	Over railroad crossing (Look-&-Listen).
42.2	67.5	Stoplight. Railroad station on right.
43.0	68.8	Over another railroad crossing (Look-&-Listen).
43.5	69.6	Careful for dip in road. Tecate brewery at right.
43.8	70.1	Here is where the traffic from town rejoins log. There is a GAS station 1/2 mile towards town that takes credit cards (when manager is in), several new hotels, a Holiday Inn Ph: (64) 14-0936 Fax: (64) 13-4194, 91-800-62333 and a good restaurant, Mr. Steak, where they roll a cart of beef out and cut your steak to your request. See Cd. Obregón Eat & Stray (page 86) for more info on accommodations. Leave prosperous town of Cd. Obregón.
44.7	71.5	Prison to left. **KM 2**.
45.7	73.1	Pemex tank farm, right.
47.1	75.4	Military base, right.
48.0	76.8	Golf club on right.
48.2	77.1	**GAS**, on left. Topes!
48.7	77.9	**GAS**, left. Pass side road (left) to Cocorít, while side road right goes to Tezopaco de Rosario and to Presa (dam) Alvaro Obregón which has a reputation for the best bass fishing in North America. Skirt edge of Esperanza (Hope). Then onto Av. Miguel Alemán (Hwy 15), Cd. Obregón's main stem. Careful for stoplights. **GAS**, left. Stop and pay toll ($32).
50.7	81.1	Cross over famous Río Yaqui whose course from the state of Chihuahua to the Sea of Cortés is 419 miles long. This is also where the Yaqui Indian Reservation begins.
51.7	82.7	Bend left and slow for *Salida de Camiones* (yield to trucks merging with highway traffic). Pass side road (right) to Est. Corral, 3 km. CAREFUL! Settlement of Tajimaroa to left.
53.1	85.0	Under pedestrian crossing. **KM 23**.

Green Angel — Adalberto Rocnín Mendivil, Calle Mango #1707, Col. Fouisste 2. Cd. Obregón, Son. Ph: 6-5894.

MI	KM	
53.5	85.6	Thru scattered settlement of Loma de Guamúchil. Guamúchil is a tree, very common in this part of Mexico, with thorny leafstalks, hairy white globe-shaped flower clusters, and black shiny seeds in spirally twisted pods from 5-6 inches long.
58.6	93.8	Pass side road, right, to Bacum. Heading NE 60. Then come to junction where the FREE ROAD JOINS HWY #15.
59.7	95.5	Pass another road, left, into town of Bacum. Canal waterfall, left.
62.5	100.0	Yaqui masks are made of dissected deer heads, wood & dried goat skin.
67.4	107.8	Pass side road (left) to Torim.
69.0	110.4	Community of Cárdenas and come now to famous YAQUI INDIAN VOCATIONAL AND AGRICULTURAL SCHOOL, left where "knowhow" is taught to Yaqui Indian kids. "Ehwi" in Yaqui means yes.
73.5	117.6	Slow thru little town of Vicam. **GAS**, left and across street **GAS**, right.
77.4	123.8	Potam exit to left. Guaymas, straight.
79.0	126.4	Pass side road (left) to Potam. Note irrigated countryside thru here — very fertile soil. Main crops — cotton, wheat soya, sunflower oil sorghum.
84.8	135.7	Pass side road (right) to Pitahaya.
94.2	150.7	Slow for sharp left curve. Now heading NE.
98.7	157.9	Livestock-shipping community of Las Guásimas.
100.5	160.8	Thru rock cut of Boca Abierta (Open Mouth).
103.5	165.6	Heading due East. The Texas Aggies finally got artificial turf for their football stadium in 1991 — two months after installing an underground sprinkler system.
106.0	169.6	Pass Cruz de Piedra (Cross of Stone) over to right on railroad. Note disabled and outdated railroad cars used now as homes. Here is where a big Yaqui Indian reservation ends and it ran for 50-odd miles from the Yaqui River just North of Ciudad Obregón. The Yaquis had a big uprising back in the late 20's and Mexico gave them this territory for a reservation.
106.5	170.4	Pass side road (left) to Playa del Sol, a beachfront development.
107.0	171.2	Veer left following Hermosillo signs. **GAS**, on left.

```
MI     KM
```

108.5 173.6 Pass side road (right) to Ortiz. Down side road a short mile is where famous NASA space capsule tracking station was located (the place that a couple of the early astronauts referred to when they remarked as they passed over, "Hello, Guaymas! Send us up some enchiladas!"). This is no longer used by NASA.

111.0 177.6 Fertimex plant, right. Pass side road (left) to beachfront community of El Cochori, 2 miles (no accommodations). Then come to toll bypass around Guaymas to right. Continue ahead on the free bypass, which is OK, unless you're in a hurry.

IF TO: Toll Bypass of town. Take an immediate right at Guaymas-Cuota sign and follow stub log below. Otherwise continue straight.

Stub Log: Toll Bypass Around Guaymas

0.0   0.0   Having turned right onto bypass, "topes" and over railroad, pass big Fertimex plant at right.
3.0   4.8   Up and over bridge over railroad.
9.0   14.4 Truck stop restaurant Los Faroles, left.
11.6 18.6 Over bridge.
12.0 19.2 Stop and pay toll (Cars $32, extra axle, 16). Then under overpass and come to junction with Hwy #15. **GAS**, diesel (SIN) & ice, left.

IF TO: San Carlos, & downtown Guaymas, Use retorno and go back on free highway for 4 miles to San Carlos turnoff, then follow San Carlos Special, for Guaymas continue ahead from there for 8 miles.

IF TO: Hermosillo, pick up Guaymas — Hermosillo Log (page 145) at mile 8.0.

End of Stub Log

113.4 181.4 **GAS** (watch 'em), left. Highway patrol, right. **KM 113.**
113.5 181.6 Ferrocarril del Pacífico station (Pacific Railroad station), right. Railroad crossing.
114.2 182.7 TOPES. Then white palm trees lining highway. Then big Anderson-Clayton complex, left.
114.8 183.7 Restaurant to right. Mount Dolly Parton to left?
115.0 184.0 Big railroad shops, right. Then slow for another railroad crossing — LOOK-&-LISTEN. Begin causeway — LOOK-&-LISTEN for DOUBLE railroad crossing. And one more railroad switch line LOOK-&-LISTEN. AHEAD on Hwy 15. Right fork is to railroad town of Empalme. And there, right, stands old engine 70 of the Ferrocarril de Sonora (Sonora Railroad), a monument to Empalme and its railroad industry.
116.2 185.9 Onto causeway alongside railroad track, left.
117.7 188.3 LP gas, right. Power plant, left. Guaymas Bay and Gulf of California on left.

Mexico calls the Gulf of California *Mar de Cortés* (Sea of Cortés).

118.0 188.8 Pass junction with side road (left) to ferries. Veer right.
119.0 190.4 SLOW FOR SCHOOL ZONE. Two big "topes."
119.5 191.2 **GAS** right. You're skirting edge of town. Another SCHOOL ZONE.
119.8 191.7 Curve to the right. Exiting left here will take you to town. **GAS**, on left. **KM 139.**
120.0 192.0 Fruit and vegetable inspection.
120.2 192.3 SLOW thru SCHOOL ZONE. Thru light. Monument to Benito Juárez on hilltop to left.
120.4 192.6 Chevy dealer. Monument at left to Heroes of Guaymas.

IF TO: San Carlos, VEER RIGHT here. Start Guaymas — San Carlos Special (page 61).

IF TO: Guaymas, RV parks on bay, TURN LEFT and start Guaymas RV Stub Log (page 15).

120.5 192.8 Stay right and veer right at obelisk. Traffic light. Motel Armida, right.
121.0 193.6 **GAS**, left. Ice. Chrysler/Dodge and VW dealer. Then Nissan and Ford dealers, left. Zerimar supermarket, left. Stoplight. Las Villas Subdivision on left.
121.1 193.8 Shopping center, right. Plaza de Viola.
121.5 194.4 Continue ahead under overpass. Pass exit left for Bocachibampo Bay (Bay of the Sea Serpents). For neat hotel Cortés with large RV park, under overpass, exit right onto Col. Miramar and continue straight to beach. For info on accommodations, see Guaymas Eat & Stray (page 84).

IF TO: San Carlos, Hermosillo, start Guaymas — Hermosillo Log.

End of Log 19

LOG 20   *START:* Guaymas, Son   *END:* Hermosillo, Son

82.5 MI or 132.5 KM
DRIVE TIME 1 1/4 — 2 HOURS
SCENIC RATING — 3
Nice flat divided highway, tolls. Ocean on your left, mountains right.

MI	KM	
0.0	0.0	STRAIGHT, PAST Miramar exit, right, to Bacochibampo Bay, Playa de Cortés Hotel & RV Park, Hotel a wonderful old place with plenty of charm. Also down this road is Leo's Inn.
0.5	0.8	Leave city of Guaymas. Motel Flamingos at right. **GAS**, left.
2.5	4.0	There's Guaymas airport over to right.
4.2	6.7	Motel Casa Blanca, left — NO. That's one White House you don't want to say you've slept in.

IF TO: SAN CARLOS, exit here, then over overpass — it's quite a nice place, sort of a gringo oasis. It's about 5 miles straight ahead on a fine divided road — you won't get lost. Watch your speed. They really have traffic cops now. Begin Guaymas — San Carlos Special (page 61).

8.0	12.8	Careful as you come to junction with toll bypass around Guaymas. Over overpass, then **GAS** & diesel, left.
9.0	14.4	Truck inspection station, right. Wide spot of El Caballo "The Horse", right.
10.9	17.4	Series of well-marked curves for a mile or two.
21.4	34.2	Watch out for posts on right side of road. DANGER!
28.2	45.1	Rancho Los Arrieros, left. Pass side road (left) to Kino Bay. (If you don't go, shame on you. It's a nice place & not too crowded.) KM 168.

IF TO: Kino Bay, turn left here and start Hwy #15 — Kino Bay Shortcut Special (page 50). It will save 1/2 hour.

30.8	49.3	White church on right. **GAS**, left.
38.2	61.1	Slow for brown-and-white cow in middle of road. This is the Dan's famous brown cow.
41.5	66.4	SHARP S-CURVE. There's about a mile more of them. Might as well tell you "heavy metal" fellows (& gals) that smokey (*el oso*?) is around and has radar! What's Mexico coming to?
44.2	70.7	Rest stop of Los Pocitos. Highway Patrol hangs out here sometimes. **KM 198**.
47.0	75.2	Whistle stop of La Pintada at left where there are supposed to be caves whose walls are carved with prehistoric hieroglyphics (though nobody seems to know about them, so look for them only if you are adventurous and speak Spanish). CAREFUL - there will be some fairly sharp curves ahead.
54.0	86.4	Those rugged mountains ahead to right are called El Pilar "The Pillar."
60.1	96.2	Shirley Temple mountains to left.
67.5	108.0	Over bridge over little dry Río La Poza, then SHARP right curve.
69.3	110.9	Notice camel hump hill over to right! Now say it 3 times, real fast.
75.3	120.5	**GAS**, left.
77.6	124.2	Police Institute right. Mexico is professionalizing its police force & some states have hired law enforcement consultants from the U.S. Welcome to Hermosillo sign.
78.0	124.8	Right to Hermosillo Ecological Park — a very worthwhile place.
78.3	125.3	Motel Del Fuego at right.
78.6	125.8	AA sign. Centro office at Garmendia and Veracruz. Ph: 4-2471. Corona distributor and ice on right. Motel Cid on left.
79.1	126.6	Shopping plaza to left.
79.2	126.7	Junction with Periférico West, right. "Periférico" means "bypass" or "loop." Right to Santa Ana & El Novillo Dam (lake), 95 miles (good bass fishing). **GAS**, right (watch 'em).

IF TO: Bypass town and on to Santa Ana, turn RIGHT and (skip Kino Bay stublog) start bypass stublog below. Otherwise skip down to mile 79.5.

IF TO: Kino Bay, turn left and start Kino Bay via Bypass stublog below.

Stub Log: To Kino Bay Via Bypass

MI	KM	
0.0	0.0	Having turned onto Periférico heading West, pass Plaza Sur shopping center.
0.4	0.6	Pass Palo Verde business park, left.
0.9	1.4	Pass automatic transmission repair shop, right.
1.1	1.8	Pass **GAS** station, left. Stoplight. Cemento Campana, left just before light.
1.2	1.9	Pass Calle Lázaro Cárdenas, left.
1.9	3.0	Amazing rock formation on left behind Las Palmas shopping center
2.1	3.4	Road goes over usually dry river and freeway to nowhere.
2.5	4.0	Another stoplight (You are now heading West). Long distance fax office on left just before light.
3.3	5.3	Another shopping center, left.
3.6	5.8	Stoplight. Plaza Satélite, left just past light.
3.8	6.1	Pass thatched mariscos palapa, right.
4.2	6.7	Pass big dry cleaner (*tintorería*) on left.

IF TO: Kino Bay, Turn left and begin Hermosillo — Kino Bay Special (page 45) at mile 2.0.

End of Stub Log.

Stub Log: From Guaymas Highway to Nogales.

0.0	0.0	Having turned right onto bypass go under overpass. Follow "Nogales" signs. **GAS**, left.
0.1	0.2	Goodyear on left. Uniroyal on right.
0.8	1.3	**GAS** on right.
1.0	1.6	VEER LEFT at Santa Ana sign (straight ahead is to Yécora and Hwy 16 to Copper Canyon). Right is to Sahuaripa. Industrial park on right. Then pass street left to downtown Hermosillo.

IF TO: Chihuahua or Copper Canyon, start Hermosillo — La Junta Special (page 50).

1.3	2.1	**GAS** on right. Cattle feed lot on right. Roll up your windows.
2.8	4.5	Railroad crossing. Curve right.
3.0	4.8	Cement plant to left.
3.6	5.8	Dangerous curve and over bridge. Railroad bridge overhead to right, then dangerous curve to left.
4.0	6.4	Get in right lane. Left lane turns to the bus station.
4.3	6.9	Baseball field on right. Soccer field on left. Careful for school zone.
4.5	7.2	**GAS**, on right.
4.6	7.4	Veer right onto one-way street, *Las Vírgenes*. Farmacia, left. AA (Spanish) Buenos Amigos at right (Alanon meetings — 4:30 til 6:00 PM, Mon & Wed).
4.9	7.8	Curve left. Then under pedestrian crossing. Again on divided 4 lane.
5.0	8.0	Over railroad crossing. Curve right.
5.5	8.8	Pemex storage facilities on left and right. Ahead, to left, is Fiesta Americana Hotel.
5.6	9.0	Firestone on right. Goodrich, left
5.7	9.1	Mobile and Chevy dealer on left. **GAS**, ahead on left.

IF TO: Nogales, turn RIGHT onto Hwy #15. Start Hermosillo — Santa Ana Log (page 147) at Mile 2.2.

IF TO: Downtown, turn LEFT.

End of Stub Log

		Continuation of main log.
79.5	127.2	Welcome to Hermosillo, (population: 449,472), capital of the state of Sonora. It's named for Colonel D. José María González Hermosillo in 1828, a leader in the war for independence.
79.9	127.5	Restaurant a Hacienda, right. Then white double domed church.
80.7	129.1	Electrical generating station, left.
81.0	129.6	Gas, regular only, right. Note monument at left to *Los Tres Pueblos* in memory of three villages on Río Sonora that were washed away years ago by a big flood. Hotel Grenada, left.
81.2	129.9	Over freeway. Pass cultural center at left. Nogales straight. Centro bus station to right.
81.4	130.2	Up and over usually dry bed of Río de Sonora. Big Rodríguez Dam & Lake upstream to right.

MI	KM	
81.8	130.9	Hotel Kino, right.
82.1	131.4	Civic center, left. Down wide two-way Avenida Rosales.
82.2	131.5	Restaurant Jo Wah. Hotel San Alberto left. Then highrise hotel Calinda.
82.5	132.0	University Plaza ahead on left. Rodríguez Library and Museum, right. Bend left past mounted statue of Don Bautista de Anza, a Sonoran military hero and explorer. He founded a little village of San Francisco, CA. in his spare time. For info on accommodations, see Hermosillo Eat & Stray (page 78)

IF TO: Nogales, Santa Ana — STRAIGHT. Start Hermosillo — Santa Ana Log.

IF TO: Kino Bay — LEFT — following "AEROPUERTO" "KINO" signs. Start Hermosillo — Kino Bay Special (page 45). Left 2 lanes are left turn only. Right 3 lanes are straight, for now, stick to middle.

IF TO: Agua Prieta & Douglas (the scenic way by Ures, Moctezuma & Nacozari) — STRAIGHT — for 8 miles on Hermosillo — Santa Ana Log, to junction with turnoff. Then start Hermosillo — Douglas Log (page 66). Don't forget to stop in Bisbee, AZ, at the Inn at Castle Rock. It's a New Age, 60's kind of place, or as the owner calls it, "a center for evolving consciousness."

End of Log 20

LOG 21   *START:* Hermosillo, Son   *END:* Santa Ana, Son

UD-126

107.1 MI or 171.4 KM
DRIVE TIME 1 1/2 - 2 HOURS
SCENIC RATING — 2

0.0	0.0	Here at University Plaza, proceed ahead past Rodríguez Museum and Library, right, and plaza of University of Sonora, left. Monument of mounted Capitán de Anza (a native of Sonora and founder of San Francisco, California) is behind you.

Rodríguez Museum and Library, Rodríguez Dam and Lake, & Rodríguez Boulevard coming up, are all named for Abelardo Rodríguez, a Sonora boy who served as *presidente* from 1932-34.

0.1	0.2	Stoplight. Restaurant Mirikon (Japanese), right. Then, Av. Madrid
0.3	0.5	KFC at right.
0.6	1.0	Come to a monument (on right) to one-armed man — General Alvaro Obregón. He was presidente of Mexico from 1920-24, a native of Sonora. Pancho Villa shot off his arm during a revolutionary battle at Celaya. Hertz Rent-A-Car, left.
0.8	1.3	Sports Palace on right. Ford clock tower & Chevy dealer to left. Straight to Santa Ana. Right to downtown Hermosillo at light. Stay in left 2 lanes — right goes to lateral only. Pass shopping center, left.
1.0	1.6	**GAS**, right.
1.1	1.8	Veer left here. Right lane is a lateral. To the left is a grocery store, "Valle Petic."
1.2-	1.9	Chrysler dealer on right. La Fiesta restaurant on left.
1.4	2.2	**GAS**, left. Laundromat on right. Mannix Cafeteria on left (fast service). Ford dealer on left. La Siesta Motel, right. Señorial hotel on right.
1.5	2.4	Motel Bugambilla, left. Hotel Petic Valle Grande, right.
1.7	2.7	Motel Encanto just beyond at right. Excellent restaurant Henry's at left.
1.8	2.9	Pretty Bancomer at left. Then well-known motel Gandara at right, 1000 Blvd. Kino.
2.1	3.4	Big Ariaza hotel at right. Highrise Fiesta Americana on right.
2.2	3.5	Come to traffic light and junction with bypass around town. Huge **GAS**, left. Periférico North, right. "Periférico" means "bypass" or "loop." This goes to Guaymas. Welcome to those folks joining us from the bypass, here at what used to be Kino Circle, back before this traffic light. Chevrolet dealer, right.
2.4	3.8	Railroad station to right. Under pedestrian crossing.
2.5	4.0	Hotel Autoparador at right, nice. Under sign "Hermosillo wishes you a good trip."
2.6	4.2	Mercedes Benz dealer on left.
4.2	6.7	Pass Motel Costa Del Sol, right.
4.7	7.5	**GAS**, right.

MI	KM	
5.2	8.3	Town of La Victoria over to right. This is a rich farming area with a lot of allied industry. Ice house, right.
6.5	10.4	Sign to Nogales Hwy 15 Cuota (Toll).
7.2	11.5	Sign to Nogales Libre. Toll road to Nogales, VEER LEFT. Free road, VEER RIGHT, following URES sign. If you want to take the Libre (free) road, be aware that it is very congested and we recommend the toll road.

IF TO: Douglas, AZ via Ures, Nacozari, turn right and start Hermosillo — Douglas Log (page 66).

MI	KM	
7.3	11.7	Having taken toll road (no toll booth here), note statue of bull at right. **KM 9.**
7.4	11.8	ITESM (technical school) to right. Statue of Capitán de Anza to left.
7.6	12.2	**GAS**, at left. Altitude 1,000 ft. **KM 10.**
23.0	36.8	Side road, right, to Pesqueíra, named after Ignacio Pesqueíra, a former governor of Sonora. Red Cross. Cafes on both sides.
33.5	53.6	Mount Cuervos over to left.
45.2	72.3	The Yaqui Indians are also natives here. Their "deer dance" is pretty neat. 'Course young folks of all tribes do "dear" dances. Like most Indians, they have a dance to celebrate the important passages in life and the seasons. It's also an excuse to socialize and relax. **KM 68.**
45.7	73.1	Up into El Oasis. **GAS**, left and ice. Emergency motel Oasis, also at left with bus station restaurant. Pass side road, right, to town of Carbo on railroad.
50.5	80.8	Mt. Amore dead ahead with radio tower.
51.5	82.4	Parador turístico to right.
52.7	84.3	Microwave tower at left, then Chapel and truck stop of "Los Chinos" (the Chinamen).
55.0	88.0	Water for radiator sign with place to right, but I wouldn't count on finding any water. **KM 84.**
55.7	89.1	Over bridge over dry Río Apache. A Texas Aggie had to make an emergency landing with his plane around here. He banged it up pretty badly. When he was pulled from the wreckage, he asked, "Why would somebody make a runway that's 100 miles wide and only 100 feet long?"
65.1	104.2	The Pápago Indians are desert dwellers. Their pottery & wood carvings are sold in "trading posts" in Phoenix & Tucson, AZ. **KM 100.**
72.5	116.0	Pass side road right to Querobabi on railroad. Hwy #82. **KM 113.**
78.2	125.1	Now up and over railroad overpass. **KM 123.**
79.9	127.8	The hand carved art works by the Seri Indians are done with *palo fierro* or iron wood. A non-Indian taught them the skill within the last 20 years. **KM 125.**
80.7	129.1	**GAS**, left and ice. Then past side road left that leads to railroad junction of Benjamín Hill. The town has an unusual name for a Mexican place especially since there's no "hill." It's named after a general in the Mexican Constitutionalist forces during the Mexican Revolution of 1910-1917. General "Hill" was the defender of the Mexican border town of Naco (South of Bisbee, Arizona) in 1914 and was of British descent.
91.4	146.2	Casa Blanca & retorno.
91.7	146.7	**GAS**, on right. Clean restrooms. Expensive refreshments.
92.0	147.2	Cross Río El Alamo (cottonwood). **GAS** and restaurant on right.
94.0	150.4	Cemetery with pearly gates on right. "Swing low, sweet chariot .... " Pass little railroad town of Estación Llano at left.
100.0	160.0	**GAS**, to left. **KM 159.**
105.0	168.0	Plaza Kennedy truck stop (RV parking sometimes allowed) and highway patrol station on left.
105.9	169.4	Sharp curve.
106.3	170.1	Restaurant El Zarape. Punta Vista RV park, left. Run by nice folks, Ana & Edgar Osuña. It's one of Mikey's favorites, humble but spic 'n span. Nice view at top of hill.
106.4	170.2	Turn right. Centro bus station. Over little bridge. At right San Francisco hotel, Ph: (632) 4-0322, and at left is hotel Elba, —MOD— restaurant (open 6 AM till 11 PM) with good food (serve 1/2 orders for those who have a small appetite), MC, VI, Ph: (632) 4-0361, 4-0178. School to left then curve to left. Downhill.
106.9	171.0	Retorno Nogales/Magdalena. Then Motel San Carlos (50 rooms and less expensive than El Camino across the highway, PH: (632) 2-1300 or 2-3697)
107.0	171.2	In Santa Ana at junction Hwys #15 & #2, past **GAS**, left.

IF TO: Nogales, veer right and Start Santa Ana — Imuris Log.

IF TO: Caborca, Sonoyta, Puerto Peñasco, San Luis Colorado (Yuma), Mexicali, Tijuana and the Pacific Ocean, TURN LEFT and start Santa Ana — Sonoyta Log (not included in this book).

End of Log 21

LOG 22   *START:* **Santa Ana, Son**   *END:* **Imuris, Son**

UD-126

26.5 MI or 42.4 KM
DRIVE TIME 30 — 45 MINUTES
SCENIC RATING — 2

MI	KM	
0.0	0.0	Here at junction of Hwy #2 West (left) to Caborca, Sonoyta, San Luis Río Colorado, Mexicali, Tijuana, etc. and Hwy #15, proceed ahead. **GAS**, left. Uniroyal at right.
0.1	0.2	Under pedestrian crossing. Curve right. Uphill and out of town.
2.8	4.5	Sign says: Tucson, 200 KM (120 MI).
5.6	9.0	Granja Santa Regina granary. **KM 175.**
7.5	12.0	Get into right lane for toll (Cuota) road or left lane for free (Libre) road.
8.0	12.8	Butane gas at left.
8.5	13.6	Toll road or free road 1 KM ahead.
9.3	14.9	Left to Magdalena. Right to Toll Bypass, right 2 lanes. Left lane exit only. Free road begins with killer "topes." The Saguaro Motel at right. Statue of "Christ" on hill on left. View of Magdalena to left. Thru Saguaro forest.
10.1	16.2	Pass turnoff (left) to Kino Hotel and Trailer Park. Then pass Ayabay Motel, right.
10.3	16.5	Enter Magdalena (population 41,000) famous as the place where the skeletal remains of the great PADRE KINO were discovered in 1966 — if you have an extra 20 minutes, don't miss this! Pottery sold here.
10.5	16.8	Slow over "topes" and past Colegio de Sonora at right.
10.8	17.3	Monument to Padre Kino on right.
10.9	17.4	Pemex **GAS** on left.
11.0	17.6	Pass series of stoplights every couple of blocks.
11.2	17.9	**GAS** on right. Large Pharmacy next on left. Moclamora Motel and restaurant, left, then Plaza del Sol with long distance phone booth. Then on right, AA Group.
12.1	19.4	Pass Tourism office, then cross bridge and past soccer field on right then more "topes."
13.1	21.0	If on toll road, stop and pay toll ($ 32), then ahead.
13.4	21.4	Nogales veer right. Magdalena, you turn. Then bypass Magdalena (pop. 41,000), **KM 187.**
14.0	22.4	San Ignacio to left.
16.1	25.8	Under power line. Over bridge over Río Tasicuri.
20.0	32.0	Careful for sharp left and right curves. Careful for next 7 winding miles.
22.1	35.4	Careful for curves.
23.8	38.1	Stone cutters on right. Very interesting. Then flashing light. Enter the fringe of Imuris (population: 8,000).
24.2	38.7	Puente Babasac. KM 205. Curve right. Jct. with Hwy #2 to the right.
26.5	42.4	**GAS**, left. Red cross. Then down and over bridge over Río de los Alisos. Come to junction of Hwy #2 from Douglas, Arizona at statue of Padre Kino and end of log.

IF TO: Nogales, AZ, start Imuris — Nogales Log.

IF TO: Douglas, AZ, turn right and start Imuris — Douglas Log (page 69).

End of Log 22

LOG 23   *START:* **Imuris, Son**   *END:* **Nogales, Az**

UP-126

48.0 MI or 76.8 KM
DRIVE TIME 50 MINUTES — 1 1/4 HOURS
SCENIC RATING — 2
Easy, winding stretch of divided highway.

NOTE: The newer border crossing via the "loop" is open from 6 AM till 10 PM only; otherwise, you have to cross at the "old" gateway via Hwy 89 downtown. Since you're not driving at night, it doesn't matter — right?

MI	KM	
0.0	0.0	Here at junction RIGHT with Hwy #2 to Agua Prieta, Mexico and Douglas, Arizona. There is a VERY neat statue at right. Take a few minutes to stop and walk all the way around it.
1.2	1.9	Thru fringe of hilltop town of Imuris (e-moo-rees). Pass Imuris' railroad depot at left.
3.0	4.8	Down past Las Viguitas on left. By the way, Mexican smokeys have ears. That's radar, son, radar, so watch your speed. Speed limit is 90 KMPH.
8.5	13.6	Railroad settlement of Cumeral, left.
11.1	17.8	Thru falling rock zone.
13.1	21.0	We have climbed to 3,400 ft.
13.8	22.1	Topped 3,500 ft. Now down. Curve right. **KM 229.**
16.5	26.4	Thru settlement of La Casita. **KM 233.**
21.0	33.6	Bear LEFT thru Cibuta and slow thru school zone. Pedestrians.
29.0	46.4	Pass *MIGRACIÓN & ADUANA* inspections station, left.

If you will not return to Mexico before your vehicle permit expires, TURN IT IN HERE. Ask for "Banjército" office. Failure to do so may result in high fines.

MI	KM	
29.1	46.6	**GAS**, right.
31.0	49.6	Thru railroad workers' settlement of Agua Zarca.
34.0	54.4	Nogales' airport over at left. **KM 260.**
36.0	57.6	Over railroad and follow alongside railroad at left.
37.0	59.2	Frequent *retornos* (turnarounds). Highway patrol station at left.
37.5	60.0	Goodyear plant left. **KM 265.**
38.0	60.8	Thru traffic light. Pass Foster Grant Americana on left. This is a big industrial zone — some big-name American plants are located here. **KM 266.**

They manufacture the first part of their products in Mexico and then ship 'em to their stateside counterparts for finishing touches — less expensive this way. They are called *maquiladoras*.

MI	KM	
38.1	61.0	CAREFUL for TOPES, Pedestrian crossing & school on left. Plaza Kino to right.
38.2	61.1	Hotel Posada Real on right. Come to stop at intersection. General Tire ahead on left. TURN LEFT.
38.7	61.9	**GAS**, and diesel station. Federal prison, left. Abandoned **GAS** on left.
39.0	62.4	Electrical generating station to left.
39.7	63.5	Nogales Technical Institute, left.
40.6	65.0	3 story building on right. Victor Muir Aduanal Agency at top of hill.
40.7	65.1	New Municipal auditorium to left. **GAS**, left.
40.9	65.4	Pass warehouse complex on left. Chamberlin manufacturing plant to right. Radio station on right.
41.6	66.6	Downhill after passing Customs. Curve right.
41.8	66.9	Cross Mariposa Canyon.
41.9	67.0	Pass town of Nogales, Sonora, mostly to right.
42.0	67.2	Texaco and Fiesta market to left.
42.3	67.7	Thru housing development. Pass La Voz Del Norte newspaper, left. Pass turnoff, RIGHT to downtown Nogales. Straight ahead thru cut. Under pedestrian walkway. School on right.
42.5	68.0	Veer right at bridge. Straight to "new" border gateway — you're entering USA. This is Nogales, AZ. The officer will ask you where you were born. (Try not to reply, "In the state of nakedness.") Where you've been. I've found most of these officers to be reasonable with a tough job to do. They may ask you to pull over and inspect your car. After customs, USA to the right.
42.8	68.5	Flashing light. School on left. Stoplight. Straight ahead for you. "N. Industrial park drive."

MI	KM	
42.9	68.6	Carl Jr's Burgers on left. Over bridge.
43.1	69.0	A right will take you downtown. This is Jct. #19. Left is to Tucson. Straight to Nogales Sanborn's office.
43.2	69.1	Vet supermarket to left. Loma Linda shopping center on right with Wal-Mart. Stoplight. Chevron at left then Mickie D's and Valley Nation bank also at left.
43.5	69.6	KFC and Arby's on right.
44.0	70.4	Cross Mariposa Canyon. Motel 6 at right. Chevron at right. Stoplight. K-Mart left. Turn left. Exxon and K-Mart on left.
44.1	70.6	Railroad at right. Stoplight. Cross "Baffert Drive."
44.9	71.8	San Luis Truck terminal at right. Bell **GAS** on left. Stoplight. Circle K at left.
45.5	72.8	Come to junction.

IF TO: Tucson, points North, East, or West, get onto IH-19. Bye-bye.

IF TO: Nogales, Sanborn's office, veer East along truck route. Turn left to Sanborn's Mexican Insurance and RV park. Having elected not to go to Tucson, ahead on US #180 (Mariposa Road). Pass Best Western Inn Suites at RIGHT.

46.5	74.4	Pass K-Mart, Safeway, and Revco drug stores. Stoplight. Turn left onto US #89. Ahead 3 stoplights.
48.0	76.8	Pass Nogales Service Center Truck stop at left. Arrive Sanborn's Mi Casa RV Travel Park.

We hope you had a dandy time. The next time someone tells you how unsafe it is to drive in Mexico, you tell 'em you know better! See us next time you go South!

End of Log 17
Hasta La Vista Baby

NOTES

Index

A

Acaponeta, Nay 31
Alamos, Son 61

B

Basaseachic, Chih 51
Batopilas, Chih 57, 58
Benjamín Hill, Son 9

C

Cananea, Son 6, 69
Cd Obregón, Son 142
Cd. Obregón, Son 18, 66
Chapalilla, Nay 37, 74, 127
Compostela, Nay 34, 74, 131
Cosalá, Sin 25, 26, 136, 137
Creel, Chih 53, 55, 57, 58, 59
Cuauhtémoc, Chih 53, 59
Culiacán, Sin 22, 23, 135, 138

D

Divisadero, Chih 55
Douglas, Az 3, 66, 69, 75

E

EAT & STRAYS
  Alamos 88
  Batopilas 104
  Cd. Obregón 86
  Creel 102
  Culiacán 93
  Divisadero 103
  El Fuerte 92
  Guadalajara 118
  Guaymas 84
  Hermosillo 78
  Kino Bay 79
  Los Mochis 90
  Mazatlán 94
  Navojoa 87
  Pto. Vallarta 110
  Rincón de Guayabitos 108
  San Blas 106
  San Carlos 82
  Tejabán 103
  Tepic 105
El Fuerte, Sin 65
Empalme, Son 16

G

Guadalajara, Jal 37, 125
Guasave, Sin 22, 138
Guaymas, Son 12, 15, 61, 141, 145

H

Hermosillo, Son 9, 12, 45, 46, 50, 66, 75, 145, 147
Huichol Indians 32, 132

I

Imuris, Son 2, 3, 7, 69, 149, 150
Ixtlán del Río, Nay 38, 128

K

Kino Bay, Son 45, 46, 49, 50

L

La Junta, Chih 50, 60
Lake Comedero 25, 26, 136, 137
Lake Domínguez 22
Lake Hidalgo 22
Las Varas, Nay 34, 72, 73, 131
Los Cascabeles, Sin 25, 136, 137
Los Mochis, Sin 19, 22, 65, 138, 140

M

Magdalena, Son 7, 8, 149
MAPS
  Alamos 63
  Cd. Obregón 17
  Creel 56
  Culiacán 24
  Douglas 4
  El Fuerte 65
  Guadalajara 44
  Guaymas 14
  Hermosillo 11
  Kino Bay 47
  Los Mochis 21
  Magdalena 8
  Mazatlán 27
  Mazatlán, North Beach 28
  Nogales 1
  Pto. Vallarta 36
  San Carlos 62
  Tepic 33
  Tequila 42
Mazatlán, Sin 23, 30, 132, 135
Mexcaltitán, Nay 32, 133

154

Moctezuma, Son 67, 76

N

Nacozari, Son 67, 76
Navojoa, Son 15, 19, 61, 140, 141
Nogales, Az 2, 150

P

Padre Kino 8
Pto Vallarta, Jal 129
Pto. Vallarta, Jal 34

R

Rincón de Guayabitos 35, 131
Río Caliente Spa, Jal 39, 126

S

San Blas, Nay 32, 70, 71, 132
San Carlos, Son 13, 61, 145
San Ignacio, Sin 26, 137
San Nicolás, Son 51, 66
Santa Ana, Son 7, 9, 147, 149
Santa Cruz, Nay 72, 73
Santiago Ixcuintla, Nay 32, 132

T

Teacapan, Sin 31, 133
Tejabán, Chih 55
Tepic, Nay 30, 34, 37, 71, 125, 129, 132
Tequila, Jal 39, 127

Y

Yécora, Son 51

If you've got a minute ...

We truly hope you had a wonderful trip and that our *Travelog* helped. You can help other folks by passing on information you may have learned. It's from your feedback that we can improve, so tell us what we did right, wrong or could have done differently. If possible, please refer to name of log, and the mile #. The whole *Travelog* covers all of Mexico & is 1,000 pages, so we need some way to track it. **YOUR PHONE #, POR FAVOR!** I may have a question, or want to thank you personally!

Praise or complaints for Mexican individuals or companies should be sent to : **Secretaria de Turismo, Direccion General de Servicios al Turismo, Presidente Masaryk – 3er Piso, C.P. 11587, Mexico D.F.** Each year, the government honors a citizen who helped tourists. Your complaint or praise will be recorded and sent to the right agency. You'd be surprised at what good it can do.

Hasta luego, "Mexico Mike" and all the staff at Sanborn's.

Today's date:______________________ Date entered Mexico: ________________ Exit date: __________________

Which Sanborn's office served you? ____

Were they friendly?________ Helpful?__________ Knowledgeable?_________ How could they improve service? ____

____

____

Did you have a good time – overall? YES! ______NO _______Was any facility or individual especially helpful? ____

Was your *Travelog* in order? YES__________NO__________ Did it make sense? YES________NO________

Excellent? ______________________________ Good? ______________________________ Fair?____________________________

Was the **HIGHWAY INFORMATION** essentially accurate?   YES______________NO______________

Do you have new info for us?____

____

____

____

Was the **EAT & STRAY** section essentially accurate?   YES______________   NO______________

Do you have new places for us, or some that should be edited?_______________________________

____

____

____

____

What would YOU like to see that WASN'T there?____

Will you return to Mexico some day?____

Name:____

Address, City, State, Zip :____

Country___________________________**TELEPHONE #** (_______)_________________________________

How many travelling?__________   First trip? YES________NO___________

Where did you hear about Sanborn's?____

____